WITHDRAWN

MIEVL X. VAVLT. MOVRIR. EN. VERTV,
QVE. VIVRE. EN. HONCTE.

THOMAS EAST

AND

MUSIC PUBLISHING

IN

RENAISSANCE ENGLAND

JEREMY L. SMITH

OXFORD
UNIVERSITY PRESS

2003

OXFORD
UNIVERSITY PRESS

Oxford   New York
Auckland   Bangkok   Buenos Aires   Cape Town
Chennai   Dar es Salaam   Delhi   Hong Kong   Istanbul   Karachi
Kolkata   Kuala Lumpur   Madrid   Melbourne   Mexico City   Mumbai   Nairobi
São Paolo   Shanghai   Taipei   Tokyo   Toronto

Copyright © 2003 by Oxford University Press, Inc.

Published by Oxford University Press, Inc.
198 Madison Avenue, New York, New York, 10016

www.oup.com

Oxford is a registered trademark of Oxford University Press

Library of Congress Cataloging-in-Publication Data
Smith, Jeremy L., 1962–
    Thomas East and music publishing in Renaissance England / Jeremy L. Smith.
        p.   cm.
    Includes chronology of East's editions.
    Includes bibliographical references and index.
    ISBN 0-19-513905-4
        1. East, Thomas, 1540?–1608?   2. Music publishers—England.
    3. Music publishing—England—16th century.   4. Music publishing—England—
    17th century.   I. Title.
ML427.E27 S65 2002
070.5'794'092—dc21   2002019632

9 8 7 6 5 4 3 2 1
Printed in the United States of America
on acid-free paper

ACKNOWLEDGMENTS

Research for this book was made possible by grants from the Meyer Foundation of the Huntington Library; the Graduate Division of the University of California, Santa Barbara; SUNY—College at Fredonia; and the University of Colorado at Boulder. Space does not permit me to extend personal recognition to all of the rare-book curators and musicologists whose individual contributions were so pivotal to the completion of research for this book. But Peter Ward Jones of the Bodleian Library; Fred Pleiester of Nederlands Muziek Instituut; Craig Wright and Nathan Link of Yale University; Jennifer Schaffner of UCLA; Roberta Zonghi of Boston Public Library; Wayne Hammond of Chapin Library; Tom Ford of Houghton Library, Harvard University; Nancy Romero of University of Illinois Library, Urbana-Champaign; Ann Simmons of Archbishop Marsh's Library; the staff of the Music Division of the Library of Congress; and Lori Johnson of Folger Library deserve my special thanks for their kind attention to an undue number of extraordinary requests. The photographic expertise of Charlotte Morse and Robert Siedentop has much enhanced the quality of the figures used in this study.

As I began this project I was especially fortunate to have the guidance of Kristine Forney, who provided me with an ideal model for my topic in her work on Susato. I wish to thank Alejandro Planchart and Robert Freeman for their generous help with my writing and research at the crucial early stages, and I am deeply indebted and most grateful to William Prizer, who served as my dissertation adviser. I profited greatly from the expert comments of Philip Brett, Donald W. Krummel, John Milsom, Katharine Ellis, Jessie Ann Owens, David Mateer, Patricia Hall, Maureen Buja, Maribeth Payne, Faith Keymer, and the anonymous reviewers of my manuscript.

I have enjoyed the special help of Nicholas Zelle, John and Judy Gainor, Temmo Koresheli, Jim Davis, Stephen Kershnar, Bruce Simon, Neil Feit, Kwasi Ampene, Tom Riis, Carlo Caballero, Daphne Leong, and Steve Bruns, to whom I am heavily indebted for their patience with me during the writing process. My interest in Renaissance music was originally sparked in seminars of H. Colin Slim and the late William Holmes of the University of California, Irvine. I thank, too, my teachers at Washington College—Amzie and Betsy Parcell, Kathy Mills, and Garry Clarke. I am grateful to Oxford University Press and the Music Library Association for permission to use previously published material: "The Hidden Editions of Thomas East," *Notes, Quarterly Journal of the Music Library Association* 53 (1997): 1059–1091; and "'From 'Rights to Copy' to the 'Bibliographic Ego': A New Look at the Last Early Edition of Byrd's 'Psalmes, Sonets & Songs,'" *Music & Letters* 80 (1999): 511–1530. Finally, I extend my heartfelt appreciation to my wife, So Young Lee, and to my parents, Jeanne and Nathan Smith. This work is lovingly dedicated to them for their constant encouragement and unflagging support.

NOTE ON PERMISSIONS AND TRANSCRIPTIONS

Throughout the narrative portion of this study the long "ʃ" is replaced with the modern "s" in quoted writings from East's era. In addition, ligatures are resolved and special typographical configurations like East's "VV" are silently replaced by "W." Otherwise, original spellings are preserved.

Contents

THOMAS EAST AND MUSIC PUBLISHING IN RENAISSANCE ENGLAND

INTRODUCTION

Beneath the seemingly placid surface of the music trade in Renaissance London was a bustling and jostling world of creativity, ambition, legal contests, and even political danger. Thomas East (1540–1608) was the premier, often exclusive, printer and publisher of music in this competitive world. This study of East's career embraces the full context of interactions among composers, tradesmen, and, indirectly, consumers; the role of patronage; and the impact of politics. It will be the first to offer a comprehensive study of music publishing at a sixteenth-century London music press, providing thereby a new and broad-based understanding of the music field in this arguably richest era of English culture.

This work is intended to complement the studies of Shakespearean publishers and join a handful of monographic studies of continental music printers that have been produced in recent years.[1] These latter works have been recognized as pivotal contributions to our understanding of the music history of this period. This book shares their agenda: to provide reference data but then to move beyond the matter of music bibliography to consider larger implications of music publishing in the context of socioeconomic and cultural history.

THE "WORLDS" OF LONDON

When asked to identify himself in a court case of 1601, East proclaimed that he was the "Citizen and Stationer of the City . . . who had the true name for the imprintinge of musicke."[2] These terms aptly described his place not only in English musical life but also in the broader environment of Renaissance London. In 1608 Thomas Milles described England's capital as a center where

> [o]ur trades do meet in *Companies,* our *Companies* at *Halls,* and our *Halls* become *Monopolies* of Freedom . . . where all our *Crafts* & Mysteries are so layd vp together, that . . . [b]y means whereof, all our Creeks seeke to one River, . . . all our Cities but Suburbs to one vast, vnweldy, and disorderly *Babell* of buildings, which the world calls *London.*[3]

In a recent study of the City itself (London was technically two cities: the City was the square mile within the Roman gates, the City of Westminster was where the royal palace and royal courts were located), Steve Rappaport reiterated Milles's synoptic view—describing London as a conglomerate mercantile society that comprised "worlds within worlds."[4] East would never produce music on the scale of his contemporaries in Paris and Venice, but one of his signal achievements in English terms was to reach across the commerce-minded City into elite Westminster and bring to-gether London's trading and musical worlds.[5]

As a freeman and "Citizen" of the Stationers' Company, East lived in the City of Companies (among ironmongers, drapers, chandlers, and so forth), with their "mys-teries" (crafts) and monopolies, as described by Milles. Each company was generally free to run its specific trade as the liverymen saw fit and to police their members through their own courts. They were each given the right to restrict others from their particular craft, to assume a legal personality in court, and to obtain wealth and prop-erty so as to strengthen their position in the city. The mayor and his court of alder-men arbitrated intercompany trading issues. Almost always, it was the wealthiest mem-bers of the most powerful companies who held such positions. All told, three-fourths of London's male population of East's day were freemen of city companies; and within the purview of the guilds were also the wives, widows, apprentices, and servants of company brethren.[6] It would not be overstating the case to suggest that until he stepped into the world of musicians East's company was the alpha and omega of his professional life.

In his own company, East held a respectable, if unremarkable, place. His posi-tion in the musical world, however, became of critical importance after England's most eminent composer, William Byrd, nominated him as his official assign in 1587 (East produced his first music editions the very next year). The special powers Byrd himself had accrued in the musical world stemmed in part from an economic advan-tage the queen bestowed on him and Thomas Tallis, in 1575. In that year, she gave to these nonstationers the exclusive rights to control the nation's music printing, printed music paper, and music importation for twenty-one years—a grant of patent that has come to be known as the music monopoly. Byrd's protégé, Thomas Morley, obtained a similar grant in 1598.[7] As members of the queen's Chapel Royal, these musicians were closely affiliated with the queen as her official courtiers. Her stated purpose was in fact to reward them for their personal service to the crown.

Putting powers of such magnitude into the hands of musicians, who were them-selves tied to the royal court, affected the normal balance of economic and social functions for publishing in London's music trade. For Tallis, Byrd, and Morley, the queen's grant was first and foremost a royal endorsement. Musicologists have been quick to seize on its potential for pecuniary benefits,[8] but the grant was a tool as much for social advancement as it was for monetary gain. One result along these lines was a boost in the composers' standing among their fellow musicians and a refine-ment of their role as the queen's most favored musical servants. It is also true that with their grant in hand the monopolists had more to gain than greater prestige. They could stand up to stationers like East with capacities unheard of on the Continent, and they were allowed to control the activities of their colleagues and competitors in music. In addition, the queen had entrusted them with a lofty cultural mission that may have proved inspirational beyond the promise of pecuniary rewards. As agents of the crown, and as the grant specifically stipulated, they were charged with "the ad-uancement of the science of musicke," a coveted responsibility that carried with it the exalted status of musical laureate.[9]

All of this gave new significance to the act of *publishing*, which must be carefully distinguished from the simple craft of music printing itself. It was primarily over issues related to publishing that stationers and courtly musicians would develop different views about the functions and advantages of a new music press. Many years ago, M. A. Shaaber sought to emphasize the economic significance of the publisher, whom he dubbed the "protagonist of the book trade."[10] As Shaaber noted, the publisher was the trade's true entrepreneur—the one who speculated on demand, negotiated with artists and craftsmen, and selected and edited the material. He or she stood to gain the most from the book's success but to lose the most if it failed. Effective publishing lined the pockets of the most creative and successful entrepreneurs. Yet even the most profitable publishing activities could adversely affect the prestige of the book's producers and authors.

The lingering patronage system ensured that musicians all over Europe experienced the tensions engendered by their rather subordinate position in the constellation of factors that controlled music publication. There were very important exceptions, such as the extraordinarily prolific and popular composer Orlando di Lasso,[11] but generally, continental musicians were rather powerless to change what occurred in the publishing arena, for they were largely at the mercy of the great publishing houses and/or their patrons.[12] Individual musicians could obtain privileges for single books, and several continental musicians had patents for larger portions of their own music. Even without privileges, musicians could of course seek to make advantageous deals with their patrons and the music presses, but unless a privilege was in place it was these latter two powers that ultimately set the terms for publishing music.[13] In East's London, musicians had a more comprehensive control of the field altogether—they could simply stop the entire nation's music presses. And since the powers were more evenly divided among authors and professional book traders, the lines between social and economic aspects of the publishing field were more sharply drawn. To a city merchant like East, publishing was basically a commercial venture: he identified a growing market segment and profited by serving it well. To a courtly composer like Byrd, however, publishing was also the means by which a reputation could be won or lost with the public and with a private-minded group of patrons, depending on whether the quality and character of the published compositions satisfied expectations.

WHEN TWO WORLDS COLLIDE

A singular enterprise was formed when the mercantile world of city stationers collided with the status-conscious environment of London's courtly musicians. If it was an unusual encounter, it was one definitely caused by the manifold enticements of the royal monopoly. For the composers, the monopoly provided the rare opportunity to profit from their compositional efforts, to govern the field of music generally, and to have what the poet Edmund Spenser so famously desired in the field of letters, "the kingdom of his own language."[14] For all this they needed a capable music press, and one that was poised to make its famous impact in their field. They needed someone like East. A royal decree determined that only a member of the Stationers' Company could provide a press for the musicians and, no less important, only he could open doors for them into the complex world of a company-controlled trade.

The monopoly looked inviting from East's side, too, although he viewed it somewhat differently than the patent holders. Deeply engrained in company wisdom was the belief that royal protections were the primary source of power in the London book trade; with monopolistic protections it was possible to nurture a single market and enjoy all its profits. Therefore, as much as the musicians needed someone like East, he would need them, too. Not only did East depend on the composers' permission to wield the monopoly over his competitors; he also looked to them to create a product that would interest his customers.

In the music-publishing enterprise, composers and book traders wove a pattern of associations based on their mutual needs and their separate skills. Because their worlds were once so far apart, the relations began with a "learning curve" for each party. Shifts in public demand, changes in the ownership of the monopoly, restructuring of the company, and major shifts in religious and governmental politics over the years led to further evolution of the relationship. The dynamic aspects of this interplay, particularly the changes over time induced by shifts in monopolistic power, are the principal points of focus in this narrative, and they dictate the basically chronological scheme of the book's organization. The pivotal year was 1588, when East entered the music-publishing field. The first two chapters serve primarily as background. Chapter 1 provides a sketch of East's life and career before he became a music printer, with attention to his role in the highly organized Company of Stationers. In chapter 2, after summarizing the history of music printing on the European continent, I outline and evaluate the state of the London music-printing trade prior to 1588. The third chapter takes up technical issues of East's music production that span his career, especially those that concern the chronology of his music books, and solves the problems of undated and misdated music prints in his output.

The next five chapters constitute a study of East's career as a music tradesman, his interactions with the composers of his era, and the adaptations each made to the changing conditions of the music-publishing environment. When East began to print music in 1588 it was under the certain terms of Byrd's music monopoly. In chapters 4 and 5, I consider, from two perspectives, the music East produced from 1588 to 1592–1593, from the year East entered the field to about the time Byrd moved from the London area to Essex (and Morley began to dominate the music trade). Chapter 4 centers on Byrd. Its purpose is to determine just how and why the composer exercised his monopoly at this juncture. Chapter 5 reveals how East quickly developed marketing strategies to enter the most popular music markets and the most competitive areas of the stationers' trade.

Morley dominated East's trade for two years (1594–1596), publishing only his own books of popular Italianate music with East as his printer. When Byrd's patent officially expired in 1596, the direct result was a true competition in the field. In September 1598, Morley obtained his own monopoly and pursued a more complicated publishing tactic. This phase of East's career is the subject of chapter 6. Chapter 7 discusses East's operations in the twilight years of the Elizabethan era, particularly as they infringed on great matters of state, including the Catholic issue and the Essex affair. In the final chapter (8), which covers the early Jacobean period, it becomes clear just how well East's original marketing stratagems served his interests. Bibliographical data that span East's career as a music printer and include a checklist of his extant works are provided in the appendices.

In this work, striking new views are offered—of the market for music, the role of the Elizabethan music monopoly, and the ways in which English composers reacted to the novel medium of print. It is demonstrated that enterprise, ambiguity, and agitation in the economic environment of East's music trade, aspects hitherto neglected or misunderstood, had a considerable effect on the publishing and musical world. As East looked to move the music of Byrd and Morley (and many others) from his shelves into the hands of London's music consumers, the musicians, in turn, encouraged or compelled him to make extraordinary uses of his press: to attempt to perfect their musical texts before they were transmitted to the public in printed form, to mass-produce music for the illegal worship needs of the Catholic minority, and to try to direct and improve the musical tastes of the English nation generally. As the power struggles among composers, publishers, and printers began to envelop East's career, moreover, a modern-day conception of copyright was foreshadowed many generations before it was law. Since the work of Carlo Ginzberg it is no longer unusual to claim that new historical insights may be gained by placing a seemingly minor figure such as East on center stage.[15] In this case, it is hoped that the effort to probe and re-create East's world will succeed in helping the general reader no less than the scholar to understand the "real workings" of an industry in the arts.

THE LIFE AND EARLY CAREER
OF THOMAS EAST

I

Lives of East's more famous contemporaries, such as Shakespeare and Marlowe, are so notoriously undocumented that entire books have been devoted to filling in the sketchy outlines.[1] While East's case will never reach Shakespearean levels of interest or controversy, in its own quiet way it, too, has stirred up a fair amount of speculation and confusion over the years. One older theory had it that East was an Italian émigré, based on his tendency to favor the spelling "Este."[2] Another rather popular conjecture was that Thomas East was the father of Michael East, the prominent composer of the early Stuart era.[3] The younger East was indeed conspicuously well published and had had his first book of music printed by his reputed father. This once promising idea was called into serious question when bibliographers noticed works printed in 1609 by "Thomas Snodham alias East." Some now assumed that East had changed his name to Snodham at the time or that Lucretia East, the stationer's wife, married a Snodham after East's death.[4] Neither guess turned out to be correct.

Subsequent scholarship was able to correct many of the older misconceptions. For example, the *Dictionary of National Biography*[5] evaluated the Italian theory and dismissed it for lack of evidence while the prominent bibliographer Henry R. Plomer brought significant documentation to bear that demonstrated the near certainty that East was an Englishman. Plomer had discovered a well-entrenched clan of Easts on the border of Buckinghamshire and Oxfordshire Counties and proposed that the stationer belonged to this group.[6] As to the Snodham alias East confusion, Edward Arber transcribed the Stationers' Company records in the nineteenth century and provided ample evidence that there were two distinct people involved.[7] With Miriam Miller's discovery of Thomas East's will (see Figure 1.1) in 1975, Snodham was finally identified properly as the stationer's adopted son; there was no mention of the composer, Michael. The otherwise attractive theory of a father/son relationship of printer and composer was now disproved.[8]

Thanks in great part to discoveries made by the eminent bibliographer Peter Blayney and the genealogist Faith Keymer, as well as to my own findings, new information about East's date and place of birth, his relationship to Michael East, and the family background of his wife and adopted son is now available.[9] From this it is possible to glean something of East's life and affairs outside the company. The other key sources of information about East are contained in the books he printed and the records of the company to which he swore allegiance.

According to court records, East was born in or about 1540. He was thus, coincidentally, almost the exact contemporary of another figure of great importance to his trade, the composer William Byrd, whose date of birth was also discovered in the

FIGURE 1.1
Original Will of Thomas East
Guildhall Library, London,
Original Wills, Box 3B
(Ms. 9052 3b), f. 61, "Will of
Thomas East, 21 July, 1607."
Reproduced by permission.

files of a civil court case.[10] In a 1584 proceeding, *Edward East vs. Richard East* of West
Wycombe, Buckinghamshire, Thomas East was described as a "London Statyoner of
the age of xliiij yeres or therabouts."[11] Beyond the birth date, the sheer number of Easts
involved does suggest that this document might contain other clues about Thomas
East's origins.

From documents in the Buckinghamshire Records Office I was able to establish
that the Easts of this case were almost certainly direct descendants of William East
of Radnage (d. 1530), who headed the most prominent family in the area.[12] In his testimony, the stationer mentioned that he had known both litigants (and Richard's father, too) for several decades. The stationer specifically mentioned that he saw them
on a Christmas visit in 1580.[13] Were it not for other information, the case would seem
to confirm Plomer's thesis about East's Buckinghamshire origins.

Thomas East may very well have had ties of kinship with the Easts of Radnage,
but in sixteenth-century England the name Thomas East was not that uncommon.
More definitive would be a precise identification of Thomas East the *stationer* and a
clear sense of where his family was clustered. Newly discovered litigation suggests
that his immediate family was centered in Swavesy, Cambridge. In a 1594 Chancery
case, *Thomas and Margaret Willet [née East] vs. Francis East* of Swavesy, Lucretia East, the
"wife of Thomas East of London Stationer," gave evidence that clarified all the relevant family connections.[14] Thanks to his wife's testimony, the stationer Thomas East
should be firmly identified as the first cousin of these Easts of Swavesy. Incidentally,

another deponent in the case was "Alexander East of London Salter," the brother of the complainant, Francis East. In 1600–1601, when the stationer was sued in an extensive litigation, this same Alexander testified that he was working in East's stationer's shop. It is now clear that the salter, long thought to be East's brother, was his first cousin.[15] Based on these discoveries, Faith Keymer, whom I was pleased to assist in the matter, developed a genealogical chart of the Swavesy East family that places Thomas East firmly within its matrix (see appendix 3).

This newly discovered information clarifies the actual relationship of Thomas East with Michael East, the composer, and also allows for an estimation of East's family wealth. Michael East had many professional links to Cambridge. Philip Brett has pointed out that before East moved to Lichfield circa 1618 the composer had worked as a lay clerk in nearby Ely Cathedral; when he published his first book of music with Thomas East, it was from the London palace of the Bishops of Ely in Holbourne.[16] Now it appears that the composer may indeed have had a specific family connection to the stationer. In his will, George East of Swavesy mentioned that his nephew Thomas (the stationer) had a brother, William. This was probably the same William East who married Mary Tayler in 1573 and baptized his first son, Michael, at Holy Trinity, Ely, in 1574. Michael East was the executor of his mother's will that was proved in Ely in 1611.[17] In the absence of any evidence to the contrary, it does seem reasonable to assert that he was also the composer and the music printer's nephew.

Some estimation of East's independent resources may be adduced from his family history. Like many London traders, East relied on his family for labor as well as for capital resources and useful connections. East held a place of pride in his immediate family; he was the firstborn son of his father, also named Thomas, and therefore likely to have had a premier claim to whatever family inheritance there might have been. The stationer's father, however, was the second son of East's grandfather (see appendix 3). Thus it was East's uncle, (another) Alexander, who commanded the chief fortunes of the East family, at least in terms of land. At one point, the Swavesy Easts owned an extensive property on the old border of Huntingdon and Cambridgeshire Counties. This land apparently included "8 messuages, a dovehouse, 8 gardens, 200 acres of land, [including] 60 acres of meadow, 30 acres of pasture, 6 acres of wood, common of pasture for all manner of cattle, fold course, free warren and free fishing in Hallywell and Nedyngworthe."[18] Unfortunately, Uncle Alexander was outlawed and lost this inheritance during Thomas East's lifetime. The latter's inheritance was certainly much more modest.

The crucial event of East's early years was his apprenticeship to the stationers' trade of London. There is no record of East's indenture, and thus the circumstances of his move to London remain a matter of conjecture. Without landed wealth but with the privileges of a firstborn son in a fairly well-to-do family, the adolescent East was on the road, at least, to possible success in the London trading world. As much as the guild system would seem to permit them, there were in fact few "rags-to-riches" stories at the time. East's slow but steady rise to the level of a liveryman and assistant in his company, though unconventional in certain ways, was no doubt due to some extent to social privileges that came from family connections. At any rate,

East was demonstrably proud of his family name. His array of type ornaments included two handsome pieces in the design of the East family heraldic seal.[19] Following up on Plomer's research, it is my contention that East looked beyond the Swavesy area to the help of other Easts to pave the way for his entry into the city.

The East family crest provides a useful starting place for the study of the sixteenth-century Easts. Examples of the family crest abound in the English visitation books of the era, and two particularly well preserved memorial brasses of an East family may be seen in their original settings from the early sixteenth century.[20] The design of the crest was of a black horse set above a chevron with three horse heads. Thomas East's particular design included a crescent (to signify his status as a descendant of a second son) and the motto "Mieux vault mourir en vertu que vivre en honcte" ("better to die in virtue than to live in disgrace"). He printed his coat of arms in colophons of a select number of prints in which his firm had special interest, which included his pivotal collection of the *Whole Booke of Psalmes* (see Figure 1.2).

The brass memorial of an East family in the parish church in Radnage, Buckinghamshire, dates from 1534. At that time, the Easts were the most prominent family of the area, and some indication of the English base of this family is suggested by the fact that members of this clan were living in the Radnage area in the fifteenth century at the latest.[21] Although he was apparently unaware of the heraldic connection, Plomer found other evidence that the printer was from that county. He discovered that a Thomas East was mentioned in the will of the prominent ironmonger Thomas Lewen, who also listed his niece, Margaret East, and a fellow ironmonger, William East, in the same document. Of these Easts, Lewen listed Thomas as his "godson and kinsman," and Lewen also mentioned another relative, David Moptid. David was the son of the ironmonger Harry Moptid and, as Plomer noted, was to become East's apprentice in the stationers' trade.[22] Plomer was convinced from this conformity of evidence that he had identified the printer of this study in the year 1554 and had determined his place of origin.

Not surprisingly, in view of the Swavesy evidence, extensive study of the parish records in Buckinghamshire produced no trace of East's birth or early life there. Nonetheless, it is clear from records of the Ironmongers' Company that Thomas Lewen's connection to a family of Easts was even much stronger than Plomer suggested. Unbeknownst to him, three members of the East family had moved to London to serve as Lewen's apprentices in the ironmongers' trade: William East (mentioned in Lewen's will) in 1527 and Robert and Christopher East in 1538.[23] Christopher may not have served his apprenticeship, but the other two men remained active traders in London for the rest of their lives.

Robert East (d. 1606) had a brilliant career. He resided in the much-admired "mansion" Lewen left to the company and became an influential landowner in the city.[24] In his business and property affairs Robert worked in productive partnerships with William Skidmore, another former apprentice of Lewen, and Sir Alexander Avenon.[25] Avenon's prominence is reflected in the fact that he served both as an alderman and as the lord mayor of London.[26] Ironmongers' Company records provide much data about Robert's own accumulation of wealth in business and property. Robert was chosen to be warden of his company several times and held the highest

¶Imprinted at London by Thomas Eſt.
the aſſigne of VVilliam Byrd : dwelling
in Alderſgate-ſtreete at the ſigne of
the black Horſe, and are there
to be ſold.

FIGURE 1.2
The East Coat of Arms
Thomas East (pub.), *Whole Booke of Psalmes,*
(London, 1592), 296. Courtesy of the Univer-
sity of Illinois Library, Urbana-Champaign.

position of master in 1591.[27] He was an ambitious and quite successful businessman
and landowner in London during most of Thomas East's lifetime.

It would seem from Robert's example alone that Thomas might be counted as
one of a number of Easts who moved to London and thrived in the trading companies of the mid–sixteenth century. Yet it is salutary to compare the evidence of his
successful entrée into the London trading world with the failures of Robert East's
brother, William. William began his career as a freeman of his company without incident, but in 1557, at the time he held the position of renter warden, he was accused
of extorting money from his company.[28] Like Robert, William resided in one of the
properties of his deceased master, Lewen. Although this arrangement was a stipulation of Lewen's will, William was evicted from his lodging by the company under the
direction of Robert East.[29] In 1582, near the end of his life, William was still insol-
vent and, consequently, the company elected to offer him a twenty-shilling quarterly
pension as an act of charity. He died within months of this small retirement offer-
ing, and his pension passed to his widow. Just a single year after his demise, his widow
remarried and surrendered her right to this meager company annuity.[30]

More data would be necessary to fully confirm Plomer's belief that William and
Robert East were closely related to the printer. At least some familial connection between Robert and Thomas East is suggested, however, by the fact that each man lived
in residences named for the East coat of arms. In his imprints, Thomas East directed
his customers to several different residences, which included his final one at Alders-

gate Street, with his "sign of the Dark Horse," an obvious reference to his crest. From the sixteenth century until the Second World War, when this area of the city was demolished by bombs, a section of Aldersgate Street where East probably ran his shop was known as "Black Horse Alley."[31] Similarly, Robert East's property near the Ironmongers' Company Hall in nearby Bread Street was known at the time, and for many years afterward, as "Horsehead Alley."[32] Further confirmation of Robert East's association with the same East family is found in the mention of him in the will of the aforementioned Richard East of West Wycombe, whom Thomas East the stationer visited on Christmas Day in 1580. Richard East was buried under a brass memorial with a design nearly identical to the one Thomas East used to advertise his firm.[33]

The career paths of William and Robert East illustrate perfectly the kinds of opportunities and obstacles Thomas East confronted as a tradesman in London. Like Robert East, Thomas seems to have started out with sparse personal means, but he was privileged to enter the trade in a flexible partnership with a brother of his company, namely, the printer Thomas Middleton. Middleton was the heir to his father's thriving business, and this led to early successes for East that probably provided a base of capital sufficient to establish his independent work in subsequent years.[34] Like William East before him, Thomas did encounter some trouble for his activities and was occasionally fined by the company. East's infringements were quite minor, however, as they involved only the printing of items that were not approved by the guild and the presenting of apprentices out of order.[35]

FREEDOM AND MARRIAGE

On 6 December 1565 the Stationers' Company clerk noted the following in the registers he maintained for his guild: "Recevyd of Thomas Heaste for his charges at his makyng fre of this Companye ... iijs iiijd."[36] By paying this standard fee, Thomas East (also spelt "Heaste," "Easte," "Est," and "Este") began his official career as a printer and publisher of London. The significance of this brief note for East's career can hardly be overestimated; company allegiance was the one constant feature of his entire career and colored virtually all his decisions as a music printer.

Formally, the Stationers' Company and the nearly 100 other livery companies of London were under state control, but they had enjoyed a tradition of autonomy that extended back to the fourteenth century. All London companies enjoyed certain measures of trading freedom and governmental protection, but they were not all equal in power. Judging by company rankings of the day, the stationers' was a fairly minor corporation. At official city dinners, for example, East's fellow book traders sat far away from the head of the table where the twelve "great" companies were positioned, and this kind of ranking tended to reflect a company's real status.[37] Without the requisite level of individual or collective wealth, few stationers rose to the rank of mayor or alderman. Thus the company had to rely on other traders to voice their concerns in city government. Still, the importance of London's book trade (that the Stationers' Company controlled) should not be underestimated. Printed books were indeed the most important means of communication in the realm. As book traders, stationers helped direct English cultural and intellectual life, and by promulgating various kinds of propaganda they also stepped into the critical area of national politics. [38]

As a company member, East enjoyed a modest but consistent rise to a relatively high position among his peers as a trader and citizen of the city. In 1594 he was elected to the livery of the company, and in 1603 he was honored with the position of assistant.[39] East operated a single press that was licensed by the government, although at the end of his life there is evidence that he also secretly employed two additional presses (a second one on Aldersgate Street and one in Cripplegate).[40] Like the much larger Day firm of stationers, East took advantage of the influx of Huguenot craftsmen to London; in particular, he hired Richard Schilders, who went on to a most prominent career as a printer in Middleburgh.[41] East also employed at various times apprentices from English families, who included the aforementioned David Moptid, who was a relative of Lewen and an ironmonger's son; Thomas Snodham, whom East adopted into his own family; John Balls and John Wiborowe, who would later serve as informants against recusant Catholics who resided at East's workplace; and the playwright Henry Chettle, who went on to become a famous colleague of Shakespeare.[42] East's workforce also included his wife, who later became his official partner; his cousin Alexander; others of his immediate family; and his servants.

East's marriage, although outside of company affairs per se, was, among other things, perhaps his most decisive single business move of the pre-1588 era. East's wife was one of several children orphaned at the death of the prosperous pewterer Thomas Hassell. Hassell was the warden of his company in 1565, and such prominence was a sure indicator of wealth.[43] The value of the match is further evident in East's eagerness to effect the marriage.

East married Lucretia Hassell circa 1568, when she was a mere fourteen years old and a ward of the city.[44] Wardships were the chief source of power in the city government. Thus it is not surprising that when the couple went to collect their rightful part of the estate from the officials East was fined, presumably for marrying someone so young.[45] It is doubtful that the guardians had any moral problems with the marriage. East had forced them to forfeit profits they could draw by collecting interest on the surety of Lucretia East's inheritance.

Several of Lucretia East's orphaned sisters also married citizens of the city. One of these sisters was the Mary Hassell who married the draper Thomas Snodham.[46] It was this couple's child whom Thomas and Lucretia East adopted after both of his parents died. See appendix 3 for East's family connections.

EAST'S PRINTS OF GENERAL LITERATURE

From 1565 to 1588, East maintained a lively career as a printer, publisher, and bookseller in London, seemingly without demonstrating any interest at all in the music trade around him. Perhaps it has even been to the detriment of a greater understanding of East's role as a contributor to the culture of his day that scholars have focused so much on his music printing. As early as 1901, East's career as a printer of general literature was the subject of an important article by Plomer, and some of the more intriguing prints by East have been amply studied in bibliographical journals and elsewhere.[47] It was also Plomer, however, who turned attention to the great impact of music printing on East's firm. Plomer demonstrated, for example, that East's general printing work was consistently pushed to a minor place in the printer's output after 1588.

If wholly deserving of separate study, East's printing of other kinds of books is often difficult to relate directly to his trade in music. Music was effectively separated from other types of book production by the two royal patents that controlled the trade, as well as by the great participation of musicians. Composers were the authors of texts and quite often the publishers of music books in print, while the primary consumers in the trade were surely musicians, although many must have been amateur performers or collectors. One common feature to both sides of East's career, however, was the Stationers' Company and, in particular, the policy of registration. Registration was a facet of the company's regulatory practice that enabled the publisher to lay claim to intellectual properties. East took full advantage of it in all of his printing endeavors, including music.[48]

Like most of his fellow freemen of London, however, East treated his company as more than just an institution with regulatory control over his trade. It was the company that recognized and ratified the official partnerships that were formed among stationers. More broadly, the company provided the social forum for establishing business networks that made so-called trade printing such a lively enterprise in sixteenth-century London.

TRADE PRINTERS AND PRINTER-PUBLISHERS

In 1929 Ronald B. McKerrow distinguished two basic classifications among the professional activities of London master printers: printer-publishers and trade printers.[49] These were distinctions common to the Renaissance trade at large. Italian book traders, for example, used the terms *editore* (publisher) and *typographico* (trade printer) to describe the two roles. Depending on their access to financial capital and their political power in the trade, as well as their entrepreneurial inclinations, printers of East's ilk situated themselves variously in one of or somewhere in between these two vocational categories. East's career as a whole shows that he most often functioned as a trade printer, but that he acted as a printer-publisher on special occasions.

In the Renaissance book trade, printer-publishers were genuine entrepreneurs. As publishers, London master printers negotiated with the writers and translators who created material for London presses. It was also the printer-publishers' responsibility to obtain and maintain the right to print the works they chose to produce, and thus they dealt extensively with issues that had to do with legal aspects of intellectual property. These printer-publishers purchased the paper, arranged for the production of the books (either by printing the work themselves or by using the services of another printer, who then served as a trade printer), and organized the distribution of their editions. Their living was determined by the market, and thus they were usually driven to action by the call of demand itself.

McKerrow conducted a study of the London stationer Edward Allde (d. 1632) as an example of the "typical trade printer." He concluded that Allde's output was largely governed by the publishing interests of other entrepreneurs in the stationers' trade.[50] The work of trade printers, like Allde, presents great challenges to the scholar who seeks to find evidence of any consistency or any conscious program of publication in the total body of works by a single printer. Trade printers entered into complicated relations with other printers and publishers. In many cases, they worked on large projects that had been divided up and the portions parceled out to a number of printers. As they worked under contract with a publisher, their output was determined by another entrepreneur. Because they worked for others, they had little reason to speculate on the demand for printed material or to try to assess and influence consumer needs.

East clearly was ambitious as a businessman but did not enjoy great resources of capital. From his first printings as a partner with Middleton until the end of his life, East wisely entered into various partnerships with his fellow stationers in order to maintain the viability of his firm. In his study of the trends of the London book trade, H. S. Bennett singled East out as a printer for whom the greatest part of his work was for other booksellers and publishers.[51] Like Edward Allde, but perhaps even more so, in his early career as a general printer East was indeed the typical trade printer of his era.

Even in his more routine work, there are aspects of East's output that merit special comment. In 1588, as he began his music printing, East settled into the residence in Aldersgate Street that he leased from the Baron Nowell Sotherton for the remainder of his life.[52] Before that time, however, East had located his trade in many different areas of the city: at Fleet Street, near St. Dunstan's Church (1566–1570); at Bread Street, at the nether end, 1568; at London Wall, by the sign of the Ship (1571–1577); and by Paul's Wharf, Thames Street (1577–1588), for example. The London trade in maritime and medical books was centered in the Paul's Wharf area of London; East produced most of his books of this sort while he lived there.[53] Also affecting East's career was his close proximity to the firm of another maritime printer of note, Henry Bynneman of Paul's Wharf.[54]

Bynneman owned several lucrative patents, as well as an interest in the music patent. East obtained convenient trade work and perhaps an overflow of copies from Bynneman's business.[55] Location may have been an important factor in East's music printing as well, at least as an incentive for East to begin this new trade. The largest stationer's firm in Aldersgate Street in the sixteenth century was that of John Day. Although his main business was in psalmbooks alone, Day was the most prominent music printer in the era before East joined the field. East did not acquire Day's music fonts but did obtain two of his most distinctive sets of initials from Day or more likely from Day's son Richard (after the latter had failed in his attempt to set up a business during his father's lifetime).[56]

There were relatively few books that East actually chose to publish rather than simply to print, but these do attest to his sharp business sense. They included a highly popular series of romances, the inaugural works of the very popular phase of Euphuism in English literature (in a partnership with the publisher Gabriel Cawood in which East appeared to have some interest in the venture), and new editions of medieval texts that enjoyed a great resurgence of popular interest in Tudor times.[57]

The most intriguing and successful of East's publications before he adopted a specialty in music were probably the series of works spearheaded by Margaret Tyler's translation of a Spanish romance by Diego Ortuñez de Calahorra.[58] The potential risk of producing the inaugural volume of this series is immediately evident from Tyler's preface. Here she carefully defended her work in what has come to be seen as a feminist position.[59] Tyler was well aware that she made herself susceptible to the criticism of her contemporaries, who viewed the act of translating as equivalent to assuming the role of author and therefore as something unsuitable for a woman. East produced a different type of apologia for his publication, choosing to defend its moral value to his readership. In this well-conceived preface, East revealed his understanding of the role he played in cultivating taste as well as maintaining a viable business in the book trade.[60]

Ultimately, as with many of East's publishing ventures, his risk in publishing Tyler's translations of Spanish romances was amply rewarded. East created a small industry out of exploiting the popular interest in Calahorra's texts. East eventually published two sequels and reprinted them frequently throughout his career. That he was indeed an astute tradesman is obvious from this single venture. His record, however, also reveals him to have been very careful about risk taking. Why then would a businessman of East's acumen commit so much of his time and effort to music printing, which, apart from simple settings of the psalms, was not highly regarded by professional printers at the time East took up the trade? What will emerge from this study as a whole is that East was attracted to the music field because of special opportunities he could obtain nowhere else within the confines of the competitive stationers' trade, opportunities to develop his capacities as an effective entrepreneur.

Music printing as an enterprise in London before 1588

 2

The European background

Music printing seems to have been introduced in Europe in the last quarter of the fif-teenthth century, and its incunabula period could perhaps be seen to linger on into the late 1520s. Among the earliest examples were sumptuous two-color folios of fifteenth-century chant; a splendid series of part-books issued by Ottaviano dei Petrucci; and the equally stunning woodcut quarto and folio editions of Petrucci's competitor An-drea Antico (the latter two printers worked in the first decades of the sixteenth cen-tury).[1] For aesthetic as well as historical reasons, such examples remain among the most treasured of printed music books. Despite these lofty achievements, however, a more comprehensive view of the field suggests that music printing was often ham-pered by technological limitations in the early years.

The kind of movable metal type that Gutenberg had famously developed for lit-erary texts in the 1450s appeared some twenty years later for music. Even by then, however, music printers apparently found it difficult to obtain the appropriate fonts and to use them effectively. Some printers had no obvious trouble with musical texts in the incunabula era. Others managed to print only the notes (or only the staves); still others left entire sections of music blank for scribes to complete by hand.[2] By the 1490s, woodcuts had emerged as an alternative means of printing music. Though perfected and championed by Antico in the early sixteenth century (and often used before and after as a convenient means by which to set musical examples), woodcut techniques never reached the kind of standardization among music printers enjoyed by movable metal type.

At the turn of the sixteenth century, there was a fundamental change in the field of music printing. After applying for a Venetian privilege for "canto figurado" (po-lyphony) and "intaboladure dorgano et de liuto" (organ and lute tablature) in 1498, Petrucci issued his *Harmonice musices odhecaton A* in 1501.[3] Thereafter, Petrucci remained committed to the music world. He followed his *Odhecaton A* with a sequel, the *Canti B,* and continued on with another forty-odd editions of music, including a series of popular *frottole,* books of masses, motets, and lute music. Petrucci was not the first to print music (as he is popularly represented to be), nor were his methods unprece-dented, but he was the first printer to specialize in polyphony (and instrumental music) rather than chant, and he set wonderfully high standards of production for nearly all kinds of music printing.

Like most other music printers of his era, Petrucci used an exacting double- and triple-impression process for printing music, one that required extra patience and care and therefore slowed considerably the time of production. Although Petrucci did have followers,[4] the field did seem to have reached a plateau—missing was a solution to the problems of printing music in multiple impressions. If type could be designed to combine notes with sections of the stave, it would permit musical texts to be printed in a single pass through the press. It turns out that type of this kind had been introduced as early as 1510 in Salzburg, where it was sporadically used to solve certain problems of melodic variance in a book of chant.[5] Later, in the mid-1520s, John and William Rastell used a single-impression font to produce several song sheets for local markets in London.[6]

The single-impression method was put to sustained use only after the Parisian Pierre Attaingnant produced his *Chansons nouvelles* of 1527/28.[7] Attaingnant enjoyed a flourishing trade in music after 1528, and his method spread quickly throughout Northern Europe. Eventually it reached Venice, where the most productive music-printing firms of the century, which included the Gardano (Gardane) and Scotto dynasties, were founded. With Parisian and Venetian music printers in the forefront, the second half of the sixteenth century witnessed a dramatic change in musical production levels.[8] Whereas Petrucci had set new standards of productivity with his 40 editions in the first two decades of the century, his successors in Venice alone put an astonishing 4,200 music editions through their presses in the years 1550–1650.[9]

THE IMPACT OF PRINT

Following in the path of print historian Elizabeth Eisenstein, music bibliographers have now grappled extensively with the advent of print culture as a Europe-wide phenomenon, treating the widespread shift from written to printed music books as a watershed event in music history.[10] In Eisenstein's view, the shift from manuscript to the medium of print opened vast new avenues for intellectual growth, provided powerful new incentives for social change, sparked decisive advances in literacy, precipitated new mixes of elite and popular art forms, and inspired more inclusive educational reforms, along with other key developments. In their studies of the music-printing industries of Venice in the sixteenth century, Mary S. Lewis, Richard Agee, and Jane A. Bernstein, among others, have contributed enormously to our understanding of the impact of print in the world of music, as an aspect of the broad phenomenon identified by Eisenstein.[11]

These same studies (and many before them), however, are also marked by attention to individuality. Not only have they tended to focus on a single music printer and that printer's musical products, but they have also sought to discover how each contributed to and was affected by the socioeconomic environment of a particular Renaissance center. This approach has proved to be a fruitful course. The cities of sixteenth-century Paris and Venice, for example, had notable differences in their socioeconomic organizational structures that affected the nature of their music publishing. Attaingnant, who held the privileged title of Music Printer to the King, looked first and foremost to musicians closest to the monarch for music to print and, as Daniel Heartz has argued, brought great publicity to the distinctly national styles that were fostered at the royal court.[12] Conversely, as they were working in a city well established for centuries as an international center of trade, Venetian music printers naturally cast their nets widely for musical material, turning as much to Roman and Neapolitan musicians as they did to the considerable musical talents they could find around them in the Veneto.[13] If distinctly varied in the kinds of musicians they promoted, what these two cities indubitably had in common, however, were economic, social, and cultural systems that encouraged expansive industries in music publishing.

For all its importance, single-impression type was not a complete panacea for the music-printing trade. Economic troubles in Rome in the late 1520s and afterward, for example, had lasting effects on the industry there. As Suzanne G. Cusick has emphasized in her study of Valerio Dorico, Rome's turbulent postsack conditions had a decidedly deleterious effect on the volume of its musical output, despite Dorico's eventual adoption of single-impression methods in 1544.[14] And for all the economic vibrancy of Antwerp and other cities in the Netherlands, it turned out that no one there would establish an industry in music printing that could truly compete with that of Venice. Certainly printers like Pierre Phalèse and Tielman Susato were highly successful music traders who had a major impact on the musical life of Leuven and Antwerp,[15] yet their individual output was decidedly less than that of Scotto and Gardano and in many ways more localized. Like many others of the post-Attaingnant era, music printing for them was more of a cottage industry.

Cultural and social historians have lately revisited Eisenstein's theories about print's revolutionary impact and have begun to look beyond quantitative aspects to consider other dimensions of its force. In the process, the "print revolution" has lost some of its appearance of uniformity.[16] Certainly there were enormously successful merchants in the field, but other book traders found it difficult to deal with uncertain markets, aggressive competition, and governmental interference, among other constraints on their trade. Furthermore, certain social and political forces opposed the press with more stubbornness than has often been credited. These latter conditions were more like those of East's London.

LONDON

At the time when Venetian and Parisian music presses were reaching new levels of productivity in their chanson and madrigal output, music printers in England had produced little more than a handful of secular music editions that have survived to this day. These include some fragments printed by John and William Rastell sometime in the late 1520s and 1530s; the anonymously printed *XX Songes* (1530); Orlando di Lasso's *Receuil* (1570) printed by Thomas Vautrollier; Thomas Whythourne's *Songs in Three, Fower and Five Parts* (1571); and the LeRoy *Instruction for Lute* (1568, 1574), printed by John Day.[17] John Milsom has argued eloquently for the possibility that a lively, and distinctly local, market for music among London citizenry existed despite this sketchy documentation, but even he concedes that the field was "frankly insubstantial."[18] Individually, the aforementioned music books do provide important clues to the later development of music printing in England and elsewhere.[19] Viewed together, they only serve to underscore the great dearth of secular music published before East's tenure as a music printer.

From the Renaissance musician's standpoint, at least, the field of sacred music printing in London was hardly more impressive in this early period. Day's publication of *Certaine Notes* (1570) was an important contribution historically. He also printed a few works that featured psalm-tune harmonizations.[20] Such editions might have demonstrated to composers that there was at least some venue to support original music in print. Before 1588, however, plainchant and the mostly static, and unattributed, tunes of the metrical psalmbooks far outnumbered more ambitious settings with polyphony. In this meager field, the Latin-texted music of the Thomas Tallis–William Byrd *Cantiones . . . sacrarum sacrae* (1575) printed by Vautrollier, and discussed later, was an extraordinarily significant publication, not only because of its quality and the standing of the two composers but also because of the prominence of its dedication to the queen herself. This was not Vautrollier's first music production in London—he had earlier printed Lasso's *Receuil*—but it is more important to note that despite the auspicious promise of the *Cantiones*, there was a striking lack of music editions to follow.[21] The Tallis-Byrd work was unanswered for thirteen years.

THE STERNHOLD AND HOPKINS *Whole Booke of Psalmes*

Throughout Reformed Europe, the institution of organized public singing had become an integral component of religious observance by mid-sixteenth-century. Congregational singing in the Protestant service was a new practice that Marian exiles (that is, those Englishmen who emigrated rather than conform to the Catholic religion of Philip and Mary) brought back to England from cities like Frankfurt, Geneva, and Emden, where they had become more firmly indoctrinated into an international brand of their faith.[22] The vigor with which this new style of worship was promoted seems clear from the following letter of 5 March 1560 that Protestant evangelist John Jewell wrote to exile Peter Martyr just after the latter's return from Frankfurt:

> Religion is somewhat more established now than it was. The people are every-
> where exceedingly inclined to the better part. Church music for the people
> has very much conduced to this. For as soon as they had once commenced
> singing publicly in only one little church in London, immediately not only the
> churches in the neighbourhood, but even in distant towns, began to vie with
> one another in the same practice. You may now sometimes see at Paul's Cross
> [in London], after the service, six thousand persons, old and young, of both
> sexes, all singing together and praising God.[23]

For Jewell, the sight of 6,000 people "all singing together and praising God" was a sure indication that the long-awaited revival of Protestantism in England had begun. Furthermore, he enthusiastically recounted the widespread growth in England of what his contemporaries described as the "Genevan" practice of congregational singing. This style of singing was apparently new to England (it was unknown in the reign of Edward VI) and was first recorded in London at a single parish church earlier in 1560 by the diarist Henry Machyn.[24] Machyn's account conforms, in substance if not with precision, to Jewell's claim that congregational singing began in "one little church in London." Thus it lends some credence to Jewell's remarks about the swift speed with which public participation in religious song had developed into a national institution.

In view of the international model and the overwhelming evidence of later practices in England, scholars have generally assumed that what was sung at events like the one at Paul's Cross described earlier was settings of the metrical psalms in English translation. As with much of the doctrine and philosophy of the Elizabethan Settlement, these poems can be traced to the courts of Henry VIII and Edward VI.[25] In the Protestant reigns of these Tudor kings there were many notable translations of the psalms, stemming from Coverdale's biblical translations and from private compilations. Thomas Sternhold, who was Groom of the Robe in both courts, set most of the psalms, and those he finished were offered to young Edward VI in a presentation manuscript.[26] Like other poets of the era, Sternhold set the psalms in a simple poetic meter (most with alternating lines of eight and six syllables). He probably expected them to be sung to courtly tunes known from an oral tradition.

It was Sternhold's metrical translations of the psalms that were first widely disseminated in print. In 1549, when he presented his incomplete collection of metrical psalms to the king, Sternhold was in the last year of his life; Day printed Sternhold's work soon after the poet's death. To finish the project, John Hopkins and others completed the translations in meter, based upon Sternhold's established method. These also went quickly into printed editions in collections that included and therefore complemented Sternhold's work.[27] From that time forward, the so-called Sternhold and Hopkins *Whole Booke of Psalmes* would exemplify the authoritative role of the press, for this one version of metrical psalms became a virtual standard and was the single most popular collection of poetry in Tudor England. For more than a century after its appearance in print this collection dominated the English marketplace.[28]

PATENTS, PIRATES, AND JOHN DAY'S *Whole Booke of Psalmes*

The psalms set to music also constituted a valuable property for those who arranged for their publication. Economic protection for the publishers of the collected psalms with music was eventually established by monopolistic patents.[29] William Seres, a founding member of the Stationers' Company, held a patent from the reign of Edward VI that gave him the privilege to print certain English translations of biblical texts. Although Seres did print prose versions of the metrical psalms, he rarely included musical notation in his editions.[30] Nonetheless, he apparently had sufficient claim to the metrical psalmbooks to bring a successful suit against Day on 2 October 1559, after the latter had printed an "unlicensed" volume of the "psalmes with notes."[31] Later that same year, Day was granted a patent, too, which he soon used to control production of the Sternhold-Hopkins psalmbooks.

Day's first patent was unusual for its open-ended coverage. It granted him the special right to exert a claim to any book "as he hath imprinted, or hereafter shall Imprint."[32] The sweeping character of the prospective clause in the grant was particularly harmful to other stationers. In 1567 Day refined his patent, focusing upon the books he printed most often and listing the "Psalmes of David in Englishe Meeter, with notes" as his exclusive property.[33]

This grant exemplified how the queen would happily bestow favor on an individual while seeming to be insensitive to the great harm it might cause her other subjects. Because the Stationers' Registers eventually served a similar function (recognizing and protecting an individual's right to any "copy" brought before the stationers' court of assistants), the confusion over the full powers of this patent led to many conflicts between Day and others in his trade.[34] By the 1570s, Day had control over thirty individual volumes, as well as several classes of books.[35] In the original struggle between Day and Seres for the right to print the psalter, Day's use of musical notation (rarely included in Seres's editions) was probably an important factor in bringing the property under his control.[36] Day's emphasis on music is clear. In his *Whole Booke of Psalmes* editions he often included a primer of instruction for musical notation, and he even took the trouble to redesign a music type with sol-fa notation to ease the problem of reading music.[37] Surely many continued to learn the texts and the music of the psalms by rote, yet it is probably some indication of a rise in musical literacy that already by the 1570s Day was reprinting editions in four-part harmonization.

This distinction between the metrical psalms "with notes" and their original presentation without notation was made official by an agreement in 1579 between William Seres the Younger (William Seres's son) with his assign Henry Denham on the one side and John Day and his son Richard on the other. Through arbitration of the Stationers' Company it was decided that

> Jhon Day and Richard Day and thier assignes shall at all and eury tyme and tymes hereafter Enioye the sole and only imprintinge of the said psalmes in meter wth note accordinge to the tenor Lymitacon and meaninge of the Queenes matie prvilege and graunt to them in that behalf amonge other thinges made and granted: without any lett clayme.[38]

Thus the company arranged that Day would control all printing of the collected psalms with music. Stationers surely associated this specific book of the psalms with Day's power and wealth. Music printing and profit were probably fixed together in the minds of many ambitious printers who envied his position.

Altogether, Day printed well over fifty editions of the Sternhold-Hopkins psalmbooks. By one contemporary account it was estimated that by selling copies at six shillings apiece he "exactethe of [the queen's] poore Subiecte fyve hundred poundes by the yeare at the leaste."[39] This was an extraordinary large sum, which was obviously still only a fraction of his annual income.[40] With such a lucrative business, it is not surprising that Day was often busy defending his rights and staving off competition from other ambitious stationers. One of Day's most grasping competitors, Roger Ward, was brought to trial for pirating 10,000 copies of Day's *ABC with Catechisms.* Ward admitted that he had hired a type founder to produce a font (probably just the initials) that resembled Day's type.[41] John Wolfe was also very keen to challenge Day, and he, too, found himself in court as a result. Having served his apprenticeship with Day and later worked for him as a subcontractor, Wolfe was very well acquainted with Day's methods. At his trial, Wolfe defended his actions not by claiming innocence— he never denied that he had printed large quantities of Day's *Whole Booke of Psalmes*—

but by arguing that he, as a citizen, had suffered unduly from the unfairness of Day's monopolistic business practices.

OPEN REBELLION AND RETALIATION

Wolfe was also the leader of a campaign mounted against Day sometime around 1577 (the actual date is a matter of some debate). A group of self-styled "poor printers" of the Stationers' Company, with East among them, joined forces to oppose the patents, and Day was their first target.[42] In their famous "Complaynt" directed to the Privy Council, they claimed that

> the privilidges latelie granted by her Majestie under her hignes great seale of England ... Concerninge the arte of printing of bookes hath and will be the overthrowe of the Printers and Stacioners within this Cittie being in number .17. Besides their wyves Children Apprentizes and families.[43]

If the rich but incomplete documentation on this struggle gives an accurate picture, this group of poor printers was hardly ignored and eventually got a full hearing of its grievances. As the Privy Council considered the case, these men continued to pirate patented books and generated a great deal of gossip and sensationalism over the case in the taverns and streets and in the courts when their cases were brought to trial.[44] Sometime in the early 1580s a commission was appointed by the Privy Council to investigate the patents. This investigation was first undertaken by Christopher Barker, the Queen's Printer, who submitted a report that evaluated all of the patents then in force. At that time Barker owned the patent for the English Bible. Thus he controlled one of the most lucrative patents of all stationers, although, ironically, he was one of the original signers of the "Complaynt." Other men of the commission, which included Thomas Hammond and Thomas Norton, were also personally involved in monopolies; they, too, could hardly have been expected to be completely impartial in their reports and recommendations.[45]

CONCESSIONS TO THE "POOR PRINTERS"

The commission itself produced a lengthy document on the patents, and three years later, in 1586, the royal court of the Star Chamber issued a decree on the subject.[46] Registers of the court of assistants at Stationers' Hall also recorded numerous discussions of the patents. Not surprisingly, the report, the decree, and much subsequent internal policy of the Stationers' Company were all designed to help protect the patent holders. Some concessions, however, were made to the poor printers. Chief among these was an order for the patentees to release certain of their titles to the rest of the company.[47] Understandably, the titles that were released were by no means the most lucrative books. In any case, Day was probably unharmed economically, because he kept the properties he printed most: the *ABC* and the *Whole Booke of Psalmes*.[48]

As a further concession to the less fortunate printers, the court of assistants of the company added two laws to the Stationers' "Court book" to help ensure that the poorer members of the company could find work. One rule restricted the size of the printed edition of any book to 1,500 copies, and the other outlawed the use of standing type, a process whereby the printer did not dismantle the type between editions but conveniently left the type in its composed state to be at the ready for further printings.[49] These conciliatory laws provide evidence of the practices of patentees, which included strategies they adopted to capitalize on the popularity of the editions they controlled.

If we judge by the newly established limit of 1,500 copies per edition, it is clear that monopolists printed very large editions of their profitable books before the restrictive law was in place. A further indication of this may be seen in the figures cited in the litigation that concerned piracy. Pirates produced the *Whole Booke* in editions of 2,000 and 4,000, and Day's *ABC* was once pirated in an edition of 10,000 copies.[50] To print such large editions was to risk squandering expensive paper if the books did not sell. For the psalmbooks and the spelling primer, however, there was apparently very good reason to expect a good return on a large capital investment in paper.

Mention of standing-type practices within the context of patent disputes presents another key to the practices of patent holders. To leave the type standing in formes indicates a bold confidence in the sales potential capacity of the volume. The printer, after all, lost access to the entire complex of preset type and thus was restrained from other concurrent production when he or she employed such a practice.[51] Of course, standing-type procedures deprived journeymen compositors of work, as did the large editions. Thus the two laws were consistent in efforts to allow more associates of the company to share the economic benefits of the more popular editions in the trade.

LAWS THAT PROTECTED THE PATENTEES

Despite some concessions, most of the actions by the Privy Council and the Stationers' Company were designed to restore order and protect the patentees. Throughout the early 1580s, a number of laws were passed to enable the company more effectively to root out instigators of piracy and to gain much greater control over the trade itself. These included limits placed on the number of presses an individual could own, the restriction of presses to master printers, and the requirement that each printer bring an actual or printed specimen of his or her firm's type, which included initials and ornaments, to Stationers' Hall.[52] Furthermore, all printers had to report how many presses they owned and also the number of apprentices and other workers they employed. If company officers suspected inaccurate reporting, they could demand to view the printer's premises. Clearly these laws were designed to deny pirates the necessary resources to produce illegal books. Most important of all, the stationers' once benign officer, the beadle, was assigned specific new duties, which included a wide range of enforcement tactics against piracy. The person in this office was given both the incentive and the opportunity to root out all piracy in the trade.[53]

It has often been noted that the appointment of Day's archenemy, Wolfe, as one of the first beadles of the company was an act of ingenuity on the part of the company but one of hypocrisy on the part of the former rebel. Wolfe had been imprisoned several times for piracy but was enticed with an award of some patents of his own to induce him to move, like Barker before him, to the side of the patentees.[54] In the late 1580s, Wolfe was an active, successful policer of the company, probably better able than anyone before him to find and destroy the books and printing equipment of those of his former confederates who continued to disregard the laws of the queen and the company.

Before Wolfe became beadle, other stationers had set about enforcing patent laws. In May 1584 Day had sent men to break into Wolfe's house and shop to destroy the latter's materials when he was suspected of piracy.[55] Four years earlier, Day destroyed a printing venture that was begun by his own son Richard, who was later to inherit his father's psalmbook patent. Richard's estranged relationship with his father and the effect this had on his career after the latter's death directly involve the patent and its operation in the immediate years before East began printing music.

RICHARD DAY, HIS ASSIGNS, AND THE *Whole Booke of Psalmes*

In 1579 Richard Day attempted to branch out from his father's shop and establish a business of his own.[56] To finance this venture, he entered into an agreement whereby his father furnished him with a printing shop, printing equipment, and a stock of books that were ready for immediate sale. Although Day permitted his son to print new editions, he stipulated that he could only produce original titles and thus gave him no right to print works like the *ABC* and the *Psalmes,* despite the fact that Richard was listed as a copatentee for these works. For the whole package Richard had to pay his father £240 over the course of several years. To Richard's dismay, he found that the stock sold to him was, not surprisingly, "dead and unsalable." In consequence, he began to pirate the *Psalmes* and the *ABC* against his father's wishes.

Day reacted to his son's piracies by bursting into his establishment, confiscating his pirated copies, and destroying his equipment (all of which was described with great relish at court). This must be seen as an unwarranted exploitation of power. In 1580 Day was the master of the Stationers' Company, and this gave him the power of "search and seizure" to regulate his industry that the queen granted to all livery companies. When John Day took such actions against his son, however, they seemed to be motivated more by personal concerns than by legitimate company business. The effect of this action was clear. Richard never (successfully, at least) set up another printing shop or personally printed any titles after 1580.[57] John Day was still not content. He later tried to remove his son's name from the patent and to remove him as an heir, although he did not fully succeed in these last draconian measures.

Richard was apparently able to regain his inheritance after 1584 through litigation, but he never achieved the position his father had held in the Stationers' Company. Perhaps because of Richard's weak position in the years after his father's death, the patent for the *ABC* and the *Psalmes* was given over to Wolfe and other stationers who were among the original group of poor printers in the rebellion; this group adopted the name "the assigns of Richard Day." Wolfe and seven other printers continued to print the *ABC* and the *Psalmes* as Day's assigns. Ironically, soon after the new syndicate of printers began to work Day's patents, several other printers pirated both of their properties. Thus the new group of printers, who were former opponents to the whole patent principle, now found themselves in court vigorously defending their own monopolies.[58] Ultimately, the psalmbook patent was so weakened by these struggles and disputes that the company was often called upon to manage these groups and to arbitrate. Eventually, the company itself began to run the patent. In 1603 the company purchased the patent from Day and thereby formalized the business arrangement that had been developing for some time.[59] From that point onward, it was the company itself that owned the royal patent.

THE *Cantiones* AND THE 1575 MUSIC PATENT

The events that surrounded the production of the *Cantiones* by Tallis and Byrd created a situation entirely different from the frenetic environment of the ubiquitous psalmbooks. This work was the only one to result (until 1588) from the conspicuously sweeping music patent that the queen granted to Tallis and Byrd in 1575:

> To all printers bokesellers and other officers ministers and subjects greeting.
> Know ye, that we for the espiciall affection that we haue and beare vnto the
> science of Musicke and for the aduancement thereof, by our letters patent
> dated the xxij of January, in the xvij yere of our raigne have granted ful priue-
> ledge an licence vnto our wel-beloued seruants Thomas Tallis and William
> Birde two of the Gentlemen of our Chappell, and to the ouerlyuer of them,
> and to the assignes of them and ouere the suruiuer of them for xxj years next
> ensuing, to imprint any and so many as they will of set songe or songes in
> partes, either in English, Latine, Frenche, Italian or other tongues that may
> serue for musicke either in Churche or chamber, or otherwise to be either plaid
> or soonge, And that they may rule and cause to be ruled by impression yn
> paper to serue for printing or pricking of any song or songes, or any bookes or
> quieres of such ruled paper imprinted. Also we straightly by the same forbid
> all printers bookesellers subjects and strangers, other then is aforesaid to doe
> any the premisses, or to bring or cause to be brought out of any forren
> Realmes into any our dominions any song or songes made and printed in any
> forren countrie, to sell or put to sale, upon paine of our high displeasure,
> And the offender in any of the premisses for euery time to forfet to vs our
> heires and successors fortie shillinges, and to the said Thomas Tallis and
> William Birde or to their assignes and to the assignes of the suruiuor of them,
> all and eurie the said bokes papers song or songes.[60]

Even if such favoritism was typical of this era, it still must have seemed unduly generous that two men were offered so much royal protection for their individual economic gain. Indeed, if any niche of the music trade remained open for others, the fullness of the description in the patent text suggests this was only the result of oversight on the part of the drafters. Due to the wide scope of musical genres covered, this grant overlapped with the patent for psalmbooks with music held by Day. The conflicting claims for these books had important repercussions for East's career after 1588, but, oddly enough, it did not affect the production of psalmbooks before East's first work in the field.

Three facets of music dissemination were noted in this patent: music printing, printed music paper, and the importation of music books. Of these, the greatest emphasis was placed upon the particular venture of music printing. Given this emphasis, it is not surprising that Tallis and Byrd, along with most modern scholars, judged the entire venture to be a failure when the first music edition of this project led to a financial disaster. The underlying social and economic forces that brought about the failure of this book in the marketplace were factors that remained vital throughout East's career.

The *Cantiones* was undoubtedly the flagship of the new monopoly. It was the second, and greatest, of the London music books printed by Vautrollier and one of the last editions in London to appear in oblong octavo format. The eye is treated to a generous, even lavish, use of space in all the six part-books. Tallis and Byrd composed every motet in this collection. Each composer contributed seventeen numbered works (for some motets the constituent parts were counted individually to render this total) to honor the queen whose reign began on 17 November 1558.[61] The number games went further, for the year of this issue, 1575, was the seventeenth year of Elizabeth's reign and the edition was explicitly dedicated to her. Richard Mulcaster, renowned headmaster of the Taylors' Company school, and the queen's favored musical courtier, Ferdinando Heybourne, alias Richardson, provided commendatory poems for the preface. The imprint of the title page announced "cum privilege," and a version of the 1575 patent text was printed in the book.[62]

Economic failure of the *Cantiones*

Even if no other data could be harnessed to make the case, the lack of music publications produced in London in the years 1575–1588 suggests that there were problems with the running of the music patent at that time. Only a few of the music editions that were printed in the years after the *Cantiones* (until 1588) survive today, and none mention the patent. Already in 1577, only two years after the *Cantiones* was produced, Tallis and Byrd appear to have forsaken the project altogether. In an appeal to the queen, they noted without hesitation that their project had met with no success. They claimed that the "lycense for the printinge of musicke ... hath fallen oute to our greate losse and hinderaunce to the value of two hundred markes at the least."[63] Testimony to the failure of the *Cantiones* continued in 1582. As discussed earlier, Christopher Barker, a member of the Stationers' Company, submitted a report to William Cecil, Lord Burghley, on the monopolistic grants the queen and her predecessors had established for printed books in the midst of the poor printers' rebellion. Barker included the 1575 music patent in his report, with the following evaluation: "[t]he paper is somewhat beneficial, as for the musicke bookes, I would not provide necessary furniture to have them."[64] Barker's negative view of the music stock substantiated Byrd's and Tallis's claim of five years before. His account goes on to mention that "this patent is executed by Henry Bynneman also."

Bynneman's involvement with the music patent has hardly been recognized in musicological studies, yet it may be more than incidental to the history of English music dissemination in the period up to 1588.[65] The fact of his involvement in the music patent yields the most compelling evidence of the fate of the *Cantiones* edition in the marketplace. In 1583, because of debts owed at the time of Bynneman's death, an inventory of his stock was recorded. One item of this inventory was "bookes of Birdes and Tallis musicke in number seaven hundred and seaventene xliiij^{li} xiiij^s."[66] This was one of 147 numbered items in the list, of which 103 items list Bynneman's books that remained unsold at his death. As Mark Eccles noted in his study of this inventory, the figure of 717 for the Byrd and Tallis work was extraordinary.[67] Only three other titles in the entire inventory had copies in quantities that exceeded 700. Furthermore, the editions with similarly large stocks were all less than two years old and thus were still relatively new. Since the *Cantiones* had been printed eight years earlier, it was certainly reasonable for Eccles to conclude from this anomaly that Bynneman "probably produced an[other Byrd and Tallis] edition about this time."[68]

It seems more likely, however, that the "bookes of Birdes and Tallis musicke" listed in Bynneman's inventory were actually from the 1575 *Cantiones* edition. Given the evidence in Byrd and Tallis's letter to the queen and Barker's report discussed earlier, it is understandable that so many copies of the first edition remained unsold even at that late date. Furthermore, there are no extant copies of another edition by Tallis and Byrd. It is unlikely that a ghost of such magnitude as a second Tallis and Byrd production, with music never before printed, would have completely escaped notice.[69] Thus it would appear that Eccles could have been wrong in his conjecture that Bynneman printed a new edition of music by these men. The 717 unsold copies lying on Bynneman's shelves in 1583 were more likely the original copies of the *Cantiones* production of 1575.

Bynneman's inventory seems to confirm what Tallis and Byrd claimed in their suit to the queen: that their first printing project of the music patent was, to say the least, an economic disappointment. But why did it fail? Certainly the quality of the music and that of the printing were not to blame. Vautrollier's work displays superb craftsmanship, and although Byrd was a relative newcomer to London, both he and Tallis were deservedly received as the finest composers of their respective generations.[70] The quality of the production and content, however, was irrelevant to the work's economic success in the London market for printed books. The composers fell victim rather to inadequate methods of distribution and a lack of public demand for the massproduced copies of their music.

PUBLICATION AND DISTRIBUTION

In their letter to the queen, Byrd and Tallis noted that they had invested the considerable sum of "two hundred markes at the least" in the production of their *Cantiones* edition.[71] This amount was certainly far more than the likely fees solicitors would charge to draft the text or scribes to copy it onto the patent rolls. It is likely that this sum of 200 marks mentioned in the letter was a figure that represented the cost of paper and other publishing expenses for the *Cantiones* (most likely in conjunction with a stock of printed music paper).[72] No other publisher was mentioned in the imprint of the edition or in the patent itself. Although the patent certainly allowed for others who might print or publish music as assigns of the two men, none were nominated in the imprint. Therefore, since the costs of publishing the edition had to fall upon someone, it follows that the composers themselves would have been the ones to pay for the paper, compensate the printer, and assume all other production costs.

Publishing the volume themselves was probably the riskiest option available to Tallis and Byrd as patent owners, for it turns out that there were other, safer ways to use the music patent for financial gain. In 1600 the composer Thomas Morley, with his partner, collected a sizable fee from George Eastland, the publisher of Dowland's *Second Booke of Songs*. Morley did no more for that project than collect his money by virtue of his patent rights.[73] Tallis and Byrd did not have the benefit of this kind of hindsight, of course, and it is impossible to know whether they attempted to find a publisher for their first music edition. It was more likely, however, that, from the start, the composers themselves wanted to be the ones to write the dedication to the queen and therefore took full responsibility for the costs of the production.

To their credit, it appears that the composers did attempt to gain professional assistance in their first effort at publishing music. The 1575 patent text had at least two separate versions, one officially recorded in the patent roll (transcribed earlier) and another version printed in the *Cantiones* edition itself. In the *Cantiones* version of the patent text, a new sentence was added. Here it was stated that the queen "commanded [the] printers, maisters & wardens of the misterie of stationers, to assist" Tallis and Byrd.[74] Despite this expression of the royal will, it is clear that there was no stationer with a vested interest in the *Cantiones* project at the outset. Vautrollier, who by all accounts did a magnificent job printing the music, appeared to have nothing to do with the sales of the volumes.[75] Joseph Kerman's suggestion that Vautrollier had assumed an active role in political affairs by that time, one that took him away from London, especially to Scotland, may explain the printer's apparent failure to market the volume.[76] Certainly Bynneman did take a professional interest in the music patent by 1582 at the latest.[77] But even if he planned to work with Byrd and Tallis to sell the copies of their edition and produce more music books, a project of that sort does not seem to have been part of the original marketing program and in any event would have been frustrated by the printer's death in 1583.

A well-honed distribution system was necessary to market music books successfully in London at that time, and it seems clear that Tallis and Byrd did not adequately provide for one. Nor did they receive much assistance from the stationers, who were royally "commanded" to give them their help. If today neglect of distribution would seem to have been an obvious flaw in the composers' plans, it may not have been so clear at that time. Byrd and Tallis were nearly pioneers of music printing in London (with the exception of psalmbooks). Distribution would not have been a matter of concern if they still thought in terms of manuscript compilations destined for a relatively small circle of admirers who had the learning and leisure to appreciate them fully and the wealth to underwrite them.

VENUE

A further problem for the *Cantiones*, which runs deeper into the underlying causes of the failure, was the restricted venue for (and purpose of) the music itself. Except for special needs of the queen herself, there were few obvious audiences for this music in Protestant England. The Latin language was certainly one key problem. It was no longer likely that many Anglican institutions within the Episcopal jurisdiction had a place for Latin-texted music.[78] Furthermore, recusant worshipers who did sing in Latin (following now a Roman rather than Sarum rite) would have only a limited use for the volume, since, in the main, the music of the *Cantiones* was not designed for liturgical observance. Joseph Kerman, in his revelatory study of Byrd's motets, determined that for this edition technical considerations of musical composition, more than any other factor, governed the composers' choice of texts.[79]

By what was then a long-standing practice, the best singers of England's churches throughout the country were recruited by the crown to serve as musicians, or "gentlemen," of the Chapel Royal.[80] Thus, in contrast to the "Queen's musik," a group of performers with an international profile, the Chapel Royal was made up exclusively of native-born Englishmen. It was no coincidence, it would therefore seem, that a note of patriotism rings through the prefatory material of the *Cantiones*, a volume with music composed by two prominent "gentlemen of the Queens chapel." At the crux of a nationalistic argument that carried through most of the prefatory material of the *Cantiones* was the claim that Byrd and Tallis stood as equals to any of the greatest musical composers of the continent.[81] The *Cantiones* music, described as "argumentae" and cast perhaps not so much in the Latin of Catholicism but in the Latin of international humanists, seemed designed to fulfill that lofty premise. The prevalence of elaborate canonic settings, works that employed *cantus firmus* scaffoldings, and motets in seven and eight parts shows that the two composers could without strain produce works that might stand comfortably alongside those of their continental rivals at the very pinnacle of compositional virtuosity.[82]

In the absence of any contemporary records to certify who performed the motets or who purchased any of the volumes, a search for the intended venue of the music must proceed deductively. Two logical choices, where the musical and linguistic challenges presented no special problem, were the Chapel Royal itself, on the one hand, and the foreign market (presumably Catholic centers on the European continent), on the other. Both of these, it turns out, were suggested by the prefatory material in the book.

With the device of a poetic quid pro quo, Mulcaster pronounced that in return for England's appreciation of foreign music the music of the *Cantiones* would be "borne through foreign lands to be appraised by the judgment of artists." This was surely a rhetorical flourish, but as the book was listed in catalogs of the Frankfurt fair it must, therefore, have been put up for sale on the continental market (probably in a reissued copy).[83] Unfortunately, there is as yet no other evidence to indicate that the work was sold in Frankfurt or that it otherwise circulated very extensively abroad. Craig Monson made this latter point clear by noting that there are a few copies of the *Cantiones* held in continental repositories today, but none were there before the late nineteenth century.[84] It may be more significant, therefore, that, unlike Mulcaster, Tallis and Byrd did not seem to anticipate an international reception for their music. Instead, they argued in their dedication solely for the high place of music in the queen's judgment.

Cast as a defense of music itself, the Tallis-Byrd dedication created a premise that music was worthy of the queen's patronage according to its place in an extensive hierarchy of meritorious subjects. Their tactic conforms to similar projections of a rational world picture that appeared in many philosophical and literary works of the Tudor era.[85] What accounted for the pervasiveness of this philosophical message was its agreement with the queen's own view of her realm and her role in its governance. Perhaps the chief point of this rehearsal of such standard rhetoric in the dedication of the *Cantiones* was to remind the queen, in the composers' own words, that "music is indispensable to the state." It was left to others, like Mulcaster, to fortify this claim and to further establish that Tallis and Byrd were the two royal subjects best suited to the task of creating such an "indispensable" commodity.

There has been no serious dispute over the supposition that the composers intended for these motets to be performed, at least initially, in a ceremony for the queen. Nomination of the queen as the dedicatee makes this seem likely, especially since the Chapel Royal itself provided such a ready performance for the task. The initial performance of the music, in light of the heavy symbolism of the number seventeen, was probably the celebration of the queen's accession on 17 November 1575, in the seventeenth year of her reign. Further uses for these works outside the royal perimeters, however, do not readily spring to mind.[86] Of course there were other possible functions for this music in the court itself that might help explain its venue and audience. This music, for example, would have been of ongoing use to the queen for diplomatic purposes. Ambassadors and other foreign dignitaries who visited the royal court sometimes mentioned the sacred music they heard there, and some noted with surprise that this music was decidedly elaborate and reminiscent of "popish" service (all of which would certainly not rule out the possibility that they heard Byrd and Tallis's motets).[87] In an era when every nuance of religious observance could attain political significance on a national as well as an international scale, it seems that Elizabeth took full advantage of the fact that she could use her court chapel to make any number of subtle conciliatory gestures to other nations.

Whether the book was intended for international, celebratory, and/or diplomatic venues is a question of great importance to its prepublication history. The most significant issue after it was produced, at least from the point of view of a trader like East, however, was how well it would sell in the stalls around St. Paul's. For anyone interested in profits, all speculation about the foreign audience for the music and possible distribution on the Continent faded well into the background in light of the aforementioned fact that 717 copies of the 1575 edition were still unsold in England in 1583. No matter what plans were considered for distributing the copies, success or failure would turn primarily on their reception in London. Here all of the compositional skill of the authors and the backing of prominent Elizabethans could not make up for the simple fact that few others in England, except the queen herself, could find a use for this music.

RESULTS OF THE *Cantiones* VENTURE

One result, as already noted, was a beautiful edition. The quality of the production, in both its music and its visual image, has been appreciated by scholars, albeit in an offhand way. The responsibility for quality rested clearly on the shoulders of the patent holders, Tallis and Byrd. With their professional reputations at stake, they were compelled to produce a good product not only in its visual appearance but in the musical content as well. This is a feature of the patent that would continue throughout East's career and has not been properly credited to the queen's monopoly policy.

A second outcome was that, viewed in different terms, Tallis and Byrd benefited from the printed edition despite its economic failure. The modern condition where publicly known marketing difficulties could destroy a person's career in music or art had no parallel in the Tudor age. If appropriately obsequious, the composers' letters to the queen that concerned their losses show no sign of embarrassment or humiliation. Of the two, Byrd, at least, was granted a new patent that was designed to compensate for the loss of his investment in the edition.[88] Evidence of Byrd's success with the work despite its poor sales is revealed by the fact that the *Cantiones* motets were copied more frequently into didactic and performance manuscripts than any others he had composed.[89] With these motets in particular, then, Byrd gained the admiration of those who would emulate, perform, and collect his work. The printed volume did not reach a sufficiently large number for direct profit, but the added exposure, presumably beyond what would have been gained with a manuscript, gave Byrd more prestige and thus a better standing in the intimate environments where he was patronized.[90]

The most tangible consequence of the *Cantiones* venture in the period before East began to print music, however, was a thirteen-year hiatus in music printing for works of that type, from 1575 to 1588. After Tallis died in 1585 and Vautrollier's music type passed to East, Byrd began to exercise his patent for the first time in an ongoing fashion. Until then, the market for music editions composed by English composers and produced by English printers remained securely restricted to a single lucrative arena, the metrical psalms with music and related publications.

PRINTED MUSIC PAPER

Despite their retreat from music printing in the aftermath of the *Cantiones* fiasco, it is possible that Tallis and Byrd profitably exercised their privilege of exclusive control over printed music paper and music importation. In the patent text, these two ventures were treated as subordinate matters. Although it is very difficult to determine Tallis and Byrd's role in the matters, there is evidence to suggest that the production and sale of music paper and the importation of music books from the Continent were lively enterprises. In a circuitous but indubitable way, these two ventures were most responsible for the first successes of music printing in 1588, for they fostered a particular demand for translated Italian madrigals among London consumers.

A monopoly for printed music paper was listed in the patent after the privilege for music printing. Here the wording was less all-inclusive, but there was the careful distinction between "bookes" and "quieres" and thus it covered two distinct methods of packaging music paper for sale in Renaissance bookshops. The term "bookes" probably described sheets of music paper bound together by standard methods that used leather, vellum, or other material; sheets sold unbound were described by the term "quire," which variously denoted a specific or generic unit of paper at this time. What was significantly lacking in this privilege for printed music paper, as Donald W. Krummel has pointed out, was any means to restrain others from the creation and distribution of music paper with staff lines ruled by hand.[91]

With the aid of a *rastrum*, a device that allowed the multiple lines of the staff to be drawn at once, it must have been nearly as efficient to prepare paper for music copying by hand as by the press. Morley noted this caveat when he lobbied after 1596 for Byrd's former music patent. He claimed that there were simply "too many devices by hand to prejudice the press" to make this protection worthwhile.[92] The inattention to this problem in the original patent contrasts with the careful treatment of music printing. This makes it seem likely that the privilege for ruled music paper was of less concern to the two composers at the time of the patent than music printing itself. Nonetheless, the patent did provide similar economic protection and therefore incentive for the two composers to produce printed music paper.

Examining the printed music paper found in the collection of music manuscripts at Tenbury, Edmund H. Fellowes noted that the initials "T.E." printed on the paper were probably Thomas East's.[93] Fellowes determined therefore that the music paper in question was related to the music patent. Iain Fenlon and John Milsom studied systematically the printed music paper in the United Kingdom from this era.[94] They discovered and described numerous stocks of printed music paper, which included seven varieties of the T.E. brand noted by Fellowes.[95] Using the repertory copied on this paper as a guide, they also attempted to date the paper, and in the process they found that some T.E. paper was probably produced after 1588. Most of the other stocks were in circulation during, and possibly before, the 1575–1588 period.[96]

With so many examples still extant, it is clear that there must have been a plentiful supply of ruled music paper in the last quarter of the sixteenth century. Evidence from the inventories of English stationers, which was not studied in the Milsom-Fenlon report, further confirms this view. As mentioned earlier, Bynneman had a large stock of music paper available in his shop in 1583.[97] In 1585 an item noted as "i Sitherne booke ruled" was recorded in the stock of Roger Ward.[98] This item illustrates the point noted in the 1575 patent that "bookes" of music paper were sold as well as "quires." Others may have bought and sold such stock: in 1600, for example, an inventory of William Barley's goods included "16 quires of Ruled [music] pap*er*."[99] Since such inventories were rare at the time and have endured only by chance, the presence of music paper in almost all printer's inventories that have survived surely suggests that music paper was a salable commodity. Unfortunately, these inventories do not specify whether this music paper was ruled by hand or at the press, and only the latter was covered by the privilege. Yet it may be significant to note that Bynneman owned part of the privilege for the music monopoly at the time of his death, that Barley had direct dealings with music monopolists at the time his inventory was completed, and that Roger Ward had been a notorious pirate of lucrative privileges in the past.

MUSIC COPYING, MUSIC IMPORTATION, AND A NEW DEMAND FOR ENGLISH MUSIC EDITIONS

Music importation was another element of the queen's music grant to Tallis and Byrd. Its role in the economics of the music monopoly is difficult to ascertain, but it too may have been of importance to the survival of the grant. The cross-fertilization of international styles found in the music of English composers after 1588 suggests that there was a flourishing commerce in the importation of music books at this time in Tudor England.[100] Even with Byrd, whose secular music was deeply rooted in the English tradition of consort song, tangible evidence of his thorough knowledge of Italian musical styles is present, most notably, in his madrigal settings, his madrigal-influenced anthems and motets, and his compositional exchanges with Philip de Monte.[101] For others, like Morley especially, the lighter forms of Italian secular music, which included the *canzonetta* and *balletto*, were integral components of their English madrigal compositions.[102]

The international interests of composers were shared by music collectors. The vast collections of foreign music books held by the Earl of Arundel at Nonsuch and by the Pastons were surely unusual for their staggering quantity.[103] These musical centers were famous enough in their own time to merit special comment from visitors.[104] Such collectors were exceptional, but it is clear from the following description by music aficionado Nicholas Yonge in his preface to the *Musica Transalpina* of 1588 (printed by East as one of his first music editions) that other, less well-to-do Elizabethans were also procuring foreign music books with similar enthusiasm:

> Since I first began to keepe house in this Citie, it hath been no small comfort vnto mee, that a great number of Gentlemen and Merchants of good accompt (as well of this realme as of forreine nations) have taken in good part such entertainment of pleasure, as my poore abilitie was able to affoord them, both by the exercise of Musicke daily vsed in my house, and by furnishing them with Bookes of that kinde yeerely sent me out of Italy and other places which being for the most part Italian Songs, are for sweetness of Aire, verie well liked of all.[105]

In this passage from the inaugural edition of Englished madrigals in London, Yonge obliquely mentioned all three elements of the music patent. His comments also signaled a new appreciation of music that would be of particular benefit to the music patentee. Yonge's description of music importation is suggestive: he mentioned that books of music were routinely "sent [to him] out of Italy and other places." But Yonge went on to describe, in detail, how he gathered together these Englished madrigals over a five-year period and diligently copied out the music and texts on music paper long before he had any designs to publish the collection. Manuscript exchange in the music field has proven somewhat difficult to trace fully in the era before 1588, but Yonge's comments go far to suggest that it was a common practice among the "Merchants of good accompt" no less than the "Gentlemen" of the city. Yonge alluded to a commerce in music copying that corresponds with the evidence of extant manuscripts and inventories.[106] It was a commerce that could well have encouraged Tallis and Byrd to value their patent for the production of printed music paper.

Finally, and perhaps most important, Yonge described a growing demand for a certain type of music among his friends and colleagues in London that could not be adequately served by manuscript copying alone. Although Yonge explained that the tastes of Elizabethans for the music of the madrigal were so strong that they were willing to make some special efforts to overcome their problems with the Italian language, it was clear that this same demand also legitimized the use of the medium of print. To meet such demand, altruistically, was Yonge's implied reason for sponsoring the publication of this collection of translated madrigals, even though he suggested that the music was actually the private property of amateur musicians and copyists. History did prove Yonge's case. His Englished madrigals were swiftly to inspire many new editions and eventually, of course, led to the composition of original English madrigals by English and Irish musicians.

It may be overstating the case to suggest that the publication of the *Musica Transalpina* caused the dam of music printing to burst, but there certainly was a distinct rise in music printing to follow. After 1588 until well into the seventeenth century, music printing in England was a constant and conspicuous element of the national book trade. Thanks to the efforts of Yonge and, perhaps, to the continued economic success of the production of printed music paper, music printing began to flourish in England. With the coming force of true demand shaping the music field, the prospects of Byrd's monopoly were amply revived. And when that occurred Byrd would bring to East's firm a patent fortified by his great prestige as a royal favorite among fellow musicians. East soon turned to music printing as the mainstay of his professional activities and established himself as the first Englishman to thoroughly specialize in the music trade.

Bibliographical Issues:
East's Music Printshop
and Chronological Puzzles

 3

Sometime around 1587, the stationer East and the composer Byrd worked out a business arrangement whereby East became Byrd's official and only assign in his music-publishing enterprise. This was the career decision that would eventually secure East a place in music history, but it was a rather risky move at the time. As the stationer Christopher Barker officially reported to the queen's Privy Council in 1582, Byrd produced music books that were among the most unrewarding commodities protected by royal patents.[1] East may not have been as discouraged by this as prudence would seem to dictate—the scope of Byrd's grant was so broad that it overlapped the jurisdiction of the royal patent specifically designed for psalmbooks with music. These were among the top-selling items in the trade. As such, however, they produced an entirely different set of troubles for the ambitious stationer. The men who ran the psalmbook patent were highly placed in the Stationers' Company and well able to defend a privilege of such magnitude.

The challenges East faced as a music printer were both immediate and long-term. Other stationers had demonstrated that Byrd's royal entitlements could sometimes be evaded, but there is no evidence that they could be ignored. Since East had officially linked himself to the composer as an assign, there was no question that he in particular had to contend directly with Byrd's royal authority. Specifically, East had to satisfy Byrd with his capability, as yet untested, to set music elegantly and accurately in type. He had also to conform to the musician's publishing agenda, which had thus far been altogether heedless of consumer demand. Neglecting the market altogether was an economic condition that East could not sustain. East's long-term strategy therefore entailed the intricate task of positioning himself advantageously between the publishing interests of royal favorites like Byrd and the company men who wielded so much power in his trade. In this chapter, I focus on the bibliographical data—the type, paper, and traces of editorial work in the music books themselves—that help to elucidate East's initial movements and long-term strategies.

By 1587, the year he worked out his partnership arrangement with Byrd, East was a seasoned stationer, with more than twenty years of experience. He had already demonstrated a willingness to explore some of the more challenging kinds of printing, such as illustrated books, for example; and he was fully equipped to handle the normal variety of projects he might encounter in London.[2] He had by then mastered all the basic skills of his craft, and he had at least one press, an attractive and suitably diverse array of type, and a competent labor force. To set up a music press East had only to obtain music type fonts and to learn new techniques for setting and correcting music at the press.

EAST'S MUSIC FONTS

East's company relations greatly facilitated his acquisition of type. As students of English printers have often noted, there was a great deal of shared printing in London that led to the borrowing of various elements of type among company brethren. Many of East's seemingly distinctive type pieces, including his famous "apostle" initial series, were once owned by other printers; East probably acquired them through his trade-printing assignments or after the death of a former partner or neighbor. The crucial business transaction that related to East's music font, however, appears to have involved East's wife, Lucretia née Hassell, and members of her extended family. A legacy created in her will of 1627 provides a newly discovered clue as to why East chose to begin a career in music printing around 1587:

> I give and bequeath unto Richard ffield and Thomas ffield the sonnes of Richard ffeild late of London Mercer deceased who was the sonne of my late deceased Sister the somme of thirtie pounds apeece to bee paid to each of them severally at such several tymes as each of them shall be made free of the Cittie of London or within one month then next followinge And my minde and will is that the said Company of Stationers shall ... paie the said legacy respectively to the said Richard and Thomas ffield as the same according to this my will.[3]

To understand the possible significance of this bequest it is first necessary to trace briefly the career of Richard Field, the London printer.[4]

In 1579 Richard Field, of Stratford-upon-Avon, was apprenticed to George Bishop, but Field worked for the first six years of his seven-year stint with the Huguenot printer Thomas Vautrollier. One of Vautrollier's first prints was musical, and he owned a handsome music font created by the Haultin firm of type designers.[5] In the year after Vautrollier's death in 1587, Field, who had just obtained his freedom the year before, married Jacqueline Vautrollier, Thomas's widow, and thereby became the successor to his former master's firm. In 1587, therefore, it was Field who owned the Haultin music font.

When East began music printing it was with the music font formerly used by Vautrollier.[6] East's acquisition of this font may have been a crucial incentive for him to print music, since it provided the only other necessary equipment he needed for the task. Until now there has been very little understanding of what may have occasioned the transfer of music type to East. If Lucretia East had a familial relationship with Richard Field, however, the move may reasonably be explained as a transaction among family members.[7] Obviously, East and Field had a special relationship regarding this equipment. When Field did print a line of music for a special edition, he borrowed the same Haultin font back from East.[8] From 1588 to East's death, Field was the only printer other than East to use this particular music font.

Although East featured the Haultin music font in almost all of his musical editions, he also owned a smaller music font, designed by van den Keere, that he used to print his books of metrical psalms. When Field reprinted the one edition he produced with music, he did not use East's Haultin font again but rather borrowed the van den Keere music font.[9] This, it would seem, establishes beyond any doubt that Field had no music font of his own after 1588 but turned to East when he needed equipment to print music. It suggests strongly that he intended to relinquish the music-printing business to his relative Lucretia East's husband when he transferred the Haultin font to him. As to the smaller font, it is possible but not at all certain that East acquired it from Richard Schilders, a Huguenot printer who worked with him in 1577. The van den Keere font also appeared in musical editions printed by Schilders.[10] Nonetheless, East did not use this font itself until 1592, and thus it is difficult to know if the striking similarity of the typefaces in East's works and editions by Schilders reveals a hitherto unknown transaction between East and his former partner.

SETTING AND CORRECTING MUSIC AT THE PRESS

With music fonts in hand, East had the basic material he needed to print music. When he created books in choir-book or table-book format (usually in upright octavo and folio editions) East could very well follow his normal style of printing texts. Most of East's music prints, however, were upright quartos in partbook format, where each part (cantus, medius, tenor, etc.) constituted a separate book with individual texts and collation.

For multi-part-book editions of music East used a technique called vertical printing.[11] Vertical printing required the compositor to set a single gathering for one part first. After setting this unit in one part-book, the compositor set the same gathering for each additional part. Thus, for example, if the tenor was the first to be set, a single gathering of the tenor part was completely set; after this, the same gathering would be set for all the other parts in turn. In this system, the compositor would complete a set unit of each part before turning to other sections. When all were done, it would be time for proofing.

Normally, the procedure at East's press involved the following steps. First the publisher delivered to the printer a manuscript version of the work in question, called the printer's copy.[12] The compositors would set the type in accordance with the manuscript, pull one or more proof copies, and turn them over to the press's designated corrector.[13] Once the corrector was given the proof copies, he or she would take note of any discrepancies between them and the original manuscript and return the corrected proof to the compositor. The latter corrected the type as required, with the printer possibly supervising but in any case bearing final responsibility for the accuracy of the work. The presses were now set in motion. During the run, detection of a fault might lead to a stop-press correction or cancellation of a forme.[14] When the machining was completed, a final check would be made to discover whether anything untoward had happened during the printing process itself. If a problem was found at this point, East might either discard the run, a very expensive proposition, or attempt to mend the flaw. He would now correct the mistakes either by having the desired characters or notes inked in by hand or by cancel-slip correction.[15] For the latter, he would print a series of impressions of the correct piece of type on sheets of waste-paper. He would then cut out single slips of the correct type and paste these so-called cancel slips over the inaccurate notes in the printed sheets.

Just how corrupt the Elizabethan correction procedure for proofing could become was revealed in a suit against East brought to trial in the royal courts and brought to scholars' attention thanks to an important article by Margaret Dowling.[16] George Eastland, the publisher of John Dowland's *Second Booke of Songs,* sued East, his printer, after he uncovered a bit of thievery among the latter's apprentices. Without concerning themselves overmuch with corrections, East's apprentices, John Balls and John Wiborowe, printed and sold a number of prints they called proof copies. These two men frankly confessed before the court that they had produced extra copies and sold them for their own gain.[17]

Although the case was based on the exploitation of so-called proof copies, there has been a remarkable lack of attention to the actual evidence about the correcting process that was discussed in the trial. East's testimony takes us into this process. He noted that he had charged the publisher for correcting a "falte in the [printer's] copie . . . not known of till the booke were fully finished" (this was uncontested by Eastland).[18] The printer's copy, whose integrity was the responsibility of Eastland, the publisher, had been prepared by eminent composers John Wilbye and Edward Johnson.[19] These men worked for Eastland, as they testified, and their job was plainly to deliver a copy of the music to East that would serve as the specimen of the text he would emulate in print. What is also clear, if not so explicitly stated, is that it was their job to ensure that the copy was faithful to some sort of musical/textual ideal. Whether it was Dowland's or someone else's, however, is difficult to ascertain. In any case, East argued that the copy they submitted was faulty, and the composers were for their part no happier about the collaboration.

Whether or not they were actually supposed to stay at East's press and correct the proofs is unclear, but there is indeed evidence that the two musicians were anxious to leave East's premises as soon as they possibly could. The problem was that, as Eastland's agents, they also had the task of physically delivering the printer/publisher contract. According to the composers, East wanted to amend the contract he had already signed without securing Eastland's approval. Such an underhanded tactic, if true, makes it quite understandable why the composers chose to be no party to East's further negotiations. The bitter mood of the moment was captured in testimony. According to the deponent Anne Rathford, a worker in East's shop who was there at the time, the composers left off dealings with the printer rather brusquely after delivering the copy and the contract to his shop. Wilbye said to East, "Heere take your noate agayne and make your bargaine with Mr Eastland your self for wee have nothinge to doe with it."[20]

East corrected the work on his own. During the machining at the press, he (or someone at the shop) discovered that the last rhythmic symbol of the lute tablature in the song "Clear or Cloudie" was incorrect. At this point, East simply stopped the press and corrected it. But then he had to go back to the uncorrected sheets and paste a slip on the page to correct them as well.[21] Significantly, the corrected item is the last note of the piece and the change is one of rhythm. The emendation would hardly affect the performance, since the last note would, of course, be held as long as the performer liked no matter what the actual note value of the print suggested. From this circumstance it is possible to speculate that East had actually found a minor "faulte" in the printer's copy but pretended it was a serious problem in order to charge Eastland more money for the extra labor of production.

The essence of East's argument was that the printer's copy, over which he had no jurisdiction, was incorrect at the time of printing. Thus the problem he felt compelled to mend was beyond his responsibilities and rested on Eastland's shoulders. East noted to the court that he was fully entitled to some compensation from Eastland for this work. In East's words, the task of mending the error involved "a whole weeke [of] worke for him & his servante for gatheringe collacioninge and mendinge [this] . . . faulte."[22] East estimated that he "and his servante did profe over foure thousand sheete or thereaboute" to fix the error in all copies of the edition. Eastland paid East twelve pence for the work. East argued that this was entirely inadequate.[23]

The rich documentary evidence from the *East vs. Eastland* litigation sheds some light on the editorial process as it might have existed throughout East's career. It shows how the responsibility for correcting music copy and proofs for the press was clearly divided between the publisher and printer but also indicates that integrity of the musical text was nonetheless the highest priority. As the story unfolds it seems clear, despite the soured relations between the parties, that the process depended on publisher and printer sharing an interest in the final product. East did make a last check of the sheets, and Eastland was willing to pay East (if not as much as he wanted) for his work correcting the error he discovered. Thus there was a structure whereby both parties shared responsibility for the accuracy of musical texts that would appear before the public. Despite his interest in overall quality, however, East was very anxious to point out the boundaries of his normal work and was keen to establish the errors for which he was not responsible and which he should not have to correct on his own time without compensation.

In this business situation, East acted as the quintessential trade printer. Illicit activities apart, East's job was theoretically limited and straightforward: a simple one-off printing assignment for a publisher who took all the financial risks. East's rate of pay was no less simply apportioned: it was based on the size of the edition and, more specifically, on the number of pages he printed. There were also the gifts of books that were customarily given to the workers, and these were the source of the problem.[24] Of course East did offer his *views* about how the book might be marketed, but this was only to suggest that the publisher had ruined his own chances to profit from the enterprise. In the normal course of events Eastland, the publisher, should have resolved all matters of editing, the paper expenses, and the fees for the privileges from the music monopolist Morley. Thanks to his problems with the musicians Eastland assigned to edit the work, the printer could argue that his adversary did not fulfil his publisher's editorial responsibilities. Eastland countered this with what seems to be the more compelling argument: by stealing the books before they were delivered to him, East's apprentices had usurped Eastland's right as a publishing entrepreneur to govern the sales and reap the resulting profits.

Paper and chronology

Once he had the appropriate type and editing skills, East could indeed print music, but this does not settle the question of his role in music publication. Generally, Renaissance books contain explicit information about their publishing circumstances: the imprint, colophon, and prefatory pages of a book customarily listed its publisher, printer, date of publication, and sponsor (the publisher's dedicatee). Publishers often went beyond mere self-acknowledgment to provide suggestive evidence as to why they chose to introduce a book to its public. In other cases, however, conflicting attitudes to print, political subversion, or monopolistic environments provided distinct incentives for printers and publishers alike to conceal this data. Obviously, any such camouflage would create a future of bibliographical confusion.

The puzzles of East's musical career begin with the 25% or so of his music books that he left un- or misdated. They continue with a series of books that were reissued with new title pages. All of these point to a gap in East scholarship: if we do know basically what he did, less often do we know when he did it. Solving that kind of problem is the second task of this chapter, where the main goal is to establish a new chronology for East's music production.

Among East's undated works were three editions of Byrd's Catholic Masses (two of which were later reprinted but still undated), two editions of Byrd's *Psalmes, Sonets & Songs*, and a treatise on music by William Bathe. The misdated works were of two kinds. The first were a series of reprinted editions wherein East purposely mimicked the date of earlier editions.[25] The extent of this mirroring at the press was such that the wrong date was, in many cases, left undetected for many years afterward (these will hereafter be termed, for convenience, East's "hidden editions"). A list of hidden editions appears as Table A1.2. The second set of misdated works among East's music prints were cases where the printer reset the title page to give the impression of a new edition while actually retaining the rest of the original sheets intact; they are commonly known as reissues. East printed editions of Giovanni Croce's sacred madrigals, Charles Tessier's chanson, and Byrd's *Gradualia* that were later (confusingly) reissued by his colleagues.

Paper was the primary bibliographical evidence I have considered in this study. An extensive examination of East's watermarks revealed that his problematic editions shared stocks of paper with works that he dated accurately. From this it was possible to suggest a solution to many problems of chronology: undated works and hidden editions were produced at roughly the same time as those sharing their stock of paper (see Table A1.3). This hypothesis had to be carefully tested; there were too many undeterminable exigencies in paper usage of the time to allow such conclusions to stand on paper evidence alone. Fortunately, type-deterioration evidence bore out the findings. There was also corroboration in archival documentation: East, it turned out, had registered music prints with his company at times that coincided with the pattern of his use of paper (see Table A1.5 for the correlation of paper and registry evidence).

Paper was mentioned repeatedly throughout the *East vs. Eastland* case: how much was involved, how it determined various rates of pay, who it was that counted the sheets (and if they could be trusted), and where it was stored. On the last issue, East argued that he had done his best to keep the valuable commodity under lock and key (although something obviously went wrong nonetheless).[26] Today it might seem strange that printers devoted so much attention to something as trivial as paper, but it would not have surprised anyone at that time. Paper entailed the most expensive outlay for Renaissance printers, its recurring cost far surpassing that of labor, plant, type, and the press itself. The publisher's primary responsibility was therefore to provide the paper (along with a suitable copy of the text and the printer's stipend). From a bibliographer's perspective, the supplier of paper *was* the publisher; and the publisher was the moving force in the engendering of a Renaissance book. Not only for music printers like East but for the Renaissance printing industry at large, paper was the mainspring of book production.

Matters of expense were undoubtedly of concern to East, for he was not one of the more prosperous stationers.[27] One way to offset the expense of paper was to join forces with another printer or find a publisher to finance the supply. Perhaps more often than was true for any other printer of his time in England, East's name appears on the title pages of his prints with a partner or as the printer for another publisher.[28] On the relatively few occasions when East acted as his own publisher and thereby took on the risk of purchasing (or obtaining, at any rate) his own stock of paper, it was for works that he clearly expected to generate a significant return for his investment.

One outcome of the exorbitant expense of paper was that Renaissance printers, unless they were of the wealthier sort, tended to use it with care and dispatch. After studying the patterns of paper use from incunabula through the eighteenth century, Allan H. Stevenson determined that the paper of an edition was likely to have been purchased specifically for the job at hand and put to use very soon thereafter.[29] Stevenson's findings have direct and powerful implications for this study. If an accurately dated work and an inaccurately dated work in East's output could be shown to share a stock of paper, it could safely be surmised that they were produced at roughly the same time—thus solving the problem of when East produced the music books he left un- or misdated. Moreover, since paper lay at the very heart of the business transactions among Renaissance printers and publishers, its study might lead the way into the more intricate realms of East's publishing activities.

The process of dating East's questionable editions with paper evidence is theoretically straightforward. After comparing watermarks in the paper of the array of his musical editions, problematic editions could then be resituated in his production schedule according to the published dates of other works that shared their paper stock. In the field, however, the process of classification was greatly complicated by the nature of watermark evidence.

Watermarks were created in handmade paper from images sewn into the wire mesh of molds. Each mold would of necessity have a unique mark, and papermakers tended to cultivate certain designs in their work at different times. Thus the watermark itself serves to differentiate stocks of paper and gives clues to where and when they were produced.[30] Many watermarks have similar designs, most are twins (this was due to the fact that paper was routinely made with two molds used in alternation in one vat),[31] and in the production process the design of the mark would gradually deteriorate, giving rise to different states. Identification of watermarks, therefore, is a delicate matter that requires special methods of measurement and comparison.[32] For purposes of this inquiry it is necessary not only to attempt to identify the watermarks in East's paper—to establish the stock of paper used for a printing project— but also to analyze East's working methods in order to determine the actual date when a distinct stock of paper was set to press. For this task we turn to another realm of paper study researched by Allan Stevenson.

Stevenson created two general categories to clarify how printers managed their paper supply.[33] The first he defined as a "run," which consisted of two subtypes. One subtype involved the condition when one mark and its twin appeared often in an edition and with enough consistency to confirm that it signified the main stock of paper for a printing. The other subtype involved the condition when two or more editions contained a stock with a small constellation of marks in common.[34] For either type of run, Stevenson found that there was little delay between the production of the paper and its use. When two editions have watermarks that represent the same running stock, it is very likely that they were produced within a short time of each other.

"Remnant" is the name Stevenson gave his second general category. It refers to the marks that occur infrequently in the print. Remnants also fall into two subtypes. Some marks seem to be truly rare, appearing haphazardly in an isolated copy or two.[35] These marks signal small quantities of paper, or perhaps even single sheets, that became part of an edition in any number of possible ways. Other remnants appear consistently in multiple copies in certain part-books and specific gatherings. In these cases, the quantity of paper in use was larger than just a single sheet or two although much less than the size of a typical stock for a run. For convenience, I refer to this subtype as a "token remnant" (a token equaled a half-ream of paper). Books with token remnants superficially resemble volumes with runs of paper with multiple marks; however, the patterns with which token remnants appear in the copies of the edition distinguish this use of paper from the other.

To demonstrate how paper evidence discloses a potential source of paper and edition chronology, it is helpful to begin with the paradigm of a simple, "best-case" scenario. Among the twelve hidden editions that appeared under East's name, the three editions of Wilbye's *First Set of English Madrigals* (dated 1598) provide perhaps the most convincing paper evidence. To begin with, of the three editions, only one shared paper with another work dated 1598. There was no problem, therefore, in determining that it was the original edition.[36] The remaining two editions shared stocks of paper with other music editions, too, but these were produced and dated many years later, in 1604 and 1610 (title pages of the three editions appear in Figures 3.1, 3.2, and 3.3; see Table A1.3 for the paper evidence). A truly lucky circumstance did arise in the case of the last of the three Wilbye editions. The *Shield*FM mark of its paper was itself dated 1610 (see Figure 3.4). This ensured beyond any doubt that this edition was produced sometime in 1610 or later.[37] It also establishes that the practice of falsely dating and reprinting musical works as hidden editions continued even beyond East's lifetime (he died in 1608), becoming the practice of his heirs.

The precision with which the paper evidence places the three editions of Wilbye's *First Set of English Madrigals* in East's (and his heir's) output at the appropriate date

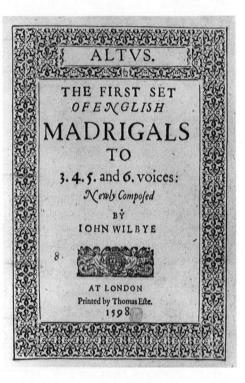

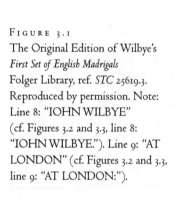

FIGURE 3.1
The Original Edition of Wilbye's
First Set of English Madrigals
Folger Library, ref. *STC* 25619.3.
Reproduced by permission. Note:
Line 8: "IOHN WILBYE"
(cf. Figures 3.2 and 3.3, line 8:
"IOHN WILBYE."). Line 9: "AT
LONDON" (cf. Figures 3.2 and 3.3,
line 9: "AT LONDON:").

confirms Stevenson's contention that paper was used expediently by printers of this era. It is clear that with these editions, as with most of his music prints, East did not overstock his supply, for, as Table A1.3 reveals, paper stocks tend to vanish rather soon after they appear in East's music editions. Here we are seeing East exhibiting his regular work habits. It is, therefore, reassuring to note that East's practice conforms so closely to Stevenson's observations. Yet even among these routine items, it is perhaps significant to find more than one book of the same year produced from a single stock of paper. Although it may have simply been the case that the same paper was still available in the London market for another publisher to purchase for East's use that same year, it is also possible that two such works were planned together and even produced concurrently.

In some cases it was possible to refine the chronology further and determine the specific order in which two works that shared paper were printed. But this was only possible in the cases where East used token remnant stocks of paper in his production. The token remnant's significance for determining chronology stemmed from its placement in the edition. In the hidden *Musica Transalpina* edition, for example, the lower parts contain a stock of paper shared with other editions of music by Damon and with Byrd's Masses. But most of the sheets for the table, title pages, and higher voices of that edition contain a small quantity of paper not otherwise found in East's output—this is the token remnant stock (see Table A1.3). The position of this remnant stock of paper in the multiple parts of a music edition was consequential. As a

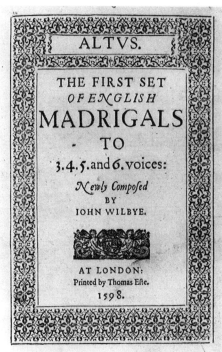

FIGURE 3.2
The 1605–1606 Hidden Edition of
Wilbye's *First Set of English Madrigals*
Folger Library, ref. *STC* 25619 copy 1.
Reproduced by permission. Note:
Line 8: "IOHN WILBYE." (cf. Figure 3.1,
line 8: "IOHN WILBYE").
Line 9: "AT LONDON:"
(cf. Figure 3.4, line 9: "AT
LONDON").

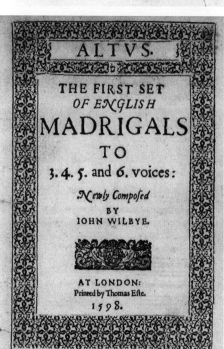

FIGURE 3.3
The 1610–1611 Hidden Edition of
Wilbye's *First Set of English Madrigals*
Houghton Library, Harvard University, ref. *STC* 25619. Reproduced by
permission. Note: Line 3: "*OF
ENGLISH*" "G" is swash (cf. Figures
3.1 and 3.2, line 3: "*OF ENGLISH*" "G"
is not swash).

FIGURE 3.4
Beta-radiographic Reproduction
of "1610" Watermark
Wilbye, *First Set of English Madrigals*, London, 1598 (hidden edition printed in 1610–1611), ref.
M1490.W66.M3 Case, Bassus;
D1–D4. Courtesy of the Library
of Congress, Music Division.

rule, the tables and title pages, if they were not part of complicated formats or half-sheet impositions, were printed last. It was a standard practice among printers of the time to save this portion of a book for the final work at the press in case substantial changes were made necessary by last-minute alterations in the layout or other unanticipated problems of production. Its placement in the edition suggests East used token remnant stocks to finish the printing project after the running stock of paper had become exhausted.[38] Thus from paper evidence alone the obvious conclusion is that any hidden edition with a token remnant was produced *after* the volume that shared its running stock of paper.

TYPOGRAPHICAL STUDIES

East's music type, and the way it was set by his compositors, has been widely discussed in books and articles on English music printing of the Renaissance. Although the main bibliographical thrust of this book has been on East's paper, its conclusions were fortified by this work on music type. Articles by H. K. Andrews and Peter Clulow bear directly on the issue at hand.[39] Focused primarily on Byrd's editions, these authors went far toward establishing a chronology for East's problematic works and generally provide an excellent source of collaborative evidence for this study. Chief among their findings is the seemingly innocuous circumstance that East varied his use of mensuration signs in a predictable fashion. The fact that in 1594 or early 1595 East began to use the unbarred semicircle rather than the barred semicircle for works in imperfect mensuration has proven most useful in clarifying a number of chronological issues.[40] This detail emerges as a completely reliable feature of East's house style.

By noting the way East corrected errors in successive editions, Andrews determined the order and general time frame for the earliest book in this series, Byrd's *Psalmes, Sonets & Songs*.[41] This volume was the first to appear under the royal patent since the pioneering Vautrollier print of 1575, and it is astonishing to note that whereas the 1575 volume was a disaster in the marketplace, this 1588 edition went quickly into second and third editions.[42] This title is the only one of the entire group of hidden editions that is likely to have been reprinted within a year of the first edition, a fact that probably reflects unexpectedly strong sales or, perhaps, Byrd's meticulous care (see chapter 4).

Undoubtedly the main focus, and the most influential component, of these Byrd studies was the use of a method known as type deterioration. Type deterioration has the potential to reveal excellent evidence for resolving problems of undated and hidden editions. Its success, however, depends on the utmost delicacy in observation and firm control over the accuracy of data.[43] As type wears down over a period of use, it produces imperfections in the impression. By comparing impressions for evidence of wear in the type, the observer is able to establish a chronological sequence of prints. Thus to bring results from a study of type deterioration the observer must find the recurrence of one specific piece of type in multiple impressions, then group these data according to the state of the type, and, finally, locate an identical condition of the type in both an undated or falsely dated work and a securely dated work.

With this methodology Andrews and Clulow solved several problems: hidden editions of Byrd's *Songs of Sundrie Natures* and Morley's *Canzonets a 3* were dated 1594–1595; the hidden second edition of the *Musica Transalpina* was dated 1593–1594.[44] Happily, these conclusions correspond to dates suggested by the stocks of paper East used in his editions (see Table A1.3). Because they were not always aware of when they were dealing with a hidden edition rather than an original version, however, it was possible for these scholars to be victimized by the false date. This would, of course, badly distort the sequence of type deterioration they were striving to establish. Such a problem occurred in the case of one of East's undated editions of Byrd's *Psalmes, Sonets & Songs*.

THE TWO UNDATED EDITIONS OF BYRD'S *Psalmes, Sonets & Songs*

East produced three editions of Byrd's *Psalmes* with the date of 1588 on the title page. He went on to reprint the work twice again in editions that appear without published dates. Andrews labeled what he believed to be a single undated edition of the *Psalmes* "B."[45] He was unaware, however, that there were actually two undated editions. Recently, I discovered that one copy Andrews listed along with other extant copies of the B edition is actually distinct. It constitutes a hitherto unnoticed additional reprinting of the collection. Since, as will be shown, it was printed earlier than the one already identified, we shall henceforth refer to it as "B1," using the designation "B2" for the edition Andrews had labeled simply B. This newly discovered edition is represented by a copy in the Britten-Pears Library (that lacks a contratenor part) and a single superius part in the Knowsley collection at the University of Liverpool. Unlike B2, which appears in a great number of copies, this newly discovered edition appears to exist only in the aforementioned two copies. Despite B1's rarity, there is little mystery about its true time of publication. The bibliographic evidence of its paper and type-deterioration is staightforward and clear. The "I" initial of this edition is in a state of deterioration that is almost undistinguishable from that of the same "I" in the original edition of Morley's *Madrigals to Fovre Voices* of 1600 (see Figure 3.6). This suggests that B1 was produced sometime around 1600. Such a conclusion is fortified by paper evidence, as a comparison of watermarks revealed that its paper is from a stock that East had usd in 1598 for the *Novæ Aliquot* by Orlando di Lasso (see Table A1.3).

There has, however, been considerable confusion over the true date of publication of B2. To investigate the problem, Andrews considered an array of evidence he found in its imprint: the spelling of East's name, the particular words used to describe the "Chapell Royal," the absence of any recognition of the music monopoly, and the unusual address posted for East's shop: "in Aldersgate street over against the signe of the George."[46] (New findings that concern East's address and the status of the monopoly will be considered at length later.) Nonetheless, the evidence Andrews considered most persuasive was the pattern of type deterioration in East's "apostle" initials.[47] From this evidence Andrews reached the conclusion that the volume was produced in 1599.[48] What corrupted his study was an undetected hidden edition of Thomas Morley's *Madrigals to Fovre Voices* that he used in his evidence. This was an edition that Thomas Snodham printed alongside the third edition of Wilbye's *First Set of English Madrigals*. Both of these hidden editions contain paper with the watermark dated 1610 (Figure 3.4).[49]

FIGURE 3.5
Type Deterioration Comparison (I)
(Note gap in sole of left foot.)

Morley, *Madrigals to Five Voyces* (1598), 'I', Tenor, sig. C3r, British Library, K.3.i.14. Reproduced by permission.

Byrd, *Psalmes, Sonets & Songs* (n.d.), 'I', Medius, sig. D1r, University of Illinois Library, x784.1 B99p. Reproduced by permission.

Morley, *Madrigals to Fovre Voices* (hidden edition, c. 1610), 'I', Altus, sig. B2v v, British Library, K.3.m.11. Reproduced by permission.

Several copies of East's accurately dated edition of 1600 are still extant, but those by Snodham that advertise the wrong date of "1600" are more plentiful today. As Figures 3.5 and 3.6 demonstrate, Andrews and Clulow must have chosen a copy from Snodham's incorrectly dated, hidden, edition for their study. Figure 3.5 is a re-creation of their type-deterioration evidence that uses East's "I" apostle initial. The deterioration appears at the base of the apostle's left foot, where there is a small gap in the bottom line. On the left is an example of Morley's *Madrigals to Five Voyces* of 1598 printed by East. This was the book used to establish the *terminus post quem* of 1598 for the undated *Psalmes* edition. In the center is the "I" from B2. Finally, at the right is the same initial as it appears in the hidden edition of Morley's *Madrigals to Fovre Voices*, the book used to establish a *terminus ante quem* of 1600 in the earlier study. Based on this evidence it is not difficult to see why the date of 1599 would have seemed readily to solve the puzzle of the true date of B2.

Figure 3.6 demonstrates, however, that the evidence was skewed by the unintended use of the hidden edition. In this figure, an "I" initial from the original edition of Morley's *Madrigalls* of 1600 appears on the left, taking the place of the 1598 example in Figure 3.5. As in Figure 3.5, however, the center image of Figure 3.6 is the "I" from B2 and the image on the right is from the hidden edition of Morley's *Madrigalls*. When reading these images from left to right and noting the pattern of deterioration at the aforementioned foot of the apostle it becomes clear that the "I" initial from the original edition of Morley's *Madrigalls* produced in 1600 is in a better condition than that of B2. Based on this evidence, B2 could only have been produced after, rather than before, 1600.

With a comparison of images from the original and hidden editions of Morley's *Madrigalls to Foure Voices*, the "1599" hypothesis may be confidently ruled out, but when

FIGURE 3.6
Type Deterioration Comparison (II)
(Note gap in sole of left foot.)

Morley, *Madrigals to Fovre Voices* (original edition, 1600), 'I', Cantus, sig. B₃ʳ Folger Library, *STC* 18128. Reproduced by permission.

Byrd, *Psalmes, Sonets & Songs* (n.d.), 'I', Medius, sig. D₁ʳ, University of Illinois Library, x784.1 B99p. Reproduced by permission.

Morley, *Madrigals to Fovre Voices* (hidden edition, c. 1610), 'I', Altus, sig. B2ᵛ, British Library, K.3.m.11. Reproduced by permission.

East actually produced this last *Psalmes* edition remains to be discovered. Once Andrews's searching methods are supplemented by new findings, the years 1606 and 1607 become the most likely candidates for the true time of printing. Figure 3.7 continues the type-deterioration study of East's "I" apostle initial. As before, the "I" of B2 stands in the center of the plate. To its left is an example from Byrd's *Gradualia II* of 1607, and on its right stands the initial as it appeared in Henry Youll's *Canzonets* of 1608. This indicates that the "I" was in nearly the same state in 1607 but had become slightly worse by 1608. Thus, type-deterioration evidence of the "I" initial compellingly suggests the year 1607 as the most likely candidate for the actual time of printing for the B2 edition.

New findings concerning East's address as it appeared in the imprints of these particular editions of the *Psalmes* (B1 and B2) seemed strongly corroborative of this dating before the discovery of B1 but less conclusive thereafter. Because the address is unique to the B imprints it is nonetheless useful to set forth these findings representing the current state of knowledge on the subject.

East's "Aldersgate street over against the signe of the George" address in the undated "B" editions of Byrd's *Psalmes* appear nowhere else in his extant works.[50] Thanks to the discovery of East's original will by Miriam Miller,[51] we now know that East had two properties on Aldersgate Street, both of which he listed as in the parish of St. Botolph's without Aldersgate.[52] Conveniently for the scholar, East included the precise inception dates for each lease.

The lease of the first mentioned of these Aldersgate properties was dated 28 October 1591.[53] East's imprints reveal that he had already set up shop at an Aldersgate street address by 1589.[54] The steady outpouring of similarly addressed books by East thereafter confirms that this lease could only have referred to his well-known press and bookshop on Aldersgate Street. It was this property that East would list more fully as "in Aldersgate street at the signe of the Black Horse" from 1589 to 1594, and where he would remain for nearly twenty years, devoting his main efforts to music printing.[55]

For the other Aldersgate Street property, East cited a lease that began on 21 July 1605.[56] In a rare 1611 survey map of London houses, a George Inn was depicted immediately next to the St. Botolph's Aldersgate parish church.[57] This inn also appears in later maps of the area, which reveal further that it was several blocks south of a tiny cluster of buildings on Aldersgate Street known as Blackhorse Court (the latter would seem a good candidate for the location of East's older lease).[58] More important, in conformity with the description in East's will, the George Inn of Aldersgate Street, and presumably a property "over against" its sign, was well within the borders of the St. Botolph's without Aldersgate parish. There was indeed a third property noted in the will, but this was "in the parishe of St. Giles *without* Cripplegate . . . in the suburbs of London."[59]

Throughout his long career, East listed the addresses of his shops in various ways. Sometimes he simply gave an address "at London," but, when necessary, he would provide a more detailed listing.[60] East was a bookseller as well as a printer and publisher, and a survey of the advertisements in his imprints suggests he sold much of the music he printed at his shop.[61] Even when he worked as a trade printer and sent the bulk of his printed work to a publisher to distribute, he found ways to retain some of the finished copies for his own retail business.[62]

There were, therefore, practical reasons that East tended to be more explicit in the advertisements of his imprints, at times, for example, when he wished to alert his customers to a new location of his shop. The detail provided in the prints of 1589 until 1594, with mention of East's sign of the "Black Horse" at his new Aldersgate street shop, exemplifies this tendency.[63] Significantly, the imprint of the undated *Psalmes* editions led East's customers to a new location for the first time in many years. There is no reason to doubt that East printed books at this new location "over against the signe of the George," as he refers in his will to the "presses coppies *letters* and ymplements" of all his residences.[64] But the identification of the "signe of the George" residence does not provide unambiguous evidence for dating B2. The lease, to be sure, is dated 1605, which would seem to support the type-deterioration evidence. Yet B1, which lists the same address, was printed about five years earlier. It is, however, quite possible that East had rented the premises five years before obtaining a formal lease, just as he had occupied his primary residence at least two years before the date of its formal lease. It would be most useful to know why East specified this address only in the case of the undated *Psalmes* editions. Further research may perhaps clarify this matter as well as the circumstances surrounding the printing and publishing of B1.

REISSUES

Once paper and typographical data were combined, it was possible to solve most of the problems of undated and hidden editions in East's output.[65] In dealing with these

FIGURE 3.7
Type Deterioration Comparison (III)
(Note gap in sole of left foot.)

Byrd, *Gradualia II* (1607),
'I', Cantus primus, sig. D3ᵛ,
British Library, D.101.c.
Reproduced by permission.

Byrd, *Psalmes, Sonets & Songs*
(n.d.), 'I', Medius, sig. D1ʳ,
University of Illinois
Library, x784.1 B99p.
Reproduced by permission.

Youll, *Canzonets* (1608),
'I', Altus, sig. B2ᵛ,
Folger Library, STC 26105.
Reproduced by permission.

editions, the basic challenge lay in the task of assembling and analyzing bibliograph-ical evidence. With reissues it was much simpler to determine when East's work was completed.

To produce a reissue, East and other stationers recast the title page of an old edi-tion.[66] The resulting book would have appeared to the public to be new, but it actu-ally represented nothing more than a re-advertised version of an older edition. Ex-amination of the respective paper stocks of the new or altered title page and the main body of the work would permit verification of its true publication status. Reissues do not really suggest anything about East's original expectations; all sorts of economies governed print runs and edition sizes. Yet when a significant period of time had elapsed between the production of the original sheets and the new title page there is some suggestion that the market interest in an earlier book was not as strong as the original publisher had hoped. It is possible to argue that someone had later gained some confidence in the music's resale value, but the purpose of resetting the title pages and advertising the reissues as new and corrected editions was clearly to revive interest in a work that had still remained unsold. Otherwise, the sheets would no longer be available for repackaging.

It is now possible to establish a new and more reliable chronology for the entire span of East's music output. This is presented in the tables of appendix 1. The reso-lution of these bibliographical issues not only contributes to an improved under-standing of publishing practices in Renaissance England but also throws considerable light on East's business practices. Falsely dated or undated editions, for example, were produced in the few periods throughout East's career when there were ambiguities in the ownership of the music monopoly. They stand as incontrovertible proof of just how closely East had to align his trade to the exigencies of the royal patent—and just how important, therefore, were his relations with composers like Byrd, the subject of the next chapter.

Music publishing during Byrd's monopoly (1588–1593)
Part I: Byrd's publishing agenda

4

In 1588, for reasons that probably had very little to do with the English navy's defeat of the Spanish Armada, East printed two large volumes of music, Byrd's *Psalmes, Sonets & Songs* and an anthology titled *Musica Transalpina I*, which consisted of Italian madrigals translated into English.[1] Thus, as the nation itself was celebrating its victory at sea with a surge of nationalistic pride, East brought an unprecedented amount of English and Englished music by Italian composers to the London marketplace. That same year East also produced five books of scholarship and general literature, which included two editions he apparently published himself. It was one of his most productive years and one in which his press produced an output of books with unusually varied topics.[2] If this seemed to point to a future career of greater variety, such a policy was soon to change. In the following year, except for some possible involvement with the issue of a sermon for another printer, East produced musical works exclusively.[3]

The decisive shift in focus from general literature to music printing so soon after the initial music editions of 1588 marked the most significant single movement of East's career. Although he remained active as a printer for other stationers, kept his press ready for special opportunities, and routinely reprinted titles to restock editions he owned that had sold out (as he had done throughout his earlier career), after 1588 music prints became the mainstay of his book trade and would remain so for the rest of his life. From 1588 to 1608, with the one possible exception of 1599, East produced at least one but often three or more music books each year, thereby distinguishing himself as the first stationer to specialize in the music of English composers.[4]

The same year of 1588, which was so crucial for East's career, was also of great consequence to Byrd in his professional advancement as a musician in Elizabethan London. Byrd's patent of 1575 had been in effect for thirteen years, but it was only in 1588 that he began to take full advantage of his exclusive right to control the publishing of music books. Byrd's use of the press for his own music after 1588 was not compulsive, for he never printed a good number of his works. Nonetheless, as an Elizabethan composer he employed the newly activated technology of music printing in a singular manner. By the end of his life, he had published numerous of his works in many different musical genres: three large volumes of devotional and secular songs with English texts; an extraordinary number of Latin-texted works, which included two sets of *Cantiones Sacrae*, three sets of Masses, and large collections of liturgical motets in the two books of his *Gradualia*; and many of his works for keyboard, which appeared in the beautifully engraved edition of the *Parthenia*.[5]

Throughout his career, Byrd maintained a special business relationship with East and his heirs. The *Parthenia* was engraved elsewhere, but that edition turns out to have been a unique case. The technique for engraving books was a rarity at this time in England, and it was a skill East's compositors apparently did not possess; the remainder of Byrd's music prints were set with type, however, and all of these were printed by East, his wife, Lucretia, and his adopted son, Thomas Snodham. Byrd employed East as his exclusive printer for the entire period from 1588 to 1596 while he owned the music monopoly, and for those eight years East's firm was the only one to serve London's musical public, except, of course, for those printers who provided the ubiquitous psalmbooks with music.

For a mere "Singingman" (to borrow a term once used by stationers), Byrd held an enviable place in London society.[6] His Catholic patrons numbered among England's most wealthy and influential. His relations with the queen herself were not only official but familiar as well. He won many highly prized royal prerogatives such as the music grant and dispensations of great financial consequence; he even enjoyed the intimacy of creative collaboration with the queen.[7] As much as we would wish to know more about such a powerful musician—perhaps the most prominent musician in Elizabethan society—nearly all of his private thoughts, to say nothing of his inner personality, are now well obscured by the distance of time (although it certainly seems fair to say that he was an obstinate and tough-minded person). But there was a public side to his personality, too; this aspect of the composer's character was fairly well documented by East's press and it awaits further exploration. As royal monopolist, Byrd held extraordinary power over the press, which offered an opportunity for financial gain. More significantly, Byrd used this power to build and maintain an extraordinary level of prestige as a public figure and musician in Elizabethan society.

Byrd's mark is easy to detect in the production of printed music during the years he monopolized the trade. Not only was his own music featured above all others, but also for a time, at least, it seems that his personal taste and his politics determined what other musical collections were allowed to go to press. From East's perspective, a royal monopoly was the means by which a stationer could rise to a position of power within the mercantile world of the Stationers' Company; for Byrd, it provided the opportunity for self-promotion and self-aggrandizement, on the one hand, and a chance to advance and even to enforce his own agenda for English music, on the other.

Byrd had close personal connections with nearly all the protagonists of the nascent music press of London.[8] Near the top of this exclusive list was Thomas Watson, the poet and publisher of the *Italian Madrigalls Englished*, who was Byrd's friend, fellow Catholic, and creative collaborator.[9] Together these men produced the broadside edition *A Gratification unto Master John Case*, which, in its pristine production, was highly atypical of the general run of street ballads that shared the same format. Byrd was also to write his only two madrigals in the true "Italian vaine" when he was given texts by Watson to set to music.[10]

Like Watson, most of the other music publishers and composers whose works went to press in the years 1588–1596 were closely affiliated with Byrd. William Damon, the composer of two large volumes of psalm-tune harmonizations (that East printed), was Byrd's colleague in the Chapel Royal. John Mundy's music publication was inspired by Byrd's first solo edition; his father, William, was another colleague of Byrd in the Chapel Royal.[11] Finally, Thomas Morley, the composer who monopolized London music printing in the mid-1590s with his English madrigal prints, was very well positioned as Byrd's former student and colleague. The road toward Morley's later control of the press was undoubtedly paved by his especially close relationship with his powerful mentor.

At the same time that he promoted the work of his friends and associates, Byrd may have exercised his power of censorship on the musical publishing program. There was a conspicuous lack of music for the lute among the editions he allowed to be published during his tenure as monopolist.[12] The lute song was the rare case of an Elizabethan musical genre in which he never composed. It has been argued often that Byrd scorned the genre, if only for the reason that his own skills at the keyboard were possibly threatened by its popularity. Later, after his monopoly had ended, a modest "rush" of lute music was to emanate from London's presses. East, too, eventually contributed several fine volumes of lute songs. Byrd's influence on the printer, however, may have slowed East's ability to maintain a competitive edge in this popular field after the monopoly had passed to others.

BYRD'S MUSIC IN COLLECTIONS OF ITALIAN MADRIGALS ENGLISHED

Personal connections with Byrd were obviously helpful to aspiring music composers and publishers during the composer's tenure as music monopolist. It would also seem that Byrd himself missed no opportunity for personal exposure. The anthologies of Italian madrigals with texts translated into English, the so-called Englished madrigals, exemplify this facet of Byrd's effect on music publishing.

Nicholas Yonge's *Musica Transalpina* of 1588 was almost exclusively an anthology of Italianate music in the conservative vein of madrigal writing. It was this musical style that had the most popular appeal in areas north of Italy. The music was less chromatic than the more avant-garde styles, but both shared a common feature: virtually every semantic nuance of the text received treatment in the music.[13] Yonge's collection was generally uniform in style, but the advertisement on the title page gave pride of place to Byrd's single, anomalous work. It offered

> [m]adrigales translated of foure, fiue and six partes, chosen out of diuers ex-
> cellent Authors, with the first and second part of *La Verginella*, made by Mister
> *Byrd*, vpon two Stanz's of *Ariosto* and brought to speake English with the rest.[14]

Byrd was unique among the composers represented in the volume, for he was the only Englishman among them. With this inclusion in the collection, he was given a special position as (at least) an equal of the exalted Italian madrigalists. This was surely meant to enhance his status among the Londoners who bought this book of madrigals.[15]

In 1590 music by Byrd appeared alongside the many madrigals by Marenzio and a few other Italians whose texts Watson translated and published in his *Italian Madrigalls Englished.* This edition featured Byrd's name in the title-page advertisement. As before, his contribution was emphasized above the others, as a special feature of the volume, wherein it was stated: "There are also heere inserted two excellent Madrigalls of

Master William Byrds, composed after the Italian vaine, at the request of the sayd Thomas Watson."[16] These two madrigals, each a setting of "The Merry Month of May," were designed as a panegyric to the queen herself, portrayed as "Elyza ... [the] Beauteous Queen of second Troy" (there was a version for four voices and one for six voices).[17] The imperial references that linked the reign of Elizabeth to a mythical Golden Age were standard tropes of the so-called Cult of Elizabeth that permeated court culture. Byrd thus contributed musically to the mode of discourse that affected much of the literature and art of the age. As a courtier who was himself the recipient of royal favor, Byrd displayed a keen political astuteness by including these works in the London publications that announced his royal privilege (and by calling attention to them in the title-page advertisements). It provided yet another chance for Byrd to remind London audiences of his special relationship with the queen. In addition, he was also prominently listed on the title page of each of these volumes as the monopolist East worked for as an assign. This was yet another form of personal advertisement, and it emphasized Byrd's exclusive position in the music trade. As a monopolist who actively published music he enjoyed an extraordinary amount of exposure in the London musical community.

EAST'S EDITIONS OF BYRD'S MUSIC (1588–1591): A PLAN FOR PUBLICATION

Byrd's central aim for controlling the press was to publish collections made up entirely of his own music. By 1587 more than a decade had passed since Byrd's music had last appeared in print and he had accumulated a large repertoire of works he apparently deemed suitable for publication.[18] He took full advantage of his privileged position as monopolist and by 1592 had published four large collections of his own music. Apparently, no other publisher was involved in these works. Byrd was most likely the single protagonist responsible for all financial matters: choosing the dedicatee, purchasing the paper, and negotiating with East, the printer. Two collections by Byrd, his Psalmes, Sonets & Songs and Songs of Sundrie Natures, featured secular and devotional music with English texts and obviously were intended to have a wide appeal. But in 1589 and 1591 Byrd balanced this conciliatory move toward the London market by imposing collections of his Cantiones Sacrae on East's press.

It was unlikely that the market for the nonliturgical Latin music of Byrd's Cantiones Sacrae was more viable in the 1590s than it had been in 1575–1588 when the edition of Cantiones coauthored with Tallis so obviously failed to sell. Throughout East's career, the publication record of the motet genre, loosely defined, was remarkably barren of reprints. Neither of Byrd's Cantiones Sacrae editions was ever reprinted by East, and later motet collections by Byrd (the two volumes of Gradualia) had to be reissued by East's heirs after their sheets had lain on East's shelves for many years.[19] As before, Byrd expected these works of compositional rigor in his Cantiones Sacrae to advance his standing as a musician in the eyes of a select few. Motets were standard fare on the Continent, but from East's point of view their audience was perhaps the most exclusive imaginable: bilingual Latinists who not only could read music but also had the talent and wherewithal to perform the most challenging compositions.[20]

By contrast, Byrd's English songs, as well as the other collections of Englished compositions East printed in the first years of the monopoly, were very successful in the marketplace. If Byrd's prefatory explanations are accurate reflections of his motivation, a certain amount of momentum from the successes of the secular editions does indeed seem to have affected his program for publishing his own music.[21] From this it might be argued that Byrd's rationale for sending Latin-texted works to East's press was to exploit an unexpected window of fiscal solvency for the London music press, but close attention to the circumstances will show that this was not the case.

As it turns out, the composer had already formed a personal agenda for publishing his music—including especially his collections of motets—soon after he became the sole owner of the music monopoly in 1585 and before he had assessed any public response to his printed editions. Byrd's preparations for the publication of his own music had begun before 6 November 1587, for on that day East paid the standard "fine" (the stationers' term for fee) of six pence to register a preliminary manuscript copy of Byrd's *Psalmes, Sonets & Songs* in the company registers.[22] This registration confirms that Byrd's collection was already planned for publication before the Armada victory, of course, and before the *Musica Transalpina* had been produced. It serves, therefore, to correct a common misconception that Byrd was influenced by the commercial success of the 1588 *Musica Transalpina* edition when producing his first secular music in print.[23] Byrd's plans to publish his own music had begun before the market was tested, and he intended to bring before the public a more substantial portion of his music than has hitherto been noted.

Byrd remarked on his publishing plans in the dedication of the *Psalmes, Sonets & Songs* itself. In this print, Byrd publicly announced to the dedicatee, Sir Christopher Hatton, the newly appointed lord chancellor of the queen's Privy Council, that he would publish more of his music soon after the edition of 1588. Here Byrd described his English works of the 1588 collection as "small" and "poore" but said that they "might happily yeeld some sweetness, repose and recreation" for Hatton and, presumably, for other listeners.[24] Byrd admitted that he was preparing works of "more depth and skill" for another publication.[25] Humility was the standard fare of dedications in printed works of this time; this, therefore, does not really provide any compelling proof of Byrd's personal disdain for his music in the 1588 collection. Nonetheless, Byrd does draw a useful comparison between certain distinct examples of his own music. One set of compositions was for recreation and devotional singing; the other was of a more serious nature, suitable for the edification of a musical connoisseur. The best candidates for Byrd's works of "more depth and skill" were his *Cantiones Sacrae* that were subsequently published in 1589 and in another collection of 1591.

Scholars have hesitated to accept the suggestion that Byrd was referring to his Latin songs in the 1588 *Psalmes.* Apparently this is because in the next year Byrd published another collection of English works in a large volume titled *Songs of Sundrie Natures.*[26] Since the *Songs* contained works similar to those in the *Psalmes* volume and so many were apparently ready to be printed, the two collections were obviously linked. Thus it would be reasonable to suppose that when he referred in 1588 to music he was preparing for publication it was the music that did appear in the next year. In the *Songs* edition itself, however, Byrd suggested a different reason for his decision to publish another volume of English music.

In 1589 Byrd claimed that the primary reason he published his second volume of English songs was because his first volume had met with great success. His reiteration of that theme in three places in the volume makes it seem that he was even slightly (and pleasantly) surprised by that success. In his words, it was "through the good acceptance of ... former endeavors," that he "became encouraged to take [the] paines" to publish the new edition.[27] This suggests that the 1589 volume was *not* planned before *Psalmes, Sonets & Songs* had been published. Byrd was surely gratified by the success of his first volume of English music; he stated that "no Science is more plentifully adorned than music."[28] But he was careful in the latter work not to overestimate the English-texted music that he had mildly snubbed earlier (even if merely to fulfill the convention of self-deprecation in dedications). Nowhere in the prefatory material of the 1589 volume does the composer claim that the compositions included in it were of a better quality than those he had formerly published, and the phrase "more depth and skill" does not reappear.

To answer the question of what music Byrd actually referred to in his publication of 1588 there is useful ancillary evidence in Thomas Morley's treatise *A Plaine and Easie Introduction to Practicall Musicke* (1597). Morley dedicated this compendious volume to Byrd, whom he praised as "the most excellent" musician. Morley claimed in his dedication that Byrd had "authority" over musical matters due to his "deep skill."[29] He wished to emphasize that Byrd's views on music were like his own and of considerable importance to him; he cited Byrd as his teacher and dedicated the volume to the composer in order to invoke his name and reputation against the anticipated criticism of others.[30] Such a gesture, self-serving though it may appear, could have been sheer flattery or an unconditional expression of respect but, in any case, provides a clear and creditable statement of Morley's wish to be closely identified with his teacher. Morley was vigorously publishing his own music in 1597 and by that time was also in the midst of a campaign to acquire Byrd's lapsed music monopoly. On several fronts, therefore, Morley was closely attuned to the work and achievement of his elder colleague.

In the section of his treatise titled "Division of Music," Morley gave a descriptive evaluation of the vocal and instrumental musical genres of his day.[31] He began with what he claimed were the most "serious" and "grave" types of vocal music and ended with those he deemed to be "light" or even "wanton." The motet was listed first. His description of the genre resonates with Byrd's notion of the motet as music of the greatest "depth and skill." Morley also gave a contemporary assessment of the specific dilemma that confronted the English composer of these works because of their limited market:

> This music [the motet] (a lamentable case) being the chiefest both for art and utility is, notwithstanding, little esteemed and in small request with the greatest number of those who most highly seem to favor art, which is the cause that the composers of music, who otherwise would follow the *depth of their skill* in this kind, are compelled for lack of Maeceanes to put on another humour and

follow that kind whereunto they have neither been brought up nor yet (except so much as they can learn by seeing other men's works in an unknown tongue) do perfectly understand the nature of it; such be the new-fangled opinions of our countrymen.[32]

Morley explicitly cited his connections to Byrd and boasted an intimate knowledge of his views on music. Therefore, when Morley used the words "depth" and "skill" similarly to describe a specific type of music the chances are very strong that this was more than mere coincidence. It may also be significant that Morley made a reference to the Roman scholar Gaius Maecenas, the famous friend and patron of Virgil and Horace, when he discussed the issue of patronage. This was certainly a hint that the generous support of English connoisseurs was necessary to promote the motet as a viable form of composition. Byrd pointedly nominated each dedicatee of his *Cantiones Sacrae* editions as his "Maecenas."[33] One gets the distinct impression that by 1597 Morley was as familiar with Byrd's remarks that related to issues of musical publication as he was with Byrd's music.

Morley helps solve Byrd's vague reference to music of "depth and skill" by pointing to the motet as the subject; this would suggest that Byrd designated the *Cantiones Sacrae* instead of the *Songs of Sundrie Natures* in the dedication of 1588. If this was the case, then he obviously planned to continue to use the press for personal advancement by publishing motets, disregarding all the problems of mass production, distribution, and sales for this genre he had experienced earlier. Obviously, if his 1588 *Psalmes* and the *Musica Transalpina* met with the same disastrous fate as his earlier music print of 1575, Byrd might never have fulfilled his promise to publish more works of "depth and skill." Nonetheless, that he would plan to publish motets at all, especially before he had experienced any success in publishing music, goes far to reveal how distant his motives were from those of someone (like East) who hoped to sell the many books that were produced at the press.

The motet volumes were advantageous to Byrd because they could serve to please and impress rich patrons of the musical arts. He dedicated the *Cantiones* to two very prominent men, Edward Somerset, fourth Earl of Worcester (1589), and Lord Lumley (1591).[34] These dedications evoke the private delectation of connoisseurs that seems and may have seemed ill-fitting for the public realm of print, because the composer refers to private music making and the intimate relationship of a patron and a musician.[35] The manuscript was the usual venue for the type of relationship Byrd hoped to create and maintain with his patrons as he presented them with his *Cantiones Sacrae*. If, as David Price has argued, the social forces that kept the greater amount of Elizabethan poetry relegated to the realm of intimate manuscript exchange applied to music as well, the *Cantiones Sacrae* would seem to represent an apparent misuse of the medium.[36] Price's theory is, however, too sweeping. The connotation of distasteful popularity had mostly to do with the private relationships cultivated among poets and their patrons and did not necessarily apply to works of scholarship and music. Byrd's privileged role as monopolist allowed him to explore this rising modification of the manuscript aesthetic without penalty.

Lord John Lumley of Nonsuch, the dedicatee of Byrd's 1591 collection, boasted an extraordinarily large library full of treasured riches of classical and humanist scholarship.[37] His collection was complemented by a substantial number of continental music editions. Much of Lumley's collection originally came from the presses of Aldus Manutius and other humanist printers as well as the musical output of Gardano, Scotto, and Phalèse.[38] By dedicating his motets to Lumley, Byrd assured himself a place in this library. Surely it was no small pleasure for Lumley to see his name so prominently displayed in a printed book that he could ceremoniously add to his rich music collection. Whereas Morley was wary of the problems that faced motets in the marketplace, Byrd was less beset with the problem; as an intimate of prominent courtiers, he could remain oblivious to the incremental profits that might accumulate through wider sales of virtually all other types of books.

Morley had some problems with patronage in 1594, and by 1597 he may not have enjoyed the favor of such well-to-do patrons as Byrd did in the late 1580s and early 1590s.[39] Morley's solution was leaving his motets unpublished. Byrd, who was successful in finding and cultivating powerful patrons, was keen to use his power over music dissemination to publish this very kind of work. He used the opportunity to present his motets in printed form to powerful men who might promote his professional career. His motet production is the most telling case of his ability to sway East's hand in the Elizabethan book trade. Surely the motets were slow to sell, but just as surely Byrd believed that by paying homage to his patrons in these volumes his own reputation as a musician would be enhanced.

Insofar as the motets were concerned, to what extent did East's firm resemble the modern-day "vanity press" for Byrd? It does seem that East performed a service similar to the one continental music printers often provided for composers who were willing to pay for all production expenses and to market their own music—what Mary S. Lewis and Richard Agee have indeed likened to the services of the modern-day vanity press.[40] The "stigma of print" factor in London publishing made it a more dubious honor to appear in print there overall, but there is no denying that self-promotion and a careerist agenda lay behind Byrd's use of East's press. Then as now, the author presumably shouldered the financial burden for production expenses. Given the fate of other motets in the London marketplace, it is also safe to suggest, finally, that no one expected sales sufficient to generate any real profits.

Nonetheless, the power relations between pressmen and authors in the vanity-press scenario was (and remains) such that authors had to succumb to the stipulations of the producers of their wares. As royal monopolist, Byrd had unprecedented powers over the press that reversed this typical account. This set Byrd apart from most continental composers and changed the function of East's press, too (as will be discussed further later). With the important exception of Orlando di Lasso and a few others whose reputations alone seem to have given them special powers, Byrd stands out for his ability to envision a long-term relationship with the music press, one that served his particular needs for musical quality as well as for various kinds of exposure.[41]

Byrd's narrow designs for the distribution of his motets frustrated East in his hopes for their widest possible sales. He did not endure this fate alone; other English printers of Latin books, especially, had long been aware of their special problems of

distribution and of authors' oblivion to their interest in the matter. As James Binns
has shown, authors and printers were very often at odds over the needs of the consumers they wished to target.[42] Unlike Byrd, London authors often had virtually to
beg stationers to print Latin works (or, presumably, pay them well), and in the end
these authors were often dissatisfied with the results of their troubles. One particular instance of this, from the many supplied by Binns, is quoted here because the basic
motives of a trade printer are so well stated from the perspective of an Elizabethan
author, in this case Richard Montagu. A translation of the original Latin appears here:

> On top of the six hundred difficulties with which we are afflicted we have un-
> fortunately had to put up with the stupidity and stinginess of the printers. For
> they are accustomed to work for profit, they are only following a mercenary
> trade. And so they load whole waggons and carts with hackneyed two-penny
> ha' penny garbage. They have no taste for serious things. Latin writings are not
> read, and as for Greek, they exclaim against them as if they were heretical.[43]

It must have been doubly satisfying for Montagu to deride his printer in this way.
Montagu could revel in the fact that the printer was setting and printing these very
words of censure against himself and his tradesmen. In this case, the author appears
to have been safe in that assumption that the printer was ignorant of Latin, for otherwise one doubts that such a diatribe would ever have passed through his press.

Byrd never criticized East's work (quite the opposite, as it turns out), but East
may have more than occasionally wished he could bend the views of the composer.
Although the separate motives of Byrd and East were probably consistent with those
of the authors and printers of Latin books, the balance of power was reversed. It was
presumably not Byrd who had to convince, coax, or cajole East to produce Latin
music but East who had to succumb to Byrd's decisions about what types of music
would be produced at his press.[44] The printer's tasks went beyond the problem of the
Latin language. He also had the responsibility of setting, and therefore understanding, the language of music. Undoubtedly, even fewer London printers than the number of Latinists among the group were musically literate. East's duties were no less
difficult than his colleagues, but unlike those printers who did set Latin or Greek, his
actions were effectively monitored rather closely; Byrd, as will be argued later, was a
vigilant "corrector" of the press.[45]

PROOFREADING AND CORRECTING THE WORK AT EAST'S PRESS

In his *Psalmes, Sonets & Songs*, Byrd very graciously exonerated East from any potential
criticism for his workmanship, particularly for setting the correct type for the musical notes of his compositions. Byrd commented on his first experience with East's
work as follows:

> In the expressing of these songs, either by voyces or Instruments, if ther hap-
> pen to be any iarre or dissonance, blame not the Printer who (I doe assure
> thee) through his great paines and diligence, doth heere deliver to thee a per-
> fect and true Copie.[46]

This statement has implications that go beyond the particular circumstances of East's production of Byrd's *Psalmes*. It is a contemporary assessment of East's work that has often been echoed by the modern editors and bibliographers who have dealt extensively with his music editions.[47] East maintained a very high standard of musical integrity in his printing work throughout his career. Although inaccuracies in written texts might be glossed over (especially if a work was mainly for reference or private reading in silence), errors in musical performances could be glaring. An unintended dissonance or stumbling block in the rhythmic flow of a work could easily embarrass the performers or at least create audible problems that would be very difficult to ignore.[48]

As a printer with his own reputation at stake, East probably felt that words from composers, like Byrd's cited earlier, would not always suffice to exonerate him as an instigator of "iarreing" musical errors in the text. East's personal quest for excellence, exemplified in his concern for his product, if impossible to document, can never be ruled out as a motive for his actions. What is clear from the evidence of his printed works, however, is that Byrd went to extraordinary measures to achieve an acceptable presentation of his music and East was somehow compelled to follow Byrd's wishes and whims. As the Byrd-East partnership developed in the late 1580s and early 1590s, Byrd—or a musician like Morley who was working for him, perhaps—experimented freely, it would seem, with different methods of monitoring and correcting the musical texts produced at East's press.[49]

There is a wealth of evidence of meticulous proofing in the editions East produced for Byrd. A preponderance of cancel slips in the edition of Byrd's *Songs*, for example, seems strongly to indicate that East went to considerable lengths to correct Byrd's music.[50] The carefully edited editions of his *Gradualia* stand as similar instances of Byrd's special influence.[51] Since comparable works, like Yonge's *Musica Transalpina*, were less meticulously redacted, Byrd may have been the decisive factor in determining East's industriousness.[52] It is not possible, however, to determine with absolute certainty that the many emendations in Byrd's editions were undertaken at the composer's behest. But in one case there is the evidence necessary to ascertain Byrd's actual role in the correction process, and this example certainly tips the scale of probabilities toward the likelihood that Byrd was an active and exacting force in the process for assuring the accuracy of his musical editions at East's press.[53]

In the preface of his *Psalmes, Sonets & Songs*, the composer gave the following supplication to his readership that explicitly announced his intentions to use the press for the purpose of correcting his musical texts:

> If in the composition of these Songs, there be any fault by me committed, I desire the skilfull, wither with coutesie to let the same be concealed, or in friendly sort to be thereof admonished: and at the next Impression he shal find the error reformed: remebering alwaies, that it is more easie to finde a fault then to amend it.[54]

It was not unusual for authors in this period to make such earnest requests to their readers. More often, however, the reader was asked to correct the errors of an edition privately and with ink.[55] Byrd's plan was different. He had East print two new editions of his collection within a few years, and in each case the most notable difference between them was the progressive treatment of errors in the text.[56] These new impressions were what Byrd had promised: errors that had been discovered were "reformed" in new "impression[s]."

Rather than attempt to amend the problems discovered after the first printing of the volume by traditional means (with cancel slips or by hand, for example), Byrd clearly decided to have East reprint the entire volume.[57] In view of the sheer amount of proofing labor involved, it is rather startling that Byrd did not cease correcting the work after the first reprint: East issued the work yet again in a third impression to incorporate further corrections to this single text.

It was in the midst of this cumbersome process of correction that Byrd noted: "[T]hrough his great paines and diligence, [East] doth heere deliver to thee a perfect and true Copie."[58] East was thus absolved of any errors that appeared in the books; the composer frankly admitted that the "true Copie" East produced was an accurate rendition of the printer's copy he was provided and could be nothing more. By such a comment the composer, as publisher, assumed responsibility for any errors that remained. This precisely describes the differences between printer's and publisher's responsibilities regarding press corrections that have been established elsewhere in this study. It also suggests that Byrd could be courteous and considerate toward his printer. But true relief from the burdens of Byrd's exacting program to ensure musical quality under the auspices of a royal monopoly would come to East only when the composer left London itself.

STONDON MASSEY AND THE CHAPEL ROYAL

The most significant event of Byrd's life in 1593 was probably the move he and his entire family made to Stondon Massey in Essex.[59] In that year, Byrd leased a house and property that had been sequestered by the crown from a recusant. The most reliable records of this move were produced in 1595 when Byrd and members of his family began to be fined for recusancy in Essex. Byrd's last fine at his former house in Harlington in Middlesex was in 1592; this serves to establish that Byrd's move most likely took place in the same year he obtained the lease.[60]

In his autobiography, Byrd's contemporary the Jesuit William Weston captures nicely the essence of the composer's change of career focus in the years after 1593, even though he was describing an event of many years earlier:

> Mr. Byrd, the very famous musician and organist, was among the company [at a recusant house]. Earlier he had been attached to the Queen's chapel, where he had gained a great reputation. But he had sacrifisied everything for his faith— his position, the court, and all those aspirations common to men who seek preferment in royal circles as means of improving their fortune.[61]

That Byrd was not listed in records of witnesses and petitioners in the Cheque Book of the Chapel Royal attests that after 1593 the composer was rarely, if ever, in London with enough frequency to fulfill an active role in the court. Contrary to Weston's claim, however, Byrd did remain a member of the Chapel Royal and probably still enjoyed many benefits of his close association with the queen.[62] After his move to Essex, however, he was undoubtedly more involved with specific Catholic patrons such as the Petres of nearby Ingatestone. The music monopoly was no longer a central concern for the composer. After 1593, most of the music Byrd was to publish was written for Catholics.

The significance of Byrd's departure was reflected in the imprints of East's music prints after 1593, where mention of his patent no longer appeared regularly as before (being found only in the 1594 edition of Mundy's *Songs and Psalmes* and in East's second edition of the *Whole Booke of Psalmes*).[63] Nevertheless, the composer did involve East in another project after his move. With East as his printer, Byrd published three Masses for the apparent use of his fellow Catholic worshipers in Essex.[64]

All of Byrd's Masses were produced in the same format. They were laid out by the pressmen so that each part fit onto a single sheet of paper. The tenor part of the three-voiced Mass, for example, appears completely on a single sheet of paper folded into four leaves with eight pages. The sheets were folded in quarto format and signed at the bottom for the binder. The three-voiced Masses were signed with an "A" and the four- and five-voiced with a "C."[65] Thus they were coded for the binder as preliminary matter, perhaps a signal that they were to be placed after the title page of another edition, or a series of editions, within a single bound book. It seems likely that one reason for this was to make it possible for them to be secretly distributed. If tucked under less provocative covers, they were usefully disguised from the authorities. Today they are nearly all bound with collections of other, less political, editions of music in the same format.[66] Consequently, none of them now has a title page of its own. It seems very likely that this omission was due to the original design of the printer's copy.

Printing the Masses was probably not taxing work, but it may have been a dangerous assignment for East. Catholic worship was illegal in England, and publishers as well as authors had been severely punished by Elizabeth from the 1580s onward for distributing religious propaganda.[67] The Masses themselves may not have been so threatening, since, as a rule, the actual liturgical material was deemed less offensive than the more confrontational and sometimes blatantly seditious political pamphlets authored by newly active English Jesuits, for example.[68] Even so, East was probably wise to take the precaution of disguising his name at the very least.

With no title pages, there is no printed date for any of these editions. East's type is there to assure us it was undoubtedly his work, but only Byrd himself was named in the Mass. The lack of basic publishing data for these works suggests the surreptitious nature of editions printed for the recusant community. Until Peter Clulow studied them in detail, the timing of their production and even the basic number of editions produced were not at all clear to music scholars. Clulow may have been the first to discover that the three- and four-voiced Masses were actually published in two editions.[69] He also used an effective method of type deterioration to date all the editions, and his results suggested very clearly that they were produced in the years 1593 to 1595.[70]

The paper of the first editions of East's Masses has marks similar to those in the paper East used in printing the two volumes of Damon's psalm-tune settings in 1591 (see Table A1.3). As was mentioned earlier, the Masses comprise very little paper, with only three to five sheets for each copy of the multipart editions. This makes the condition that they shared paper with these other editions in East's output rather unremarkable. It is not hard to imagine a scenario whereby Byrd and East decided to use leftover paper from the Damon productions, rather than purchase new paper, to produce the Masses.

As will be discussed in more detail later, Morley had taken over East's music press at the same time that Byrd sent his Masses to East for publication. Byrd's lack of participation in the mainstream of activities at East's music press was one way in which their relationship had begun to change. For the remainder of his career Byrd would deal with East as a longtime business associate rather than as an indirect servant of the crown. It is fitting that the Masses would herald the new association. Rather than conform to the monopoly's original designs (as most of the other books East produced could be said to have done), the Masses ran against the stipulations of "courtly compromise" implicit in royal monopolies. Today it could easily be argued that the Masses did much to "aduance the science of Musicke," but at the time they drew Byrd away from the queen and into the treasonous realm of illegal Catholic worship. Byrd himself argued that his motets had purely musical purposes (even though they were also pointedly political), but he made no such claim for his Masses. Freed from the strictures of the royal monopoly, Byrd created a new program for the press. Significantly, it was at this point that East exerted his own independence by producing an edition in a hidden format.

A HIDDEN EDITION OF THE *Musica Transalpina*

Like the *Psalmes, Sonets & Songs* before it and seven other editions East would later produce, the *Musica Transalpina* edition was reprinted so that the original date was represented again on the title page (see Table A1.2). With the same study of type deterioration Clulow used to date editions by Byrd, he concluded that a second edition of the *Musica Transalpina* was not printed at the stated time, 1588, but in 1593–1594.[71] According to his data, Damon's psalmbooks, Byrd's Masses, and this hidden *Musica Transalpina* edition fit especially close together in East's printing schedule.[72]

East produced these three editions with the same stock of paper. These data corroborated Clulow's evidence on the printing schedule of the Masses and led logically to the hypothesis that the *Musica Transalpina* (a volume of little apparent use to Byrd in Essex, it would seem) was published by East with paper also skimmed from the Damon prints.

Byrd might conceivably have been a party to East's method of skimming paper from the Damon editions in the case of the Masses that he himself surely published. But was Byrd aware of the additional use East made of the same paper to produce the *Musica Transalpina?* Probably not. In 1588 Byrd did participate in a similar reprinting venture with East. His motive then was most likely to correct errors in the original issue of his *Psalmes,* and for that purpose the composer himself probably sponsored the multiple editions that appeared in that year.[73] Although there was, in fact, a noticeable problem in the table of the first *Musica Transalpina* edition (which East took the opportunity to correct when reprinting the volume), no editorial program comparable to Byrd's desiderata for editing the *Psalmes* can be found in the *Musica Transalpina* editions.[74] Without a compelling editorial incentive and because it was done five years after the original (rather than in the same year or so, as with Byrd's *Psalmes*), the reprinting of the *Musica Transalpina* was more likely to have been solely for the traditional reason: the work had sold out from East's shelves but remained in demand among London consumers.

If the *Musica Transalpina* was reprinted to address a surge of demand, then the central problem becomes its false date. Why did East not re-advertise the volume when he printed it again? By 1593 East may have at least partially owned the 1588 edition. In two cases for which documentation survives, East did specifically attempt to secure property rights for second editions from other publishers, and, significantly, he never claimed more rights to these works beyond that of reprinting them.[75] What probably stood in the way of East's full disclosure of his activities at this juncture was Byrd's ambiguous position as an inactive monopolist. As patent owner, Byrd could exact a subsidy from East for the right to print a new edition of music.[76] If East was attempting to hide his activities, it would fit well with the evidence of Byrd's movements in 1593. When Byrd was removed from London and less concerned with his monopoly, he was most prone to overlook East's independent actions.

The hidden edition of the *Musica Transalpina* may indirectly point to the dilution of monopolistic power during a period of ambiguity over the supervision of the patent. After his move to Essex in 1593, Byrd still found the monopoly useful, but he treated it with new circumspection. His single project for the music press, as it was still nominally under his control, was the production of his Masses. East complied with Byrd's wishes by producing three different Mass editions in close succession. But even if Byrd was still able to control East's output, the printer probably found the circumstances of the composer's move propitious for his own entrepreneurial designs. When Byrd was unable to supervise the work, it would seem that East took the opportunity to publish a new edition of the *Musica Transalpina* disguised as an older version.

MUSIC PRINTING DURING BYRD'S MONOPOLY (1588–1593) PART II: THE BENEFITS TO EAST

5

As music monopolist, Byrd had personal goals that shaped much of the enterprise of music publishing in England. His interests began with his own music, and only after he considered that music did he consider other music publications that might advance his own standing or that of his friends and colleagues. Especially when producing Byrd's music, East was probably inconvenienced by the composer's unusual capacity to control the presentation of his music in print. Byrd fostered an experimental yet meticulous approach to the accuracy and integrity of his musical texts, seemingly at the expense of East's labor.

In the face of such pressures, one natural recourse for East would have been to retreat to a familiar and more comfortable position, that of the trade printer who works for a fee. Acting simply as a printer, with no entrepreneurial aspirations (that is, with no means to independently sell music or publish it), would have allowed East to escape the problems of music volumes that were slow to sell. As he had done for many publishers in the past, he might simply have put his presses and his pressmen at Byrd's disposal for a printer's fee. We know how such arrangements worked. In the Dowland case, discussed earlier, the contestants explained the precise fee Eastland paid to the printer for his craftsmanship, and the evidence there is revealing: whereas East was paid ten pounds for the labor of printing, his two apprentices had quickly earned four pounds by selling illegally just thirty-three copies.[1] The better tactic for a businessman in East's position was obviously to have an interest in the success of the books in the marketplace, but he would only benefit from sales if the music books were desired by the London public.

At the outset of the Dowland project, East assumed a role as trade printer. Yet even here (and perhaps especially so) he demonstrated entrepreneurial ambitions in the music trade. His contract with the publisher George Eastland specified that the intellectual property would revert to East after the first edition sold out.[2] For the first music editions after the 1575 *Cantiones* fiasco, when music printing was at its riskiest, East took a possibly stronger financial stake in the publishing of music. He listed himself not only as the printer but also as the bookseller.[3] Unlike Christopher Barker, the queen's printer, who in 1582 explicitly stated that he would not provide the necessary furniture to produce music books and put them on his shelves, East was actively selling and promoting his music editions from the very first one he produced, with his address prominently displayed on the title page.[4]

Professionally, East was deeply committed to music printing, and despite all of its adverse features it was undoubtedly the monopoly itself that attracted him to the enterprise. To enjoy the benefits of the monopoly, he was dependent on Byrd's willingness to use his printing shop exclusively. Unfortunately, we have no record of the earliest business arrangements between composer and printer. Whatever precise form these arrangements took, Byrd and East were clearly partners in the music trade long enough for each to find advantages in the monopolistic system. Byrd's interests have already been discussed; this chapter considers two main subjects illustrative of the benefits that accrued to East. The first involves the editions of Byrd's *Songs* and how they were packaged for the market. The second focus is on the collected and individual musical settings of the psalms in the editions East printed.

ADAPTING BYRD'S CONSORT MUSIC FOR THE PRESS

In the prefatory remarks in the editions of his own music, Byrd makes several points clear about his motives for publishing music as well as his plan to present much of his own music in print. In a motet volume and the volumes of English songs, he noted that although he had a store of compositions he wished to print, he needed to make certain changes in the music before it could be published. For the motets the composer did not specify exactly what these changes would be, and thus we must speculate on what he may have done to prepare this music for the press.[5] Byrd did specify more concretely how he revised his English music. By adapting consort songs to an a cappella performance medium he may have made at least some concessions to what the Renaissance stationer called vendibility.

Byrd announced in the "Epistle to the Reader" of his *Psalmes* that his songs were "originally made for Instruments to express the harmonie, and one voyce to pronounce the dittie" but "are now framed in all parts for voyces to sing the same."[6] All of the works in the 1588 collection were scored for five parts, and in many of these songs there is printed text in the header to designate "[t]he first singing part," the single part for voice in the original consort song.[7] Studies have shown that Byrd adapted other consort songs as well, but they do not provide this convenient clue.[8]

Byrd's adaptations have generated a great deal of discussion in musicological scholarship, not for their compositional implications directly but because of the light they shed on his role in the birth and growth of the English madrigal. As many have discovered, Byrd's music was quite unlike the madrigal. His songs were typically strophic and much less attentive to every semantic nuance of the text. The latter characteristic was a virtual hallmark of the contemporaneous madrigal. It would be wrong to claim that Byrd was not sensitive to the poems and prose texts he set or even to claim that his music was generally devoid of madrigalisms, but his style of secular song was clearly of a different species than the madrigal.[9]

The stylistic differences between Byrd's songs and the madrigal had not been fully appreciated by modern scholars even by the mid-twentieth century. The primary reason for this was not the result of any deception by the composer. He surely hoped that his music would coexist with madrigals in performance, but he did not suggest that his musical style was in any way similar.[10] Byrd composed two sterling examples of madrigals in Watson's anthology of 1590; otherwise, he took little personal interest in the genre. East would surely have had even more profitable books on his hands if Byrd had risen to the demand and composed new English madrigals in sufficient number for separate printed collections. Unlike many of his colleagues, friends, and students, Byrd never composed enough madrigals for a separate collection.

By adapting his consort songs to an a cappella format, however, Byrd did provide East with the chance to profit from the sales of his songs. This was one reward of East's career move to the field of music printing. Another was his rise in social status. From his first music editions, shrewdly dedicated to Christopher Hatton, the sudden star of Elizabeth's court, East, on Byrd's coattails as his assign, was drawn into the rarefied and jealously sought realm of the royal court.[11] This was an environment rarely frequented by printers of East's rank. Beyond the sheer glamour of such an occupation, there were enduring political benefits, somewhat analogous to those gained more directly by the queen's official printers.[12]

East's connection to royal powers was explicitly advertised in his editions as Byrd's assign and in his role as London's exclusive music printer. From this he would gain a useful reputation as a specialist among music publishers, composers, and consumers. As the only official center that distributed music paper as well as music books for eight years, his shop was probably frequented by many musicians, both amateur and professional. From the outset, East had particular economic reasons to cultivate these relationships, one of which was to set himself up as a viable publisher of Sternhold/Hopkins psalmbooks. It was through musical connections fostered by the music monopoly that East positioned himself favorably with the largest social group of all, the comprehensive consumer base for those books.

As it was written, the music monopoly overlapped with the patent for the psalmbooks. At this time, the psalmbook patent was nominally held by Richard Day but actually was run by a syndicate of stationers who listed themselves as Day's assigns.[13] It seems very likely that East planned from the start to use his position as Byrd's official assign to exploit this single facet of the music monopoly and followed a consistent plan to mesh the psalm-tune settings with other privileged music printing. The ultimate result of this strategy was East's well-timed publication of his *Whole Booke of Psalmes* (1592). In several ways the appearance of this volume marked the pinnacle of his career.

The legality of printing psalms under the music patent

The psalmbook patent was among the most vigorously contested and jealously guarded monopolies of the stationers' trade.[14] Perhaps because the music patent was a recognized failure by 1577, there had been no attempt to reconcile the coverage of the Byrd and Tallis patent with that of the psalmbook patent until 1598. The music grant listed in its purview "[all] set songe or songes in partes, either in English, Latine, Frenche, Italian or other tongues that may serue for musicke either in Churche or chamber, or otherwise to be either plaid or soonge."[15] Theoretically, the owner of the Tallis/Byrd patent could claim the right to print music for the church, including the metrical psalms with "notes."

The duplication in coverage appears to have been an oversight on the part of the drafters. It might easily have been rectified if challenged in court, since the Day firm could establish prior rights to the property. John Wolfe and his partners, the de facto owners of the psalmbook patent, constituted a powerful syndicate of stationers who had already defended their legal rights several times before the royal courts by the end of the 1580s. East would not have been wise to challenge such a group directly. In 1598 Morley, as holder of the music monopoly, did attempt to outflank this syndicate by printing a direct challenge to the psalmbook patent in a work by Richard Allison.[16] Morley was immediately contested by Day, who won an effective, and what was surely a damaging, injunction against the music patentees.[17] It was a sign of East's business acumen that when he set out to exploit this window of legal opportunity he proceeded cautiously. Unlike Morley, East did not openly provoke the syndicate of printers but slowly constructed a defensible case for his right to print the metrical psalms under the umbrella of the music patent.

It should be emphasized here that East's 1592 production of the *Whole Booke of Psalmes* was very risky, precisely because it rested on such a thin legal foundation. Ultimately, he harnessed all of his new standing in the court and the musical world to publish the collected psalms. East's choice of Sir John Puckering, Keeper of the Great Seal, as the dedicatee of the 1592 book (and therefore its nominal protector as well as patron) was undoubtedly a key decision. Like Hatton and other dedicatees of music books, Puckering was an immensely powerful figure.[18] If East's new connections in the court had made such an alliance possible, that alone might have made the whole enterprise of music printing worthwhile. East wrote the following to Puckering in his dedication:

> I present it [the volume] unto your Honour, as to a maintainer of godliness, a
> friend to Virtue, & a louer of Musick: hoping of your Lordships favorable ac-
> ceptance, crauing your honorable Patronage & countenance, and praying unto
> God long to continue your Lordship, a protector of the iust, and the same
> God to bee a protector of your Lordships welfare for euer.[19]

Much as he might have hoped to gain from it, East was obviously too cautious to rely on Puckering's influence alone. Using the text of Byrd's music patent as a shield, East brought the psalmbook patent under the music patent by the Fabian tactic of avoiding direct confrontation while progressively printing more and more settings of the metrical psalms. One or more of these tactics must have been effective, for there is no record of any attempt by Day's assigns to challenge East's intrusions into the psalmbook market.

METRICAL PSALMS IN MUSIC EDITIONS BY EAST

Musically, there were two types of editions of the psalms. Monophonic settings were the more prevalent and probably best served the utilitarian needs of consumers, but there were also polyphonic versions of the same poems and tunes. Even John Day (who had little professional interest in composers or the musical world in general) had found that at least some amateur performers wished to break out of the bounds of monophonic settings.[20] This smaller group sought the more musically enriched settings of the psalm tunes with harmonizations. Theoretically, and perhaps intentionally, this market was one with which the spirit of the music patent coincided, for these arrangements did promote the art of music, at least in that they enriched the Anglican service.

The narrow segment of the public that desired more challenging music was rather little nurtured by John Day and ignored by Richard Day and his assigns. Thus there was a potential consumer demand for psalm-tune settings with harmonizations that emphasized musicality. This was the vulnerability East exploited in order to arrogate to himself eventually a segment of the Day firm's market. At first, East did not threaten the large market for monophonic settings. Even so, his strategy was a risky one, as is revealed in the cautiously worded registration of the first music book East printed in the Stationers' Registers:

> Thomas East: Receaued of him for printinge. *Bassus, Sonnettes and songes made into musick of fyve partes : By* William Burd &c/ PROVIDED ALWAIES that this entrance shalbe void if it be hurtfull to any priuilege &c [21]

On 6 November 1587, the same day that East took his first music book to Stationers' Hall, John Wolfe also visited there to register a copy of one of John Day's former privileged books. This coincidence may explain the discrepancy between the registered title *Bassus, Sonnetts and Songes* and the actual title of the music book East printed: *Psalmes, Sonets & Songs.* Wolfe was the legal owner and most powerful defender of the Day patent that covered the psalms with music. If East had registered Byrd's music advertising the correct title of the *Psalmes,* Wolfe would then have had the legal foundation to accuse East of piracy, even if Byrd had not composed a full complement of psalms and thus had no intention of actually producing a psalmbook. The evidence that concerns intent to deceive, however compelling, is circumstantial. Byrd did mention in the preface that he had composed new works for the collection, and perhaps these included the ten settings of the metrical psalms that were a featured part of the printed edition.[22] If these were already part of the copy that East registered under the misleading title, it would be possible to imagine an innocent explanation. But the likelihood of that is rather small. In legal terms, as they may be tentatively reconstructed, the final version of the book that East printed would seem indeed to have been "hurtfull to [a] priuilege," for it contained settings of the metrical psalms and thus competed in content with the music protected by the psalmbook patent. Even more telling a case is made by the marketing of the work. East's title page, in stark contrast to the registered title, prominently mentions the psalms, and it was probably no coincidence that they appeared first in the collection.

Once he had established a precedent with Byrd's music, East moved against the Day firm with more confident steps. After about 1589, when he had already gone to considerable trouble to print the works of Latin motets and songs for Byrd, East began to exploit more fully the market opportunity of printing more and more psalm-tune settings under the auspices of Byrd's patent. Byrd himself contributed a number of new settings of metrical psalms in his *Songs* of 1589.[23] These were soon followed by two versions by William Damon (both of 1591), titled:

> The Former (and Second) book of the music of Mr. William Daman . . . containing all the tunes of Davids psalms: as they are ordinarily sung in the church: most excellently by him composed into 4 parts.[24]

EAST'S *Whole Booke of Psalmes*

It has been pointed out by Donald Krummel that 1592 was a propitious year for East to bring out his most provocative volume of psalm-tune settings (that is, the so-titled *Whole Booke of Psalmes*). This was because the patent for the psalmbooks was then in a state of transition.[25] East prepared his book as an octavo edition of almost 300 pages of music and text. The main part of the volume was set with his ten-point roman type, which was well suited to its small, octavo format. He also used the small and elegant van den Keere music font, which had not appeared in his books before.[26]

Beyond its handsome appearance (an unmistakable feature of East's volume, which set it apart from almost all of Day's editions), the book was also distinguished by its focus on musical quality in the four-part harmonizations of its tunes. As East described it, his volume was filled with the music of outstanding composers, who were men he believed to be "expert in the Arte & sufficient to answere such curious carping Musitions, whose skill hath not bene employed to the furthering of this work."[27] These ten musical experts were John Dowland, Richard Allison, John Farmer, George Kirbye, Edward Johnson, Michael Cavendish, Giles Farnaby, Edward Blancks, William Cobbald, and Edmund Hooper.[28]

The *Whole Booke* was a difficult enterprise.[29] East took the opportunity to add nine tunes to the existing repertory and claimed that these had not been included in earlier editions.[30] Presumably he was making a direct reference to the Day versions of the same title, for several of the nine "new" tunes had earlier appeared in East's own edition with music by Damon.[31] These were the tunes with place names such as "Oxford" and "Southwell," and so forth, and for the initiation of this practice credit has been given to East.[32] Also a novelty for him, and a special challenge, as he maintained, was his decision to present the parts together in choir-book format. The logistics involved in dealing with so many composers presented yet another complication. Altogether, this was a project he had to plan thoroughly and implement carefully. It probably took considerable time.

In the prefatory section of the volume, East was explicit about the special requirements of the task and permitted himself a few complaints about the work it entailed. He noted in his dedication the "paynes [of those] that compyled" the volume, and in the preface to the reader he cited his own "trauayle." He maintained that he was willing to go through such trouble for two reasons: first, for "the furtherance of Musicke, in all godly sort, & to the comfort of all good Christians," and, second, and more broadly, for the general "publique benefit." As part of the latter reason, he suggested that his concern for the commonweal should be interpreted as a gesture of altruism, since it operated to the detriment of his own "private gaine."[33]

East could not easily be challenged on the first account, for his work probably did cause the "furtherance of Musick," whether or not he was consciously attempting to resonate with the text of the royal grant. His *Whole Booke of Psalmes* was a musical triumph of its kind, and eventually its settings would displace all others, to become the standard text for several generations to follow. When it was finally revised, it became known as the "Old Version" of the psalms. This was never fully excised in the Anglican service, although it was effectively replaced by the Tate and Brady "New Version" in the time of Henry Purcell.[34]

THE SUCCESS OF EAST'S *Whole Booke of Psalmes*

Like others before him, East argued that by producing a work of quality he had to sacrifice the larger gains that he might expect from a cheaper, more popular work.[35] Undoubtedly East's *Whole Booke of Psalmes* was for a time less popular than the monophonic versions that continued to emanate from the presses of Day's assigns, but it was clearly a volume that had great appeal among London's consumers. Already in 1594 East had brought out another edition of the work, and East and his heirs produced similar collections again in 1604, 1611, and 1621. Furthermore, this was the single work by East that was treated to a most telling compliment for its popularity: in 1599 it was pirated by William Barley.[36]

East's strategy in producing his *Whole Booke of Psalmes* edition makes it seem very likely that he, like Byrd, had particular goals for his own use of the music monopoly. Almost surely he had planned to exploit the possibility of printing the *Whole Booke* from the outset of the venture. He began to realize this plan soon after he entered into partnership with Byrd in 1587, and traces of his strategy were found in several volumes that featured musical settings of the metrical psalms before 1592. Byrd had his own prestige uppermost in his agenda, and East served him well in this regard. But the printer did not neglect his own interests; East found a way to great profit through the sales of psalmbooks to a large group of consumers.

Byrd and East had separate designs as they attempted to monopolize the music trade, but it is not unlikely that their goals might also have overlapped to some extent. It is tantalizing to note, on the one hand, that Byrd would take such measures as to compose a laudatory setting for Watson's poem that honored John Case. Case was a strong proponent of the best available music in the church, and he certainly would have endorsed the use of East's psalter over other editions as part of the Anglican service.[37] And, of course, Byrd's own pleas for the lofty place of music in his editions represents the composer's recognition of both his own and his printer's need for a wide market for music in order to survive.[38] On the other hand, East is not really a good fit for the label of pure mercenary that many authors routinely pinned on their printers. He, too, may have taken pride in the meticulously corrected volumes he produced with Byrd. The impressive quality of East's own production of the psalter surely was not a trivial matter to the printer, who may have striven for excellence in his work quite apart from the issue of pecuniary reward.

In the next phase of East's career, when he began to deal more extensively with Thomas Morley, his course was to change significantly. For the first time he encountered a competitive environment in music printing. In this era his own position as a music tradesman was strengthened as he added to his accumulated experience, but he was clearly threatened by the vigorous activities of Morley and others. Morley was a particular problem because it was he who eventually gained the power Byrd once held as the sole Elizabethan composer to monopolize the English music trade.

THE MORLEY ERA:
COMPETITION IN LONDON MUSIC PRINTING AND PUBLISHING (1593–1602)

6

In Commendation of the Author . . . by I.W.

A noise did rise like thunder in my hearing,
When in the East I saw darke clowdes appearing:
Where furies sat in Sable mantles couched,
Haughty disdain with cruel enuy matching,
Olde *Momus* and young *Zoylus* all watching,
How to disgrace what Morley hath auouched,
But loe the day star with his bright beams shining,
Sent forth his aide to musicks arte refining,
Which gaue such light for him whose eyes long houered,
To find apart where more lay undiscouered,
That all his workes with ayre so sweet perfumed,
Shall live with fame when foes shall be consumed.

R. A. Harman suggests that "I.W." is John Wootton, a poet featured in the English *Helicon* anthology;[1] the musician John Wilbye might be another possibility. In any event, this poem appeared as the last of three commendatory verses to introduce Morley's *A Plaine and Easie Introduction* of 1597. Unlike the two other poems on the same page, which simply praised the composer in standard laudatory terms, this verse offered a theatrical image: the dramatic triumph of the personified force of good over evil. The poet's device was an allegory at daybreak, and its point is clear. Morley is cast as the hero, and we witness his moment of victory over darkness. The foes, whom the narrator hears as cacophonous musical competitors with evil intentions, are watched, approvingly no doubt, by the Roman gods of criticism, Momus and Zoylus. These carping deities were no strangers to print; they served as foils for many writers of Elizabethan dedications to express their angry disdain for critics and other detractors.[2]

The poem was chosen to introduce this chapter for two reasons. First, through the use of puns (see line 10: "where *more lay* undiscouered"), the poet may have intentionally named the protagonist of this study, Thomas East, when he referred to the location of the dawn (see line 2: "When in the *East*").[3] From 1588 to 1596, when East worked under the auspices of William Byrd's music monopoly, his shop at Aldersgate Street was the legal center for all English printed music and printed music paper.[4] In 1597, one year after Byrd's monopoly expired and when East was functioning as a prominent force in the music trade who worked sometimes for and sometimes against Morley, it is quite reasonable to suppose that Wootton would imagine that the lesser musical lights, with their competing musical works containing real or implied criticism, would be clustered around East's press in their "Sable mantles." Second, this poem alludes to the competitive spirit among musicians and music printers at this time. Criticism mattered because competition became a new and vital force in music printing in the years 1593–1602, which figured in East's career as the Morley era.

To suggest today that there was any kind of competition in the musical world of Morley and East is to challenge a well-entrenched view among scholars, namely, that the English music-printing industry at this very time was a completely lackluster affair. [5] The apparent dearth of reprints and the sluggish production of new musical editions by London presses, especially when compared to the activities of continental firms, formed the cornerstone of this evidence. If correct, the very idea of competition among the producers of music would hardly be tenable.

A closer scrutiny of the Morley phase of East's career offers evidence to the contrary. Renaissance London could indeed never compete in music printing with Venice, Paris, or the Netherlands. However, an awareness of the full scope of East's previously unknown hidden editions opens a much richer perspective for the possibility of a competitive environment than had previously been imagined. Not only were these editions true reprints, which indicated a livelier market than hitherto believed, but also their publishing status, once determined, reveals that East's strategy was in direct opposition to Morley's interests. A fuller appreciation of the interactions of East, Morley, and other music printers and publishers strengthens the view that competition played a significant role in shaping the musical world of the time.

THE REGULATORY ENVIRONMENT IN CRISIS

There was a complex set of regulations and controls for music printing in late Elizabethan London. The field was governed by three competing monopolistic forces that covered music: two patents granted by the queen—one for psalms with music and the other for general music—and a set of Stationers' Company privileges. Throughout the Morley era, the royal psalter patent was owned and run by a syndicate of stationers, the assigns of Richard Day. The royal music patent, however, was in a state of flux. There was a gap between Byrd's and Morley's successive ownerships of this grant (Byrd: 1575–1596; Morley: 1598–1602), and printers like East and William Barley took full advantage of the resulting ambiguities in power. If the field was somewhat stabilized when Morley gained control of the patent (in 1598), the composer's entrepreneurial ambitions only increased with his new power: once he had obtained the music patent itself, he used that opportunity to push brazenly into the lucrative area of psalter publishing, formerly the sole domain of the syndicate of Richard Day and his assigns.

During this era, Morley, East, and other printers and publishers became involved in intricate relationships whereby printers were pitted against one another and new strategies emerged, which allowed some to capitalize on special advantages or exploit weaknesses of particular competitors. Quite contrary to the impression of an apathetic market environment, the energy of these men gives telling testimony to the lively interest in gaining control of what was clearly perceived to be an attractive industry. If the degree of interest was not sufficient to yield reprinted books in numbers that rivaled those of Continental firms, there can be no doubt that the confrontations among authors, printers, and publishers amounted, inter alia, to an incipient struggle for the control of what would now be called intellectual property, or copyrights. The London music field, if seemingly small, was a battleground for one of the most coveted privileges of modern society: the author's rights to his or her own creative properties.

MORLEY

In 1593, at the same time that Byrd retreated from London society, Morley became a rising figure at Elizabeth's court. Like Byrd, Morley, too, was probably a Catholic, but along with others of Byrd's acquaintance, including Thomas Watson for example, Morley was involved in complicated adventures that tend to make his own personal convictions rather obscure to us today. It would seem that at one time he was an informer, or double agent, in religious politics.[6] Philip Brett has advanced the hypothesis that one of Morley's escapades as a religious informant helped him to attain the highest position of the era for an English musician. Swiftly following on his service to the Privy Council, Morley was awarded a lofty position as a "gentleman of the Chapel Royal."[7] He began to publish music at East's press in 1593, and his participation increased noticeably over the next two years. In 1595, just one year before Byrd's monopoly was to end, the productivity at East's music press rose to new heights. This was due entirely to Morley's energy as a publisher. In that year East brought out four music books, the largest number he had ever produced in a single year. All were devoted exclusively to Morley's musical works. The composer was rather curiously inactive in 1596 but returned to music publication with his earlier vigor in the following year, publishing three music books of his own and sponsoring two others. Morley went on to gain the patent of the music monopoly in 1598 and continued to publish music until his death in 1602.

Morley's interest in music printing from 1593 onward leaves little room for doubt that the composer had already made plans to assume the place Byrd once held as the most powerful figure of the music trade in London. It was a project Morley probably developed from the first years he began to publish music. Not surprisingly, Morley's acuity in business matters is a well-known aspect of his life that has been studied in some detail.[8]

The main thrust of Morley's printing program in his first years (1593–1596) was a calculated attempt, through the publication of his own music, to bring the English madrigal itself in line with the more popular types of music in the markets of the European continent.[9] Lighter styles of music were often derided and dismissed as inferior and ephemeral by the musical authorities and sometimes even by the composers who wrote such pieces, but this style of music was clearly the mainstay for European music publishers of the era.

Ironically, when he functioned as a theorist Morley was apt to dismiss the lighter forms of music that sold so well on the Continent. By the mid-1590s, he was an acclaimed "Bachelor of Music" from Oxford, organist at St. Paul's, and had recently joined the queen's Chapel Royal.[10] He also was the author of a musical treatise, the *Plaine and Easie Introduction*. This not only was a compendious primer for musical composition and understanding but also offered a notable example of Elizabethan musical criticism. From Morley's writings it would seem clear that he treated the lighter forms of secular music with the disdain of a scholar, but beneath this one finds his basic understanding of the whole business of music as a commodity in trade.[11] Morley knew which types of music should be praised by a theorist, but he also knew which kinds would sell best when mass-produced. Furthermore, he knew that the two types did not mesh. It was no more inconsistent for Morley to offer his best praise for the motet and choose never to publish any than for him to dismiss the lighter forms of the English madrigal as ephemeral but publish as many of them as he possibly could.

With hindsight it appears that not all of Morley's marketing decisions were auspicious. In a brilliant analysis of the conditions of publication of Morley's *Madrigalls to Fovre Voyces*, which East printed in 1594, Thurston Dart discovered that the composer may have had a special problem with its dedicatee. Possibly at the urging of East or perhaps by exploiting his printer's connection, the composer attempted to dedicate the edition to Sir John Puckering, who had already received the dedication for East's *Whole Booke of Psalmes*.[12] Puckering was probably in a strong position to assist Morley financially and to provide political protection if any were necessary, but in the end Puckering's dedication was excised from the edition. Dart believed that the dedication was withdrawn because Puckering was heavily beset with dedications in 1594 and was too annoyed by them to accept any new financial obligations or responsibilities.[13] Ultimately the composer must have lost some potential rewards, for all extant copies of the work appear without a dedicatee.

Morley's Italian-texted ballets and canzonets also represent something of an entrepreneurial miscalculation. It is typical of Morley's ambitious nature that he would attempt to reverse the trend of Englished madrigals by repackaging his English works with Italian texts, presumably to attract an international consumer base for his music. Since East never reprinted these editions, it seems likely that they were not selling as well as his Englished works. Morley may have simply overestimated the interest in English music among continental consumers, but it is more likely that he overestimated East's capacity and desire to pursue an international market for his works.

If he had problems with patrons and international markets, Morley's analysis of the continental scene itself and its untapped implications for a publisher of music in England was ingenious and wholly successful. The English-texted ballets Morley composed and published were modeled on the immensely popular works of Gastoldi that by 1640 had been reprinted an astounding twenty-three times.[14] Morley's own music proved to be a favorite among the London consumers, and his works, too, were reprinted many times by East and other music printers.[15]

The new popularity of music editions in England was a condition that East, as distributor and publisher, and Morley, as composer and publisher, worked together to create. This was the phase when East's music presses were preoccupied with the English madrigal, a genre that Morley had almost single-handedly developed into a popular form of original composition by English composers.[16] Like Byrd before him, Morley proved to be a creative and a self-interested monopolist whose ultimate goals were to advance music in various ways through the medium of print, but the particular interests of these two composers could not have been more different. Byrd valued the medium for the command it gave him over his work, and he directed his music toward an elite audience. Morley was much more concerned about the basic economic benefits to be gained first by cultivating and then by meeting the needs of a popular market. Thus Morley's concerns for music publications, unlike Byrd's, were rather closely shared by East himself.

EAST AS MUSIC PUBLISHER IN 1596

No music books by Thomas East advertise the year "1596" in their imprints. Information from the archives of the Stationers' Company, however, and the bibliographical evidence of type and paper in East's extant work suggest that East was not only printing music in that year but was also operating independently as a music publisher on the most ambitious scale of his career. East's registrations of music books and his practice of producing hidden editions (both of which occurred in 1596) were integral components of his new publishing policy. East acquired property rights to music editions through the registrations and took it upon himself to arrange for the expenses (chiefly the paper) of their production through a practice he developed in his hidden edition policies.

One of East's publishing ventures in 1596 was a rather modest book. It was a reprinted production of the well-known Irish musician William Bathe's theoretical treatise, *A Brief Introduction to the Skill of Song.* The work was not dated, but East registered his copy in 1596 and probably produced it in that year.[17] This was the first time he had operated independently in the music field, and it may have taken Morley by surprise. *A Brief Introduction* was one of two treatises that evidently spurred Morley onward his decision to bring out his own voluminous treatment of the subject in 1597. More important to Morley than the competitive aspect of Bathe's manual, however, was the circumstance that East chose to enter the volume in the Stationers' Company Registers before producing it in print.

Registration was a proto-copyright procedure established and enforced by the Stationers' Company. Although well known to be a crucial factor in the emergence of copyrights for the intellectual property of plays, for example, in the realm of music the registers have been largely misunderstood by modern scholars. These registers functioned significantly in the distribution of power within the Renaissance London music-printing trade. They stood as a counterforce to the queen's two distinct monopoly grants (or patents) that controlled the field. To fully understand their significance in the competitive environment of the Morley era, their effect on matters of copyright, and the advantages they brought to East as a publisher, it is necessary to explain their function in some detail.

The registration of books in Elizabethan England

Registering books in Renaissance London was an uncomplicated process. It began when a stationer (or, for a brief period in the pre-1580 era, any citizen interested in printing or reprinting a text of a work) brought a copy of the work he or she wished to print to the clerk and wardens of the Stationers' Company. Then, if the text was deemed suitable for public consumption, its title was noted in the company's registry books, together with an indication that the standard administration fee had been paid for the "entrance."[18] The formal act of registration, or entrance, in the Stationers' Registers was straightforward; the Elizabethan practice has proven difficult to understand today, however, because of the various ways this single list of titles was treated.[19]

The registers contain a rare body of useful evidence. Many works extant today are listed there in various states of prepublication. More important still, they provide a list of printed works that are now lost, as well as a fascinating group of texts that were considered for the press but never produced.[20] Historically, they served the active needs of several different institutions and individuals. In the form of licenses, the registrations were an effective tool for Tudor government.[21] Basic control over the press was still possible in the early years of the sixteenth century when the entire output of the English national press was manageable.[22] Licensing all books before they were mass-produced in printed form gave Tudor monarchs, who were represented by their most trusted bishops, strong power over the press. In the years when there was mandatory registration of all books for the purpose of licensing, the distribution of propaganda against the government was a difficult and dangerous business.

Given the constant threat of opposition from Catholic and Puritan forces, it is not surprising that Queen Elizabeth's policy did not radically change in regard to the registration of books as her reign progressed. In some fashion or other, the government continued to use the valuable resource of the Stationers' Company Registers to monitor the activities of the press throughout the Elizabethan era (and beyond). As the volume of printed matter expanded, however, the bureaucratic task grew too large for busy government officials, and the monitoring function was delegated to the Stationers' Company. Company officials seemed to be prudent enough to call on the bishops for advice on especially sensitive texts, but otherwise they accepted their task as a part of their function as a self-regulating industry.[23] This was in keeping with the routine power the monarchy bestowed on all London livery companies, granting to them the means to establish a fair and prosperous trade in the realm.[24]

In the late 1570s, when it was monitoring the national press through its registry, the company was beset by a struggle over the ownership rights of printed property. This was the famous revolt within the guild over the queen's own policy of granting monopolistic patents. The music monopoly, of course, was only one of many such grants. One important outcome of this struggle was that these same registers became a tool for the legal demonstration of property rights. When a book was registered, it was no longer permissible for anyone else to print it. Thus the registers became a separate concern of the Stationers' Company of great consequence to its members but, in this regard, of little import to the monarch. Still, the queen was deeply involved: it was the monopolistic patents she granted to individual stationers that inspired them to establish an economic, rather than political, use of the registers.

At the time of company strife, the registers began to function more and more as a means of protecting the more powerful individuals of the company from their competitors. (Most of the queen's patents for monopolies in books were granted to stationers, and these patent owners were typically the richer members of the company—or they quickly became richer as the economic benefits of their patents came to fruition.) This led to a negative function of the registers; they came to serve primarily as a clearance check required of all printers to ensure that no patents were illegally breached before any texts were produced in print. Happily, this benefit for the richer stationers was balanced by a positive role for the registers that the whole company could enjoy. Individuals who established rights to "copy" (that is, the text for printed matter) by whatever method they could also had the opportunity to pay a fee and list their property in the registers. In this way, on a basic level, the proprietors of smaller firms enjoyed the same protection from competition as their more prosperous brothers in trade.

East's role in this history of the Stationers' Company Registers was distinctive. What set him apart from most of his brothers of the Stationers' Company after 1588 was his involvement with the music patent. As previously noted, this was a rare monopoly for books owned by grantees who were not members of the Stationers' Company. In his particular registration of 1596, East used his special status as a member of the company to gain a certain advantage over composers like Byrd and Morley, who published most of East's music books yet were not members of any trading firm.

EAST'S LARGE-SCALE REGISTRATION OF 1596

East did not register any music books in the years 1588–1596, when he worked as Byrd's assign, but in 1596, when the monopoly had expired, he registered nearly the entire collection of music editions he had premiered at his press. (Table A1.4 is a list of the books East registered in 1596.) Beyond the fact that East avoided the registers at certain times, there are larger, more complicated issues related to this registration and East's property rights. The most compelling aspect of this registration of 1596 is its size: East may have been "fined" (that is, charged a fee equal to) the price of ten books, but the list actually includes twelve books and the relisting of a formerly registered title.[25]

To explain East's registrations of music books, some scholars have argued that they were done solely for licensing purposes, that is, to comply with the censorship requirement imposed by the government. If this were true, the registrations could be explained without reference to any business agenda.[26] East certainly dealt with Catholic, and therefore controversial, material that he may indeed have wished to clear with the authorities. But there is otherwise little proof to substantiate the theory that his registrations were determined by rules for licensing and some convincing evidence against it. East's 1596 registration came long after the government had delegated the licensing function of registration to the company; economic motives for registration were already commonplace by this time.[27] Militating further against the licensing theory is the evidence that East registered no music books during Byrd's monopoly. This immediately suggests that East had a subordinate standing in relation to music property during the term of the patent. If the purpose of registration were only to obtain licenses that certified political acceptability, East most likely would have availed himself of such useful protection with respect to these books. Registrations, as licenses, would protect both East and Byrd from the government. In addition, even with the political works that East did produce, and which it would have been prudent to clear with the bishop, his behavior was inconsistent. On the one hand, he failed to register the Masses by Byrd, which could be seen as indirect recognition of the censorship function of registration, given that this Catholic music was politically sensitive. On the other hand, East registered Byrd's Latin motets in 1596 and, despite the momentous political events that occured in Elizabeth's last years and the early years of the new reign, he did the same with both volumes of *Gradualia* with settings of Mass Propers by Byrd in 1605[28] and 1607.[29] Although it is possible that East may have felt compelled to bring all his musical editions to the company for licensing, there is no special evidence of this. Economic, rather than political, motives were more likely the cause of his large-scale registration of music books in 1596.[30]

It now seems apparent that East sought to enter every property he felt he had the right to list in broad view of his colleagues in the company. Since almost the entire collection of printed music was in the list of 1596, this conclusion is primarily based upon an analysis of the smaller number of works the printer did not register. The largest volumes stand as the most glaring exceptions (the two volumes of music by Damon and East's own *Whole Booke of Psalmes*) and offer the real key to East's motives for registering music copy. The works by Farmer and Whythourne were probably not of as much concern to East, and, more important, they were not East's to sell. In both cases, the addresses of the musical composer was given on the title pages as the location to buy copies.

Although they were probably even more salable than the other titles, the large items East failed to list in 1596 shared a common feature that distinguishes them from the rest of the registration: they were complete musical settings of the metrical psalms, and East advertised them as alternatives to the more common monophonic psalmbooks. As such, these books would have seemed most offensive to the owners of the still active psalter patent, who could claim the legal right to confiscate them as piracies of their property. East was obviously confident that some of his books with metrical psalm texts (and with music by Byrd and Mundy) would be allowed to him. But this was because of the diversity of the musical genres in these collections.[31] In all other cases, he must have believed that music editions that featured settings of the metrical psalms were too dangerous for him to list or even to advertise as his property in 1596.

This confirms that East's position at the close of Byrd's monopoly was rather tangled. The sheer number of psalter editions in East's output leaves little doubt that Byrd's monopoly had given him an opportunity to print music with settings of metrical psalms despite the competing monopoly that expressly forbid East to do so. Obviously, Byrd's power, stemming as it did from the queen herself, protected East to some degree here. The registrations, however, indicate that although East was interested in using the Stationers' Company books to guard copy that he had previously published, he had not the means to protect his rights to the psalter books that were of such value to him. He was restricted altogether from such privileges after Byrd's monopoly had ended. Thus each patent presented advantages and drawbacks for his firm. When East was no longer the assign of a music monopolist, he could consolidate his ownership of music copy per se by using company registers, but he could not extend this protection to his psalter publications because of the direct challenge it would pose to the company's interests. This shows, generally, that the two music monopolies, with their overlapping coverage and shifts in power, shaped East's publishing strategies and, more specifically, that the threat represented by the psalter patentees in 1596 was palpable.

East dared not cross the psalter patentees at this juncture, but the registers would otherwise serve their traditional function: to announce his property claims as a warning to and injunction against any would-be book pirates. Thus East by this maneuver thwarted the competitive interests of other stationers in his music prints. Furthermore, with these registrations East could effectively ward off Morley's competitive interests in the music he had printed before Byrd's monopoly lapsed.

All of this leads, finally, to a noteworthy fact of East's career that relates to registrations, one that has escaped notice: namely, that his most conspicuous registrations of music tend to coincide with the gaps, or shifts in power, in the music monopoly (see Table A1.5). I believe that East had found within the company's proto-copyright system of registration a way in which to develop a publishing strategy of his own. His purpose was to capitalize on the periods of free trade in the music field and thereby participate on the entrepreneurial level of a publisher in the music field, even though he never actually owned a music patent.

MORLEY'S MANEUVERS

Bibliographical evidence from East's misdated works has established that he printed two hidden editions in 1596: Morley's *Canzonets a 3* and Byrd's *Songs of Sundrie Natures*. He printed these as part of a strategy that included his registrations of books in that year.

Whether Morley was aware of East's actions is uncertain; had he been, he surely would have wished to retaliate. The frustrating aspect of the situation was that in 1596 Morley had no recourse to prevent East from publishing his *own* music, a fact to which the presence of Morley's *Canzonets* in East's list of hidden editions provides clear testimony. The music monopoly, which once gave Byrd such extraordinary power, was not to be Morley's until 1598.[32] During the gap in the ownership of the monopoly, Morley had no legal backing from a patent. East, however, did have access to the registers; and, unlike the situation with psalmbooks, stationers would have had no reason to object to East's plan to appropriate Morley's music.

Since it would give its owner such an advantage in matters of copyright over a stationer like East, one might well wonder why Morley did not take quicker steps to obtain the actual monopoly. Perhaps Morley was caught off guard? He may have assumed that Byrd was intending to renew the patent himself. Morley should have been somewhat wary of such an assumption; Byrd had removed himself from London already in 1593 and no longer had ready access to the queen. In any case, such a grant would not have been easy to acquire. Not only was there the Elizabethan equivalent of time-slowing "red tape," but also obtaining patents often required considerable payments to the right people or the granting of certain kinds of favors in return.

By the time Morley did obtain the patent in 1598, he had indeed been subject to the give and take of court politics. That Christopher Heybourne, the queen's preferred musician, was to become Morley's silent partner was surely the consequence of such a compromise.[33] No doubt Morley had bettered his own chances for success as a suitor for the grant by giving the queen a chance to reward her favorite in this patent, but Morley's financial sacrifice—halving his own profits—was considerable.

To fully understand Morley's position as an ambitious music publisher in the 1596–1598 era (that is, between the time his mentor, Byrd, owned the grant and when he acquired it for himself), it is necessary to consider the sum of circumstances he faced. His primary objective was to control music printing, but this was difficult to achieve in short order. He needed first to concentrate his efforts on positioning himself to be the natural candidate for the music monopoly patent. In the meantime, he was confronted with competitors. These were men who may not have had similar monopolistic ambitions but were nonetheless clearly willing to take advantage of every moment of free trade in the music field. Morley would need to squelch their efforts. This duality of purpose manifests itself in Morley's editions of 1597. The telling references to court affairs in the texts of the music and the dedications, the ostentatious recognition of Morley's greatness as a musician in the laudatory poems of his treatise, and the preference given in his publications to composers who were well known to the queen betray his intense lobbying effort for the royal patent. Yet these same works provide searing criticisms of his opponents, not only on an intellectual level but on matters of business ethics as well. Competition from East's firm was something Morley would address and rectify later. Where the composer's first retaliatory maneuvers are most evident is in his dealings with two newcomers to the music trade—William Barley and Peter Short.

MORLEY AND SHORT VERSUS BARLEY

Barley, like East, was an ambitious and active music publisher and thus a direct competitor to Morley. In 1593, when Byrd moved away from London, Barley registered and may even have published a music book in direct defiance of Byrd's monopoly (a now lost edition of the anonymous *Pathway to Music*).[34] This was at the very time when Morley himself had just entered fully into the music-publishing arena. Barley and Morley crossed paths again at the official termination of the music monopoly in 1596. While Morley was preparing his voluminous music treatise for the press, Barley had published two primers of music that included a good portion of musical repertoire: the aforementioned *Pathway to Music* and the *New Book of Tablature*. Both of these volumes were to figure as sources of contention for Morley.

Barley was a novel force in the music-publishing field. He was neither a musician nor a member of the Stationer's Company in 1596 (although the latter situation would change in the next century).[35] He was rather a member of the Drapers' Company, a rival company with many book traders among its members. As such, Barley was not as easily controlled by the Stationers' Company, especially in matters of copyright. By the very essence of his status as a "freeman" it was perfectly lawful for a draper to trade in books rather than the cloth of his formal company affiliation, but the stationers had deep misgivings about this arrangement (they later took steps to curb these rights).[36] Thus Barley's status as a freeman of the city introduced a troublesome new wrinkle in the Elizabethan music trade. Morley reacted to Barley's perceived effrontery by venting publicly some rather harsh criticisms of the publisher. Perhaps the most damning appeared in Morley's *Plaine and Easie Introduction* of 1597. In a comprehensive and scathing critique of Barley's *Pathway*, Morley simply demolished his rival's work, concluding that "[v]ix est in toto pagina sana libro" ("There is scarcely a page that makes sense in the whole book").[37]

Morley's tirade found resonance in other musical publications of the same year. Anthony Holbourne, the celebrated "Gentleman Usher to Queen Elizabeth," took issue with Barley's *New Book of Tablature*.[38] Holbourne's music was featured in Barley's print but apparently without his consent. Thus in 1597 he complained of "a wrong proffered from a meere stranger unto me, who (without my knowledge of either man or meane) hath delivered in common to the worlds view certaine corrupt coppies of my Idles."[39] This response was in fact a trenchant insult in more ways than one. By insisting that he was but a "meere stranger" Holbourne emphasized Barley's lowly social status in London, especially as compared to Morley and Holbourne, who were familiar figures at court.[40]

In his vastly popular *First Booke of Songs*, John Dowland was yet another critic of Barley's publishing efforts. This volume was closely associated with the intimacies of court life, for like Morley's *Canzonets for Five to Sixe Voyces*, the Dowland volume was dedicated to George Carey, Lord Chamberlain of the Household.[41] Dowland complained of Barley's unauthorized, and corrupt, use of his music in 1596. Because of Barley, he wrote, "there have been diuers Lute-lessons of mine lately printed without my knowledge, false and imperfect." The onslaught against Barley seems to represent something of a unified front by three composers who were numbered among the most respected musicians of their generation. All three were intimately associated with the court, and, among other connections, all had their 1597 volumes of music printed by another East competitor, Peter Short. [42]

The extraordinary output of seven music editions that Short produced in a single year of 1597 set a record for the field in England and topped East's output of any given year. [43] There were three music books in this list authored or published by Morley himself and, as already indicated, two others were by authors linked rather closely to him. The only work not discussed thus far was an edition of Hunnis's *Seven Sobs* with music. Although it was not so clearly associated with Morley, this volume may help explain why Short so suddenly became a music printer of great importance in London.

Like East, Short was a member of the Stationers' Company, and it was this affiliation that best explains his role in the music-publishing field. Short had inherited the rights to the Hunnis book as the successor of the London stationer Henry Denham, who first issued the work with music in 1587.[44] More important, Short also acquired Denham's music font, which had lain idle for more than eight years while Byrd and East enjoyed their effective monopoly over music printing.

With some links to music publishing in property matters and with the necessary equipment in hand already by 1589, Short had a new opportunity to exploit in 1596. In that year not only was the field of music publishing in London suddenly thrown open by the absence of Byrd and the termination of his monopoly, but thanks to Morley, Short was in a position to enjoy the kind of alliance East had once had with a musician of the queen's court. This alliance had its clear benefits for a stationer's mercenary interests as well as many benefits for the source material of Elizabethan music. Short's editions were very well produced, attractive, and musically correct.[45] All in all, in quality they surpassed the contemporaneous work of East himself.

Through the use of Short, Morley could attack Barley effectively in a public arena as well as establish himself as the logical successor to Byrd in the eyes of the queen and her court. Short would also serve Morley's other needs. As a fellow stationer, Short was in a position to effectively thwart East in the very strategies the latter had developed to capitalize upon his double role as music printer and stationer. Short could force East's hand through the company laws both men had pledged to follow. For example, once he had registered a copy of Morley's music, Short could count on East not to interfere with its production.[46]

Morley's exclusive use of Short's firm and tight grasp on the market for the most established composers of London had a clear effect on East's career. No longer able, thanks to Morley, to feature composers like Dowland or Holbourne, East was at least free from the wants and whims of a music monopolist during the ambiguous period while the patent lay inactive. He took this opportunity to expand his clientele, attracting a class of lesser-known (but soon to be prominent) composers. By opening his firm to a group of tyros East found a solution to his dilemma. The scheme had larger historical implications as well. If East's intentions were perhaps mercenary at heart, the result of his willingness to risk his time and efforts on younger, untested composers was the bringing of some of the era's finest music to more consumers than was possible otherwise. Since many of these pieces were of the greatest worth to future musicians, and many have survived in East's prints alone, it also brought this music to its ultimate place in the canon.

EAST'S MUSIC PRINTS OF 1597–1598: "THE TRUE IMPRINTINGE OF MUSICKE"

Short's prolific output in his "miraculous year" of 1597 was nearly matched by East himself. Until the monopoly had passed from Byrd's hands, East was generally producing two or three music volumes a year. In 1597 he produced five music books, and he continued this more ambitious production schedule with four new editions in 1598. There were a number of features of the volumes he produced in these years that make them cohere as a group, but it is worth emphasizing that this period of 1597–1598 represents the first, and nearly the last, time in East's career that his press was unencumbered by the overriding agenda of a third party in the form of a music monopolist. The gap in monopoly ownership of the late 1590s created a special opportunity for him to function as a London-based specialist in music printing. In these few years, East's music presses were available to anyone who had the means and the need to partake of his services.

East once made a revealing statement about how he viewed his position in the competitive market for music. He described himself proudly as the one printer in London with the "name for the true imprintinge of musicke."[47] It turns out, however, that he was not measuring up to anything very worthy at the time he made this boast. The statement was made in his trial of 1601, and after this introduction East had to go on to defend himself against the charge that he had not effectively stopped his apprentices from stealing music books from the publisher Eastland.[48] Even so, for modern historians East was not exaggerating his claim when he described his position. Through a mix of strategy and stubbornness, he was the most stable and most productive printer of music in London in 1601, just as he claimed. In 1597, however, after eight years of a monopoly with Byrd, and when it probably mattered more, East was surely even more determined to make it known that he was the "true" printer of music. He seems to have relied to some extent on his reputation as a means to survive in a field newly populated by competitors.

East's music editions of 1597–1598 are among the most diverse of his career. They include not only a rare collection of French and Italian music by Charles Tessier (1597) but also the duos of Orlando di Lasso (1598). The duos represented the first full collection of Latin music by a single continental composer printed in England. To produce this volume, East copied the original Munich print of 1577 very closely, although by 1598 Lasso's music had appeared in more than a handful of continental editions.[49] There is no dedication in the work, and no editor is named. Thus it would seem likely that this very popular didactic volume from the Continent was another example of East's quiet style of self-publication in the field of music.

The Lasso volume by East may be a clue to an audience he began to embrace actively in the years 1597–1598. If the choice of the work was East's, then it reveals that he had the foresight to develop current and future customers with primers of music composition. These duos were primarily didactic and thus presented a way for East to actively meet the basic needs of a musicians' market.[50] His target audience during the years when no monopolist controlled his trade would seem to have been young aspiring musicians who patronized his shop, including a number who were probably students from the Inns of Court and the universities. Music was standard fare both in the curriculum and throughout the extracurricular program at the Inns of Court, which were conveniently near St. Paul's and East's Aldersgate Street shop.[51] If Morley and Short would attract the most prominent composers, East was surely able to draw on a market of youthful musicians for the musical copy he printed in these years.

The chance survival of three holographic letters, as well as a copy of the actual dedication title page of Charles Tessier's edition, has given us a rare glimpse into the underlying reasons for a special musical publication East printed.[52] These letters inform us that in 1597 the young French musician was trying to secure a professional post in the household of an English grandee and had decided to use the press to advance his qualifications. Charles was the son of Guilliaume Tessier, who himself had professional connections in England and was, perhaps, the instigator of the project.

Like his father before him, Charles hoped that a well-timed, and appropriately dedicated, publication would better his chances of obtaining a position in London.[53] He dedicated his work to Penelope Rich. Rich was a famous music patroness in London circles and the sister of Robert Devereaux, the Earl of Essex.[54]

Today there are too many unfilled gaps in the picture to determine how the whole business turned out for young Tessier.[55] In his letters of appeal he did not write directly to Rich but rather to Anthony Bacon. Bacon was the most trusted secretary and patronage broker of the earl himself. What Tessier received for his troubles and if ever he was employed by anyone in London remains a mystery.[56] It is reasonable to assume that in turning to East to promote his accomplishments the printer's reputation may have been the deciding factor. By 1597 East would have been the natural choice for the average citizen of the city.

If the results of Tessier's strategy remain murky, the epistolary evidence makes it clear that he was a young musician who sought to use East's press as a means of self-promotion in London. Tessier's quest sets a pattern that was followed to some degree in East's editions by George Kirbye, John Wilbye, and Thomas Weelkes. All three of these Englishmen were young, and all were associated with musical establishments less glamorous than the Chapel Royal, to be sure, but of some substance nonetheless. Kirbye was featured in East's *Whole Booke of Psalmes* and therefore may have been the person to introduce Wilbye to East at that time. Kirbye worked in Rushbrooke near Bury St. Edmonds, only a few miles from Hengrave Hall, where Wilbye served as a resident musician. In 1597 Kirbye dedicated his work to the daughters of Sir Robert Jermyn from this landowner's seat in Bury St. Edmonds.[57] In the next year the musician married and settled in the same area, perhaps on the strength of his new reputation as a published composer.

Wilbye may have been slightly more ambitious than Kirbye. Wilbye's work was produced in London and dedicated to the prominent courtier Sir Charles Cavendish. But he signaled his position when he signed his dedication from Hengrave Hall in Austin Friars, London, where he was employed by the Kytson family.[58] The musical establishment there was well served not only by Wilbye himself but also by Edward Johnson, another featured composer of East's *Whole Booke of Psalmes*.[59] Johnson and Wilbye acted together as music correctors for the production of Dowland's *Songs* at East's press in 1600, when they worked for the novice music publisher Eastland.[60]

Of the three English composers to be featured in individual collections at East's press in 1597–1598, Weelkes was the most youthful and perhaps the most ambitious. In 1597 he was only twenty-one, although he was expert enough at that age to prepare two volumes for the press and submit them to East. Weelkes's dedications in 1597 and 1598 were to prominent men: George Phillipot of Compton near Winchester (1597) and the London-based courtier Edward Darcy (1598), who was very well placed as the groom of the queen's Privy Chamber.[61] At the end of 1598, Weelkes was appointed organist of Winchester College, no doubt due to the efforts of his dedicatee Phillipot and perhaps at the urging of Darcy, too. Thus one result of Weelkes's publication program with East was apparently an advancement in his career.

Weelkes returned to East's shop in 1600, after problems had arisen in his position at Winchester. Joining with East in concocting an unusually grasping scheme of

dedicating a single publication to two men, George Brooke and Henry Lord Wind-
sor, Weelkes obtained a new position as an organist the very next year in Chichester.[62]
Weelkes, it would clearly seem, had special and rather effective uses for East's press;
like Tessier before him, he turned to East specifically to find new positions as a professional musician. As the operator of a freely governed music press, East was thus to
provide a useful service to young musical talents of London, and in some cases his
efforts were handsomely repaid.

If they originally presented a greater economic risk, it is possible to judge from
his further operations that East did not altogether waste his energy on these young
men. Weelkes did business with East repeatedly, proving himself to be a reliable author for the press. Wilbye was less active in his personal quests through the press, but
his *First Set of English Madrigals* was of immense value to East's firm. For his own profit,
East reproduced it as another hidden edition (see Table A1.2). His heir, Thomas
Snodham, produced it again in the hidden edition format in 1610, around the time he
also printed the composer's famous *Second Set of English Madrigals*. That both men would
take such a publisher's interest in this single volume testifies to the great popularity
and commercial value of Wilbye's *First Set*.

Not surprisingly, because of the narrow focus of its intended audience and with
its French and Italian texts, Tessier's music was not particularly popular in London
and was never reprinted by East as his own property. It seems that faced with a stock
of unbound and unsold sheets of the music, East took steps simply to dispose of the
work. He printed slips with the name of a new publisher and removed the sheets of
dedicatory material, which were no longer relevant to or appropriate for a new market for the copies.[63] East printed the name and address of his fellow stationer Christopher Blount on the slips and pasted them on reissued sheets of his original publication. Perhaps Blount had a special audience in mind. For whatever reason, it was
Blount, rather than East, who advertised Tessier's music in the reissue and sold the
extra copies of the edition.[64]

EAST, MORLEY, AND THE MADRIGAL, 1597–1598

In 1597 East began to focus attention not only on a youthful group of composers but
also on the madrigal genre that he had done so much to popularize. By now it was a
commodity he must have thought to have been fully tested for its viability in the marketplace. (At this time, Morley was quite active in producing music for the lute.) East's
books in this era included sets of English madrigals by individual composers: Kirbye
(1597), Weelkes (1597), and Wilbye (1598), and collections of Englished madrigals by
a variety of composers in Yonge's *Musica Transalpina II* (1597) and Morley's anthology
of *Madrigals to Fiue Voyces* (1598).

The second volume of *Musica Transalpina II* (1597) was one of East's few sequels
in music printing. For this second installment of "transalpine" music East collaborated again with Nicholas Yonge, who served as the publisher. Not surprisingly, Yonge
noted that the reason a second volume was produced was the good "acceptance" of
the first.[65] The evidence therefore suggests that Yonge and (indirectly at first) East
had good reason to be fully confident of the market for English madrigals. Unlike

the first *Musica Transalpina* volume, however, the second was never brought out by East as a hidden edition; its popularity apparently did not match that of its predecessor.

One possible repercussion of East's rather conservative focus on madrigals in 1597 was that it gave Morley a good reason to choose him to print his own collection of Englished madrigals in 1598. Morley may even have been excited into action by East's 1597 publication. What is clear is that after he collected his own Englished madrigals in 1597–1598, Morley decided that it was East's shop rather than Short's (or even Barley's) that would best attract his prospective customers. By choosing East to print the volume, Morley placed his anthology in the hands of a printer whose trade was most familiar to the London customers who bought works of that sort.

Overall, the years 1597–1598, when the monopoly was not officially owned by Morley (or anyone else for that matter), represent a small but vibrant interlude not only for East but also for the English music-publishing trade in general. Not only were more presses than ever before producing music for English consumers, but also, thanks to Morley especially, musical quality was not to suffer as much as it might have if the music-printing enterprise had been run otherwise. Morley's strategic use of the Short firm seems to have been a positive stimulus for East, too. East decided at that point to increase his efforts, thereby developing further his madrigal market and attracting a crop of young aspirants of the musical world to his, rather than to Short's, shop. Already by 1598 East could also boast the printing of works by Morley, who was exploring the advantages of making new alliances with former opponents.

After Byrd's era, when musical quality had been, perhaps, overemphasized to the detriment of salability, it is surprising that a central concern of the next phase was on musical standards, both in production and in the selection criteria for music that went to press. Clearly it was the team of Morley and Short who could boast of the best product in music printing, but East's press was not far behind. Furthermore, Barley's work, if probably deserving some of the criticism it was given, might never have been so closely evaluated by his competitors if Morley was not so determined to overpower him in the music-printing field. During the years he had no official position as a patent holder, Morley's strategy was to show himself as the one best suited to protect musical quality. This noble stance gave way, however, to a more practical pursuit of his economic position when he would finally control the press as a monopolist. Once he gained the patent, Morley concentrated on two of the most lucrative types of music editions, the collected psalms with music and the reprintings of proven popular titles. For both endeavors, he found he had to turn to Barley and East, as well as to Short, to satisfy his ambitions.

Morley and the royal monopoly for music (1598–1602)

The first incontrovertible record that reflects Morley's effort to assume his mentor's former place as a music monopolist appeared in a summary note of a letter Morley wrote to the attorney general in July of 1598 (by which time the process was already well under way).[66] After negotiations, Morley finally obtained the grant in September of 1598.[67] On 6 October, he brought his new patent to Stationers' Hall to communicate his new powers to the music printers of the company.[68]

Morley was keen to make his patent operate more effectively than its predecessor. He obtained changes in the patent that affected both its enforcement and coverage. In matters of enforcement, Morley established much stiffer fines against pirates by raising the rate of penalty from forty shillings to a quite severe ten pounds.[69] In terms of its coverage, Morley's patent strengthened the wording to better protect his rights to control music importation, music printing, and printed music paper. In the matter of ruled music paper created by the press, Morley was particularly anxious to point out to the patent drafters that he was aware of the competition from manuscript copying. He also gave some evidence, both in the lengthy discussion of the paper clause in the letter of July and in the final draft of the patent, that he believed the provision for paper to be of great economic importance. His patent tends to emphasize music paper more than its predecessor, especially in connection with its importation.[70] As far as the competition with manuscript copying was concerned, however, there was no attempt to place any injunctions on the use of *rastra* (a common device used to create staff lines). If Morley did wish to eradicate the copying of music on hand-ruled paper, he did not succeed, but how such a barrier to copying might have been enforced at all is certainly not easy to imagine under any circumstances.

In matters of music printing, Morley attempted to broaden the coverage of his own patent to include the wording "all, every and any music," in the place of the phrase "or any otherwise to be sung or played."[71] Here he was unsuccessful. The attorney general did not endorse the new phrase, and evidently he was not to be swayed from his objections. All this shows that Morley understood well the most profitable elements he might exploit in the music monopoly. For each actual or proposed change, whether subtle or blatant, Morley's purpose was to make the patent both more comprehensive and more specific in its coverage. In particular, he wished to extend the patent beyond its normal confines and enter into the most profitable trade of the time, that of the psalter with music.

THE METRICAL PSALMS

In 1599 Morley took the surprising step of forming an alliance to publish music with his former rival Barley. At that time, the Stationers' Company was enforcing the psalter patent. East and Short, as stationers, were subject to the company's discipline. Barley lacked this disability: he was not a stationer and was therefore was well situated to carry out Morley's enterprise. The new partners brought out two productions in 1599. One was a pocketbook edition with the same title as and based to a great degree on East's *Whole Booke of Psalmes.*[72] The other was a beautiful folio volume with music by Richard Allison, which featured settings of the tunes for lute and voice.

Barley's partnership with Morley began as a fruitful venture, but it ultimately miscarried. Rather than hide behind the conflicting claims of the two music patents, as East appeared to do in the early 1590s, Morley and Barley openly challenged the Day patentees. They decided to print an excerpt of Morley's music patent in the Allison volume of 1599 and made the further claim therein that they had exclusive rights to the psalter property.[73] Consequently, Morley did not even leave room for sharing the patent with the stationers who were its true owners. Instead, he tried blatantly to overtake the competing monopoly. Not surprisingly, Richard Day was provoked into action by Morley's maneuver, challenging its legality.

There is only a brief notice that serves as evidence of a contest between Morley and Day.[74] This evidence, however, contains other materials that expand our understanding of the event. The notice was addressed from Bishop Bancroft to Elizabeth's chief minister, William Cecil, and appears as follows: "I can in no wise agree them, both of them standing peremptorily upon the validity of their several letters patent from her Highness, which Mr. Morley saith the common law must decide, and Mr. Day will have the matter determined by the Lords in the Star Chamber."[75]

Morley's aim was to seek a hearing of the matter in a court of common law, where he might well have cited East's publications in the early 1590s as a precedent for his own program. The publishing record of the psalter at this time makes it clear, however, that Day's argument was to prevail; Morley and Barley never published another one. More significantly, neither East nor Short published any editions under the auspices of a music monopoly. It is thus clear that no one associated with the music patent in the remaining years it was run by Morley had the legal right or took the risk to publish the psalter.

MORLEY'S FINAL YEARS (1600–1602)

East's career as a music printer was placed in jeopardy when Morley became the music patent owner in 1598 and entered into partnership with Barley a year later. Morley then had the power to stop East's music presses; for the first time since 1588 East had no legal right to print music of any kind, and, as mentioned earlier, he produced no music dated 1599. But he was not without recourse, even though he could not openly compete with Morley. East had the power to prevent the composer from reprinting popular works premiered at his press.

With registrations standing in the stationers' records to clearly identify which musical property he owned, East could protect his claim to certain prints even when music printing was monopolized. As a result, Morley could only prevent East from producing reprints of editions premiered at his press, but he could not take possession of East's copy or intellectual property. Therefore, despite the monopoly, Morley was unable legally to produce second editions of his own music, since the original copy was registered with East. The printer's registration tactic restricted Morley's choices. It led to a situation where the composer was unable to use his power over the music press fully to capitalize on the popularity of music he originally wrote and published himself.

Soon after 1599, therefore, Morley was faced with a dilemma: despite the composer's obvious wish to run the patent as a profitable business, the two most lucrative texts of music (reprints and metrical psalm-tune settings) were no longer available to him. Morley's solution was to abandon Barley as a partner—since the collected psalms venture had led to an injunction against him—and to work again with East and Short, since these men could produce second editions of music proven to be popular with the London audience. Morley drew up three-year contracts with Short and East in 1600, and both men agreed to print music as Morley's assigns.[76]

It cannot really be claimed that Morley's entrepreneurial energy diminished in his last years (1600–1602). His *Triumphes of Oriana* (1601) was the first anthologized collection of English madrigals to be published and amply reminds us of Morley's extraordinary contribution to the birth and growth of that musical genre. But it is not surprising that both East and Short, when acting as the authorized music printers in the years 1600–1602, mostly set about reprinting their registered music for Morley. Having secured the royal monopoly and with two printers of the Stationers' Company who had registered his works under contract, the composer finally had a firm claim to his formerly printed material and a clear road to its publication.

In this last compromise arrangement, that is, the contract of 1600, it is difficult to determine whether East or Morley benefited the most. Certainly after enduring the effects of Morley's strategies in 1599, East had good reason to join forces with the composer. He was effectively shut out of music printing in 1599, and, if only to continue printing music (which was surely his favored product after twelve years in the field), he no doubt welcomed the new contract. East was probably glad to know that his registrations had pressured Morley to resume their relationship. Yet as a partner with Morley he was also forced to make a powerful sacrifice. When he joined forces with the astute composer-businessman, he had to relinquish for a time his special opportunity to act as a music publisher and thus could not function as a true entrepreneur in the music-printing field. This, of course, was why Morley benefited, too, when he joined forces with East; for now, Morley (who was the author of the music, the original publisher, and the music monopolist) was able to profit fully from the positive reception of his own work. East, in contrast, was relegated to his familiar, but lesser, role as a simple trade printer of music.

East and Morley were engaged in an intense struggle during much of the period under review. Each wished to capitalize pecuniarily on the sale of printed music, a trade that was essentially new to London at this time. Morley's strategies differed significantly from East's. East looked to the markets themselves, rather than relying solely on his well-established reputation for music printing. He sought to expand and diversify his consumer base by publishing popular works as hidden editions and bringing out madrigal collections by up-and-coming composers of his day. Morley, for his part, consistently emphasized the quality of product he could deliver as the helmsman of a national publishing industry. It was surely the royal music monopoly, awarded with the express purpose of promoting musical life in England, that inspired Morley's qualitative stance as a competitive publisher. This first surfaced in the years 1596–1598, when Morley was lobbying for the monopoly and therefore publishing the music of composers well known at court. It continued into the next era as well. Even when he was engaged, unsuccessfully in the end, in the blatantly mercenary effort to evade the psalter patent, part of Morley's strategy to do so was clearly to position himself as the protector of quality, as the Allison volume provides witness. Because he had to struggle for his position, Morley was much more interested in "rights to copy" than Byrd before him, who basically enjoyed an uncontested monopoly. Like his mentor, however, Morley, too, seemed to grasp well the benefits at hand when an author, rather than a mere trader, possessed the power to control the destiny of his art as it was prepared for dissemination among the public. The final compromise of the erstwhile competitors, embodied in the contract of 1600, had not only rewards for East and Morley but also very significant benefits for the quality of music printing itself. From this perspective, Elizabeth's music monopoly may be judged to have had a generally salubrious, rather than negative, impact on the expansion and quality of the music industry in England, even during periods of free trade.

THOMAS EAST AND THE SPHERE
OF PUBLIC AFFAIRS IN THE TWILIGHT YEARS
OF THE ELIZABETHAN ERA

7

After Thomas East and Thomas Morley formalized a mutually beneficial contract in 1600, the music printer's production schedule, uncharacteristically barren in 1599, seemed to resume its normal pace. As if expressing pent-up energy, East's output in 1600 was particularly strong: two openly acknowledged reprints of works by Morley (*First Booke of Balletts, Madrigals to Fovre Voices*), two original works by younger composers (Dowland's *Second Booke of Songs*, Weelkes's *Madrigals of 5 & 6 Parts*), another edition of Byrd's *Psalmes, Sonets & Songs*, and two hidden editions (Byrd's *Mass a 3* and *Mass a 4*). In 1601 East printed the *Triumphes of Oriana*, the famous collection of madrigals that extolled the queen, which had been assembled, edited, and published by Morley. In 1602 East brought out a reprint of Morley's *Canzonets a 3*. The special, and rather remarkable, feature of this brief period, however, was the involvement of East and his establishment in high affairs of state.

Through his music printing and publishing activity, East became entangled in two major elements of late sixteenth-century politics: the so-called Catholic question and the Essex Revolt. Two aspects of the first issue are relevant here: (1) Robert Persons's project to shape English Catholic views on the succession at the turn of the seventeenth century and (2) the distribution of music for illegal Catholic Masses by William Byrd.[1] Persons was the leading English Jesuit exile and the most important English Catholic educator and controversialist of his time, second only to Cardinal William Allen. Byrd's Masses number among his most important musical contributions, and their publication history has intrigued scholars for several generations.[2]

The second element was the famous Essex Revolt spearheaded by Robert Devereux, the Earl of Essex, and its relationship to specialized publishing ventures in London in the year 1601.[3] A close relationship between East's music printing and the affairs of Essex has been broadly argued in two articles by Lillian Ruff and Arnold Wilson.[4] Their position is controversial, as will be discussed later, but it does afford a useful platform for further discussion of East's role in the political affairs of his era.[5]

In the virtual absence of evidence to the contrary from parish records, recusant rolls, or litigation papers, it must be considered that East was not, at least in any overt way, a religious dissenter or a Catholic recusant.[6] Nor is there documentation to suggest that the printer had any special commitment to Essex, although the immensely popular courtier was the dedicatee of more books than any other patron in England at this time, including a number of books printed by East.[7] The path toward an understanding of the printer's involvement in these political affairs leads, rather, to his stationer's trade in London. What first must be established is the type of musical works that would bring East into contact with political groups, like the Catholic activists, on the one hand, and Essex's men, on the other. Second, the difficult question of how markets for these special groups developed and who developed them must be resolved. Third, there is the problem of determining what economic enticements in these ventures would have had the power to draw East into such markets in the first place.

Of particular importance to an understanding of all of the issues noted here is the determination of the precise role the printer played in the dissemination of his books after they were produced. Was he the publisher or the printer in these ventures? Did he sell them himself or were they distributed by others? In addition, the lack of immediate data for East's production schedule in printing two editions of Masses by Byrd presents a specific bibliographic problem for this inquiry. The findings of this study are partially negative, for evidence suggests that the printer was not as involved in the affairs of the Essex Revolt as it might otherwise seem. There is strong indication, however, that East had ventured far enough away from the safe position of trade printer to leave his establishment open to involvement in a great controversy over the succession among English Catholics of the late sixteenth century. East's business dealings with political activists of his day go back to his participation in the dissemination of music for Catholic worship in the first years he worked as a music printer.

ENGLISH CATHOLICS AND EAST'S PRINTS

Discovering which editions in East's output would have the potential to attract Catholic agitators to his operations is not a particularly difficult task, for unlike nearly all of his London colleagues in the Stationers' Company, he consistently produced books of specific interest to the Catholic community in England. These were the sacred, Latin-texted musical works by Byrd, which included the two volumes of Byrd's *Cantiones Sacrae* printed in 1589 and 1591; Byrd's undated Masses for three, four, and five voices; and the two volumes of *Gradualia* that were printed for Byrd in 1605 and 1607.[8] In addition, Byrd's collection of *Psalmes, Sonets & Songs* contained a fine setting of the English poem "Why do I use my paper inke and penne?" attributed to Jesuit martyr Henry Walpole. This collection, too, might therefore have been of special interest to Catholic audiences. As noted earlier, East did reprint Byrd's *Psalmes* in circa 1600. This hitherto unnoticed edition was probably produced in very close proximity to, or perhaps at the same time as, the two new editions of Byrd's Masses (that will be discussed in detail later in this chapter). Whether or not the newly discovered edition of Byrd's *Psalmes* was published in *conjunction* with these editions of Masses, however, is a tantalizing possibility that I have been unable to confirm thus far.

As music appropriate for worship (if not always so intended), with sacred texts in the Latin language of their faith, certainly all of East's editions of Latin-texted music in this list were of potential interest to English Catholics. Furthermore, there is a growing conviction among musicologists that these works had deeper ties to that particular community. After considering the texts of Byrd's motets, Joseph Kerman argued that Byrd made specific allusions to the plight of English Catholics and the Jesuit mission through his choice of texts in sixteen of his motets.[9] In a complementary study, Philip Brett suggested that Jesuits had a role in the publication of Byrd's *Gradualia*.[10] Finally, in a recent article Craig Monson has discovered numerous occasions where Byrd's texts echo what were, at the time, the well-known words of Jesuit primers and martyrologies.[11] The mounting evidence of a strong connection between Byrd and the Jesuits is particularly valuable for this study. More directly germane, however, is the question of whether there was a sufficient audience for these political pieces by Byrd to draw the printer into their distribution.

Kerman's careful analysis of the music and texts of the two *Cantiones* collections by Byrd has shown it to be difficult to pinpoint their venue. Certainly these pieces would have been ideal for special occasions, like the gathering to receive the Jesuits Henry Garnet and Robert Southwell at Hurleyford on 14 July 1586, which Byrd himself attended.[12] Byrd's music in the *Cantiones* is very elaborate and would have been perfectly suitable for this momentous occasion. Nonetheless, such complex music would have been difficult to prepare on a regular basis, especially in the conditions of secrecy maintained at illegal meetings of Catholic worshipers.

The music of the *Cantiones* was probably too challenging and elaborate for routine use by the broader population of East's special Catholic niche in his market for music in print. The texts of these motets also narrowed the prospects for their widespread dissemination. It is true that Kerman and others have shown that Byrd had various criteria, which included political alignment with the Jesuits, for choosing the texts to set in these collections. But whereas Byrd consistently chose texts for expressive and political purposes, he seems never to have chosen them specifically to satisfy liturgical needs.[13] All of this suggests that Byrd intended his works of the *Cantiones* for performances that were occasional and had less to do with routine religious worship than might seem at first glance to have been the case.

Lacking ongoing liturgical purpose, the *Cantiones* collections may not have been of great interest to the larger membership of the Catholic community. Instead they may have been more to the taste of refined musicians whatever their religion. John Milsom has shown, for example, that these *Cantiones* collections were demonstrably of interest to Protestant musicians who apparently sang them without regard for their religious agenda. He also noted that there were instrumentalists who redesigned the works for performances without their texts.[14] Significantly, East's involvement in these particular motet volumes was rather modest; they number among the dwindling list of musical works he produced that were never reprinted at his press, although the printer did go to the trouble and expense of registering these books with his company.[15] By the same token, Byrd's music for the Mass had a very different profile and would have been of greater use to English Catholics.

The three editions of Byrd's settings of the Ordinary of the Mass and the two volumes of Mass Propers of his *Gradualia* are quite different from the *Cantiones* in their text, style, and likely venue. The texts have an obvious place in the service, and the brevity of musical lines and generally homorhythmic musical texture made them eminently suitable for performances by the small groups of singers who sang in chapels designed for secret Catholic worship.[16] Whereas the Latin motets of the *Cantiones* might have been crafted for special occasions and performed in any number of innocent circumstances, the music Byrd wrote for the Mass had the obvious specific connection to its celebration in the liturgy. In the early 1580s, new measures were taken to outlaw the celebration of the Catholic Mass in England; by then it was well known that willingly hearing or performing this music was illegal.[17] East, as a printer, took steps to protect himself when he handled the sensitive problem of producing music books that were intended directly, and unambiguously, for the unlawful use of English Catholics.

Although Byrd, who as the composer was theoretically even more culpable, was to sign his name as "W. Byrd" in the Masses, East remained anonymous.[18] In addition, he never registered these works with the Stationers' Company. They stand as the only music books East never registered with his guild, except for some small editions and the volumes of psalm-tune settings that were covered by other monopolistic patents. As a further measure to conceal his role, East produced the Masses without title pages.[19]

For Byrd's *Gradualia* volumes East did provide title pages with all of the customary information about the printer, the date of printing, and the address where the books were to be sold.[20] Yet for these as well, he decided to take precautions, albeit of a very different kind. Despite their undisguised Catholic purpose, East registered both copies with Richard Bancroft, the reigning Bishop of London.[21] In 1605 and 1607, among his many other duties, Bancroft served as the official censor of London presses.[22] It was unusual that the bishop personally signed his authorization for Byrd's *Gradualia* in the Stationers' Company records. The venturesome religious nature of the volumes was undoubtedly the main reason for this special treatment. It turns out that by 1605 Bancroft had long been engaged as an activist in the politics of religion.

Bancroft's appointment was arranged by the courtier-statesman Robert Cecil in 1598.[23] Functioning in this case as Cecil's deputy, Bancroft was directed to control London presses in order to prevent the dissemination of propaganda against the Tudor government. Bancroft not only monitored the output of London presses as censor, but he also played an active role in turning them against threatening propaganda that emanated from Jesuitical publications.[24] Following Cecil's lead, Bancroft's tactic was to encourage a factional struggle among Catholics themselves; it entailed "remarkable leniency … towards the [anti-Jesuit] faction … as an apparent reward for their divisive role."[25]

Bancroft encouraged four printers of the Stationers' Company, Thomas Creede, Felix Kingston, Richard Field, and Adam Islip, to produce prints designated for English Catholics and thus to nourish the factionalism among recusants involved in the so-called Archpriest Controversy.[26] These printers all worked for the publisher Thomas Man, who was known as Bancroft's "familiar." East also did extensive trade-printing work for Man.[27] His adopted son, Thomas Snodham, continued this tradition and often worked for Man with this specific group of printers.[28] There is, therefore, the distinct possibility that East (probably unknowingly) was another, hitherto unrecognized, participant in Bancroft's agenda for publishing Catholic prints. Although there was surely no need for East and Bancroft to have consulted on the strategy, East may have unwittingly contributed to Bancroft's devious scheme to use Byrd's *Gradualia* as an indirect means to gather intelligence about English Catholics.[29] If his agenda in endorsing the *Gradualia* was similar to his known motives in sponsoring other Catholic publications, Bancroft must be seen as Byrd's enemy. He seems to have hoped to use Byrd's volume not for the composer's purpose—to enhance the worship activities of those of his faith—but to root out other Catholic dissidents. Extreme secretiveness would be necessary for such a plot to work; thus it would seem unlikely indeed that either Byrd or East would know of this devious plan.

For whatever reason, like the Ordinaries of Byrd's Masses but in a wholly different manner, the *Gradualia* copies were exceptional among East's prints in terms of their entrance status: these were the only musical publications by him to have been deemed so sensitive as to have their registrations actually signed by Bancroft. It is unlikely that Byrd was the one who prompted the special registration of these books; the composer never had any qualms about revealing his contributions to the Catholic cause in music. It was obviously East, not Byrd, who needed the assurance of his company that he would not encounter any trouble as the result of his producing these two volumes of music for the Propers of the Mass. Unfortunately, the precaution was to no avail; soon after they were printed, it seems that Byrd had to withdraw the volumes from circulation.[30]

If the number was small, the musical style, liturgical texts, and especially the precautionary measures East took to protect himself in the production of Masses indicate that East did bring forth music editions that were specifically designated for the use of Catholics in England. These precautions would appear to indicate that East was attempting to disassociate himself from Byrd's music, rather than to encourage their trade. This is especially true in the cases where no title page was produced. East's role in the distribution of these volumes in particular appears to have been minimal. Nonetheless, there is evidence to suggest that the printer was the publisher, or at least a copublisher, of certain hidden editions of Masses. Bibliographical data serve to establish a refined date for the hidden editions, and other documentary evidence provides a possible context for their publication and distribution.

EAST AND HIS STOCK OF CATHOLIC PRINTS

Although it is generally safe to conclude that East was a distributor of most music editions he printed, the first editions of Byrd's Masses are hardest to place on the printer's shelves. Because they were produced in the very period when Byrd moved to Essex to become involved in the recusant activities of his coreligionists in that area, it is likely that the composer himself may have undertaken single-handedly to distribute these works. Byrd had the pressing need to provide music for his own worship and that of his fellow Catholics once he arrived in Essex.[31] Based in London and presumably less in contact at that time than Byrd with Catholic markets for music, East would have had little need to retain copies of Byrd's Masses to sell at his shop after the composer himself had moved away from the city.

Distribution needs for Byrd's Masses did not cease with the first editions, however. It was Peter Clulow who discovered that the three- and four-voiced Masses were subsequently reprinted in separate editions.[32] (No evidence is extant to suggest that the five-voiced Mass was ever reprinted in Byrd's lifetime.) Clulow's contribution was valuable but incomplete. He discovered two hidden editions, but he brought to light a new problem. Since the Masses were the most disguised and least advertised of all of East's prints, it is difficult to discover who next published them and for what purpose.

The second editions were almost completely unaltered from their original versions. The close typographical similarity to their originals links these newly discovered editions of the Masses with East's other hidden editions. Even among this curious group of prints by East, however, they are peculiar; unlike all other hidden editions, there is no false date in these second editions. East closely imitated the older versions he had at hand. Because the first editions of the Masses had no title page and thus no printed dates, it was not necessary for East to falsify the dates, as he did in other cases. Thus it is frankly puzzling why he chose to emulate the first editions so closely. Nonetheless, it is obvious that East reproduced the three- and four-voiced Masses from the original editions with such care so that they could remain quite hidden. Clulow's study confirmed that they did indeed escape discovery until very recent times.

DATING THE HIDDEN EDITIONS OF BYRD'S MASSES

Bibliographical evidence, although intricate, does establish important chronological facts about the undated hidden editions of Byrd's Masses. In his study of East's type, Clulow noted that several of the apostle initials East used to set the hidden editions of the Masses had appeared before in East's editions of Weelkes's *Balletts and Madrigals* and Morley's *Madrigals to Fiue Voyces* of 1598.[33] In those latter editions, Clulow noted, the initials appeared in a better condition than in the Masses. He then found that the same type initials appeared again, but in a worsened condition, in two books East produced in 1600: Dowland's *Songs* and Weelkes's *Madrigals of 5 & 6 Parts*.[34] With these data, Clulow narrowed the possible times of production to a specific period of East's schedule between the works of 1598 and those of 1600.

Clulow did not attempt to determine East's schedule in any more detail beyond the year each edition was produced (based on East's printed date), although he did sometimes suggest East's order of printing works within a calendar year. Thus it is not the whole year of 1598 that may be seen as among the possible times the Masses were produced according to Clulow's evidence but, rather, some undetermined time after East produced the Morley and Weelkes editions. The later part of Clulow's range has a similar ambiguity. Clulow established that the Masses could not have been printed after the Dowland and Weelkes works of 1600, but he did not attempt to narrow the range any further. Clulow set 1599 as the correct date for the two editions of Masses.[35] That date, 1599, is the only one of the three years in Clulow's range where no other of East's music editions predated or postdated the Masses, and it was also the only year East did not produce any other music with a printed date.

With the study of his paper, on the one hand, and his dealings with the publisher Eastland and the music monopolist Morley, on the other hand, additional data beyond Clulow's findings become available to answer the question of when East printed the hidden editions of Byrd's Masses and to suggest a slightly later date of early 1600.

Paper evidence helps to refine the earlier part of Clulow's range of possible dates. The paper East used in the hidden editions of Byrd's Masses was from a stock he also used in 1598 in a set by Wilbye (which furnished ambiguous typographical data for Clulow).[36] When printing hidden editions it was East's policy to use a stock of paper he had obtained from another book. The hidden edition with a shared stock of paper appeared after the volume with the same paper stock in his schedule in every case where this could be proven. It would be reasonable to assume, therefore, that the Masses followed this pattern and therefore that they were also produced *after* the Wilbye set of 1598.

With regard to the year 1600, the upper perimeter of Clulow's range, it is possible to make more definitive statements about East's schedule. This is because of all the years in which East printed music, there is none more documented than the last year of the sixteenth century. In his extensive litigation with Eastland, the publisher of Dowland's *Songs*, East mentioned to the court the precise day when he had finished that edition: 2 August 1600.[37] Therefore, the Masses had to have been produced before that time. But Clulow's typographical evidence revealed that the Weelkes edition that East printed in 1600 predated the Dowland edition in his schedule. The exact date he printed the Weelkes edition within the year is not documented, but it is still possible, by reference to East's contract with Morley, to refine its time of production to a period from the first of June through July of 1600.

In his litigation with Eastland, East explained that his contract with Morley began on 29 May 1600.[38] Because he listed himself as the assignee of Morley in the Weelkes edition, as well as in all of the works he dated 1600, East obviously did not print them before this time.[39] It is clear, therefore, that the Weelkes edition must have been produced after East and Morley's formal agreement. Paper evidence helps to establish an even more refined estimation of East's music-printing schedule in 1600.

Grouping East's prints of 1600 by their paper stocks creates the following two pairs of music editions: (1) Weelkes's *Madrigals* and Morley's *Madrigals* and (2) Dowland's *Songs* and Morley's *Balletts*.[40] Studies by Allan H. Stevenson have shown that paper used by printers at this time was usually purchased and used for specific projects.[41] The music books paired together by paper here were therefore probably produced sequentially or even concurrently at East's press. Since the Dowland and Weelkes editions were not printed on the same paper stock, it is unlikely that they were produced close upon each other in his schedule.

All of these data show that the summer of 1600 was a busy time for East in terms of his music printing. All four musical editions were begun after 29 May. At least three but possibly all four were completed by August of 1600, depending on East's scheduling of the second pair. With a similar caveat, here based on an undetermined internal order within the first pair, there is a distinct possibility that East began printing the Weelkes edition as soon as his contract with Morley permitted, that is, in June of 1600; if so, the bibliographical evidence shows that the Masses were produced by 29 May 1600 at the very latest. (This is because the Weelkes edition had type in a worse state than it appeared in the Masses.) Further evidence, fascinating in its own right, suggests the possibility that the Masses may have been printed in a period from 11 to 23 April, when it turns out that Catholic recusants were visiting East.

THE MEETING OF RECUSANTS AT EAST'S ON 23 APRIL 1600:
A FOILED DISTRIBUTION PLAN FOR BYRD'S MASSES?

A series of official interrogations, preserved in the records of the State Papers, revealed that at five o'clock on the morning of 23 April 1600, Edward Forset, a Catholic
recusant from Billesby in Lincolnshire, was called to East's house in Aldersgate Street
to read and discuss a letter by Robert Persons that concerned the succession.[42] It was
addressed to the Scottish nobleman Lord William Douglas, the tenth Earl of Angus,
who, like the Jesuit, was a notoriously powerful Catholic active in the affairs of an officially Protestant nation.[43] Attending the meeting were two prominent recusants
from Lincolnshire, John Thimbleby and his son Richard, both of whom had been re-
siding at East's house for twelve days prior to the event.

The letter had been delivered to East's house by the servant of Gervase Pierrepont, who was also an established recusant. It was confiscated by the government officials after the episode had been reported to them by two of East's apprentices, John
Wiborowe and John Balls.[44] Like many informants of this time, these boys had spied
on their Catholic countrymen and reported their activities to a more and more in-
tolerant Protestant government. What is immediately significant to this study, of
course, is that the Catholic activists had met at East's residence and were reported to
the government by his apprentices.

The meeting at East's was an event of great magnitude in the public affairs of
the time. A rich store of archival material reveals that Forset, the Thimblebys, and
Pierrepoint, in particular, were activists for the Catholic cause. Forset and the Thimblebys were known not only as staunch recusants but even as agitators.[45] Pierrepont
played a prominent role in the most threatening operations by English Catholics in
the Elizabethan era and maintained connections to many of the most prominent
of his coreligionists (he had a notorious role in the famous Campion affair, for example).[46] John Thimbleby and Pierrepont had been jailed and confined to special
centers for recalcitrant recusants.[47] These men knew each other well and had relations
prior to the episode at East's shop. Even in prison, Pierrepont was active as a Catholic instigator. During his term in the Marshalsea, he conducted illegal Masses, collected and distributed Catholic books, and corresponded with other recusants.[48] It
would be difficult indeed to find a group of English Catholics in a better position to
disseminate news such as Persons's letter. If there were a network of Catholics involved in the distribution of Byrd's Masses as well, it would have had great potential
for success if it were headed by men as energetic and well connected as Pierrepont
and the Thimblebys.

The government learned of the event through the spying activities of two of
East's rather enterprising apprentices, Balls and Wiborowe.[49] These young men came
in succession to eavesdrop on the visiting Catholics who were reading and discussing
Persons's letter.[50] When the printer's employees went before the Privy Council, they
pieced together their reports to give a full accounting of the episode at their master's
house in Aldersgate Street. Government officials acted with dispatch. Even though
Balls and Wiborowe were only apprentices and East's was not a large trade, this intelligence was processed rapidly and efficiently. By the end of the same day as the read-

ing, 23 April 1600, the authorities had arrested the three Catholic recusants who were involved in the meeting, confiscated Persons's letter, and taken official examinations of all parties.[51] Second examinations of Balls and Wiborowe were conducted the next day, and the imprisoned Catholics were reinterrogated a week later.[52] That these examinations were handled by some of the most powerful jurists of Elizabethan England is a matter that speaks further to the stature of the Catholic agitators who met at East's establishment, as well as to the intensity of the government's concern about all matters that affected the succession.[53]

Persons's letter concerned the succession of the English crown, and thus it spoke to an issue of the utmost significance to English Catholics at the turn of the century.[54] If James would reconcile himself to the Catholic Church and the pope, Persons was willing to become an enthusiastic supporter of the king's claims to the English throne. Adding to the significance of this letter was the fact that Persons's effort to realign his politics in favor of James was based on more than wishful thinking.[55] Forset, Pierrepoint, and the Thimblebys were therefore conspiring to discuss and disseminate news of great importance to English Catholics and of enormous interest to a suspicious government. Once these events began to unfold on 23 April, it was unlikely that East would have had anything further to do with the Masses. This would therefore establish a newly refined *terminus ante quem* of 23 April 1600 for Byrd's Masses in their second edition.

The evidence at hand suggests that the Thimblebys elected to stay with East because they were involved with him in the production and distribution of the hidden editions of Byrd's Masses. The date of 23 April 1600 fits neatly into the chronology established by bibliographical evidence outlined earlier. In April of 1600, East's distribution needs were clear. By this time two years had passed since East had printed any other music, and, although East continued to print general literature in these years, it was almost exclusively for other publishers. There is the testimony of Balls and Wiborowe to suggest that the distribution of books was a matter of particular interest to Richard Thimbleby. According to the boys, Thimbleby specifically discussed the "means of sending over or receiving certain books" after reading Persons's letter.[56]

The length of the Thimblebys' stay, twelve days, would have been sufficient time to produce two editions of Byrd's Masses. (In the one case where his production schedule was documented, East explained that he spent just over two weeks on another, larger, music-printing project.)[57] Furthermore, since the meeting of Catholics did occur in East's workhouse at the unusual hour of five o'clock in the morning and not in East's living chambers, these men were obviously familiar with East's printing operations, and they must have had special access to his press.[58]

The evidence discussed earlier has been cited to support the conclusion that the Thimblebys were at East's house in April of 1600, at the very time when East either was producing or had recently produced (since the year 1599 cannot be ruled out with bibliographical evidence) a large stock of Catholic music that was ready for dispersal. Even though the letter itself is the more tangible item in the documentation and it was more provocative to the authorities, it seems possible, in the end, that it was incidental to the larger project of producing Masses at East's press.[59]

The two spies among East's pressmen may have foiled the original plan of distribution altogether. After they were examined by Lord Chief Justice Sir John Popham and his colleagues of the King's Bench, all three recusant Catholics were sent to prison without further trial.[60] Soon after this, they were put in the so-called close quarters of the Tower and therefore made to suffer some of the harshest conditions available in that institution.[61] Eventually, however, the men were treated with some lenience. All three were given certain liberties when they became ill, and on 14 November 1601 they were released.[62] Presumably East was left to deal with the surplus stock of Byrd's Masses that he had recently printed.

It has been established here that some entanglement with English Catholics was a fact of East's career. The timing of the Catholic assemblage at his premises, combined with what can be reliably surmised about the likely production date of the Masses, establishes a strong circumstantial case for his role as their publisher or co-publisher. After we consider the whole of East's music editions, we may infer that this facet of his career was initiated in the late 1580s when, for economic reasons, he began to work as music printer for the Catholic musician Byrd, who owned the music monopoly. Without the monopoly, it is doubtful whether Byrd could have brought so many of his own Catholic works to East's press and had them printed.

Since East's entrepreneurial energies were equal to dealing with the many contingencies of the music monopoly, it would not be surprising to discover that he found a way to exploit a market for the Catholic music by Byrd that he had printed. One probable reason for his willingness to embrace such ventures was that his resources were limited. East had no patents of monopoly of his own; he registered only a single press with the company; and he leased, rather than owned, the property where he lived and worked. Whether encouraged by economic necessities of his limited capital or simply following the dictates of his style as a tradesman, East did often expend his energies on special projects other stationers tended to ignore, music printing itself being one such undertaking.

It was in the more obscure realms of his trade that East developed a market among English Catholics for his editions, but with his relationship to the Essex Revolt this study moves to the very mainstream of London stationers' interests as printers and publishers. As the thrust of Elizabethan politics shifted decisively in 1600 to the court from a previous focus on international threats from Spain and from men like Persons, a new series of manuscripts appeared in London that drew the attention of the most prominent of London stationers. Unlike Catholic material, which was difficult to distribute, books associated with the factions of the court were virtually unparalleled for their popularity in the City of London.[63] In particular, it was Lord Essex and his famous revolt that captured the attention of the London populace.

Essex and the stationers

After the tragic death of Philip Sidney in 1586 on the field of battle in Liège, it was Lord Essex who took Sidney's place as the most popular contemporary figure among Elizabeth's courtiers in London. Not only was Essex the Earl Marshall, a military commander of great fame, and a champion at the tilts, but he was variously known as a Protestant hero, a sponsor of Puritan clergymen, and even a friend of English Catholics.[64]

More Elizabethan books were dedicated to Essex than any other figure of his time; the queen herself ranked second.[65] They underscore the depth of his influence over the entire trade of publishing.[66] Even more than his military successes or his reputed benevolence and wealth, it was the queen's special relations with Essex that made his life so intriguing to the London populace. From his early years he had a turbulent relationship with the queen. He once reached for his sword after she had boxed his ears, yet he wrote effusive love poems to her afterward, and she was reported to have wept openly as he left England to command a military campaign in Ireland against the renegade Earl of Tyrone.[67] When Essex returned from Ireland to visit the queen in 1599, however, it was against her express orders, and the subsequent events of his life were those that led to his revolt, which is of direct concern to this study.

Essex failed in Ireland and had signed an unauthorized treaty with Tyrone before he revisited the queen. After his ignominious return, there began a long period of decline in royal favor. In May of 1600, he was officially deprived of his offices and put under house arrest. In a second trial, after he had lobbied for the queen's forgiveness, he was allowed more freedoms but was blocked from access to the queen and her court.

Essex's plans became more desperate after September, when the queen chose not to renew his lucrative monopoly for sweet wines. After this he began to consider more radical actions to reestablish his position, and on 8 February 1601 he and a group of his most loyal followers began their infamous revolt. Devereux and his men marched through the streets toward Westminster and the queen, but they never reached her palace. They were stopped by Bancroft (who had solicited the help of a group of city pikemen), arrested, and charged with the crime of high treason. After a long and acrimonious trial, Essex and several of his coconspirators were sentenced to death and executed in the Tower courtyard. Bancroft quickly established a special political censorship to outlaw the publication of any tracts that sympathized with Essex.[68] The execution of the much-admired courtier was notoriously unpopular, but it did not provoke the feared backlash of popular outrage against the queen and her court.

Essex's life, and particularly his last years, proved irresistible to later English playwrights and historians; modern interpreters have argued that Essex was also an extraordinarily conspicuous presence in the works of contemporary poets, historians, and playwrights of England. Although many such studies rely on the slippery evidence of allusion and political allegory, the findings are sometimes quite persuasive.[69] David Bevington, while critical of its excesses, has provided a convenient summary of this historiographical tendency in the first half of this century. He noted that among the politically charged works of the time modern scholars have found the greatest number to have concerned Essex.[70] Support from documentation is scarce in these interpretations, and many arguments have proven too tenuous to stand the test of time.[71] Nonetheless, there is strong evidence that certain late Elizabethan works about Richard II, especially Shakespeare's play and John Hayward's *The First Part of the Life and Raigne of King Henry IV*, were thinly veiled allusions to Essex and his agenda.[72] These works were greatly in demand and amply show how effectively London stationers could profit from the exploitation of public interest in Essex's fate.[73]

ESSEX AND MUSIC PRINTING

English historians have noted well that Essex's popularity in London was greatly to benefit stationers, like John Wolfe (the publisher of Hayward's history), who sold works that were known to relate to the courtier's life and interests. Lillian Ruff and Arnold Wilson have argued that Essex's behavior had a similar effect on musical works.[74] By comparing the number of music volumes that appeared in Elizabethan England each year with the events of Essex's life, these scholars concluded that the entire enterprise of music printing and, indeed, of London musical composition in general was determined to a great degree by the dramatic rise and fall of Essex's career. Thus in a single effort these scholars have followed the same trajectory of the larger movement of literary history in their attempt to show the meshing of politics and art in Elizabethan history.

Since East printed the majority of the works considered by Ruff and Wilson, their conclusions are of a fundamental concern to this study. These scholars begin their discussion with East's first music editions of 1588, and they end with a discussion of the lute song publications and madrigals printed after East's death in 1608.[75] Although they focus mainly on the texts of the musical compositions, this study stands as the most extensive work on London music publishing available today, and it was the first to argue comprehensively that political forces had a powerful effect on the Elizabethan music trade.

Problems with Ruff and Wilson's theory, exacerbated by the ambitious scope of their undertaking, have long been known and are difficult to ignore.[76] They argued that the volume of music publishing in England depended on Essex's standing, and this is a position that does correspond with Essex's proven effect on the larger book trade. Nonetheless, economic forces that have to do with the music monopoly better explain the behavior of London's music presses at each juncture. For example, the dates of 1596–1597 that Ruff and Wilson assign to Essex's rise coincide with the first gap in the ownership of the music monopoly. Whereas Ruff and Wilson point to Essex's great military triumph in Cadiz as the cause of the efflorescence of music prints in those years, it was more likely due to the effects of a sudden window of free trade in an otherwise restrictive economic environment.[77]

DOWLAND'S *Second Booke of Songs* AND ESSEX

Dowland's *Second Booke of Songs*, however, does appear to have ties to the Essex movement, and thus it stands as a link between East's operations and the Essex Revolt. To begin with, this edition was produced in the summer of 1600 and thus in the very midst of Essex's crisis. It was at that point that Essex enjoyed his fullest popular support and was still attempting to plead his case with the queen, rather than to pressure her by force. Furthermore, as Ruff and Wilson noted, there is the specific reference to Wanstead in a song of this collection.[78] Wanstead was Essex's childhood home, and he did spend some time there after he was released from house arrest in 1600.

The texts in the Dowland set may well allude to Essex's relations with the queen. The tone of several songs in this collection matches that of Essex's letters to her. In both texts, the apologetic agenda is unmistakable.[79] Were these songs meant to allude to Essex's plight or even to serve as a means of communication with Elizabeth? Unfortunately, neither hypothesis can yet be proven. Still, as much as the clear allusions to Essex in the history of Richard II may have threatened the queen, nothing would have better reflected Essex's appeal in the form of a lover's apology than the affecting texts and music of Dowland's *Second Booke*. If anyone at the time cared to view the matter as such, the songs of Dowland's set would have captured the spirit of Essex's well-known attempts to plead for Elizabeth's forgiveness just as obviously as the Richard II plays and books did so clearly refer to his alternative plan of reestablishing his position by the military force of a coup d'ètat.

The dissemination history of the Dowland *Second Booke of Songs* is surprisingly rich, but the links between the Dowland set and the popular political events that surrounded Essex are tenuous. On the surface, it would appear that the Dowland set was an oddly unpopular edition of secular music among East's prints. Odd because the previous item Dowland brought to the press was the most reprinted title of music in the entire era, whereas the *Second Booke* was never reprinted by East or even by his heirs.[80] Why East failed ever to print this great collection in new editions, hidden or otherwise, may never fully be known. Some of the mystery might be removed, however, by bringing to bear the testimony of East and the publisher Eastland in their litigation over the printing of Dowland's *Songs*.

In the *East vs. Eastland* trial, the issues at hand were the problems Eastland allegedly encountered as a publisher who was attempting to distribute Dowland's music books. One salient question was that of professional expertise: Eastland was a novice publisher, whereas East had already dealt extensively with some of the most clever entrepreneurs among London's stationers and musicians. Eastland's ineptitude as a publisher was mentioned several times in depositions by East and his workers.[81] In their view, Eastland would have profited from the venture if he had not charged so much for the volumes and if he had not waited so long to distribute them. He explained, however, that the reason he temporized was to make special presentations of the book to certain individuals in London. These were people, Ruff and Wilson insinuated, who were associated with Essex, but the only person Eastland named was the dedicatee, Lucy Harrington, the Countess of Bedford.[82] The Bedfords were certainly associated with Essex, but the evidence suggests only that Eastland wished to follow the custom of the time of sending a special copy to the person who helped to finance the production. Based on evidence from this case alone, a more reasonable conclusion is that Eastland waited until he had an audience with Lady Bedford before selling the edition to the public and that this is what had hindered his sales.

The printers of East's firm consistently argued that Eastland mismanaged the distribution of Dowland books. Eastland countered this by accusing East and his workers of outright thievery. Astonishingly, Balls and Wiborowe confessed to committing the crimes alleged by Eastland. These were the same apprentices who had acted as spies in the Catholic escapade at East's house in April of 1600. Each admitted that they had indeed printed extra copies of the Dowland set and sold them before the edition was delivered to Eastland on 2 August 1600.[83] But they claimed to have pilfered 35 copies, whereas Eastland testified that they printed 500 copies for themselves. How many they actually printed is indeterminable, but why the two confessed may be surmised. Although it is possible that these apprentices of East's press confessed in reliance on the goodwill they believed they had earned as spies earlier in the year, it is more likely that they were simply trapped by the testimony of several stationers in London who bought the stolen volumes from them.

The few customers for the illicit music books of Balls and Wiborowe were actually deponents in the *East vs. Eastland* trials, and these men represent the only direct purchasers of East's editions known to us through documentation. Unfortunately, their information is less valuable than it might otherwise seem, for most of them were only middlemen. One William Frank, a leather seller who obviously served as a bookbinder, bought several books from William Cotton, a servant of the stationer William Leake.[84] Frank sold bound copies back to Cotton for resale and also gave a copy of the book to Thomas Fanshaw. Fanshaw, who was a lawyer of the Exchequer and actually involved in the *East vs. Eastland* case, stands as the only person mentioned in the trial who did not acquire the book with the purpose of reselling it; there is no conclusive evidence that Fanshaw was affiliated with the Essex faction.[85]

Two of the younger members of the Stationers' Company, Matthew Selman and John Smethwicke, bought a few dozen of Dowland's books, and another youthful stationer, John Flaskett, was shown several books, but he apparently declined to purchase them.[86] Despite suggestions by Ruff and Wilson, therefore, there is no information from the examinations that concerned the Dowland volume to reveal that these buyers were specifically involved in the Essex affair. Rather, the profile of the men who bought the volumes from East's apprentices (a youthful, relatively poor, and therefore ambitious group) conforms to what has been discussed elsewhere as an "Elizabethan black-market" established by journeymen and stationers' apprentices.[87] Judging by the evidence of the first customers of the Dowland book, the efforts of Balls and Wiborowe do seem too amateurish to have been at the forefront of the publishing ventures that surrounded the Essex affair.

The path of distribution for the Dowland volume that is traceable today offers no direct connection to Essex, yet there is ample evidence that there was a great pre-publication interest in the Dowland work. That Balls and Wiborowe decided to print their own copies and sell them before the publisher received his copies is not insignificant as a measure of the anticipated market for these works. East himself also took the extraordinary step of registering the copy as his own property in the Stationers' Company books even though Morley owned the official music monopoly at the time.[88] This was the first musical volume that East registered during a period when the grant of a music monopoly was in force, and for this registration his purpose was unambiguous. He explained in the trial that his agreement with Eastland stipulated that after the original edition of 1,025 copies was sold he could reprint the volume as his own property.[89] Obviously, East registered the title to ensure that his colleagues in the company would be aware that he had a claim to this property.

Apparently, Eastland never recovered his alleged losses from East, but the latter was not to escape unscathed. The costs of the litigation at King's Bench, the Chancery, and the Court of Requests must have dampened East's enthusiasm to exploit the potential market for Dowland's *Second Booke of Songs*. It is therefore quite possible that the litigation itself kept East from exploiting the popular market for the Dowland print that had seemed a promising item for sale in August of 1600, when Essex was still famously beseeching the queen's forgiveness.

It is tantalizing to note that a short month after East had printed the Dowland set, in September, Essex's agenda shifted to a more antagonistic tack. By that date the Dowland volume, for all its magnificent music, would have been out of step with the aims of the Essex faction. Thus Eastland's decision to wait before selling the copies could indeed have been the cause of the distribution problem he complained of in his case against East. By the time Eastland was prepared to sell the copies of his publication, the message of Essex's apologies in musical allusions would have been out of touch with the issues at hand; in September the Essex faction had turned from a strategy of appeasement to the more exciting prospects of a coup d'état, as alluded to in Shakespeare's *Richard II.*

EAST AND LORD CROMWELL

Ruff and Wilson suggest that the politics of the Essex affair colored the reception of Dowland's music and affected the outcome of the *East vs. Eastland* trial. From the evidence of the case itself, however, this is difficult to substantiate. But in the aftermath of Essex's execution, the connections between East and those involved in the Essex Revolt went far beyond the tenuous relationship of the Dowland work and the aims of the Essex faction. At that time East's residence was chosen as the location for the house arrest of Lord Cromwell, Essex's coconspirator.

After the thwarted revolt and trials, several of Essex's coconspirators were executed with their leader. In the interests of minimizing the repercussions of the coup, Elizabeth soon pardoned the wealthiest of Essex's supporters after a short imprisonment.[90] The peers and grandees of the Essex Revolt whom Elizabeth pardoned in 1601 included the Earl of Rutland, Lord Sandys, Lord Cromwell, and Sir William Parker. All of these men were freed from the Tower in August of 1601 and put under house arrest. Of this group, Cromwell was assigned to stay at "one John East's, a printer in Aldersgate Streete."[91] A search of the Stationers' Company records and parish records of the London area revealed that there was no John East who lived on Aldersgate Street and worked as a printer at this time. Since Thomas East had the correct address and trade, the obvious conclusion is that the Privy Council mistakenly wrote the name "John" instead of the correct appellation, "Thomas," when they referred to "a printer in Aldersgate Street."

Edward Cromwell was the third of an illustrious line that began with his grandfather Gregory, the first Baron Cromwell.[92] Gregory was the one so honored with the title, but he owed his position to the great achievements of his father, the famous Thomas Cromwell, who served as a powerful minister under Henry VIII. Like Essex himself, Edward Cromwell was a military man. He had served under Essex in several campaigns and had even attempted to establish himself as a marshal of the English army in Ireland at the time Essex was there. After the revolt, Cromwell was brought to trial on 5 March 1600 with Lord Sandys, another peer who was closely associated with Essex. Why Cromwell was assigned to East's house in particular presents special problems.

Obviously, Cromwell was well above East's station. He was a distinguished peer of the realm, whereas the music printer was not even particularly conspicuous as a member of the company of stationers, which was itself a relatively minor livery company in the City of London. Most likely, therefore, it was the fact that Balls and Wiborowe were still in residence at East's house that disposed the government to choose this location for Cromwell's house arrest. By August of 1601, these two apprentices were known to the Elizabethan courts not only as thieves but also as reliable informants. Perhaps, in the end, East's involvement in two of the most intriguing and important political episodes of his era owed almost as much to the behavior of these two grasping apprentices as to the political implications of the musical works he printed.

In the period that followed Cromwell's detention at East's shop and the prior episode with Catholic agitators, East took the opportunity to print and publish an uncommon number of books of a political nature (although none were musical). He also used the occasion to introduce the publishing activities of his adopted son, Thomas Snodham, whose books were produced and sold at his firm. The works printed by East and Snodham included several politically charged works that dealt with Angus's conspiratorial behavior, Persons's views on the succession, and the Essex Revolt.[93] They also printed an account of James's visitation to Theobalds en route to his accession in London and a very popular work on the tobacco controversy so famously incited by the new king.[94]

After 1603, East's firm ceased to specialize so conspicuously in political matters and returned to its regular routine. But, as will be shown in the next chapter, changes in England's economic systems for the book trade in the new Stuart era turned out to have a lasting effect on music printing, the field East had most firmly incorporated as a specialty from 1588 onward.

EAST'S LAST YEARS, HIS LEGACY, AND THE TWO MUSIC PATENTS OF THE EARLY STUART ERA (1603–1611)

8

The accession of James VI of Scotland to the throne of England in 1603 brought with it new prospects for East's firm. It is well known that one of the greatest achievements of the early reign of James I was the abolition of many of the most abhorred monopolies established by his predecessors.[1] For East, however, what was more significant were the opportunities opened to him not by the abolition of monopolies but by shifts in power in the music patents that controlled his trade. The Stationers' Company established a publishing corporation called the English Stock that assumed the ownership of the patent for the psalter with music and significantly altered the publishing conditions for that class of books. At nearly the same time, there were new developments in the general music monopoly after the death of Morley in 1602 that turned out to have a lasting effect on the relative strength of this grant.

Although each music patent had survived James's antimonopolistic legislation of this era, they developed along very different trajectories in the early Stuart era. For a short time after Morley's death, the general music patent experienced a period of ambiguous ownership. As before, this attracted new competitors to East's trade. By 1606, however, the music patent had passed into the hands of a nonmusician, William Barley, who attempted to restore the monopoly. Yet under Barley the power of this grant was systematically diminished in the first decades of the seventeenth century. In 1612 Morley's widow nominated Edward Allde, a stationer, as the owner of the music monopoly.[2] By then the idea of musicians controlling a monopoly was a distant memory.

Conversely, the psalter patent was greatly fortified by the advent of a new publishing conglomerate in 1603. East's position was seemingly compromised by this shift in ownership of the psalter patent, since he had officially lost his former power to publish his own version of the collected psalms with music. In actuality, however, the establishment of this new publishing firm had auspicious results for him as well, for he received special treatment from this institution. It offered him not only opportunities for well-compensated work as a trade printer but also the means to establish a level of reliable financial security as the owner of a share of stock in the books he helped to produce. Such security had no parallel in East's earlier career.

East carefully positioned his firm against the changing condition of both music patents. He also protected his own rights outside their jurisdiction. These achievements demonstrated the music printer's uncommon skills as an entrepreneur. By his death in 1608, East had made his firm solvent and established a strong economic basis for its continued success. His heirs, whose subsequent careers brought to fruition the very strategies East had begun to formulate in the last years of his life, reaped the benefits. The restructuring of music monopolies in the years 1603–1608, which affected not only East's work but nearly all music publishing in this era, is the central focus of this chapter, which covers the last years of East's work in the music trade of London and the burgeoning careers of his heirs in the music field.

THE ENGLISH STOCK OF THE STATIONERS' COMPANY

In the year of his accession, King James granted to the Stationers' Company a patent of monopoly that made it unique among London's merchant guilds. The company had already supervised the publication of psalms set to music for the past two decades, but this grant formalized the transfer of control and established within the institution itself an official publishing concern that was run as a joint stock trading company.[3] The books of the newly established firm were listed as "Prymers Psalters and Psalmes in meter or prose with musycall notes or withoute notes both in greate volumes and small in the Englishe tongue," as well as "all manner of Almanackes and Prognosticacons whatsoever in the Englishe tongue."[4] Due to its special coverage of English books, this patent became known as the English Stock, and soon it would represent only one, albeit the first and largest, of the Stationers' Company's monopolies in the book trade.[5] No other London livery company had ever operated as a conglomerate trading firm, and the new powers bestowed by the grant itself served to reshape the organization's internal structure as well as its external functions. Most important, the stock was run by the same elected officials who dealt with all guild affairs, and therefore its business was intertwined with other functions of company governance.[6]

When the English Stock was officially brought into being by the 1603 grant, it was composed of properties from a number of the most lucrative patents formerly owned by individuals of the company and by others who worked outside its jurisdiction.[7] Soon after 1603, the Stationers' Company purchased six warehouses to hold the supply of printed books that were to be sold in the interests of the company.[8] They appointed a treasurer and stock keepers in the same year, and a ruling group designated as the "Table" was established that met fortnightly to discuss company matters. At these meetings the Table discussed and decided the usual issues faced by publishers: what books would be printed for the company stock, where and how the paper would be acquired for the printing, and who among their colleagues would print the chosen volumes. As a publishing venture, the English Stock was extraordinarily successful, and it remained, in some vestige of its original form, a viable institution into the post–World War II era.[9]

East was a founding member of this new stock company, and he participated extensively in its activities. This brought him not only economic benefits but also new opportunities as a printer. As a stockholder with a livery share, East was paid a generous dividend for the remainder of his life. His widow, Lucretia, received an assistant's share for each of the nineteen years she outlived her husband (by 1611 the shares were divided into livery, assistant, and yeoman shares at £320, £160, and £80 respectively).[10] Even without other resources, this was sufficient income for Lucretia East to retire from printing completely within two years after East's death. The annual share must have been a great boon to East in the last years of his life when he was also profiting from other printing ventures both related to and independent of the English Stock.

THE ENGLISH STOCK AND EAST'S *Whole Booke of Psalmes*

The stationers chose East to print for their new stock almost immediately after their trading firm was formalized. Under these new conditions, East brought out an impression of his *Whole Booke of Psalmes* in 1604 with the significant change of publisher noted in the imprint of the title page but otherwise presenting essentially the same content. East's heirs continued to print the volume "for the Stationers' Company" at fairly regular intervals throughout the first quarter of the seventeenth century.[11]

The Sternhold/Hopkins *Whole Booke of Psalmes* was one of the most valuable, and therefore most important, items of the stock in the early seventeenth century.[12] Despite its musical character, this property, which until 1603 was still formally owned by Richard Day and managed by the group of stationers who worked as Day's assigns, was never officially associated with the general music patent. In various ways, East, Barley, and Morley, among others, had all found it possible to bring out editions of the psalter under the dubious authority of the music patent, but this was never completely condoned by either the Stationers' Company or the royal courts that dealt with patent matters.[13] East's new productions of the psalter therefore reveal that he was able to rejoin the field only after the monopoly for psalms set to music was sold to the company in 1603.[14]

East was to gain further advantage from the new arrangements. In 1604 he produced a monophonic setting of the collected psalms in quarto format for the Stationers' Company.[15] In 1607 he printed part of a folio edition of the monophonic music again; here his type appears along with that of the music printer John Windet.[16] It seems to have been the first and only time East produced a musical work as a shared effort with a stationer from another firm.

There is evidence that these monophonic editions were prepared in conjunction with various editions of the *Book of the Common Prayer* published by the king's printer, Robert Barker. Among other editions, Barker's printers produced a quarto edition of the Common Prayer in 1604 and a folio edition in 1607. That East's printing was possibly done in cooperation with the Common Prayer project is evident not only from the fact that all extant copies of these editions are bound with Barker's editions of the Common Prayer but also because the two editions of each set share the same paper stock.[17] It would seem from this evidence that East's and Barker's printers collaborated for the two projects. This type of sharing was typical for master printers of the time, but having two separate publishers for a single volume was unusual.

The royal printer traditionally had the sole right to print the Book of Common Prayer, including the psalter therein. This rule seems to have been temporarily suspended, however, with the establishment of the English Stock. The publisher of East's editions is unambiguous. In the imprint, it is clearly stated that they were printed "for the Stationers' Company."[18]

The early ventures of the English Stock temporarily changed the publishing status of the psalter. Because East's books of the collected psalms in the years 1604 – 1608 included volumes associated both with the music monopoly and with the patents traditionally owned by the royal printer, his music printing at this time uncovers the full extent of the company's powers as a publishing firm in the early stages of the stock's history.[19]

East was also employed for other work on books covered by the English Stock. Earlier in his career he had produced the famous prophesies of Erra Pater, and this probably influenced the Table of the stock when they chose him to print several of the lucrative editions of the almanacs and prognostications that were covered in their grant.[20] From the year 1606 until his death in 1608, East printed several such editions for the company in his new capacity as one of their privileged printers.[21]

East was probably treated very well by this new conglomerate publisher. His membership and participation in the English Stock alone would have been sufficient to leave his heirs in a comfortable economic position, but other indicators suggest his printing work was also well rewarded. While most of the early records of the English Stock transactions no longer survive, the extant traces of their dealings show that the company was very generous to those who helped to produce the books of their stock. In 1614, for example, one of three correctors of a single volume was paid an additional "£33 13s 14d" beyond his (undisclosed) normal pay for his "great paines."[22] East was probably well compensated for his efforts, since they were surely more appreciated by the company than the work of a corrector, although the aforementioned transaction must have been based on extraordinary circumstances to justify such a bountiful expenditure.

East's participation in the production of psalmbooks (as well as prognostications and almanacs) for the company was undoubtedly a reflection of the respect he had gained as a master printer who had served his public and his company for nearly forty years. Despite his advancing age and the great security and comfort afforded to him by his role in the prospering English Stock, East did not surrender his entrepreneurial aspirations in other types of music editions in the last years of his life. He took new strides in establishing his own position as a music publisher. After a short period of seeming disinterest in music printing (apart from the psalmbooks), East began to advance his own standing as an independent printer and publisher after 1603 and became less restricted by an active music monopoly.

THE MUSIC MONOPOLY IN THE EARLY STUART ERA

Thomas Morley's death in 1602 created a novel condition for the music patent. Traditionally, it had always been in the hands of the queen's finest musicians. There was, however, no one of the king's newly established Chapel Royal able to take Morley's place in 1603, if indeed any musician was interested in taking on the trouble and risk for what surely would have been an expensive new patent. By design, this grant was to remain active from its inception in 1598 until its twenty-one-year term expired in 1619.[23] Nonetheless, for a four-year period, 1602–1606, the monopoly stood inactive.

Not surprisingly, music printers who were working before Morley's death in 1602 continued to print music in the years just after his death, although they did so cautiously.[24]

East, Barley, and Short were the London music book traders active during Morley's brief period as a music monopolist (1598–1602). Of these men, Barley had worked most extensively with Morley in the final years of the sixteenth century. It was East and Short, however, who had worked with Morley continuously until his demise. These two printers had official contracts with the composer to remain in force until 1603, whereas after 1599 Barley was not to be involved in the music field to any great degree again until 1606.[25] In Short's case, Morley's contract was at least nominally honored in a music book the year after the composer's death. In his 1603 edition of John Dowland's *Third Book of Songs*, Short noted that his work was allowed "by assignment of a patent granted to [Morley]."[26] This was Short's last music publication. The printer died later that year, and his widow, Elizabeth, printed only one music edition (in 1604) before she married Humfrey Lownes and began to print music that advertised the name of his firm.[27]

East, whose press was otherwise occupied with political works in 1603, printed Robinson's *Schoole of Musicke* in that year, but he did not recognize Morley's patent therein.[28] Unfortunately, the precise date of the Robinson work within the year is not known. East's three-year contract with Morley expired by June 1603, so it is unclear whether he was violating the partnership terms by this publication.[29] Significantly, his edition of 1603, like that of a growing number of others at this time, had been published by a professional book trader, Simon Waterson. East's role in the publication was that of a trade printer, and this may have kept him from having to be concerned about property rights. It also meant that he sacrificed opportunities to profit exclusively from the sales of this particular work.

The presence of new professional book traders in London's music trade after 1603 is evident in East's record although far less so than in that of his adopted son, Thomas Snodham.[30] After he took over East's firm in 1609, Snodham printed music extensively for the music publisher John Browne, who soon became his partner.[31] Except for his edition of music for Waterson in 1603, East himself worked with only one other professional publisher in the music trade: in 1606 he printed an edition of John Danyel's *Songs for Lvte* for Thomas Adams.[32] He never laid claim to this property; rather, Danyel's edition was entered by Adams in the Stationers' Company Registers.[33] It stands as an exceptional case, as it was the only work of music East produced that he allowed another stationer to register before he had entered the book himself. Neither he nor anyone else ever registered Robinson's *Schoole of Mvsicke*. Apparently East did not do so because Waterson had the claim to this property as its publisher. Perhaps it was because of the questionable status of the music patent in 1603 that Waterson himself never chose to exercise his right to enter the music book in the company registers.

In 1603, the year after Morley's death, East's interest in music printing seemed to have dwindled. For the first time he was willing to surrender his rights to musical property to other stationers. In the final four years of his life (1604–1608), however, he began vigorously to reassert his own special claims in the field of music publishing. East's renewed interest in the music field may be seen in a series of his registrations in the Stationers' Company in 1604. These were followed by two hidden editions and a reprinting of Byrd's *Psalmes, Sonets & Songs* in another undated edition.

THE SECOND GAP IN THE MUSIC MONOPOLY (1604–1606)

In 1604, when East had no need to recognize the music monopoly, he returned to music printing with an entrepreneurial scheme similar to that of the late 1590s when Byrd's grant had lapsed. First, East took the opportunity of Morley's death and the resulting ambiguity in the ownership of the music patent to register music books in the stationers' registers as his own property. Second, bibliographical evidence suggests that East brought out the last and largest group of his hidden editions to accompany the registrations of 1604. Since Morley and East had concentrated on reprinting several of the more popular of East's music editions during Morley's tenure as monopolist, there were actually only a few additional works of music that he needed to register for the first time in this interim, namely Weelkes's *Madrigals* and the *Triumphes of Oriana* that he had printed for Morley in 1601. East also registered every music book he printed in the years 1604 to 1606.[34]

From the evidence of their paper stocks, three hidden editions appear to have been produced in this era (see Table A1.3). They fall into two sets according to their paper. One includes John Wilbye's *First Set of English Madrigals* (first printed in 1598) and the *Triumphes of Oriana* (first printed in 1601). East reprinted both of these titles with what remained of a single stock of paper he had originally used to print Thomas Bateson's *English Madrigales* in 1604.[35] The other consisted of a hidden edition of Morley's *Balletts*, which he had originally produced in 1595. For this East used paper from the following three paper stocks: (1) a running stock from the original printing of the *Triumphes* in 1601, (2) a token remnant from a stock he used to print an edition of Michael East's *Madrigales* in 1604, and (3) a few remnant sheets from the Bateson edition of 1604, paper that also appeared in the other two hidden editions of this era.[36]

The publishing history of the *Triumphes* edition has puzzled modern scholars. Edward Arber noted that the book was first registered three years after its date of printing.[37] He attributed the delay to a withholding of the publication and, since he did not know that there were in fact two separate editions, he must have believed that East's edition dated 1601 was actually produced in 1604. To explain this, Arber argued that the queen did not appreciate any reference to herself as Oriana, and thus the *Triumphes of Oriana* was suppressed for political purposes that had to do with the queen's personal tastes and then was brought out only after her death.[38]

Even though they were aware that East had indeed reprinted the *Triumphes*, Lillian Ruff and Arnold Wilson accepted Arber's contention that the volume was registered later than its publication because it was suppressed.[39] Unlike Arber, however, these scholars pointed to the exigencies of the Essex Revolt to explain the circumstance. In their view, the Essexians controlled music printing to such an extent that the publisher of the music sought to minimize the circulation of the work due to its flattering references to the queen, especially since it appeared so soon after Essex's execution. Traditionally, the appearance of a new edition signaled the music's success in the market, yet Ruff and Wilson argued that the first edition had been purposely kept from circulation (and perhaps destroyed).

East actually had other reasons for not registering the edition at the time of its original issue and waiting instead until 1604 to do so. His policy from his first music printing of 1588 until 1606 was to print music books without registration during the periods when the monopoly was in force. In 1601, when the original *Triumphes* edition was produced, Morley was the official owner of the monopoly. Thus East waited to register this work as he had done for many others. There is no reason to attribute the delay of registration to special political circumstances that involved the queen or her rival Essex but rather to economic factors that had to do with the shifting status of intellectual property for Elizabethan music.

A hidden edition was a new publication, and as I have suggested throughout, all the patterns of production suggest that the publisher of hidden editions was East himself. Although one can imagine a number of possible reasons that a stationer would publish a new edition, the most likely is that he wished to sell copies of the book in question, perhaps to a special market but just as likely directly to his anticipated general run of paying customers.[40] The pattern for the reprinting of the *Triumphes* was similar to that for all East's hidden editions. Like Wilbye's *Madrigals*, also reprinted at this time, the *Triumphes* should be counted among the many collections of English madrigals that reached a level of marketability among London consumers so great as to merit a new edition in the surreptitious style of East's hidden edition format. Contrary to what prior scholars have suggested, it was probably widely disseminated both before and after Queen Elizabeth's death in 1603.

In addition to his production of hidden editions in the years 1605–1606, East also resurrected his trade relations with the composer Byrd for a rather large undertaking. From the time Byrd had taken his Masses to East to print in the mid-1590s, the composer had not ventured to publish any more music collections until 1605. In that year, however, Byrd brought to East the first of two volumes of his extensive *Gradualia*. This collection of Mass Propers was the largest single collection of music East was to print, and Byrd's second volume, which he printed in 1607, was nearly as large.[41] Byrd had less evident power over East in 1605, since at this time he was only a publisher, not a monopolist. East's work for the composer was nonetheless as exacting as it had been before.

The *Gradualia* copies extant today provide ample evidence of meticulous proofing at East's press. These include typographical alterations between sections of text normally left standing between part-books; stop-press corrections, often to change spellings of words that probably otherwise would have been allowed to stand by most Renaissance correctors of Latin; and a number of cancel slips, where East painstakingly corrected errors not detected until after the sheets were printed.[42] The combination of its great length and the high level of proofing makes this one of the most time-consuming projects of East's career as a music printer.

New considerations that surrounded Byrd's participation in the publication of his *Psalmes, Sonets & Songs* arise with the likely prospect that the last edition (B2) was also produced in the years 1606 or 1607, as bibliographical evidence overwhelmingly suggests (see chapter 3). In this context, Byrd's intermittent relationship with the press is noteworthy: gaps in his output range from four to thirteen years (his prints appear in 1575, 1588–1595, 1605–1607, and 1611–1613). The newly established date places the *Psalmes* in the midst of some of East's and Byrd's most intense work together.[43] David Mateer has suggested that the *Gradualia* was financed with a loan from Byrd's patron Sir William Petre; now it may be further conjectured that the loan covered the expenses of this *Psalmes* edition as well.[44] Significantly, too, the last edition brought with it some further and important improvements to the musical texts themselves, including an effective resolution of certain mensuration problems with which Byrd had long struggled. Since East and Byrd had recently renewed their former working relations, it would not seem too far afield to suggest that these editorial changes were introduced at Byrd's behest, revealing that the composer was quite consistent in his approach to print as a vehicle he could experiment with and ultimately bend to his own particular needs.

EAST, BARLEY, AND THE MUSIC MONOPOLY (1606–1608)

East had demonstrated a renewed interest in music printing in the years when the monopoly was in flux, and this continued even when the music monopoly passed into Barley's hands in 1606.[45] No music editions before this date mentioned the draper as the monopoly owner. Yet in June 1606 when East and Barley appeared before the court of assistants of the Stationers' Company to resolve a dispute over the printing of music, Barley's ownership of the music patent was already a key issue. The first part of the report of this contest mentions the "letters patente granted of Musick booke by the late Quene Elizabeth to Tho. Morley whose Interest therein the said William [Barley] claymeth to haue."[46] By the end of the arbitration, it was clear that Barley was indeed the recognized owner of the patent. East and his wife, Lucretia, who was listed as a partner in East's firm, were ordered by the court to pay Barley twenty shillings before printing certain editions of music and to deliver to Barley six sets of every music edition they printed within a week of their completion.[47] Following the court's judgment, Thomas and Lucretia East consistently recognized Barley's position; in nearly all of East's remaining music books, he duly listed himself as Barley's assign. Lucretia East listed herself as the "assign of William Barley" when she printed the third edition of Byrd's *Songs of Sundrie Natures* in 1609, the year after East's death.[48]

As a draper whose main trade was in books, Barley was one of more than a dozen members of his company who, at the behest of the Stationers' Company itself, had officially translated their allegiance to the latter guild. Of these men, he had been one of the more troubling to stationers before his translation. He had apparently not only been involved in the wholesale publishing of books protected by royal patents and the stationers' guild but also had worked with a fellow draper, Simon Stafford, who was actually printing these books in pirated editions.[49] If publishing and selling books was a trade stationers wished to regulate, printing itself was a prerogative they guarded with special zeal. To bring men like Stafford and Barley under their control, the stationers' plan was to force them to join the company. In 1600 they won their point before the London court of aldermen. Many of the drapers who traded in books were officially transferred to the Stationers' Company at that time, but Barley was one of the last to take this step.[50] It was not until he and East appeared before the court of assistants on 25 June 1606 that Barley became an official brother of the Stationers' Company.

In the 1606 settlement, East seems to have been compelled to pay Barley for the privilege of printing music; for this reason, bibliographers and musicologists have generally seen the results of the *East vs. Barley* dispute as a victory for Barley.[51] But the events were not nearly so one-sided. What has not hitherto been recognized by scholars is that Barley's dispute with East centered on his hidden editions. Two issues were before the court: East's policy of registering music books and his right to print them. As the reigning music monopolist, Barley argued that it was not East but he who had the right to this property. Therefore, he brought East's scheme of printing hidden editions to the full attention of the court.

It was decided by the stationers that Barley had to be paid whenever East or his wife decided to "prynt" what were described as his "copies Registered," that is, the reprints of older editions that East might produce—that he had indeed been producing—as hidden editions as late as 1605–1606.[52] Thus East seems to have lost the advantage he had with his earlier hidden editions that he published without paying any fees. Nonetheless, he had never produced hidden editions when the music monopoly was in full force, and Barley's challenge may therefore have been unnecessary. If East did recognize Barley as the true owner of the monopoly after 1606, he would in any case normally not have risked publishing any hidden editions from that time forward.

One matter is clear: the threat Barley perceived was that East would begin publishing his registered books after 1606, either as hidden editions or perhaps even in an aboveboard manner with the correct date. If East actually had plans to avoid paying the monopolist's fees, Barley did indeed stop such a scheme with this arbitration.[53] But it was only East's *potential* publishing policy that was frustrated by Barley before it began. Essentially, after this arbitration East did not have to change his position at all in the music trade. Furthermore, he was awarded certain rights that better served his own standing in the music field.

In the first place, East's use of the registers for their traditional purposes was fully recognized by the company. Barley was advised that he "shall not Deale or intermeddle with the printinge of any of [East's registered books]."[54] If it were ever in doubt before, here East unambiguously won the proprietary rights to the music that he had premiered at his press and registered in the company books. It is quite understandable why Barley, as the music monopolist, would have questioned East's rights. The music patent was clearly worded to cover all music printing regardless of any prior claims. But Barley had just become a stationer, and from that day forward he was forced to conform to the guild's rules. East's problem of the past, when monopolists answered only to the queen or king, was thereby dissolved. This constituted a major turning point for East, simplifying the economic environment and reducing the constraints to trade. The Stationers' Company, for its part, also gained palpably in this outcome: by establishing jurisdiction in a dispute that involved the royal monopoly, the guild registered a signal advance in its ongoing struggle to counteract the power of the royal patents that affected so much of its members' trade.

The second advantage for East established by this arbitration involved the fees he had to pay to Barley as a music printer and publisher. Most scholars have assumed that these fees were simply those Barley was ordered by the court to charge all publishers of music for the rights to use his patented property.[55] If this were true, Barley's fees were significantly lower than Morley's (the forty shillings Morley charged for printing music was halved to twenty shillings, the six-shilling rate per ream of paper used in the production was eliminated, and, finally, instead of twelve copies of printed music as a honorarium for each edition Barley was to be given only six).[56] What has not been properly noted, however, is that the fees outlined in the arbitration were specifically associated only with East's registered music books. This settlement did not necessarily apply to Barley's relations with other music printers and publishers, nor did it concern East's printing of music books that he did not register. By the simple act of registering books before printing them East could ensure that he would pay the more favorable fees.

How much East was influenced by the fees in changing his policy for his registrations is unclear. Well before this time he had found a solution to the problem of the monopolist's fees, as may be seen in his earlier litigation with Eastland: he simply passed them on to the publisher before the printing began.[57] The arbitration agreement does seem to have eventually inaugurated an era of reduced fees paid to the music monopolist. This was surely a boon to the industry, for there would have been greater incentive for publishers to bring music manuscripts to the press. The most important immediate result of the contest between East and Barley, however, was that it gave Thomas and Lucretia East the full rights to republish the music they had printed in earlier years.

East's defense in his litigation with Barley illuminates his precise motive for using the registers throughout his earlier career. Until 1606 he must have considered the stationers' method of protection insufficient in the eyes of nonstationers; hence he falsely dated the editions he produced after such registrations. But after 1606, all the people involved in the music trade were stationers. Among members of this group, East had the advantage of his many years in the company and the wise decision he had made earlier in his career to register his music copies. It is difficult to know if the court was fully aware of all the advantages East accrued in this settlement. But there is no question the printer perceived an entirely new role for the Stationers' Registers after this 1606 arbitration. Throughout his career, he had only rarely ventured to register music books during the official reign of the music monopoly, but for all the remaining books that he printed after 1606 he routinely registered the titles with the Stationers' Company before he printed them.[58]

The precipitating event that led to the hearing before the court of assistants in June 1606 is unknown. The best available clue comes from the recently established likelihood that East printed an undated new edition of Byrd's *Psalmes* in 1606–1607, at about the time the dispute with Barley was under way or, in any event, not long after its settlement.[59] It would have been thoroughly in character for East to exploit the uncertain status of the monopoly by surreptitiously bringing out new editions of popular works. His renewed collaboration with Byrd on the *Gradualia* would have served as a reinforcing stimulus. If Barley had somehow learned of the work in progress, it might well have incited him to protect the monopoly he claimed by finally submitting to the jurisdiction of the stationers and bringing charges.

If the work were produced *after* the arbitration settlement and therefore in direct defiance of the ruling that East recognize Barley's grant, which indeed the printer honored in every other case, it would seem most unlikely that the motive were simply to avoid payment of the monopolist's fees and delivery of six copies of the work in question. Two other considerations seem more salient. First, it is possible that East simply refused in principle to share with anyone his publisher's interest in a volume that had virtually symbolized his historic commitment to music printing, a collection of songs that he had gone to considerable trouble and expense to produce and protect throughout his twenty-year regime as the premier printer of music in London. The second possibility is that he was more concerned about the reactions of the English Stock than those of Barley. Given the presence of metrical psalms in the volume and the trouble he had already encountered in registering the work, East may have found the path of subterfuge a wiser course than to test the authority of the Stationers' Company, which had just further strengthened its power over the intellectual property of psalmbooks by drawing the music monopolist Barley under guild supervision.

Once the 1606 stationers' court legislation was in place, the Easts finally had the opportunity to restock the most popular items on their shelves by openly publishing reprints of music editions, without resort to evasive stratagems. In 1606 East printed a new edition of Morley's *Canzonets a 3*, in 1608 he printed a new edition of Weelkes's *Balletts and Madrigals*, and in 1609 Lucretia East printed Byrd's *Songs of Sundrie Natures* as Barley's assign. These volumes have not been given much attention in bibliographical studies, but in publishing terms they were among the most unusual prints of Renaissance London. In bringing them out openly and at their own discretion, the Easts undertook the expense and risk normally associated with publishers. Among their European counterparts this was a common practice, but not so in London, where the complex environment of monopolistic patents and conflicting jurisdictions of guilds and royal courts militated against it. Because the Easts were traders who actually sold, as well as printed, music, their advantages as music publishers were clear. As booksellers of music for over twenty years, they were in the best position of all the London publishers to judge the salability of their product. After a long and productive career as a music printer, it is fitting that East was finally able to operate without the least subterfuge when he took the last of his many opportunities to replenish his stock of music books.

LUCRETIA EAST, THOMAS SNODHAM, AND
THE MUSIC MONOPOLY AFTER EAST'S DEATH IN 1608

In 1607 East wrote an extensive will, which bequeathed his personal and business properties to his wife and to his adopted son, Thomas Snodham.[60] Legally, this would have been the natural outcome of events even if East had died intestate, but it is important to note that, in business terms, Lucretia East and Snodham were well versed in his trade and therefore deserving of his estate. The record of the *East vs. East-*

land trial and other documentation of East's career in the Stationers' Registers reveal that his wife and his son had many responsibilities within the firm for a number of years prior to his death. Officially, Lucretia East was East's partner for the last years of his life.[61] Snodham, too, had been conspicuously active at East's firm. In 1603 he had already used East's presses to print material with the firm's type.

From his will, it is obvious that East's plan was to pass his business to his adopted son, while protecting his widow's financial security. To do this, he left to his wife the Aldersgate Street residence and another dwelling where he secretly operated a press in Cripplegate, with provision that it pass to Snodham only after her death. But East also stipulated that the business was to be freely operated by Snodham, who would pay Lucretia East a £200 bond for the use of her property.[62] As she passed the firm on to her adopted son, Lucretia East soon found many economic incentives to retire from printing altogether.[63] The arrangement she made with Snodham was officially ratified when the latter appeared before the court of assistants to register himself as a master printer in East's place.[64]

Snodham had entered East's firm as Lucretia East's orphaned nephew. He was the son of a draper, who may have had relations with the many booksellers of that company, and he was probably related to several other stationers of the same name.[65] In addition, soon after his adoptive father's death Snodham had married Elizabeth Burby, the daughter of the very influential Cuthbert Burby, who was a warden of the Stationers' Company and the treasurer of the English Stock at this time.[66] With Elizabeth's dowry, as well as the returns from his own efforts in publishing music, Snodham must have been able to raise quickly the sum of £200 so that he could post the bond required to run his former master's shop in Aldersgate Street. Beyond the physical property, however, Snodham also had to negotiate with his aunt and adoptive mother for East's registered books, and this led finally to new complications in the music trade that Snodham seems to have remedied through his own publication of hidden editions.

THE ASSIGNMENTS OF EAST'S PROPERTY

As East's executee Lucretia East inherited East's house and savings. Written at the bottom of East's will is the figure "£482–8s-3d."[67] If this was an estimate of the financial estate that he left to Lucretia, it would have added considerably to her position at this time. But the larger inheritance that Lucretia East obtained after her husband's death was from East's share of the English Stock that brought her an annual income of £160 per year and copies of the books that he had entered in the Stationers' Registers. The value of the latter commodity was determined by the interest other stationers might have had in his registered books, for Lucretia East herself was apparently not in a position to print them after 1609.

Not surprisingly, it was Snodham who was the first to negotiate with Lucretia East for the rights to print East's registered copies. On 17 June 1609, Snodham entered thirty books not related to music that his father had published earlier. These are listed in the Stationers' Registers with the note that they were entered "with the consent of mistress East."[68] More so than his father, Snodham was an active printer of books of general literature. At Snodham's own death, his widow assigned over 100 books, of which only about 20% contained music.[69]

Snodham became an important general printer as well as a music specialist, but his immediate concern in the years 1609–1610 was music printing. In 1609 alone, Snodham brought out two volumes of music by Ferrabosco and an edition of music by Rosseter for the publisher Browne, an edition of Ravenscroft's *Deuteromelia* for Adams, and the exquisite collection of Wilbye's *Second Set of English Madrigals* published for the composer.[70] Judging from his printing activities in 1609, Snodham was probably eager to obtain the music books formerly owned by his father, but this turned out to be a difficult endeavor.

Lucretia East did not choose simply to award East's music books to Snodham. Rather, she sold them to the publisher Browne, who had been accumulating a list of music books throughout the first decade of the seventeenth century. On 22 December 1610 the stationers' scribe recorded that "19 Copyes" of East's registered music books were entered to Browne "by assignemente of Mistres East."[71] But this was a provisional registration. Under the list the scribe noted further that it was "[p]rovided that yf any question or clayme be made for any of these Copyes, That then the sayd John Browne shall therein stand to the order of the mayster, wardens, and Assistants or the more part of them."[72]

The records of the stationers' court of assistants, where disputed claims were usually logged, contain no references to this transfer of East's music books to the publisher Browne. Yet on 3 September 1611 the same music prints, with the addition of one or two others, were entered again, this time to three stationers: Browne, Matthew Lownes, and Snodham.[73] From that time forward, these three men printed and published a considerable amount of music together, although, as Miriam Miller has pointed out, the precise nature of their partnership now remains somewhat obscure.[74] Snodham was sometimes listed in the imprints as the printer "for" the other two stationers, but at other times he is listed as the publisher as well. Certainly Snodham was the printer for this group; the music type in all of the part-books produced by this partnership was the font Snodham had inherited from East.

HIDDEN EDITIONS BY THOMAS SNODHAM

Snodham produced two hidden editions sometime after 1610, and the evidence of these two assignments of music books suggests it may have been due to Browne's registration of East's former copies of that year. Snodham's two hidden editions of this era were new editions of Wilbye's *First Set of English Madrigals* and Morley's *Madrigals to Fovre Voices.* There is little doubt that these were chosen for their popularity as musical collections; each had already been reprinted earlier by East. The Morley set was first printed in 1594, and the second edition was published by Morley himself, who added two madrigals. Under Morley's auspices, East accurately dated the second edition of Morley's *Madrigalls* in 1600, and it was this reprint that Snodham carefully emulated as a hidden edition. The Wilbye set was a rather special case. In 1604 or 1605, East had already reprinted it with the false date of its original edition (1598).[75] They were obviously popular titles, yet both of Snodham's hidden editions were doubly veiled: not only did he falsify the dates of these reprintings as their originals, but he also incorrectly listed his father, East, as their printer.

The strongest of the array of paper evidence for dating problematic works in the entire group of hidden editions occurs in these reprints by Snodham. Both volumes were produced with paper that has a watermark with the date "1610" in its design (see Figure 3.4).[76] There is, however, no assurance from this fortuitously dated watermark that the books were produced in that year. As was common for London stationers, Snodham had to rely on the importation of paper from Europe.[77] Therefore, the date of this paper's manufacture in France in 1610 and its use by him in England could very well have been at some distance in time. Nonetheless, there is the distinct possibility that the paper of these hidden editions was used in 1610. This is because the 1610 and 1611 registrations serve to explain why he resorted to the hidden edition format he had apparently learned from his adoptive father.

If he wanted the full benefits of East's legacy, Snodham was surely threatened by Browne's registration of East's former music books in 1610. This should have kept him from the lucrative trade of reprinting older editions. Since they were both stationers, Snodham could not easily ignore Browne's rights. His only recourse was to pirate Browne's property. Conversely, Browne himself did not have the means to print music, and Snodham's recourse to hidden editions revealed his willingness to use his press to find alternatives to Browne's rights. A collaboration was needed. In a partnership Browne could maintain his position as a publisher with the rights to copy, whereas Snodham would be mollified because he could affirm his standing as a music printer with a publisher's interest in his product.

Once the firm of Browne, Lownes, and Snodham was established in 1611, there would have been little reason for Snodham to resort to the hidden edition format for reprinting popular titles. His actions after 1611 demonstrated his new position in matters of the entered copies. As the proper owner of the rights to the title, for example, Snodham, like East himself, printed Morley's *Canzonets* as a fully acknowledged new edition. It was published and accurately dated in 1619 by Snodham.[78] The 1611 registration therefore sets the *terminus ante quem* for Snodham's two hidden editions of this era.

Snodham entered into partnership with the music publishers Browne and Lownes to protect his rights to publish as well as to print music. The partnership apparently further weakened Barley's position. Professional publishers like Browne and Adams, who entered the picture after Morley's death, rarely troubled to recognize Barley's patent.[79] Contrary to the claims of other scholars, Gerald Johnson has noted that Barley's patent was almost always ignored in the music printed by Snodham (variously published by him and the others of his partnership).[80] If, as music publishers, these men happily avoided Barley's fee, it was probably the musicians who took their music to Snodham's press to be printed who stood to benefit the most from this situation. Not only would publishers be more interested in finding new music to print at this time, since the monopolist's fees were eliminated, but also musicians who wished to publish their own music could enjoy the same economic incentive.

REISSUES OF EAST'S PRESSWORK

The indications from Browne and Snodham's registrations in the company books, and the subsequent hidden editions by Snodham, suggest that East's property was considered valuable by these stationers, since they went to considerable trouble and expense to establish and protect this intellectual property. If this leads to a rather optimistic view of the salability of music in print in this era, that contention is mitigated by a consideration of the reissues of East's original printing that occurred at approximately the same time that Snodham printed his hidden editions.

Reissues of East's original music books were produced by resetting the title page to give the impression of a new edition while actually retaining the rest of the original sheets intact. It is important to note that these reissued books contained the same sheets of paper East had printed before, with the crucial exception of the title page and prefatory material. This minimal printing activity of setting and printing the title and dedication pages effectively served to advertise these reissues falsely as new and corrected editions. Giovanni Croce's sacred madrigals and Byrd's motet collections were treated this way, following a similar tactic East himself had once used for an edition of music by Charles Tessier.[81]

In the case of the magnificent collections of Byrd's *Gradualia*, stationers after East's death seem to have found it difficult to unload the unsold sheets that made up the volume. In the British Library copy of the 1610 reissued *Gradualia II* (K.2.f.8), there are wormholes that skip every other leaf, indicating that the paper was not bound for a considerable time. This rather strongly confirms Philip Brett's suggestion (in regard to the 1605 edition) that their sheets were unbound and shelved for the entire period between the original printing (1607) and the reissue.[82] Even one of the last works to appear at East's press may have had such troubles in the market: the 1608 sheets of Croce's *Musica Sacra* were similarly reissued in 1611.

Although the books reissued from East's originals have been reasonably mistaken for new editions, the assertion that a measure of popularity may be seen here precisely reverses the real situation. The recasting of the previously printed sheets under a new title page only very tentatively indicates an anticipated rise in popularity for an edition, but it indubitably reveals a lack of success for a first edition. For these reissues, the purpose was to revive a poorly selling volume by recasting the material to reintroduce it to a market clearly driven by its preference for freshly produced editions. This reissue tactic provides rich data on the marketability of certain musical genres. They confirm with negative evidence the suggestion of East's hidden edition policies that it was music with English texts of a secular nature, composed by well-known English composers who had succeeded in the London market. The reissues are all by foreign composers, or the texts are in a foreign language. Like the hidden editions, but in a very different way, the deceptive "new editions" stand among East's music books to indicate the true range of practices available to the Renaissance printer. The modern bibliographer must be aware of the entire spectrum to properly assess the printing enterprise of that era.

CONCLUSION

East's professional relations with English composers, as they affected musical dissemination and composition, form the cornerstone of his contribution to music history. To appreciate this, one must recall the situation in London before 1588, when East's first musical editions were put up for sale at his firm. Although several London printers had demonstrated excellent capabilities for printing music, there was very little fruitful interaction between musicians and printers in the entire pre-Armada era. To be sure, there were special editions of music produced in London before 1588, yet the majority of them appear now to have been experimental and economically unsuccessful. Psalmbooks with music were another matter altogether. Stationers so valued the traditional tunes that made up the Sternhold/Hopkins volumes that they could occasionally contemplate simple ensemble arrangements. But, essentially, musicians who might compose new music of any kind were in the way.

Powerfully illustrative of this situation was the experience of composer Thomas Whythourne in having his *Songes in Three, Fower and Five Parts* printed by the London stationer John Day (1571). When the venture proved an economic failure, Whythorne bitterly blamed the printer for the poor sales, citing negligent workmanship, spiritless marketing, and faulty proofreading.[1] Music printing for living composers was not a completely neglected trade, of course, but Whythourne's lament, unopposed by contrary evidence, can be taken to indicate that there was an extraordinary gap between music printers and musicians of this era.

Against this background, it is surprising how important East's professional relationships would be with many of the best composers of his era after he began to print music. We have seen how unusual was the practice of musical editing carried out at his shop. Elizabethan composers themselves were conspicuously involved in the editorial aspects of East's production process, an involvement undoubtedly prompted by their special power over the press as monopolists and publishers. The process was not all one way, however. When East commissioned works for his own publication in 1592, he used his power as an active sponsor and promoter of musical composition to actively direct the work of composers.

East's position in the history of music printing in the London milieu has never been seriously challenged. But ever since the incredibly rich output of the continental music presses has been properly understood, much ink has been spilled over the peculiarly delicate and feeble condition of music publishing in Renaissance England before, during, and after East's tenure. One generally accepted theory is that the music monopoly was one of the main causes of this situation.[2] This theory contends that because of the monopoly the composers had interests in music publishing that obstructed the fluid interaction of supply and demand for Elizabethan music.

Direct evidence to support the theory is easily found. The Tallis/Byrd fiasco of 1575 and Byrd's retreat from printing thereafter heads the list of gloomy indicators, of course. Even after 1585, Byrd was primarily interested in printing his own music and the music of his friends. Morley was indeed a clever businessman who realized the potential of the press, but he chose to exploit his patent by imposing a stiff charge on anyone who wanted to publish music. This would naturally have had a chilling effect on the supply of music books for the market. Even the qualitative index seemed to decline: with Barley, any vestige of the queen's original purpose to encourage the advancement of music in her nation had evaporated, for Barley was probably not a musician, as the inaccurate lute music he published strongly suggests.[3]

The periods in East's and Snodham's careers when there was freedom of the press were never without auspicious result. The years 1596–1598, 1604–1606, and 1609–1610 were strong in the music field, not only because other printers were involved but also because East and Snodham concentrated even more than their usual efforts on its publication. The most activity in music printing occurred at those very times when the monopoly was inactive and windows of opportunity were opened for free trade. It is a simple fact that in these periods printers produced more music than at any other time.

Looking at the issue from a slightly different angle, Donald Krummel has found an ingenious way to exculpate the patentees by downplaying the significance of the market's exuberance in periods of free trade.[4] He argues that the market niche for music was a small one and therefore amply filled by official printers for the music patentees. In his view, the monopoly was unnecessary, but the very fact that it was there served to attract the jealous interest of a group of entrepreneurs from other realms of the English printing trade. When the monopoly was not fully enforced, these printers were attracted by the imagined profitability that they associated with a monopoly and not by real demand. Although both the general theory about the baneful influence of the music monopoly and Krummel's refinement of it are in large part correct and each provides excellent insights about the trade, neither offers a fully satisfactory solution.

Once properly understood, the publishing careers of East and his heirs shed new light on the whole issue of Elizabethan music publishing, the monopoly, and the demand for English printed music. Although, prior critical studies of East's output concede that after 1588 he was printing a steady flow of new musical works, these studies have tended to focus on the lack of reprints among his editions.[5] Without the recognition of East's and Snodham's hidden editions, the picture does indeed seem bleak. Not only is the overall number of reprints meager, but also the problem appears to affect all genres, including English madrigals that were once thought to be so much in demand. Once we include the hidden editions among the reprints, which is appropriate since they must now be seen as odd but genuine new editions, a different picture of the role and scope of reprinting emerges. East and his heirs engaged in a program of concealed reprinting that expands significantly the scope of their known music-printing enterprise. The legal disputes that involved both East and

Snodham show that whenever it was possible, both men were zealous to establish and defend their perceived right to publish music themselves. Engaged in by such seasoned businessmen, this effort would seem to speak volumes about the perceived profitability of the music printing and publishing enterprise.

East's career does reflect the deleterious effect of the monopoly yet also demonstrates that it was not foolproof. Whenever the monopoly was weakened and an opportunity arose, East and his heirs took advantage of this to produce more music editions than has hitherto been known. Since he registered so many of his books, it now seems likely that East produced even more hidden editions than the number extant today. A constraining factor, however, was surely the cost of paper and the limits on the supply of it that East seems to have been able to skim from former editions. After securing the rights to the various works, he and his heirs then had to make a critical assessment of the market in order to select for reprinting those titles that seemed most likely to sell well.

A new demand for the rather large number of works that he reprinted as hidden editions was surely the determining criterion for selection. After many years of experience in the music trade, East and his heirs were strategically well positioned to judge the Elizabethan and early Stuart market for printed music. Thus one of the trends that their hidden editions and other publications bring into focus is the workings of demand for music in the London marketplace. They show that the musical styles of the English madrigal and the lighter forms introduced by Morley were so well adapted to a wide audience that the composer himself could not control their dissemination, even with the power of the queen's patent on his side.

Finally, with some of its more restrictive features shown to be less effective than once thought, the English music monopoly itself, especially while it was in the hands of Byrd and Morley, seems to require new appraisal. The special care taken in the production of East's music books shows that both composers were keen not only to profit from their monopolies but also to achieve the best possible printed versions of their own music and the music of others. For this reason the patent holders also functioned as East's editors, but they did so from a uniquely powerful vantage point. In the Renaissance era, it was a very special circumstance that the editor was also the composer, who, in addition, had control over the printing of his music. How such authority translated into the actual musical notes, texts, and images on the printed page is sometimes quite difficult to determine, but whatever the result and however traditional the motivations of composer/editor, the implications were remarkably modern: musical ideas were deemed too valuable simply to be abandoned to the workings of a press, as they normally would be. At East's, on many occasions, composers were attentively and actively negotiating with the exigencies of print medium to affect the ways in which their music was ultimately presented to their publics. Shakespearean scholars would find this unusual, for it rarely occurred in dramatic texts of the time, but such authorial control over the press was almost routine during East's tenure as music printer—unlike the situation on the Continent, where musicians had such power only exceptionally—and it is an aspect of the monopoly that has been underestimated. Nevertheless, when the market was strong and the monopoly was weak, East was willing to jeopardize his relations with these composers. For his own profit the printer found a surreptitious but effective way, first through his hidden editions and later by using the technique of in-house publication, to keep these composers from obstructing the dissemination of their own works with costly fees and self-interested programs. Thus it was East and his heirs, on those occasions, who did the most to bring their music to the London public.

But any sweeping statements about the industry lose force in the realization that the publication process was so personalized by the monopoly. It is true that the mercenary and the musical goals of composer and printer were indelibly meshed. For his part, East found he could protect his economic privileges by promoting the nation's music. The composers, in turn, found that they needed the mercenary outlook of a city trader in order to market the art over which they exerted such control. But the ways in which these compromises manifested themselves reveal more about the individuality of the people in question than the strength of their basic motivations.

In the case of Byrd, the most revealing period was the mid-1590s, when he had moved to Essex. As we look back, it seems it was at this point that the equitable partnership between composer and printer began to dissolve. Byrd had published most of the music he had composed before 1588 during the remarkable years 1588–1591. Though he marked his move away form London with a publication of his Masses, surely a sign of a new direction in his work, he may have grown weary of meeting the constant compositional and editorial demands of an active music press. It is significant that his next engagement with the process did not occur until 1605. However one looks at it, the partners' interests in music publishing had grown far apart over the eight years of their management of the monopoly. East's penchant for independence and his plainly mercenary designs for music publishing became more and more evident as Byrd's interest in the London market began to wane. By the end of his patent period, Byrd had turned fairly sharply away from any commercial considerations; he clearly wished to explore how the press might be used to serve the illegal needs of his fellow recusant Catholics. He seemed perfectly willing to allow his student Morley to take his place as the reigning music monopolist in London.

As much as Byrd looked beyond the marketplace to fulfill his ambitions for the press, Morley was through and through the artist as entrepreneur. His true colors emerged when Byrd's patent officially expired in 1596. To mark the moment of free trade, Morley turned immediately away from East and found new partners among a group of printers who had been attracted to the formerly monopolized field. He then promoted a kind of music that was geared most carefully to the court in an obvious ploy to capture the grant for himself. Once Morley did obtain his own monopoly in September 1598, he kept his various marketing designs in place, but, unlike Byrd, he openly competed with members of the Stationers' Company for the sole rights to control the great market for psalms with music. In the end, it was Morley, more than anyone else, who led the music-publishing field into and through its most competitive phase in the Elizabethan/early Stuart era.

For his part, East reacted to the competitive environment by exploiting new markets of his own devising and inviting an otherwise neglected group of youthful aspiring musicians to his press. It was only in the early years of James I, when the Elizabethan monopolies were under pointed scrutiny, that East's more long-term designs for the music press finally rose to the surface. East's involvement in the elaborate scheme whereby the Stationers' Company used the king's patent to formalize a publishing conglomerate within its own ranks was a key feature of his music-publishing career. Thanks to his participation in the music trade, East quickly rose to new levels of importance within the company as this event took place. In an intracompany dispute, he helped to draw the music monopoly itself into the folds of the new publishing firm. Under company auspices, East enjoyed a position of unprecedented power in music publishing, but the victory also represented the end of a long period of shared powers among stationers and musicians.

When the music monopoly was folded into the company, it helped East to realize long-held ambitions. For musicologists, however, it marked the end of a very special moment in music history. When empowered by the queen's monopoly, musicians as important as Byrd and Morley encouraged or compelled East to make extraordinary uses of his press: to closely monitor their musical texts as they were transferred from manuscript to printed form before they were transmitted to the public, to mass-produce music for the illegal worship needs of the Catholic minority, and to direct and improve the musical tastes of the English nation generally. By focusing too narrowly on the quantitative superiority of its continental counterpart, scholars have depicted the English scene as anemic and dispirited. This book has found a very different situation: the music-publishing trade was a sharply competitive arena full of clever and ambitious entrepreneurs and composers. Musicians did indeed have the opportunity to advance their careers. They benefited not only in the standard way of "getting their name and their music out to the public" but also from the chance to explore a kind of protection for intellectual property and an extensive control over the editing of their music, precisely *because* of the unique privileges the queen bestowed on certain musicians.

East's special contribution to the field of music printing and publishing stemmed from his willingness to adapt to the twofold pressures of the monopolistic environment that confronted his trade. As a meticulous corrector of the texts he produced and as an adventurous spirit in the face of religious politics he amply met the particular demands of the musical luminaries, Byrd and Morley, who occasionally controlled his press. As a mercenary entrepreneur, however, East also helped to satisfy the very London public whose tastes established a system of mass consumerism in music. This more general public, willing, in a burgeoning capitalistic society, to buy music that suited its tastes, eventually gained the respectful attention of the elite musical community. This in turn created a base of support for the economic livelihood of a larger constituency of London's musicians as a whole. To East's credit, his efforts were almost equally divided between serving the most important needs of each of these groups—the public no less than the composer-monopolists.

ABBREVIATIONS AND SIGLA

Aberdeen University	Aberdeen University Library, Scotland
A.P.C.	*Acts of the Privy Council of England*
Archbishop Marsh's Library	Archbishop Marsh's Library, Dublin, Republic of Ireland
BE	William Byrd, *The Byrd Edition*, 20 vols. edited by Philip Brett (London: Stainer Bell, 1976–)
Bibliothèque nationale	Bibliothèque nationale, Paris, France
Bibliothèque Sainte-Geneviève	Bibliothèque Sainte-Geneviève, Paris, France
Bodleian Library	Oxford University Bodleian Library, Oxford, England
Boston Public Library	Boston Public Library, Massachusetts
Briquet	Charles-Moïse Briquet, *Les Filigranes, Dictionnaire historique des marques du papier des leur apparition vers 1282 jusque'en 1600. Avec 39 figures dans le texte et 16, 112 fac-similés de filigranes*, 4 vols., 2d ed. (New York: Hacker art Books, 1966)
British Library	British Library, London, England
Britten-Pears	Britten-Pears Library, Aldeburgh, England
Cal. S.P. Dom.	*Calendar of State Papers, Domestic Series*
Cal S.P. Scot.	*Calendar of the State Papers Relating to Scotland*
Cambridge University	Cambridge University Library, England
Chapin Library	Williams College Chapin Library, Williamstown, Massachusetts
Cashel Cathedral	GPA-Bolton Library, Cashel Cathedral, Ireland
Christ Church, Oxford	Oxford University Christ Church, England
Churchill	W. A. Churchill, *Watermarks in Paper in Holland, England, France, etc., in the XVII and XVIII Centuries and Their Interconnection*, 2d ed. (Amsterdam: M. Hertzberger, 1967)
Com.	compartment
DNB	*Dictionary of National Biography*, 21 vols. (London: Oxford University Press, 1917–1938)
Edinburgh	National Library of Scotland, Edinburgh
Edinburgh University	Edinburgh University Library, Scotland
ESTC	*English Short-Title Catalogue* (on-line) (London: British Library, 2000)

Folger Library	Folger Shakespeare Library, Washington, District of Columbia
Glasgow University	Glasgow University Library, Scotland
Hamburg	Hamburg Staats- und Universitätsbibliothek
Harvard University	Harvard University Libraries, Cambridge, Massachusetts
Heawood	Edward Heawood, *Watermarks, Mainly of the 17th and 18th Centuries*, 2d ed. (Hilversum: Paper Publications Society, 1969)
Huntington Library	Henry E. Huntington Library, San Marino, California
JAMS	*Journal of the American Musicological Society*
Jesus College, Oxford	Oxford University Jesus College, Oxford, England
John Rylands Library	John Rylands University Library of Manchester, England
Kassel	Murhard'sche Bibliothek der Stadt Kassel und Landesbibliothek
King's College, Cambridge	Cambridge University King's College, England
Kirwood	A.E.M. Kirwood, "Richard Field, Printer, 1589–1624," *The Library* 4th ser., vol. 12 (1931): 3–39
Lambeth Palace	Lambeth Palace Library, London, England
Library of Congress	Library of Congress, Washington, District of Columbia
Lincoln Cathedral	Lincoln Cathedral Library, England
Liverpool Central Library	Liverpool Central Libraries, England
Liverpool University	The University of Liverpool Library, England
Manchester Central Library	Manchester Central Library, England
McKerrow	Ronald B. McKerrow, *Printers' and Publishers' Devices in England & Scotland 1485–1640* (London: Bibliographical Society, 1913)
McKerrow & Ferguson	Ronald B. McKerrow and F. S. Ferguson, *Title-Page Borders Used in England & Scotland 1485–1640* (London: Bibliographical Society, 1932)
Meynell & Morison	Francis Meynell and Stanley Morison, "Printers' Flowers and Arabesques," *Fleuron* 1 (1923): 1–43
Nederlands Muziek Instituut	Nederlands Muziek Instituut, den Haag
Newberry Library	Newberry Library, Chicago, Illinois
New South Wales	State Library of New South Wales, Sydney, Australia
New York Public Library	New York Public Library, New York
NG	*The New Grove Dictionary of Music and Musicians*, 29 vols., edited by Stanley Sadie and John Tyrell (New York: Grove, 2001)
Orn.	ornaments (including headpieces, tailpieces, devices, etc.)
Plomer	Henry R. Plomer, *English Printers' Ornaments* (London: Grafton, 1924)

Princeton University	Princeton University Library, Princeton, New Jersey
PRO	Public Records Office, London
RISM	*Repertoire internationale des sources musicales*
Royal Academy of Music	Royal Academy of Music Library, London, England
Royal College of Music	Royal College of Music Library, London, England
Ti.	title-page border
tp	title page
Trinity College, Cambridge	Cambridge University Trinity College, England
STC2	Alfred Pollard, *A Short-Title Catalogue of Books Printed in England, Scotland, & Ireland and of English Books Printed Abroad 1475–1640*, 2d ed., 3 vols., revised and enlarged, begun by W. A. Jackson and F. S. Ferguson, completed by Katherine F. Pantzer (London: Bibliographical Society, 1976–1991)
University of Birmingham	University of Birmingham Library, England
University of Illinois	University of Illinois Library, Urbana
University of London	University of London Library, Senate House
University of Michigan	University of Michigan Library, Ann Arbor
Western Reserve	Western Reserve Library, Cleveland, Ohio
Woodfield	Denis Woodfield, *Surreptitious Printing in England 1550–1640* (New York: Bibliographical Society of America, 1973)
Yale University	Yale University Libraries, New Haven, Connecticut
York Minster	York Minster Library, York, England

*STC*2 LIBRARY SIGLA

The British Library, London (L), Royal College of Music, London (L7), London University (L30), Cambridge University Library (C), Trinity College, Cambridge (C2), Bodleian Library, Oxford (O), Christ Church Library, Oxford (O3), Edinburgh University Library (E2), Aberdeen University Library (A), University of Glasgow Library (G2), Lincoln Cathedral, Lincoln (LINC), York Minster Library, York (YK), Central Library, Manchester (M3), Archbishop Marsh's Library, Dublin (D2), Bibliothèque nationale, Paris (PARIS), Folger Shakespeare Library, Washington, D.C. (F), Huntington Library, San Marino (HN), Library of Congress, Washington, D.C. (LC), Harvard University (HD), University of Illinois, Urbana (ILL), Newberry Library, Chicago (N).

APPENDIX 1
TABLES

TABLE A1.1   MUSIC EDITIONS PRINTED BY THOMAS EAST

Composer/Publisher	Short title	Date	STC2 #
William Byrd	*Psalmes, Sonets & Songs*	1588	4253
Nicholas Yonge (pub.)	*Musica Transalpina I*	1588	26094
William Byrd	*A Gratification vnto John Case*	1589	4246
William Byrd	*Cantiones Sacrae I*	1589	4247
William Byrd	*Songs of Sundrie Natures*	1589	4256
Thomas Watson (pub.)	*Italian Madrigalls Englished*	1590	25119
Thomas Whythourne	*Duos, or Songs for Two Voices*	1590	25583
William Byrd	*Cantiones Sacrae II*	1591	4248
William Damon	*The Former Booke of the Musicke*	1591	6220
William Damon	*The Second Booke of the Musicke*	1591	6221
John Farmer	*Diuers & Sundry Waies*	1591	10698
Thomas East (pub.)	*Whole Booke of Psalmes*	1592	2482
William Byrd	*Mass a 4*	[c. 1593]	4250
Thomas Morley	*Canzonets a 3*	1593	18121
Thomas East (pub.)	*Whole Booke of Psalmes*	1594	2482
William Byrd	*Mass a 3*	[c. 1593–1594]	4249
John Mundy	*Songs and Psalmes*	1594	18284
Thomas Morley	*Madrigalls to Foure Voyces*	1594	18127
Thomas Morley	*First Book of Balletts*	1595	18116
Thomas Morley	*Il Primo Libro delle Ballette*	1595	18118
Thomas Morley	*First Book of Canzonets a 2*	1595	18119
William Byrd	*Mass a 5*	[c. 1595]	4251
William Bathe	*A Brief Introduction to the Skill of Song*	[1596]	1589
Charles Tessier	*Chansons*	1597	23918
George Kirbye	*English Madrigalls*	1597	15010
Thomas Weelkes	*Madrigals*	1597	25205
Nicholas Yonge (pub.)	*Musica Transalpina II*	1597	26095
John Bull	*Oration*	1597	4032.5
Orlando di Lasso	*Novæ Aliquot*	1598	15265
Thomas Morley (pub.)	*Madrigals to Fiue Voyces*	1598	18129
Thomas Weelkes	*Balletts and Madrigals*	1598	25203
John Wilbye	*First Set of English Madrigals*	1598	25619.5
William Byrd	*Psalmes, Sonets & Songs*ᵃ	[c. 1599–1600]	not in STC2
John Dowland	*Second Booke of Songs*	1600	7095
Thomas Morley	*First Booke of Balletts* (2d ed.)	1600	18117

continued

TABLE A1.1   *Continued*

Composer/Publisher	Short title	Date	STC₂ #
Thomas Weelkes	*Madrigals of 5 & 6 Parts*	1600	25206
Thomas Morley	*Madrigals to Fovre Voices* (2d ed.)	1600	18127
Thomas Morley (pub.)	*Triumphes of Oriana*	1601	18130
Thomas Morley	*Canzonets a 3* (2d ed.)	1602	18122
Thomas Robinson	*Schoole of Mvsicke*	1603	21128
Thomas East (pub.)	*Whole Booke of Psalmes*	1604	2515
Thomas East (pub.)	*Whole Booke of Psalmes*ᵇ	1604	2514
Michael East	*Madrigales*	1604	7460
Thomas Bateson	*English Madrigales*	1604	1586
William Byrd	*Gradualia I*	1605	4243.5
Francis Pilkerton	*Songs or Ayres*	1605	19922
John Danyel	*Songs for Lvte*	1606	6268
Thomas Morley	*Canzonets a 3* (3d ed.)	1606	18123
William Byrd	*Psalmes, Sonets & Songs*ᵈ	[c. 1606–1607]	4254
Thomas East	*Whole Booke of Psalmes*ᶜ	1607	2522.3
William Byrd	*Gradualia II*	1607	4244.5
Giovanni Croce	*Musica Sacra*	1608	6040
Thomas Weelkes	*Balletts and Madrigals*	1608	25204
Henry Youll	*Canzonets*	1608	26105

NOTES: This list is based on the editions cited in the STC₂ and includes extant editions only. It does not include East's hidden editions, which appear in Table A1.2. Allan Sopher provides a list of the editions East registered in the Stationers' Company entrance books but for which no copies now exist (these "ghosts" are not reflected in the table, although it is entirely possible that East produced them); see "A Handlist of Works Printed by Thomas East" (Diploma in Librarianship diss., University of London, 1959), 51. Musical editions in Sopher's list of ghosts include: Thomas Morley's *Canzonets to Two Voices* [Italian version], Nathaniel Patrick's *Songs of Sundry Natures*, Thomas Robinson's *Medulla Music*, William Byrd and Alfonso Ferrabosco's *Medulla Musicke*, and John Wilbye's *Lessons for the Lute*.

ᵃ With copies in Britten-pears and the Knowsley collection of the University of Liverpool (an imperfect superius part-book—[A]1, tp and A1 verso).

ᵇ This is a quarto edition with monophonic settings of the metrical psalms.

ᶜ This is a folio edition with monophonic settings of the metrical psalms, printed by East and John Windet.

ᵈ See chapter 3 for a discussion of this undated work and the theory that it was printed in 1606–1607.

TABLE A1.2   HIDDEN EDITIONS BY THOMAS EAST

Composer, Short title	Nominal Date	Probable Date	STC2 #
Byrd, *Psalmes, Sonets & Songs*	1588	1588	4253.5
Byrd, *Psalmes, Sonets & Songs*	1588	1588	4253.7
Yonge (pub.), *Musica Transalpina I*	1588	1593–1594	26094.5
Byrd, *Songs of Sundrie Natures*	1589	1596–1597	4256.5
Morley, *Canzonets a 3*	1593	1596–1597	not in STC2
Byrd, *Mass a 4*	n.d.	1599–1600	4249.5
Byrd, *Mass a 3*	n.d.	1599–1600	4250.5
Morley, *First Booke of Balletts*	1595	1605–1606	not in STC2
Morley (pub.), *Triumphes of Oriana*	1601	1605–1606	18130.5
Wilbye, *First Set of English Madrigals*	1598	1605–1606	25619
Wilbye, *First Set of English Madrigals*	1598	1610–1611	25619.3
Morley, *Madrigals to Fovre Voices* (2d ed.)	1600	1610–1611	not in STC2

NOTES: *STC2* lists the repositories where copies of hidden editions are currently held but only for those that appear in the catalog. See "Checklist of music printed by Thomas East" in appendix 4 for the repositories with copies of hidden editions not listed in the *STC2*.

TABLE AI.3   DATING EAST'S MUSIC EDITIONS BY HIS USE OF PAPER

Composer, Short title	Mark	Run/Remn.	Edition type	Nominal date	Probable date
Byrd, *Psalmes, Sonets & Songs*	*Circle* IB	run	original	1588	1588
Byrd, *Songs of Sundrie Natures*	*Circle* IB	remnant	original	1589	1589
Byrd, *Cantiones Sacrae I*	*Crown*IB	run	original	1589	1589
Byrd, *Songs of Sundrie Natures*	*Crown*IB	remnant	original	1589	1589
Damon, *Former Booke . . .*	*Fleur-de-lis* 1a	run	verifying	1591	1591
Byrd, *Mass a 4*	*Fleur-de-lis* 1a	run	original	n.d.	1592–1593
Yonge, *Musica Transalpina I*	*Fleur-de-lis* 1a	run	hidden	1588	1592–1593
Damon, *Former Booke . . .*	*Fleur-de-lis* 1b	run	verifying	1591	1591
Damon, *Second Booke . . .*	*Fleur-de-lis* 1b	run	verifying	1591	1591
Byrd, *Mass a 3*	*Fleur-de-lis* 1b	run	original	n.d.	1592–1593
Byrd, *Mass a 4*	*Fleur-de-lis* 1b	run	original	n.d.	1592–1593
Morley, *Il Primo . . . Ballette*	*Letters*GB	run	verifying	1595	1595
Morley, *First . . . Canzonets a 2*	*Letters*GB	run	verifying	1595	1595
Byrd, *Songs of Sundrie Natures*	*Letters*GB	run	hidden	1589	1596–1597
Morley, *Canzonets a 3*	*Letters*GB	run	hidden	1593	1596–1597
Kirbye, *English Madrigalls*	*Letters*GB	remnant	verifying	1597	1597
Tessier, *Chansons*	*Letters*GB	remnant	verifying	1597	1597
Byrd, *Songs of Sundrie Natures*	*Letters*AM	token remn.	hidden	1589	1596–1597
Morley, *Canzonets a 3*	*Letters*AM	token remn.	hidden	1593	1596–1597
Morley, *First Booke of Balletts*	*Pot*PBD	run	original	1595	1595
Weelkes, *Madrigals*	*Pot*PBD	run	verifying	1597	1597
Yonge, *Musica Transalpina II*	*Pot*PBD	run	verifying	1597	1597
Weelkes, *Balletts and Madrigals*	*Crown* 1	token remn.	verifying	1598	1598
Wilbye, *First Set . . . Madrigals*	*Crown* 1	token remn.	original	1598	1598
Weelkes, *Balletts and Madrigals*	*Fleur-de-lis & Star*	run	verifying	1598	1598
Wilbye, *First Set . . . Madrigals*	*Fleur-de-lis & Star*	run	verifying	1598	1598
Byrd, *Mass a 3*	*Fleur-de-lis & Star*	run	hidden	n.d.	1599–1600
Byrd, *Mass a 4*	*Fleur-de-lis & Star*	run	hidden	n.d.	1599–1600
di Lasso, *Novæ Aliquot*	*Grapes*	run	verifying	1598	1598
Byrd, *Psalmes, Sonets & Songs*	*Grapes*	run	undated	n.d.	1599–1600
Weelkes, *Madrigals of 5 & 6 Parts*	*Crown & Oval*	run	verifying	1600	1600
Morley, *Madrigalls to Fovr Voices* (2d ed.)	*Crown & Oval*	run	original	1600	1600

continued

TABLE A1.3   *Continued*

Composer, Short title	Mark	Run/Remn.	Edition type	Nominal date	Probable date
Morley (pub.), *Triumphes* . . .	Crown 2	run	original	1601	1601
Morley, *Canzonets a 3* (2d ed.)	Crown 2	run	verifying	1602	1602
Morley, *First Booke of Balletts except* Cantus, Altus, Quintus, C	Crown 2	run	hidden	1595	1605–1606
East, M., *Madrigales*	Fleur-de-lis 3	run	verifying	1604	1604
Morley, *Canzonets a 3* (3d ed.)	Fleur-de-lis 3	run	verifying	1606	1606
Morley, *First Booke of Balletts only* Cantus, Altus, Quintus, C	Fleur-de-lis 3	token remn.	hidden	1595	1605–1606
Youll, *Canzonets*	Fleur-de-lis 3	run	verifying	1608	1608
Bateson, *English Madrigales*	Crown 3	run	verifying	1604	1604
Morley (pub.), *Triumphes* . . .	Crown 3	run	hidden	1601	1605–1606
Wilbye, *First Set . . . Madrigals*	Crown 3	run	hidden	1598	1605–1606
Morley, *First Booke of Balletts*	Crown 3	remnant	hidden	1595	1605–1606
Bateson, *English Madrigales*	LetterR	run	verifying	1604	1604
Morley (pub.), *Triumphes*	LetterR	run	hidden	1601	1605–1606
Wilbye, *First Set . . . Madrigals*	LetterR	run	hidden	1598	1605–1606
Croce, *Musica Sacra*	Shield & Castle	run	verifying	1608	1608
Wilbye, *Second Set . . . Madrigales*	Shield & Castle	run	verifying	1609	1609
Wilbye, *First Set . . . Madrigals*	Shield & Castle	remnant	hidden	1598	1610–1611
Morley, *Madrigals to Fovre Voices* (2d ed.)	ShieldFM	run	hidden	1600	1610–1611
Wilbye, *First Set . . . Madrigals*	SheildFM	run	hidden	1598	1610–1611

N O T E S : In this table East's music editions with similar marks are listed together. The list includes hidden editions that are falsely dated, the original editions they were based on, and the prints used to establish the actual date of printing. The editions outside of the group of hidden editions and their originals are listed as "verifying" editions. Where the mark signifies a "run," there were frequent recurrences of the mark in the edition. "Remnants" and "token remnants" signify small quantities of paper that occurred infrequently in the edition. See "Checklist of music printed by Thomas East" in appendix 4 for the specific locations of paper within the editions.

TABLE A1.4   EAST'S LARGE-SCALE REGISTRATION OF MUSIC BOOKS IN 1596

Composer, Short title	Date
Byrd, *Psalmes, Sonets & Songs*	1588
Yonge, *Musica Transalpina*	1588
Byrd, *Cantiones Sacrae I*	1589
Byrd, *Songs of Sundrie Natures*	1589
Watson (pub.), *Italian Madrigalls Englished*	1590
Byrd, *Cantiones Sacrae II*	1591
Morley, *Canzonets a 3*	1593
Mundy, *Songs and Psalms*	1594
Morley, *Madrigalls to Fovre Voyces*	1594
Morley, *First Booke of Balletts* (English and Italian)	1595
Morley, *First Book of Canzonets* (English and Italian)	1595

SOURCE: Edward Arber (ed.), *A Transcript of the Registers of the Company of Stationers of London, 1554–1640 A.D.*, 5 vols. (Birmingham: The editor, 1875–1894), vol. 3, 76–77.

TABLE A1.5 CHRONOLOGY OF ELIZABETHAN MUSIC PUBLISHING, 1575–1611

Time Line	Music Monopoly and Its Personnel	Recognition in the Imprint	Registrations at Stationers' Hall	Hidden Editions (Production)
1575	1575 Grant to Tallis and Byrd	1575 Vautrollier prints as the assign of Byrd and Tallis		
1580				
1585	1585 Tallis dies		1587 East registers Byrd's *Psalmes, Sonets & Songs*	
	1588 Byrd begins publishing music	1588–c. 1593 East prints as the assign of Byrd	1588–1596 No registrations	
1590				
	c. 1593 Byrd moves to Essex; Morley begins to publish his own music	c. 1593–1596 East does not mention Byrd as the patentee (except in *STC2* 18284)		c. 1593–1594 *Musica Transalpina* (with Byrd's undated Masses)
1595				
	1596–1599 *Gap in patent ownership*	1596–1600 No patentee is mentioned	1596 East registers 13 preprinted music books	c. 1596–1597 1. Byrd's *Songs* 2. Morley's *Canzonets a 3*
	1597–1599 Morley lobbies for patent, prints with Barley		1597–1600 East registers 6 music books before printing	
	1599 Morley is granted patent			c. 1599–1600 1. Byrd's *Mass a 3* 2. Byrd's *Mass a 4*
1600	1600 Morley makes contracts with East and Short	1600–1602 East and Short print as the assigns of Morley	1600 East registers 1 book (of 4 produced that year) Dowland's *Second Booke*	
	1602 Morley dies			
	1603–1606 *Gap in patent ownership*	1603–1606 No mention of the patent	1603 East registers 5 books (1 preprinted and 4 before printing)	c. 1604–1605 1. *Triumphes* 2. Wilbye's *Madrigals* 3. Morley's *Balletts*

continued

TABLE A1.5 *Continued*

Time Line	Music Monopoly and Its Personnel	Recognition in the Imprint	Registrations at Stationers' Hall	Hidden Editions (Production)
1606	1606 Barley acquires patent and makes an agreement with East 1608 East dies	1606–1608 East prints as the assign of Barley 1609 East's heirs print music as assignees of Barley	1606–1608 East registers all music books before printing	
1610	1610 Lucretia East sells music property to John Browne		1610 John Browne registers East's former music property	c. 1610–1611 Thomas Snodham prints 1. Morley's *Madrigals* 2. Wilbye's *Madrigals*
1611	1611 Formation of the partnership of Snodham, Browne, and Lownes	1611–1614 Infrequent mention of Barley's patent	1611 Official transferral of Browne's property to the partnership of Snodham, Browne, and Lownes	

APPENDIX 2
OBSERVATIONS ON TYPOGRAPHICAL VARIANTS
AMONG EAST'S HIDDEN EDITIONS
AND THEIR ORIGINALS

Although they were completely reset, East's hidden editions have a striking visual similarity to the original editions on which they were modeled. The gathering structures of hidden editions tend to mimic the first edition. They most often have the same line endings, and nearly every piece in the hidden edition is headed by a decorative initial of the same design as that of the original volume.[1] There were some substantial changes between editions, but most of the variants were relatively minor: some small errors were mended (and, of course, a few new errors crept into new editions); spellings of words varied greatly in many cases; placements of accidentals in the music and stem directions for notes on the middle line also varied often.[2]

Hidden editions of smaller books (in terms of their paper and content) generally seem to have the most in common with their exemplars. These include the two editions of Byrd's Masses, Wilbye's *Madrigals*, Morley's *Canzonets a 3*, *Madrigals to Fovr Voices*, *Balletts*, and the modestly sized *Triumphes of Oriana*.[3] Of these, however, the *Triumphes* and the hidden editions of Wilbye's *Madrigals* do have significant variants in the hidden editions that may be seen to distinguish them more readily from their originals. Hidden editions of the larger anthologies, that is, Byrd's *Psalmes*, his *Songs*, and Yonge's *Musica Transalpina*, tend to deviate more noticeably from their original editions.

East may have had special, but as yet undetermined, reasons to closely imitate certain works more than others, but it is also possible that the more extensive anthologies simply presented more opportunities for unintentional (or incidental) compositorial variance.[4] Unlike in other hidden editions, the types of changes in Byrd's *Psalmes* volumes, however, indicate that the new volumes were produced to fulfill an editorial, rather than an economic, need.[5] The remaining works have relatively fewer changes, and even though some intentional amendments were made to them as a matter of course, the works were most likely reprinted to address a rise in consumer demand for the music of each volume.

The following discussion is intended only as a preliminary guide to patterns discovered in certain variants among editions and as a treatment of some more substantial changes. Small changes (discovered in a cursory comparison of these volumes) among the editions may have been unintentional or might have been the result of the individual habits and inclinations of different music compositors. Among these, patterns were discovered that seemed to be prominent enough to warrant discussion. These tend to occur with particular pairs of hidden editions and may further reveal how closely the editions of such pairs followed each other in East's schedule.

The method of setting musical accidentals among the original and hidden editions of Morley's *Canzonets a 3* and Byrd's *Songs* was handled similarly. In the two hidden editions accidentals were placed almost exclusively to the left of the note in question (whereas in the original editions of both volumes they were usually set above or below the note). East owned two kinds of type for setting musical accidentals: a conglomerate piece, which consisted of the note and its accidental above or below it with staff lines; and a piece that contained only the accidental and the staff lines that had to be combined with the note in question. It was the latterly described piece that had to be placed to the left of the note. The compositors of hidden editions had to account for the extra space they added to the musical line in each case when they used accidentals. Due to this tendency (caused perhaps by the limited array of type in a particular worker's case), many slight changes in text settings obtained between the original settings and the hidden editions. Occasionally the additional space was sufficient to cause the line to end in a different place in the hidden edition than in the original setting. When this happened, however, the compositor made the requisite adjustments to ensure that the next line ended in the same place as the original.[6]

Another pattern of note among variants was discovered in the pair of hidden editions created at Thomas Snodham's shop sometime around 1610 or 1611. In the original editions of Morley's *Madrigalls to Fovre Voices* and Wilbye's *First Set of English Madrigals*, the compositors followed a policy of presenting every note placed on the middle line of the staff with its stem facing upward. In the hidden editions, however, this policy was frequently ignored.[7] Despite the fact that the orthography and other typographical details of the original were followed especially closely in these latter works, notes on the middle staff line were rather often set with their stems facing downward.

Patterns of accidentals and stem directions among East's and his heirs' editions may eventually prove of some value for explaining broader issues that surround their careers. It is possible, for example, to hypothesize from the two patterns in the variants noted earlier that the two hidden editions in each case were set by the same compositor and/or were produced concurrently.[8]

LARGE-SCALE CHANGES

There are major typographical changes between the hidden editions and their originals, most of which have been hitherto discovered by other music bibliographers.[9] In his study of Byrd's *Psalmes*, H. K. Andrews discussed in detail the changes in mensuration sigla among its different editions.[10] He argued persuasively that these changes were made to correct the music of the first edition. These editorial changes stemmed from Byrd's preferences as the composer of the music. They were changes, as argued here, that he could impose on East because of his position as music monopolist. Although conclusions to this effect must ultimately remain hypothetical, it is salutary to attempt to determine whose interests were served by the intentional changes in other volumes.

In the *Musica Transalpina* editions, a problem was created in the original volume that seemed to be of greater concern to the printer than to the composer. In the first edition, Alfonso Ferrabosco's "Susanne Faire" was cast-off and printed on one page in the cantus part, whereas the work appeared on two pages in all other parts (see *STC2* 20694: cantus; C2). Consequently, the Ferrabosco work and the version of "Sussane Fair" by Orlando di Lasso that followed it were placed in a different order in that part. Although they are numbered 19 and 20 throughout the edition, the two works in question appear out of order (20, 19) in the cantus book of the original edition.

In the table of the Cantus part of the original edition, performers were instructed to "sing this [the Lasso "Sussane"] for the 19. song" (*STC2* 20694; cantus; H4v). This may have served to alert musicians to the problem. It probably created extra work for East's compositors, however. In other parts, the table was a page of type that had been left standing during production. As noted elsewhere in this study, because East followed vertical printing methods in his production of music in part-book format the use of standing type made his work more efficient. To accommodate the different text of the cantus table (as well as the nonconforming layout of the whole part-book), however, East's workers had to stop presswork and reset the type before machining the sheets. It is probably significant, therefore, that when the entire work was reset the madrigals in the cantus part were recast to conform to the order of other parts. Methods of vertical printing could be accomplished more effectively at the press for the hidden edition after the cantus book was brought into conformity with the other parts (see *STC2* 20694.5; cantus; C).

In the two hidden editions of Wilbye's *Madrigals,* the dedication page that appeared in all parts of the original edition was reprinted only in the tenor and sextus parts (see *STC2* 25619 and 25619.7). On the one hand, it is possible that the dedication page was excised from some part-books and kept in others to simplify the printing process.[11] On the other hand, since the original dedicatee no longer had a role in the publishing process of the hidden edition, it is possible that this change was made to correct a misconception about the proper dedicatee (an issue about which East and Snodham were obviously not overly concerned, since they retained the dedication page in two part books of Wilbye's editions).

A different madrigal verse for George Kirbye's contribution to the *Triumphes* appears in the hidden edition (see madrigal 20 of the *Triumphes* in *STC2* 18130 and *STC2* 18130.5 [D4v]). The original version contained the poem "Bright Phoebus Greets More Clearly," but this poem was replaced by a poem that began "With Angel's Face and Brightness" in the second (hidden) edition.[12] In an edition of Kirbye's music, Edmund H. Fellowes noted that the latter poem was also set by Daniel Norcombe (madrigal 1) in the *Triumphes.* Fellowes suggested that Morley or East may have therefore substituted the new verse in the original setting of the edition to avoid a duplication of texts in the anthology. Fellowes's further hypothesis was that Kirbye "resented the substitution of other words, which certainly much marred the subtler points of his madrigal, and that the original words were replaced as a result of his protest."[13] Such a scenario, if difficult indeed to prove, is certainly within the realm of reasonable conjecture.

Finally, it has been of great service to modern bibliographers that some of the hidden editions produced after 1594 were based on original editions of 1588–1593. It was sometime after 1594 that East completely changed his practice of setting works in imperfect mensuration with a cut C and began using C instead. As noted by Andrews and Clulow, East's consistent use of C in the hidden editions of Byrd's *Songs of Sundrie Natures* and Morley's *Canzonets* neatly sets them apart them from their originals. It also establishes their *terminus post quem.* It is Andrews's intriguing theory that when East thoroughly changed his house style after 1594 it was at the urging of Morley, whose influence over East's press was strong at this time and whose theoretical work dealt extensively with mensural practices.[14]

Appendix 3
The East-Hassell-Snodham-Field
Connection

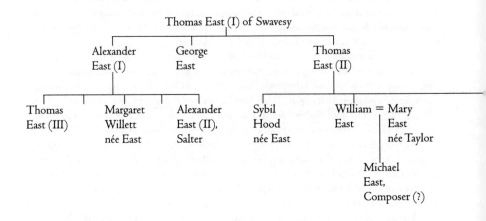

NOTES: This table is an abridged version of data that was provided in part by Faith Keymer, who has kindly given permission for its use. For more details on the East family, including the theory that Michael East was Thomas East's nephew, see F. Keymer, "Thomas East, Citizen & Stationer of London: The Reconstruction of a Tudor Family Using Public Records," *PROphile* 11 (2000): 3–10. The best source of information about the Hassell family is the original will of Agnes Hassell née Lamotte (Guildhall Library, Commissary Court of London, Ms 9172/10d f. 143). Lucretia East née Hassell listed Richard Field (II) and Thomas Field (II) as her beneficiaries in her will of 1627 (Great Britain, Public Records Office, London, Probate Records, PROB 11/56/61, "Will of Lucretia East," 1627). Although I suspect they were related, I have thus far found no connections between these Fields and the stationer Richard Field who married Jacqueline Vautrollier, a music printer's widow, in 1587.

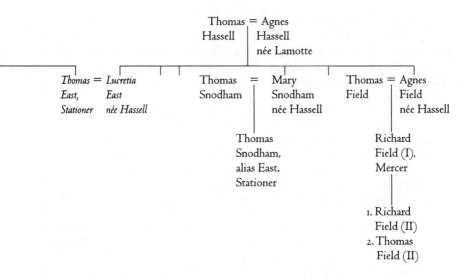

APPENDIX 4
CHECKLIST OF MUSIC EDITIONS
PRINTED BY THOMAS EAST

This checklist provides a bibliographical overview of East's musical production.[1] A complete census of the extant copies proved to be an unattainable goal. The effort to reach it did prove fruitful, however, in identifying a considerable number of uncataloged items that I have used to supplement the works indexed in *RISM, ESTC, STC2*, and individual research library catalogs. With these augmented lists in hand I could identify the whereabouts of a large number of East's works for in situ study. For many of the copies that I was unable to consult, I received invaluable information from many kind research librarians and researchers at various locations here and abroad.

The chronology of East's musical production is a crucial part of the printer's professional biography. This list was designed in part to present evidence for my theories about the chronological aspects of East's production. Undated works, including both editions of Byrd's Masses, for example, are listed where bibliographical evidence suggests they fall in East's output. Another function, prompted by the mimetic nature of East's hidden editions and the misrepresentations of publishing status among his reissues, is to present in close proximity those of East's editions with special relationships (pointing up bibliographical features they have, or fail to have, in common, e.g., typography versus paper). The main citation for a hidden edition or a reissue appears with a subheading ("a" or "b") under the original edition with which it shares bibliographical material. Hidden editions are also relisted (by short title only) in their appropriate place according to their time of printing.

There are five basic descriptive components for each edition in the list: (1) a quasi-facsimile title-page transcription; (2) a statement of collation; (3) an identification of the paper stock via watermarks; (4) a list of locations and shelfmarks of known copies; and (5) an *STC2, ESTC*, and *RISM* listing, wherever applicable. Each title-page transcription (1) and statement of collation (2) is based on a representative copy (or copies) within the edition (the separate part-books are noted within parentheses). Throughout the list, line endings are indicated with an " | " symbol, the long "s" appears as "ſ" in the transcription, and "vv" is not resolved to "w" (ligatures and abbreviations, however, have been silently realized). Ornaments, compartments, and title-page borders that appear in the title pages are described later. An abbreviated reference to the description of the ornament (compartment or title-page border) appears within parentheses in the title-page transcription (as Orn. 1, Com. 1, Ti. 1., etc.). In some cases, East reset more than just the heading of a part-book in an edition. For these I have included a separate transcription of the dissimilar material in these part-books beneath the main transcription (I should quickly report that I doubt very much that I have discovered all such cases of variance). Part-books listed within brackets are the surprisingly few books among East's editions that apparently no longer exist. Three of East's editions were reissued by Humphrie Lownes (*44a, 47a, 52a*). For reasons that are explained in the note of *44a*, my transcriptions of these works are based on one specific title page among the part-books.

Watermarks that help to distinguish a paper stock of East's musical editions are described in some detail below the collation statement. To describe them, I have used the methods of watermark identification suggested by Stephen Spector.[2] A statement of the watermark's design is followed by its measurements (height by width in millimeters); unmarked paper is provided with an approximate measurement of the chainlines. East used quarto format most often for music printing. In this format, the mark will usually appear on two separate pages of a single gathering. In these cases, I have described both "halves" of the mark with semicolons separating them and provided measurements set against the attendant chainlines, with brackets indicating the two chainlines that stand near the perimeter of the mark. The "|" character is used to indicate chainlines that fall within the mark's design. Following the description of the mark and its measurements, there is a note of an extant copy with those specific features (the nature of watermark evidence prohibits any sweeping statements about the similarity among marks in other copies of the edition). This is occasionally followed by: (1) a reference to a standard book of watermark tracings, (2) a similar description of other important marks in the edition, or (3) a discussion of other aspects of the paper stock.

In the list of locations, I have attempted to include the precise shelfmark of the specific copy (within parentheses) as well as to list the part-books that are held in that collection. It certain cases, it has also been possible to report something about the condition of the books in question. Many, but not all, of the editions of this list are briefly listed in *STC2*, the recently developed on-line version of this resource, *ESTC* (which is relatively new but designed eventually to replace the *STC2*), and *RISM*. The final component of each description is a listing of the relevant reference number for each of East's editions that appear in these resources.

ORNAMENTS, COMPARTMENTS, AND TITLE-PAGE BORDERS
Ornaments (Including Headpieces, Tailpieces, Strips, Devices, Printer's Marks, etc.) (Orn.)

1. 110 x 84, crest of Sir Christopher Hatton with "Pro cerva charrissima et gratissimus hinnulus" (a smaller version is McKerrow 229)
2. 17 x 45, King David with lyre in center flanked by men playing horns
3. 6 x 55, strip with initials ER flanked by two 6 x 7 fleur-de-lis
4. 6 x 55, strip with fleur-de-lis flanked by two 6 x 7 honeycombs (in Plomer 23)
5. 6 x 55, strip with repeating ribbon design and a rose in center (Woodfield D18) flanked by two 6 x 7 roses
5a. 6 x 54, Orn. 5 flanked by two 6 x 7 roses in fuller bloom
6. 17 x 44, winged figures holding a crowned globe
7. 25 x 25, mask with branches and scrollwork
8. 16 x 44, crowned rose with spray
9. 26 x 105, winged boy flanked by devils blowing flames in spray (in double-ruled frame)
10. 21 x 102; vase (center) with "A" scrolls, boys in foliage, squirrels, and other small animals (Plomer 50 & Kirwood.7)
11. 6 x 63, strip of repeating chains flanked by two 6 x 7 stars (in Plomer 22)
12. 16 x 44, mask in spray with dragons at sides
13. 59 x 50, rake, pitchfork, and scythe in grass with "Sed adhuc mea messis in herba est" (McKerrow 305)
14. 28 x 112, (Humphrie Lownes's) Tetragrammaton, plumed heads at corners (McKerrow & Ferguson 179, 180 top compartment only)
15. 6 x 72, (Humphrie Lownes's) strip with masks and flowers
16. 20 x 45, (Humphrie Lownes's), King David with lyre at center with scrollwork, masks and fruit at sides (in McKerrow & Ferguson 181)

Compartments (Com.)

1. 23 x 107, a single strand of 6 x 9 fleuron type ornaments (Plomer 66)
2. 22 x 60, scrollwork with crowned flowers in corners
3. 24 x 58, scrollwork with tassels

Title-Page Borders (Ti.)

1. 192 x 132, strand of 6 x 9 fleuron type ornaments (Plomer 66) with compartment at top
1a. 190 x 132, Ti. 1 without compartment
2. 176 x 112 (to 188 x 128), four horizontal strips: Orn. 5 and Orn. 6 (top and bottom); four vertical strips: 87 x 6 repeating flowers, vines and bells (sides)
3. 169 x 114, Royal Arms, Fame, Victory, Stationers' Arms, lion and dragon. Initials HD (Henry Denham) at bottom (formerly HB: Henry Bynneman) (McKerrow & Ferguson 160 [b])
4. 140 x 83, Com. 2 (top), Com. 3 (bottom); 140 x 10, 3 vases of roses, bottom vase is hand-held (right-hand side); 140 x 10, 3 vases of acorns, strawberries, roses, bottom vase is hand-held (left-hand side)
5. 193 x 133, single strand of 6 x 9 (or 9 x 6) fleuron type ornaments (Meynell & Morison 19) in a ruled frame, with compartments at top and bottom
6. 193 x 129 half-strand of 6 x 9 (or 9 x 6) fleuron type ornaments (Meynell & Morison 19) in a ruled frame
7. 193 x 129, double strand of 6 x 9 (or 9 x 6) fleuron type ornaments (Meynell & Morison 19) in a ruled frame, with top and bottom compartments and two calligraphic ornaments of four ovals (under the top compartment and above the bottom compartment)
7a. 190 x 126, Ti. 7, without ornaments
7b. 191 x 130, Ti. 7, with uneven strands of fleuron ornaments at sides and an index finger under the top compartment (only)
7c. 190 x 129, Ti. 7, with five-point star ornaments for both compartments
7d. 191 x 129, Ti. 7c, with two index fingers pointing toward the part-book headings in the bottom compartment
8. 185 x 125, single strand of 6 x 9 (or 9 x 6) fleuron type ornaments (Meynell & Morison 19) in a ruled frame, with a top compartment and a calligraphic ornament of four ovals under the part-book heading
8a. 185 x 127 (width ranging from 115 to 128), Ti. 8, with an index finger under the part-book heading
8b. 185 x 129, Ti. 8, with a five-point star under the part-book heading
9. *c*150 x 102, single strand of 6 x 9 (or 9 x 6) fleuron type ornaments (the top section is cut off in the original)
10. 269 x 178, cherubs holding cornucopias, David with lyre and Samson in bottom panels, compartments at top and bottom (McKerrow & Ferguson 132a)
11. 168 x 148, architectural compartment with cherubs at top and trophies of arms at sides (McKerrow & Ferguson 123)
12. 235 x 112, Orn. 14 at top with four women kneeling at sides and Death enthroned at bottom (McKerrow & Ferguson 181)

CHECKLIST OF MUSIC EDITIONS PRINTED BY THOMAS EAST

1. Byrd, *Psalmes, Sonets & Songs*, 1588

   SVPERIVS. (MEDIVS., CONTRA TENOR., TENOR.) | Pſalmes, Sonets, & ſongs of ſadnes

and | pietie, made into Muſicke of fiue parts: whereof, | ſome of them going abroade among di-
uers, in vntrue coppies, | are heere truely corrected, and th'other being Songs | very rare and
newly compoſed, are heere publiſhed, for the recreation | of all ſuch as delight in Muſicke: By
William Byrd, | one of the Gent. of the Queenes Maieſties | honorable Chappell. | [Orn. 1] |
Printed by Thomas Eaſt, the aſsigne of VV. Byrd, | and are to be ſold at the dwelling houſe of
the ſaid T. East, by Paules wharfe. | 1588. | *Cum priuilegio Regiæ Maieſtatis.*

BASSVS. | . . . by Paules wharfe. | *Cum priuilegio Regiæ Maieſtatis.* (n.d.)

NOTE: li. 4: "abroade"; li. 5: "th'other"

4° upright. Superius: [A]₂, B–F₄, G₂ [$3 (C₃ unsigned) signed]. Medius: [A]₂, B–F₄, G₂ [$3
signed]. Tenor, contratenor, bassus, the same.

*Circle*IB: 3[I 15]9; 2[B 26] (British Library: medius: C), see Briquet 8073.

Bodleian Library (2 copies) ([MS] Mus.Sch.E.453–457; 85.d.8). British Library (K.2.f.1, lacks bassus). Cambridge University (Syn 5.58.10, superius). Harvard University (STC 4253, superius).
Library of Congress (M1490 S69 no. 8, bassus). New South Wales (L3/M, superius, medius).
Trinity College, Cambridge (VI.2.60 [1], lacks bassus). University of Illinois (uncat. 1588,
contratenor). York Minster (P/12.1, 3–4, medius, tenor, bassus).

STC2 4253; *ESTC* S122507; *RISM* B-5209

1a. Byrd, *Psalmes, Sonets & Songs,* 1588 [*c*1588–1589]

SVPERIVS. (MEDIVS., TENOR.) | Pſalmes, Sonets, & ſongs of ſadnes and | pietie, made
into Muſicke of fiue parts: whereof, | ſome of them going abroad among diuers, in vntrue cop-
pies, | are heere truely corrected, and th'other being Songs | very rare and newly compoſed, are
heere publiſhed, for the recreation | of all ſuch as delight in Muſicke: By *William Byrd,* | one of
the Gent. Of the Queenes Maieſties | honorable Chappell. | [Orn. 1] | Printed by Thomas Eaſt,
the aſsigne of VV. Byrd, | and are to be ſold at the dwelling houſe of the ſaid T. Eaſt, by Paules
wharfe. | 1588. | *Cum priuilegio Regiæ Maieſtatis.*

NOTE: li. 4: "abroad"; li. 5: "th'other"

4° upright. Superius [A]₂, B–F₄, G₂ [$3 signed]. Medius, tenor, the same.

*Crescent*B: 5[crescent B 16 | 17]5; 5[16 | 15]7 (Royal College: D), cf. Briquet 5253.

British Library (1+ copies) (55.b.20 [1], medius; Harl. 5936 [357], medius tp). Folger Library (STC
4253, superius, medius). Royal College of Music (I.D.1 [4], tenor).

STC2 4253.3; *ESTC* S124483

1b. Byrd, *Psalmes, Sonets & Songs,* 1588 [*c*1588–1589]

SVPERIVS. (MEDIVS., CONTRATENOR., TENOR., BASSVS.) | Pſalmes, Sonets, & ſongs
of ſadnes and | pietie, made into Muſicke of fiue parts: whereof, | ſome of them going abroad
among diuers, in vntrue coppies, | are heere truely corrected, and th other being Songs | very
rare and newly compoſed, are heere publiſhed, for the re- | creation of all ſuch as delight in
Muſick: By *William Byrd,* | one of the Gent. of the Queenes Maieſties | honorable Chappell. |
[Orn. 1] | Printed by Thomas Eaſt, the aſsigne of VV. Byrd, | and are to be ſold at the dwelling
houſe of the ſaid T. Eaſt, by | Paules wharfe. 1588. | *Cum priuilegio Regiæ Maieſtatis.*

NOTE: li. 4: "abroad"; li. 5: "th other"

4° upright. Superius [A]₂, B–F₄, G₂ [$3 signed]. Medius, contratenor, tenor, bassus, the same.

*Crown*B 18[crown 5 | 23 | 2]21; 2[B 20]1 (British Library: K.2.f.1: bassus: C), see Heawood 999;
mixed with other crescent and crown marks including *Crescent* 2[crescent 18]1 (British Library:
K.2.f.1: bassus: D), see Heawood 847.

British Library (3 copies) (K.2.f.1, bassus; D.101.d, bassus; R.M.15.d.3, contratenor). Folger Library (STC 4253, tenor, bassus). Glasgow University (Euing R.a.10). Harvard University (STC 4253, superius tp). Huntington Library (79637, superius [−G], medius, contratenor [−[A], G], tenor, bassus). Lincoln Cathedral (Mm.4 5−9, superius [−[A], G], medius, bassus [−F, G]). University of London (Littleton 5815). York Minster (P/12.2s, contratenor).

*STC*2 4253.7; *ESTC* S122507

2. *Musica Transalpina I,* 1588

[Ti. 1] MVSICA TRANSALPINA. | CANTVS. (ALTVS., TENOR., QUINTVS., SEXTVS., BASSVS.) | Madrigales tranſlated of four, fiue and ſixe partes, | choſen out of di-uers excellent Authors, vvith the firſt and | ſecond part of *La Verginella,* made by Maiſter *Byrd,* | vpon tvvo Stanza's of *Ariosto,* and brought | to ſpeake Engliſh vvith | the reſt. | *Publiſhed by* N. Yonge, *in fauour of ſuch as | take pleaſure in Muſick of voices.* | [Orn. 2] | Imprinted at London by Tho- | mas Eaſt, the aſsigné of William | Byrd, 1588. | *Cum Priuilegio Regiæ Maiestatis.*

  NOTE: li. 3: "partes"; li. 6: "tvvo Stanza's"

4° upright. Cantus: A_2, A–H$_4$ [$3 (+ B, F, H$_4$) signed]. Altus: A_2, A–H$_4$ [$3 signed]. Tenor: A_2, A–G$_4$, H$_3$ [$3 signed]. Bassus: A_2, A–G$_4$, H$_3$ [$3 (+A, B, C, E, F$_4$) signed]. Quintus: A_2, A–G$_4$ [$3 (B$_2$missigned D$_2$) signed]. Sextus: A_2, A–B$_4$ [$3 signed].

Column: 9[Column 16 | 13]12 (Archbishop Marsh's: cantus: [A]), see Briquet 5242.

Archbishop Marsh's Library (Z.4.3.9, lacks quintus, sextus). Bodleian Library ([MS] Mus.Sch.E. 453−458). Britten–Pears (11 Ba 4, tenor). Cambridge University (Syn.5.58.7, sextus, tenor [A–H]). Folger Library (STC 26094). Glasgow University (Euing R.a.12, tenor). Harvard University (STC 26094, altus, tenor, quintus, sextus). Huntington Library (20120, cantus, altus, quintus). Library of Congress (M1490 Y65 M9 bk., altus, tenor, bassus). Royal College of Music (I.D.33, cantus, quintus). Trinity College, Cambridge (VI.2.60 [3], lacks bassus). University of Texas, Austin (Pforz 1104, quintus). Yale University (BEIN VL 30 4, quintus).

*STC*2 26094; *ESTC* S120367; *RISM* 1588/29

2a. *Musica Transalpina I,* 1588 [*c*1593−1594]

[Ti. 1] MVSICA TRANSALPINA. | CANTVS. (ALTVS., TENOR., QUINTVS., SEXTVS., BASSVS.) | Madrigales tranſlated of foure, fiue and ſixe parts, | choſen out of diuers excellent Authors, vvith the firſt and | ſecond part of *La Verginella,* made by Maiſter *Byrd,* | vpon two Stanz's of *Ariosto,* and brought | to ſpeake Engliſh with | the reſt. | *Published by* N. Yonge, *in fauour of ſuch as | take pleaſure in Muſick of voices.* [Orn. 2] Imprinted at London by Tho- | mas Eaſt, the aſsignè of William | Byrd, 1588. | *Cum Priuilegio Regiæ Maiestatis.*

  NOTES: li. 3: "parts"; li. 5: "two Stanz's"

4° upright. Cantus: A_2, A–H$_4$ [$3 signed]. Altus, tenor, bassus, the same. Quintus: A_2, A–G$_4$ [$3 (B$_2$missigned D$_2$) signed]. Sextus: A_2, A–B$_4$ [$3 signed].

*Fleur-de-lis*M: 9[flower 18.5 | .5] 20.5; 9[M 14]2 (British Library: K.3.i.19: cantus: D), cf. Briquet 7007, 7008.

Bodleian Library (2 copies) ([MS] Mus.Sch.E.453−458 [12]; Tyson Mus. 1380 [2], altus [−G2-4, H]). British Library (2 copies) (R.M.15.e2 [1]; K.3.i.19). Cambridge University (Syn.5.58.7, lacks sextus, tenor *A*). Edinburgh University (De.6.98−99, 104 & 106, tenor, altus, quintus, sextus). Harvard University (STC 20694, cantus, bassus). Huntington Library (20120, tenor, sextus, bassus). Library of Congress (M1490 Y65 M9 bk, cantus, quintus, sextus). Manchester Central Library (BR470.1 Yn 21). Newberry Library (Case VM1579 Y57m). Royal Academy of Music (Spencer Collection, sextus). University of Illinois (uncat. 1588, altus, bassus, quintus, tenor [imp]).

STC2 26094.5; *ESTC* S120367

3. Byrd, *Songs of Sundrie Natures*, 1589

[Orn. 3, Orn. 4] SVPERIVS. [Orn. 5, Orn. 5a] (MEDIVS., CONTRATENOR., SEXTVS., TENOR., BASSVS.) | ₵Songs of ſundrie natures, ſome of | grauitie, and others of myrth, fit for all compa- | nies and voyces. Lately made and compoſed in- | to Muſicke of 3.4.5. and 6. parts: and pub- | liſhed for the delight of all ſuch as take plea- | ſure in the exerciſe of | that Art. | By VVilliam Byrd, one of the Gentlemen | of the Queenes Maieſties honorable | Chappell. | [Orn. 6, Orn. 7, Orn. 8] | ₵Imprinted at London, by Thomas | Eaſt, the aſſigne of William Byrd, and are to be | ſold at the house of the ſayd T. Eaſt, being in | Alderſgate ſtreete, at the ſigne of the | blacke Horſe. 1589. | Cum priuilegio Regiæ Maiestatis.
    NOTE: li. 5: "Muſicke"; li. 6. "plea-"; li. 14: "Eaſt"; "be"; li. 15: "Eaſt"; "being"

4° upright. Superius: [A]$_2$, B–H$_4$ [$3 signed]. Bassus, the same. Tenor [A]$_2$, B–H$_4$ [$3 (H$_2$ missigned G$_2$) signed]. Medius: [A]$_2$, B–D$_4$ [$3 signed]. Contratenor: [A]$_2$, B–F$_4$ [$3 (C$_2$ missigned E$_2$) signed]. Sextus: [A]$_2$, B$_4$, C$_2$ [$3 signed].

Mixed paper stock with a constellation of IB, AF, circle and crown marks, including: *Circle*IB: 3 [I 15]9; 2[B 28] (University of London: sextus: C), see Briquet 8073; *Crown*IB: 3[I 12]13; 3[B 10]15 (Christ Church: bassus: [A]); and *Crown*AF: 2[A 23]; 4[F 21] (Christ Church: bassus: H).

British Library (3 copies) (K.2.f.3; R.M.15.d.2; K.3.h.7, tenor, sextus). Britten-Pears (uncat. lacks sextus). Cambridge University (Syn.6.58.12, superius). Christ Church, Oxford (489–494). Glasgow University (Euing Ra. 9, lacks sextus). Harvard University (STC 4256, sextus). Huntington Library (34006). Library of Congress (M1490 S69 no. 4, bassus). Royal Academy of Music (RBa 1/1). Trinity College, Cambridge (IV. 2. 60/4). University of London (Littleton Strong).

STC2 4256; *ESTC* S106995; *RISM* B-5212

3a. Byrd, *Songs of Sundrie Natures*, 1589 [c1595–1596]

[Orn. 3, Orn. 4] SVPERIVS. [Orn. 5, Orn. 5a] (MEDIVS., CONTRATENOR., TENOR., BASSVS., SEXTVS.) | ₵Songs of ſundrie natures, ſome of | grauitie, and others of myrth, fit for all compa- | nies and voyces. Lately made and compoſed in- | to Muſick of 3.4.5. and 6. parts : and pub- | liſhed for the delight of all ſuch as take | pleaſure in the exerciſe of | that Art. | By VVilliam Byrd, one of the Gentlemen | of the Queenes Maieſties honorable | Chappell. | [Orn. 6, Orn. 7, Orn. 8] | ₵Imprinted at London by Thomas | Eſte, the aſſigne of William Byrd, and are to bee | ſold at the house of the ſayd T. Eſte, beeing in | Alderſgate ſtreete, at the ſigne of the | blacke Horſe. 1589. | Cum priuilegio Regiæ Maiestatis.
    NOTE: li. 5: "Muſick"; li. 6. "pleaſure"; li. 14: "Eſte"; "bee"; li. 15: "Eſte"; "beeing"

4° upright. Superius: [A]$_2$, B–H$_4$ [$3 signed]. Tenor, bassus, the same. Contratenor: [A]$_2$, B–F$_4$ [$3 signed]. Sextus: [A]$_2$, B$_4$, C$_2$ [$3 signed].

*Letters*GB: 9[B 9]4; 9[G 9]4 (Bodleian: medius: B), see Briquet 9290; mixed with token remnant *Letters*AM: 5[A 10]13; 3[M 18]6 (Bodleian: medius: C).

Bodleian Library ([MS] Mus.Sch.E. 453–458). British Library (K.4.g.12, sextus, tenor). Britten–Pears (11 Ba 2). Glasgow University (Euing Ra. 9, sextus only). Folger Library (2 copies) (STC 4256.2 copy 1; STC 4256.2 copy 2, contratenor, bassus). Lincoln Cathedral (Mm.4.6 & 9 [2], bassus, medius). Royal Academy of Music (uncat.; Spencer Collection, sextus).

4. Byrd, *Cantiones Sacrae I,* 25 Oct. 1589

[Orn. 9] SVPERIVS. (MEDIVS., CONTRATENOR., TENOR., BASSVS.) *Liber primus* | SACRARVM CANTIO- | num Quinque vocum. | *Autore Guilielmo Byrd Organista* | *Regio, Anglo.* | [Orn. 10] | *Excudebat Thomas Est ex aſsigna-* | *tione Guilielmi Byrd.* | *Cum priuilegio.* | *Londini, 25. Octob.* *1589.*

4° upright. Superius: A–D₄ [$3 signed]. Medius, contratenor, tenor, bassus, the same.

*Crown*IB: 3[B 10]12; 1[I 14]11 (Trinity College: tenor; E), see Briquet 9282.

Bodleian Library (2 copies) (Tenbury Mus. e.16; G.P. 1742 [1], contratenor). British Library (2+ copies) (K.2.f.4; 55.b.20 [2], medius; Harl. 5963 [367], contratenor tp). Britten-Pears (uncat. lacks contratenor). Cambridge University (2 copies) (Syn.6.59.3/12, superius, contratenor; Syn.6.58.11, superius). Trinity College, Cambridge (VI.2.60/2, lacks bassus). Chapin Library (Music: 2 Byrd). Christ Church, Oxford (489–493). Folger Library (2 copies) (STC 4247 copy 1; STC 4247 copy 2, superius, medius, tenor). Glasgow University (Euing Ra. 9). Huntington Library (79636). Lincoln Cathedral (Mm.4.5–9). University of Illinois (uncat. 1589, superius). York Minster (2 copies) (P2/1–5s; P5/1–5s).

*STC*2 4247; *ESTC* S106990; *RISM* B-5211

5. Byrd, *A Gratification vnto Master John Case,* 1589

₵A gratification vnto Maſter Iohn Caſe, for his learned booke, lately made in praiſe of Muſicke | CANTVS SECUNDUS ([CANTUS PRIMUS], [ALTUS], [TENOR], BASSVS, [SEXTUS]).

(Bassus colophon)

₵Imprinted at London by Thomas East, the aſsigne of William Byrd, and are to be ſold at the house of the ſaid T. Eaſt, being in Alderſgate ſtreete, at the ſigne of the blacke Horſe. 1589.

1°: [Cantus primus], cantus secundus, [altus, tenor], bassus, [sextus].

Grapes: 12 × 19 (Cambridge).

Bodleian Library (Don.a.3 [3], bassus). Cambridge University (Broadsides. 8.58.1, cantus secundus).

*STC*2 4246; *ESTC* S108198; *RISM* B-5222

6. *Italian Madrigalls Englished,* 1590

[Ti. 2] SVPERIVS. (CONTRATENOR., TENOR., SEXTVS., BASSVS.) [Orn. 11] | ₵*The firſt ſett,* | Of Italian Madrigalls Englished, | not to the ſenſe of the originall dittie, | *but after the affection of the* | *Noate.* | *By Thomas Watſon Gentleman.* | There are alſo heere inſerted two excellent | Madrigalls of Maſter VVilliam | Byrds, compoſed after the | Italian vaine, at the requeſt | of the ſayd Thomas | Watſon. | ₵Imprinted at London, by Tho- | *mas Eſte, the aſsigné of William Byrd,* | & are to be ſold at the houſe of the ſayd T. Eſte, | being in Alderſgate ſtreet, at the ſigne | of the black Horſe. 1590. | Cum Priuilegio Regiæ Maieſtatis.
  MEDIVS. ₵*The firſt ſett, ...* ₵Imprinted at London, by Tho- | *mas Eſte, the aſsigné of William* | *Byrd.* 1590. | Cum Priuilegio Regiæ Maieſtatis.

4° upright. Superius: [A]₂, B–D₄, E₂ [$4 signed]. Contratenor, tenor, bassus, the same. Medius: [A]₂, C₄, C₄, E₂ [$4 (E₂ signed D₂ in some copies) signed]. Sextus: [A]₂, B₄ [$4 signed].

Horn: 21[5 | 26]; 3[23 | 5] 21 (Glasgow: tenor: B), see Briquet 7837.

Bibliothèque nationale (Rés. Vm⁷ 651, superius). Bodleian Library (2 copies) 30.d.8; Mal.973). British Library (K.3.k.12). Cambridge University (Syn.5.59.12). Folger Library (3 copies)

(STC 25119 copy 1; STC 25119 copy 2, medius, contratenor; STC 25119 copy 3, sextus). Glasgow University (Euing R.a.14). Harvard University (STC 25119). Huntington Library (14217). Manchester Central Library (Br.470.1.Wn.21). Library of Congress (M1490.S69 no.6 Case, bassus). Newberry Library (Case Vm 1579 m23 fi). Trinity College, Cambridge (VI.2.60/5, lacks bassus).

STC2 25119; ESTC S119493; RISM 1590/29

7. Whythourne, *Duos, or Songs for Two Voices*, 1590

[Ti. 1a] CANTVS. (BASSVS.) | Of Duos, or Songs for tvvo voi- | ces, compoſed and made by *Thomas Whythorne* | Gent. Of the which, ſome be playne and eaſie to | be ſung, or played on Muſicall Inſtruments, & be made | for yong beginners of both thoſe ſorts. And the | reſt of theſe Duos be made and ſet foorth | for thoſe that be more perfect in ſing- | ing or playing as aforeſaid, all the | which be deuided into three parts. | That is to ſay: | The firſt, which doth begin at the firſt ſong, are made for a man | and a childe to ſing, or otherwiſe for voices or Inſtruments | of Muſicke, that be of the like compaſſe or diſtance in ſound. | The ſecond, which doth begin at the XXIII. ſong, are made for | two children to ſing. Alſo they are aptly made for two treble | Cornets to play or ſound: or otherwiſe for voices or Muſicall | Inſtru- ments, that be of the lyke compaſſe or diſtance in ſound. | And the third part which doth begin at the XXXVIII. ſong, (be- | ing all Canons of two parts in one) be of diuers compaſſes | or diſtances, and therefore are to be vſed with voices or In- | ſtruments of Muſicke accordingly. | Now newly publiſhed in An. Do. 1590. | Imprinted at London by Tho- | mas Eſte, the aſsigné of *William* | Byrd. 1590.

4° upright. Cantus: A–F₄, G₂ [$3 (+A, E₄) signed]. Bassus: A–F₄, G₂ [$3 (+ A, C₄) (D₃ mis- signed C₄) signed].

Fleur-de-lis: 3[Flower 22]4; 7 [base 10]10 (British Library: cantus: F), see Heawood 1408.

Bodleian Library (Douce W subt. 30, bassus). British Library (K.4.c.3). Cashel Cathedral (E. 09. 26. 2).

STC2 25583; ESTC S102968; RISM W-993

8. Byrd, *Cantiones Sacrae II,* 4 Nov. 1591

[Orn. 6, Orn. 7] | [in Com. 1] SVPERIVS. (MEDIVS., CONTRATENOR., TENOR., BASSVS.) | *Liber Secundus* | *SACRARVM CANTIONVM,* | *Quarum aliæ ad Quinque, aliæ verò ad* | *Sex voces æditæ ſunt.* | Autore Guilielmo Byrd, Organiſta | Regio, Anglo. | [Orn. 11] | *Excudebat Thomas Eſte ex aſsigna-* | *tione Guilielmi Byrd.* | Cum priuilegio. | *Londini, quarto Nouemb. 1591.*

[Orn. 7, Orn. 12] | [in Com. 1] SEXTVS. | *Liber Secundus . . .*

4° upright. Superius: [A]₂, B–E₄ [$3 signed]. Medius, contratenor, tenor, bassus, the same. Sex- tus: [A]₂, B–C₂ [$3 signed].

Unmarked, chainlines c27.

Bodleian Library (G.P. 1742 [2], contratenor). British Library (3 copies) (K.2.f.5; D.101.a; 55.b.20 [3], medius). Cambridge University, (Syn.6.59.13, superius). Christ Church, Oxford (489– 494). Folger Library (STC 4248, bassus, sextus). Huntington Library (56257, tenor, sextus). Lincoln Cathedral (Mm.4.5–9, lacks sextus). York Minster (P5/1–5 [2], lacks sextus).

STC2 4248; ESTC S104835; RISM B-5216

9. Damon, *The Former Booke of the Musicke*, 1591

[Ti.3] CANTVS. (ALTVS., TENOR., BASSVS.) | [rule] | The former Booke of the | Muſicke of M. William Da- | mon, late one of her maieſties | Muſitions: conteining all the tunes | of Dauids Pſalmes, as they are ordina- | rily ſoung in the Church: moſt excellent- | ly by him compoſed into 4. parts. | In which Sett the Tenor | ſingeth the Church | tune. | Publiſhed for the recreation of ſuch | as delight in Muſicke : | *By W. Swayne Gent.* | Printed by T. Eſte, the aſsigné | of W. Byrd. | [in Ti. 3] 1591.

4° upright. Cantus: [A]₂, B–G₄ [$3 signed]. Altus, tenor, bassus, the same.

*Fleur-de-lis*M: 9[flower 18.5 | .5]20.5; 9[M 14]2 (British Library: K.3.m.4: altus: B), cf. Briquet 7007, 7008: a related mark or distinctive twin is *Fleur-de-lis*: 5[flower 16]5 (British Library: RM.15.f.1 [1]: altus: B).

Bodleian Library (Tanner 303, bassus). British Library (2 copies) (R.M.15.f.1 [1]; K.3.m.4). Christ Church, Oxford (1083–1084). Edinburgh (Cwn. 1037 [1, 2 & 4], cantus (−[A]), altus, bassus). Folger Library (STC 6220). Huntington Library (60597).

*STC*2 6220; *ESTC* S105154; *RISM* D-830

10.　Damon, *The Second Booke of the Musicke,* 1591

[Ti. 3] *CANTVS. (ALTVS., TENOR, BASSVS.)* | [rule]. | The ſecond Booke of the | Muſicke of M. William Da- | mon, late one of her maieſties | Muſitians: conteining all the tunes | of Dauids Pſalmes, as they are ordina- | rily ſoung in the Church: moſt excellent- | ly by him compoſed into 4. parts. | In which Sett the higheſt part | ſingeth the Church | tune. | Publiſhed for the recreation of ſuch | as delight in Muſicke: | *By W. Swayne Gent.* | Printed by T. Eſte, the aſsigné | of W. Byrd. | [in Ti. 3] 1591.

4° upright. Cantus [A]₂ B–G₄ [$3 signed]. Altus, tenor, bassus the same.

Fleur-de-lis: 5[flower 16]5 (Christ Church: cantus: E).

Bodleian Library (2 copies) (Tanner 303, bassus [imp]; Vet. A1 e.11, cantus). British Library (2 copies) (R.M.15.f.1 [2]; K.7.a.3). Christ Church, Oxford (1083–1084). Edinburgh (Cwn. 1037 [3], tenor). Folger Library (STC 6221).

*STC*2 6221; *ESTC* S111040; *RISM* D-831

11.　Farmer, *Diuers and Sundry Waies,* 1591

Diuers & ſundry vvaies | *of two parts in one, to the number* | of fortie, vppon one playnsong: some- | times placing the ground aboue, & two parts | beneath, and other while the ground beneath and | two parts aboue: or againe otherwiſe the ground | ſometimes in the midſt betweene both, like- | wiſe other conceites, which are plainly ſet | downe, for the profite of thoſe | which would at- taine | vnto knowledge. | Performed and published by Iohn Farmer | in fauour of ſuch as loue Muſicke, | with the ready way to per- | fect knowledge. | *Imprinted at London by Thomas* | Este, the aſsigne of William Byrd, and | are to be ſould in Broadſtreete neere | the Royall exchaunge at the | Authors houſe. | 1591.

8°: A₄, B–D₈ [$5 signed].

Fleur-de-lis: 4[flower 20]4; 7[base 12]7 (Bodleian: C), see Briquet 6986.

Bodleian Library (Wood 90 [−A1, D5–8]). New York Public Library (Drexel 3825).

*STC*2 10698; *ESTC* S111790; *RISM* F-106

12.　*Whole Booke of Psalmes,* 1592

[Ti. 4] [li. 1-3 xylographic, in Com. 2] THE | WHOLE BOOKE OF | PSALMES: | WITH THEIR WON- | ted Tunes, as they are ſong | *in Churches, compoſed into* | *foure parts:* | All vvhich are ſo placed that foure may ſing, | ech one a ſeueral part in this booke. VVherein the Church | tunes are carefully corrected, and thereunto added other | short tunes uſually ſong in London, and other places of | this Realme. VVith a Table in the end of the | booke, of ʃuch tunes as are nevvly added, | vvith the number of ech Pʃalme pla- | ced to the ʃaid Tune. | COMPILED BY SONDRY AVTHORS, | vvho haue ʃo laboured heerein, that the vnskilfull | vvith ʃmall prac- tice may attaine to ʃing | that part, vvhich is fitteʃt | for their voice. | [Orn. 2] | IMPRINTED AT LON- | DON by Thomas Eʃt, the aʃʃigné | of William Byrd: dwelling in Alderʃgate | ʃtreete at the ʃigne of the black Horʃe, | and are there to be ʃold. | [in Com. 3] 1592.

8°: A₂, B–T₈, V₄ [$5 signed].

Fleur-de-lis: 4[Flower 22]3; 9[Base 9]8 (Bodleian: *A*), see Heawood 1391.

Bodleian Library (Don.f.211). British Library (K.2.c.7). Cambridge University (SSS.26.1). Edin- burgh (Cwn.786). Glasgow University (Euing F.e.23). John Ryland's Library (R 128431). Uni- versity of Illinois (uncat. 1592).

STC2 2482; *ESTC* S115453; *RISM* 1592/7

13. Byrd, *Mass a 4,* [*c*1593–1594]

no title page.

4° upright. Cantus: 𝄴₄ ($3 signed). Altus, tenor, bassus, the same.

Fleur-de-lis: 5[17]5; (Lincoln: bassus), cf. Briquet 7068: a possible twin is *Fleur-de-lis:* [flower 18]8; [base 16]10 (Lincoln: altus).

British Library (RM.15.d.5, lacks altus). Christ Church, Oxford (489 & 491–493 [6b]). Folger Li- brary (*STC* 4250). Library of Congress (M1490.S69 Case, bassus). Lincoln Cathedral (Mm.4. 5 & 7–9 [8]).

STC2 4250; *ESTC* S126107; *RISM* B-5207

14. Morley, *Canzonets a 3,* 1593

[in Ti. 5] CANZONETS. | OR | LITTLE SHORT | *SONGS TO THREE* | *VOYCES:* | NEWLY PVBLISHED | BY | THOMAS MORLEY, | *Bachiler of Muʃicke, and one* | of the Gent. of hir Maieʃties Royall | *CHAPPEL.* | [in Com. 3] 1593. | ❡*Imprinted at London by Tho: Est,* | the aʃʃigné of William Byrd: dwelling | in Alderʃgate ʃtreet, at the ʃigne | *of the black Horʃe, and are there* | to be ʃold. | [in Ti. 5] CANTVS. (ALTVS., BASSVS.)
  NOTE: li. 16 "be ʃold"

4° upright. Cantus: [A]₂, B–F₄ [$3 signed]. Altus, bassus, the same.

CrownAI: 6[Crown 11]4 (British Library: RM.15.e.2: cantus: [A]), cf. Heawood 1049a.

British Library (2 copies) (K.3.i.7, cantus; R.M.15.e.2 [4]). Huntington Library (13101 v.2, altus). Kassel (4° Mus. 2). Library of Congress (2 copies) (M1490.S69 no.1 Case, bassus; M1490.M85.C33, bassus). Nederlands Muziek Instituut (In: kluis B 20 [1–2]). Royal College of Music (I.D.20 [b]).

STC2 18121; *ESTC* S112994; *RISM* M-3691

14a. Morley, *Canzonets a 3,* 1593 [*c*1596–1597]

[in Ti. 5] CANZONETS. | OR | LITTLE SHORT | *SONGS TO THREE* | *VOYCES:* | NEWLY PVBLISHED | BY | THOMAS MORLEY, | *Bachiler of Muʃicke, and one* | of the Gent. of hir Maieʃties Royall | *CHAPPEL.* | [in Com. 3] 1593. | ❡*Imprinted at London by Tho: Est,* | the aʃʃigné of William Byrd: dwelling | in Alderʃgate ʃtreet, at the ʃigne of the | *black Horʃe, and are* | *there to* | bee ʃold. | [in Ti. 5] CANTVS. (ALTVS., BASSVS.)
  NOTE: li. 16 "bee ʃold"

4° upright. Cantus: [A]₂, B–F₄ [$3 signed]. Altus, bassus, the same.

*Letters*GB: 9[B 9]4; 9[G 9]4 (Marsh's: cantus: C), see Briquet 9290; mixed with token remnant *Letters*AM: 4[A 9]14; 3[M 13]10 (Marsh's: cantus: B).

Archbishop Marsh's Library (Z4.3. 14 [9–10], cantus, altus). Bodleian Library (4 copies) (Ten. Mus. d.11; Douce Mm 361 [5], bassus; Douce HH 216, altus; Harding Mus.e. 700 [1], cantus). British Library (K.3.i.7, altus, bassus). Huntington Library (13101 v.2, bassus). Folger Library (STC 18121 [−cantus [A], E₄, F₄]). Library of Congress (M1490.S69 no.1 Case, cantus (−[A1]). Royal Academy of Music (Spencer Collection, altus).

15. Byrd, *Mass a 3*, [*c*1593–1594]

no title page.

4° upright. Cantus: A₄ ($3 signed). Tenor, bassus, the same.

Fleur-de-lis: 5[17]5; (British Library: bassus), cf. Briquet 7068: mixed with unmarked paper, chain-lines *c*27.

British Library (RM.15.d.4). Christ Church, Oxford (493 [6a], bassus). Folger Library (STC 4249.2). Library of Congress (M1490.S69 Case, bassus).

STC2 4249; *ESTC* S112707; *RISM* B-5206

Musica Transalpina I, 1588 [*c*1593–1594]

16. *Whole Booke of Psalmes*, 1594

[Ti. 4] [li. 1-3 xylographic in Com. 2] THE | WHOLE BOOKE OF | PSALMES: | WITH THEIR WON- | ted Tunes, as they are ſung | in Churches, compoſed into | foure parts: | Being so placed, that foure may ſing each | one a ſeueral part in this booke. VVherin the Church tunes | are carefully corrected, & thervnto added other short tunes | vsually sung in London and most places of this Realme. | VVith a table in the beginning of this booke, of | ſuch Tunes as are nevvly added, vvith the | number of each Pſalme placed to | the ſayd Tune. | COMPILED BY X. SVNDRY AVTHORS, | vvho haue ſo laboured heerein, that the vnskilful vvith | ſmall practice may attaine to ſing that part, vvhich | is fittest for their voyce. | [Orn. 2] | IM-PRINTED AT LONDON | By Thomas Eſt, the aſsignè of William | Byrd: dvvelling in | Alderſgate ſtreete at the ſigne of the black Horſe, | & are there to be sold. | [in Com. 3] 1594.

8°: [A]₂, B–S₈, T₄ [$5 signed].

Fleur-de-lis/Cross: 5[flower 21]4; 7[cross 18]3 (British Library: C), see Briquet 7045 (and Briquet 1387, for an example with a cross).

Bodleian Library (Ps verse 1594 f.1). British Library (Gren. 12151). Cambridge University (A.8.57). Edinburgh (Cwn. 147). Harvard University (STC 2488). Huntington Library (13079). Library of Congress (STC 2488). Trinity College, Cambridge (NQ.16.171 [2]).

STC2 2488; *ESTC* S102258

17. Mundy, *Songs and Psalmes*, 1594

[Ti. 6] SVPERIVS. (MEDIVS., CONTRATENOR., TENOR., BASSVS.) | [rule] | *SONGS* | AND PSALMES | compoſed into 3. 4. and 5. parts, | for the vſe and delight of all | ſuch as either loue or learne | *MVSICKE:* | BY | *IOHN MVNDY* | Gentleman, bachiler of Muſicke, | and one of the Organeſt of hir | Maieſties free Chappell of | *VVINDSOR.* | [Orn. 8] | *Imprinted at London by Thomas Eſt,* | (the aſsigne of William Byrd,) dwelling in | Alderſgate ſtreete, at the ſigne of the | black Horſe. 1594.

4° upright. Superius: [A]₂, B–E₄ [$3 signed]. Tenor, bassus, the same. Medius: [A]₂, B–C₄, D₂ [$3 signed]. Contratenor: [A]₂, B₄, C₂ [$3 signed].

Unmarked, chainlines *c*27.

Bodleian Library (2 copies) (Mus. 2e. 2–6; Douce Mm 361 [3], superius). British Library (2 copies) (K.2.a.3; RM.15.f.1 [3]). Cambridge University (Syn.6.59.4). Christ Church, Oxford (489–493 [9]). York Minster (P14/1–5 s).

STC2 18284; *ESTC* S105466; *RISM* M-8143

18. Morley, *Madrigalls to Fovre Voyces*, 1594

[in Ti. 7] MADRIGALLS | TO | FOVRE VOYCES | NEWLY PVBLISHED | BY | THOMAS MORLEY. | THE | FIRST BOOKE. | [Orn. 6] | IN LONDON | BY THOMAS EST IN AL- | derſgate ſtreet at the ſigne of the | black horſe. | [rule] | M. D. XC. IV. | [in Ti. 7] CANTVS. (ALTVS., TENOR., BASSVS.)

4° upright. Cantus: [A]₂, B–E₄, F₂ [$3 signed]. Altus, tenor, bassus, the same.

*Crown*IB: 1[I 14]11; 3[B 10]12 (British Library: K.3.i.13: altus: B), see Briquet 9282, mixed with unmarked paper, chainlines *c*27.

Bodleian Library (Mus. 17e.15, altus). British Library (3+ copies) (RM.15.e.2 [3]; K.3.i.12; K.3.i.13; Harl. 5936 [366], altus tp). Edinburgh University (De.6.100–101 [1], cantus, bassus). Folger Library (STC 18127, tenor). Glasgow University (Euing R.b.8). Huntington Library (13100). Library of Congress (2 copies) (M1490.M85 M34 1594; M1490.S69 no.2 Case, bassus). Trinity College, Cambridge (VI.2.60 [6], contains an excised dedication to Henry Puckering). York Minster.

STC2 18127; *ESTC* S112991; *RISM* M-3695

19. Byrd, *Mass a 5*, [*c*1595]

no title page.

4° upright. Superius: ₵₄ ($3 signed). Contratenor, tenor primus, tenor secundus, bassus, the same.

Unmarked, chainlines *c*27.

Bodleian Library (Douce MM 361 [15]). British Library (3 copies) (K.2.f.12; K.8.d.12, lacks contratenor; RM.15.d.6). Christ Church, Oxford (489–493 [6c]). Library of Congress (M1490.S69 Case, bassus). Lincoln Cathedral (Mm.4. 5–9).

STC2 4251; *ESTC* S112709; *RISM* B-5208

20. Morley, *First Book of Canzonets a 2*, 1595

[in Ti. 8] CANTVS. (TENOR.) | OF | THOMAS MORLEY | THE FIRST BOOKE OF | CANZONETS | TO | TWO VOYCES. | [Orn. 7 | IN LONDON | BY THOMAS ESTE. | [rule] | CIꓕ. Iꓕ. XC. V.

[A]₂, B–D₄ [$3 signed]. Tenor, the same.

*Letters*GB: 9[G 9]4; 9[B 9]4 (British Library: cantus: B), see Briquet 9290.

Archbishop Marsh's Library (Z4.3.14). British Library (K.3.i.8). Folger Library (STC 18119, cantus). Hamburg (Scrin. A/585 [2]). Huntington Library (62708). Library of Congress (M1490 M85 Case). Royal Academy of Music (Spencer Collection, tenor). Royal College of Music (I.D.14 [12]).

STC2 18119, *ESTC* S113004, *RISM* M-3701

21. Morley, *First Book of Balletts*, 1595

[in Ti. 8] CANTVS. (ALTVS., QVINTAS., TENOR., BASSVS.) | OF | THOMAS MORLEY | THE FIRST BOOKE OF | BALLETTS | TO | FIVE VOYCES. | [Orn. 13] | IN

LONDON | BY THOMAS ESTE. | [rule] | CIƆ. IƆ. XC. V.

NOTE: Ti. 8 (with a calligraphic ornament of four ovals under the part-book heading); Orn. 13 perfect

4° upright. Cantus: [A]$_2$, B–D$_4$, E$_2$ [$3 signed]. Altus, quintus, tenor, bassus, the same.

*Pot*PBD: 23 [pot 2 | 25]1; 5[base PBD 14]5 (British Library: K.3.i.5: altus: B), cf. Heawood 3576, and see *The Marsh Lute Book c. 1595*, with an introduction by Robert Spencer (Kilkenny: Boethius, 1981), xviii. Only Archbishop Marsh's Library has a copy with the following mark: *Letters*GB: 9[G 9]4; 9[B 9]4 (cantus: [A]), see Briquet 9290.

Archbishop Marsh's Library (Z4.3.14 [5-6], cantus, quintus). British Library (2 copies) (K.3.i.4, cantus, altus, bassus; K.3.i.5, cantus, altus, quintus, tenor [E]). Library of Congress (M1490 S69 no. 3). Royal Academy of Music (Spencer Collection, quintus). Royal College of Music (I.D.19, cantus). University of California, Los Angeles (M1585. M86b).

*STC*2 18116, *ESTC* S110042; *RISM* M-3697

21a. Morley, *First Book of Balletts*, 1595 [*c*1605–1606]

[in Ti. 8a] CANTVS. (ALTVS., QVINTAS., TENOR., BASSVS.) | OF | THOMAS MOR-LEY | THE FIRST BOOKE OF | BALLETTS | TO | FIVE VOYCES. | [Orn. 13] | IN LONDON | BY THOMAS ESTE. | [rule] | CIƆ. IƆ. XC. V.

NOTE: Ti. 8a (with an index finger under the part-book heading); Orn. 13 imperfect

4° upright. Cantus: A$_2$, B–D$_4$, E$_2$ [$3 (−B$_3$, D$_4$ missigned D$_3$) signed]. Altus: A$_2$, B–D$_4$, E$_2$ [$3 signed]. Quintus, tenor, bassus, the same.

Crown: 19[crown 5 | 24 | 5]19; 19[base 5 | 24 | 7]17 (British Library: K.3.i.5: bassus: C); with a token remnant in gathering C of the cantus, altus, and quintus parts: *Fleur-de-lis:* 5[flower 18]4; 4[base 18]3 (Christ Church: quintus: C).

Bibliothèque nationale (Rès vm^7 657, cantus). British Library (2 copies) (K.3.i.4, tenor, quintus; K.3.i.5, tenor [−E], bassus). Bodleian Library (2 copies) (Vet.A1.d.21, 22, cantus, tenor; Harding Mus. E 700 [2]). Christ Church, Oxford (242–246). Edinburgh University (De.6.98–99, 104, tenor, quintus, cantus). Folger Library (2 copies (STC 18116 copy 1; STC 18116 copy 2, cantus, quintus). Harvard University (STC 18116, altus). Huntington Library (62693). Newberry Library (Case VM 1579 M866). Royal College of Music (I.D.19, altus, quintus, tenor). Yale University (2 copies) (Eliz.141; uncat. [temp: 20010228-h]).

22. Morley, *Il Primo Libros delle Ballette*, 1595

[in Ti. 8] CANTO. (ALTO., TENORE., BASSO., QUINTO.) | DI | TOMASO MORLEI | IL PRIMO LIBRO DELLE | BALLTETE | A | CINQVE VOCI. | [Orn. 13] | IN LON-DRA | APPRESSO TOMASO ESTE. | [rule] | CIƆ. IƆ. XC.V.

4° upright. Canto [A]$_2$, B–D$_4$, E$_2$ [$3 signed]. Alto, tenore, basso, quinto, the same.

*Letters*GB: 9[G 9]4; 9[B 9]4 (British Library: alto: B), see Briquet 9290.

British Library (55.b.20 [4], alto). Folger Library (STC 18118, canto). Huntington Library (16540). Jesus College, Oxford (I.Arch.2.4, canto).

*STC*2 18118, *ESTC* S110044, *RISM* M-3697

23. Bathe, *A Brief Introduction to the Skill of Song* [*c*1596]

[Orn. 5] A BRIEFE INTRO-| duction to the skill of Song: | *Concerning the practiſe, ſet forth* | *by William Bathe* | *Gentleman.* | In which work is ſet downe X. ſundry wayes of 2. parts | in one vpon the plaine ſong. Alſo a Table newly ad- | ded of the compariſons of Cleues, how one followeth |

another for the naming of Notes: with other neceſ- | ſarie examples, to further the learner. | [Orn. 8] | *Fabius.* | *Musica eſt honeſtum et incundum oblectamen-* | *tum, liber alibus ingenijs maxime dignum.* | LONDON | Printed by Thomas Eſte.

8°: A–C₈, D (D is a fold-out page) ($5 signed).

Vase: 2[vase 24]5; 4[base 20]3 (Harvard: C).

Bodleian Library (Douce B 193). British Library (2 copies) (K.1.e.5; 1042.d.36 [1]). Cambridge University. Harvard University (STC 1589). King's College, Cambridge. Lambeth Palace Library. University of California, Los Angeles (MT855.B33).

> *STC*2 1589; *ESTC* S113169
> Byrd, *Songs of Sundrie Natures,* 1589 [*c*1595–1596]
> Morley, *Canzonets a 3,* 1593 [*c*1596–1597]

24. Bull, *Oration,* 1597

[Ti. 9] The oration of Maiſter | Iohn Bull, Doctor of Mu- | ſicke, and one of the Gentle- | men of hir Maieſties Royall | CHAPPELL. | *As hee pronounced the ſame, bee-* | fore diuers Worſhip- full perſons, | *Th'Aldermen & commoners of the Citie* | of London, with a great Multitude of | *other people, the 6. day of October.* | 1597. | In the New erected Colledge of Sir *Thomas* | *Gresham* knight, deceaſed: made the commenda- | *tion of the ſaide worthy Founder, and the* | excellent Science of Muſicke. | [Orn. 7] | ❡*Imprinted at London by* | Thomas Eſte.

8°.

British Library (Harl. 5936 [356] tp).

*STC*2 4032.5; *ESTC* S124480

25. Tessier, *Chansons,* 1597

[in Ti. 8a] SVPERIVS. (CONTRATENOR., TENOR., BASSVS.) | LE | PREMIER LIVRE | de Chanſons & Airs de | court, tant Enfrançois qu'en | Italien & en Gaſcon a | 4. & 5. parties: | mis en Muſique par le ſieur | Carles Teſsier, Muſitien | de la Chambre du | Roy. | [Orn. 6] | *Imprimes a Londres par Thomas Eſte,* | *Imprimeur ordinaire.* | 1597.

4° upright. Superius: [A]₂, B–E₄, F₂ [$3 (B₂ missigned B₃, C₂ missigned B₂) signed]. Contratenor: [A]₂, B–E₄, F₂ [$3 signed]. Bassus, the same. Tenor: [A]₂, X, B–E₄, F₂ [$3 signed].

Mixed stock of IB, AF and grapes marks, including: *Crown*DG: 2[D 12]10; 1[G 12]3 (Bibliothèque nationale: contratenor: D), see Briquet 9380.

Bibliothèque nationale (Rés. Vm⁷ 235). Bibliothèque Sainte-Geneviève (Vm 169).

*STC*2: 23918.3; *ESTC* S96200; *RISM* T-594

25a. Tessier, *Chansons,* 1597 (reissue)

[in Ti. 8a] SVPERIVS. (BASSVS., CONTRATENOR., [TENOR]) | LE | PREMIER LIVRE | de Chanſons & Airs de | court, tant Enfrançois qu'en | Italien & en Gaſcon a | 4. & 5. parties: | mis en Muſique par le ſieur | Carles Teſsier, Muſitien | de la Chambre du | Roy. | [Orn. 6] | *Imprimes a Londres par Thomas Eſte,* | *Imprimeur ordinaire.* | 1597. | Les preſents Liures ſe treuuent ches Edouard Blount Libraire | demeurant au cimitiere de Sainct Paul deuant la gran | porte du North dudit S. Paul a Londres.

> NOTE: [A]–B1: newly printed pages with commendatory poems and dedications to Pene- lope Rich

Huntington Library (17264, superius, bassus). Lambeth Palace (Ms 661. No. 15, contratenor tp).

*STC*2: 23918.3; *ESTC* S96200

26. Kirbye, *English Madrigalls,* 1597

[in Ti 8a] CANTVS. Primus (CANTVS. Secundus, ALTVS., TENOR., BASSVS., SEXTUS.) |
The firſt ſet | OF ENGLISH | *Madrigalls,* | to 4.5. & 6. voyces. | *Made and newly publiſhed* | *by* | *George
Kirbye.* | [Orn. 6] | LONDON | *Printed by Thomas Eſte* | dwelling in alderſgate | ſtreet. | 1597.

4° upright. Cantus primus: [A]₂, B–D₄ [$3 signed]. Cantus secundus, tenor, bassus, the same.
Altus: [A]₂, B–C₄, D₂ (−D₂) [$3 (B₂ missigned C₂) signed]. Sextus: [A]₂, B₄ [$3 signed].

*Crown*DG: 2[D 12]10; 1[G 12]3 (British Library: K.1.e.6: cantus primus: D), see Briquet 9380.

Bodleian Library (Douce Mm 361 [1], altus). British Library (2 copies) (R.M.15.e.2 [6]; K.1.e.6).
Folger Library (2 copies) (STC 15010 copy 1; STC 15010 copy 2, tenor, sextus). Huntington
Library (62178, lacks altus). Library of Congress.

*STC*2 15010; *ESTC* S109353; *RISM* K-627

27. Weelkes, *Madrigals,* 1597

[in Ti. 8a] CANTVS Primus. (CANTVS Secundus., ALTVS., QVINTAS., SEXTVS.,
BASSVS.) | MADRIGALS | TO | 3. 4. 5. & 6. voyces. | *Made & newly publiſhed* | BY |
THOMAS VVEELKES. | [Orn. 6] | AT LONDON | Printed by Thomas Eſte. | 1597.

4° upright. Cantus primus: [A]₂, B–D₄ [$3 signed]. Cantus secundus, altus, bassus, the same.
Quintus: [A]₂, B₄, C₂ [$3 signed]. Sextus: [A]₂, B₄ (−B₄).

*Pot*PBD: 23 [pot 2 | 25]1; 5[base PBD 14]5 (Bodleian: bassus: A), cf. Heawood 3576.

Bibliothèque nationale (Rés. Vm⁷ 652, cantus primus). Bodleian Library ([MS] Mus.Sch.E.470–
473, lacks cantus primus and sextus). British Library (2 copies) (K.3.k.15; 55.b.20 [5 & 8]), cantus primus, altus). Folger Library (2 copies) (STC 25205 copy 1; STC 25205 copy 2 vols. 1–2,
altus, quintus). Glasgow University (Euing R.a.45, cantus primus, altus, sextus, bassus). Harvard University (STC 25205, sextus). Kassel (4° Mus. 104). Library of Congress (M1490 W.42
M3 Case, bassus [imp]). Royal College of Music (I.D.26, altus, quintus, sextus, bassus).

*STC*2 25205; *ESTC* S103293; *RISM* W-480

28. *Musica Transalpina II,* 1597

[in Ti. 8a] *MVSICA TRANSALPINA.* | CANTVS. (ALTVS., BASSVS.) | THE SECOND
BOOKE | OF | *Madrigalles, to 5. & 6. voices:* | *tranſlated out of ſundrie* | *Italian Authors* | & |
NEWLY PUBLISHED | BY | *NICOLAS YONGE.* | [Orn. 6] | AT LONDON | Printed by
Thomas Eſte. | 1597.

[in Ti. 8a] *MVSICA TRANSALPINA.* | QVINTVS. (SEXTVS., TENOR.) | . . . *NICHOLAS
YONGE.* | . . .

4° upright. Cantus: [A]₂, B–D₄ [$3 signed]. Quintus, altus, tenor, bassus the same. Sextus: [A]₂,
B₄ [$3 signed].

*Pot*PBD: 23[pot 2 | 25]1; 5[base PBD 14]5 (Royal College: I.D.35: bassus: C), cf. Heawood 3576.

Archbishop Marsh's Library (Z4.3 10-13b). Bibliothèque nationale (Rés. Vm⁷ 657, cantus, quintus
[−D₃-4]). British Library (1+ copy) (R.M.15.e2 [2] [−tenor C₄]; Harl. 5936 [344], quintus
tp). Christ Church, Oxford (913–918). Edinburgh University (De. 6. 98–106, lacks bassus).
Folger Library (*STC* 26095). Glasgow University (Euing R.a.13). Harvard University (*STC*
26095). Huntington Library (20121). Newberry Library (Case Vm 1579 Y57mu, altus, bassus,
quintus). Royal Academy of Music (uncat.). Royal College of Music (2 copies) (I.D.34;
I.D.35). University of Illinois (uncat. 1597). University of Texas, Austin (Pforz 1105, sextus).
Western Reserve (M1490 Y66 M8 1597). Yale University (M1490 Y57 M98).

*STC*2 26095; *ESTC* S120387; *RISM* 1597/24

29. di Lasso, *Novæ Aliquot*, 1598

[in Ti. 8a] CANTVS. (BASSVS.) | NOVÆ ALIQVOT ET AN- | TE HAC NON ITA VSI-
TATÆ AD | DVAS VOCES CANTIONES SVAVISSIMÆ, | omnibus Muſicis ſummè vtiles:
nec non Tyronibus | quàm artis eius peritioribus ſummopere | inſeruientes. | ⟨AVTHORE |
ORLANDO DI LASSO, | Illuſtriſsimi Bauariæ Ducis Alberti | Muſici Chori Magiſtro. |
Summa diligentia compoſitæ, correctæ, & nunc | *primùm in lucem editæ.* | [Orn. 6] | ⟨LONDINI. | Ex-
cudebat Thomas Eſte. | 1598.

4° upright. Cantus: A–B₄, C₂ [$3 signed]. Bassus the same.

Grapes: 4[grapes 17]3 (British Library: cantus: C), cf. Heawood 2307.

British Library (K.3.m.9). Folger Library (STC 15265, cantus). Huntington Library (89033).

STC2 15265; *ESTC* S109338; *RISM* L-1013

30. *Madrigals to Fiue Voyces*, 1598

[in Ti. 8a] CANTVS. (ALTVS., TENOR., QUINTVS., BASSVS.) | MADRIGALS | TO |
fiue voyces. | *Celected out of the beſt approued* | *Italian Authors.* | BY | Thomas Morley Gentleman | of
hir Maieſties Royall | *CHAPPELL.* | [Orn. 6] AT LONDON | Printed by Thomas Eſte | 1598.

4° upright. Cantus: [A]₂, B–D₄ [$3 signed] Altus, tenor, quintus, bassus, the same.

Unmarked, chainlines c26.

Bodleian Library (2 copies) (Douce Mm 361 [8]; Mal. 976). British Library (K.3.i.14). Folger Li-
brary (STC 18129, cantus). Huntington Library (62692). Library of Congress (M1490.M85
M33 1598 [Case]). University of California, Los Angeles (M1583.M86 1606). Yale University
(M1579.5 M864 M18).

STC2 18129; *ESTC* S110062; *RISM* 1598/15

31. Weelkes, *Balletts and Madrigals*, 1598

[in Ti. 8a] CANTVS. (ALTVS., QUINTAS., TENOR., BASSVS) | BALLETTS | *AND* |
MADRIGALS | TO | fiue voyces, vvith | *one to 6. voyces: newly publiſhed* | BY | Thomas
Weelkes. | [Orn. 6 | AT LONDON | Printed by Thomas Eſte, | 1598.

4° upright. Cantus: [A]₂, B–D₄ [$3 signed]. Altus, tenor, bassus, the same. Quintus: [A]₂, B–D₄,
E₂ (−E₂) [$3 signed].

Fleur-de-lis & Star: 10[flower 14]6; 8[star 15]10 (Royal College: altus: B), see Briquet 6964. Includes a
token remnant with the following mark: *Crown:* 10[12]5; 9[13]5 (Royal College: altus: [A]), cf.
Heawood 992.

Bibliothèque nationale (Rés. Vm⁷ 653, cantus). Bodleian Library ([MS] Mus.Sch.E. 453–457).
British Library (55.b.20 [7], altus). Folger Library (STC 25203, cantus). Huntington Library
(16520, bassus, altus, sextus [imp]). Royal College of Music (I.D.27).

STC2 25203; *ESTC* S111685; *RISM* W-481

32. Wilbye, *First Set of English Madrigals*, 1598

[Ti. 8a] CANTVS. (ALTVS., TENOR., BASSVS., QUINTVS., SEXTVS.) | THE FIRST
SET | *OF ENGLISH* | MADRIGALS | TO | 3. 4. 5. and 6. voices: | *Newly Compoſed* | BY |
IOHN WILBYE | [Orn. 6] | AT LONDON | Printed by Thomas Eſte. | 1598.
   NOTE: li. 3: "G" is not swash; li. 9: "WILBYE" (no period); li. 11: "LONDON" (no colon)

4° upright. Cantus: [A]₂, B–E₄ [$3 signed]. Altus, bassus, the same. Tenor: [A]₂, B–D₄ [$3
signed]. Quintus: [A]₂ B–D₂ (−D₂) [$3 signed]. Sextus; [A]₂, B₄ [$3 signed]. Dedication to
C. Cavendish is missing in some copies.

*Fleur-de-lis & Star:*10[flower 14]6; 8[star 15]10 (British Library: sextus: B), see Briquet 6964. Includes a token remnant with the following mark: *Crown:* 10[12]5; 9[13]5 (British Library: sextus: [A]), cf. Heawood 992.

British Library (Hirsch III.1150, altus, sextus). Folger Library (STC 25619.3). Royal College of Music (2 copies) (I.D.29a, tenor; I.D.29, bassus).

STC2 25619.5; *ESTC* S125575; *RISM* W-1065

32a.　Wilbye, *First Set of English Madrigals*, 1598 [*c*1605–1606]

[in Ti. 8a (cantus tp with unruled border)] CANTVS. (ALTVS., TENOR., BASSVS., QUINTVS., SEXTVS.) | THE FIRST SET | *OF ENGLISH* | MADRIGALS | TO | 3. 4. 5. and 6. voices: | *Newly Compoſed* | BY | IOHN WILBYE. | [Orn. 6] | AT LONDON: | Printed by Thomas Eſte. | 1598.
　　NOTE: li. 3: "G" is not swash; li. 9: "WILBYE." (period); li. 11: "LONDON:" (colon)

4° upright. Cantus: A–D$_4$ [$3 signed]. Altus, bassus, the same. Quintus: A–B$_4$ C$_2$ [$3 signed]. Tenor [A]$_2$, B–D$_4$ [$3 signed]. Sextus: [A]$_2$, B$_4$ [$3 signed]. Tenor and sextus with dedication to C. Cavendish.

Crown: 19[crown 5 | 24 | 3]21; 16[base 8 | 24 | 5]19 (British Library: Hirsh III.1150: quintus: C), see Heawood 1020.

Bodleian Library (Tyson Mus. 1380 [2], tenor [D2–4]). Boston Public Library (M. Cab. 2.13, vol. 1, bassus). British Library (2 copies) (55.b.20, altus; Hirsch III. 1150, quintus). Britten–Pears (11 Ba 4, tenor). Folger Library (4 copies) (STC 25619 copy 1; STC 25619 copy 2, quintus, altus; STC 25619 copy 3, altus; STC 25619.2, sextus). Princeton University (M1490 W66 M3.1598, sextus). Royal Academy of Music (Spencer Collection, altus). University of Illinois (uncat. 1598, tenor).

STC2 25619; *ESTC* S101316

32b.　Wilbye, *First Set of English Madrigals*, 1598 [*c*1610–1611]

[in Ti. 8a] CANTVS. (ALTVS., TENOR., BASSVS., QUINTVS., SEXTVS.) | THE FIRST SET | *OF ENGLISH* | MADRIGALS | TO | 3. 4. 5. and 6. voices: | *Newly Compoſed* | BY | IOHN WILBYE. | [Orn. 6] | AT LONDON: | Printed by Thomas Eſte. | 1598.
　　NOTE: li. 3: "G" is swash; li. 9: "WILBYE." (period); li. 11: "LONDON:" (colon); li. 13: "8" (wrong size)

4° upright. Cantus: A–D$_4$ [$3 (A$_3$ missigned B$_3$) signed]. Altus: A–D$_4$ [$3 signed]. Bassus, the same. Quintus: A–B$_4$ C$_2$ [$3 signed]. Tenor [A]$_2$, B–D$_4$ [$3 signed]. Sextus: [A]$_2$, B$_4$ [$3 signed]. Tenor and sextus with dedication to C. Cavendish.

*Shield*FM (1610): 17[shield 3 | 20 | 20 | 6]14; 15[tail '1610' 5 | 15] 20 (Bibliothèque nationale: C), it is similar to Heawood 571. See Allan H. Stevenson, "Watermarks Are Twins," *Studies in Bibliography* 4 (1951–1952): 74 and Fig. 3.4. Remnants include: *Shield & Castle:* 3[shield 18 | 20 | 18]3; 1[tail 20]1 (Royal College: altus: A); it is similar to Heawood 578 and Churchill 264.

Bibliothèque nationale (Rés. Vm^7 649, cantus). Bodleian Library (Mal. 972). Boston Public Library (M. cab. 2. 13, vol. 1, altus). British Library (2 copies) (K.3.k.17; Hirsch III.1150, cantus, tenor, bassus). Britten–Pears (11 Ba 4, cantos, altus, quintus, bassus). Edinburgh University (De. 6.98-99, 104, tenor, quintus sextus). Glasgow University (Euing Ra.50, cantus, altus, tenor, bassus). Harvard University (STC 25619). Library of Congress (M1490 W66 M3). Newberry Library (Case Vm. 1579 W66). Princeton University (M1490 W66 M3.1598, lacks sextus). Royal Academy of Music (Spencer Collection, tenor). University of Illinois (uncat. 1598, cantus, altus, sextus). University of London (Littleton Strong).

STC2 25619.3; *ESTC* S95848

33. Byrd, *Mass a 3* (2d ed.) [*c*1599–1600]

no title page.

4° upright. Cantus: A$_4$ ($3 signed). Tenor, bassus, the same.

Fleur-de-lis & Star: 8[star 15]10; 10 [flower 14]6 (Christ Church: cantus: A), see Briquet 6964.

Bodleian Library (Douce MM 361 [15], bassus). British Library (K.8.d.10). Christ Church, Oxford (490–491, 493, cantus, tenor). Folger Library (STC 4249).

STC2 4249.5; *ESTC* S126106

34. Byrd, *Mass a 4* (2d ed.) [*c*1599–1600]

no title page.

4° upright. Cantus: ₵$_4$ ($3 signed). Altus, tenor, bassus, the same.

Fleur-de-lis & Star: 8[star 15]10; 10 [flower 14]6 (British Library: bassus: B), see Briquet 6964.

Bodleian Library (Douce MM 361 [15], tenor). British Library (K.8.d.11). Cambridge University (Syn.6.58.13, cantus).

STC2 4250.5; *ESTC* S116696

35. Byrd, *Psalmes, Sonets & Songs* [*c*1599–1600]

SVPERIVS. (MEDIVS., TENOR., BASSVS.) | Pʃalmes, Sonets, & ʃongs of ʃadnes and | *pietie, made into Muʃicke of fiue parts: whereof,* ʃome | of them going abroad among diuers, in vntrue coppies, | are heere truely corrected, and th'other beeing Songs very | *rare and newly compoʃed, are heere publiʃhed, for the recrea-* | *tion of all* ʃuch as delight in Muʃick: By William Byrd | one of the Gent: of the Queenes Maieʃties | Royall Chappell. | [Orn. I] | *Printed at London by Thomas Eʃte,* | dwelling in Alderʃgate ʃtreete, ouer | againʃt the ʃigne of the George.

4° upright. Superius: [A]$_2$, B-F$_4$, G$_2$ ($3 signed). Tenor, Bassus, the same. Medius: [A]$_2$, B-F$_4$, G$_2$ ($3 (B$_3$ missigned B$_2$) signed).

Grapes: 3[grapes 19]5 (Liverpool: F), cf. Heawood 2307.

Britten-Pears (11 Ba 2, superius, medius, tenor, bassus). Liverpool University (Knowsley Pamphlets 526 (20), superius —[A]I).

36. Dowland, *Second Booke of Songs,* 1600

[Ti. 10, with canonic setting "Praise GOD vpon the Lute and Viol (Ps. 150)" in top compartment] THE | SECOND BOOKE | of Songs or Ayres, | of 2.4. and 5. parts: | VVith Tableture for the Lute or | Orpherian, with the Violl | *de Gamba.* | Compoʃed by *IOHN DOVVLAND* Batcheler | of Muʃick, and Luteniʃt to the King of Den- | mark: Alʃo an excelent leʃʃon for the Lute | and Baʃe Viol, called | *Dowland's adew.* | Publiʃhed by George Eaʃtland, and are | to be ʃould at his houʃe neere the greene Dragon | and Sword, in Fleetʃtreete. | [in Ti. 10] LONDON: | Printed by Thomas Eʃte, | the aʃigne of Thomas | Morley, 1600.

2°: A–M$_2$, N$_1$ [$2 signed].

*Pot*VO: 65 × 26 (Royal College: B), see Heawood 3549.

Bodleian Library (Tenbury Mus. c.83). Boston Public Library (XG.400.52 Folio). British Library (K.2.i.5). Folger Library (STC 7095). Huntington Library (59101). Lincoln Cathedral. Liverpool Central Library (imp.). Manchester Central Library (RF.410.Ds.406). Royal Academy of Music (Spencer Collection). Royal College of Music (II.k.6).

STC2 7095; *ESTC* S106688; *RISM* D-3483

37. Morley, *First Booke of Balletts* (2d ed.), 1600

[in Ti. 8a] CANTVS. (ALTVS., TENOR., BASSVS., QVINTVS.) | OF | THOMAS MOR-
LEY | THE FIRST BOOKE OF | BALLETTS | TO | FIVE VOYCES. | [Orn. 12] | IN
LONDON | BY THOMAS ESTE, | the aſsigne of Thomas Morley. | [rule] | 1600.

4° upright. Cantus: [A]$_2$, B–D$_4$, E$_2$ [$3 signed]. Altus, [tenor], bassus, quintus, the same.

PotVO: 2[vase 24]; 3[base 17]6 (British Library: cantus: B), see Heawood 3549.

Bodleian Library (Vet. A1 e.104, cantus, altus). British Library (1+ copies) (K.3.i.6, cantus, bassus); Harl.5936 [361], altus tp). Folger Library STC 18117 (cantus, quintus, bassus). Hamburg
(Scrin. A/585 [3]).

STC2 18117; *ESTC* S107515; *RISM* M-3699

38. Weelkes, *Madrigals of 5 & 6 Parts*, 1600

[in Ti. 8a] CANTO. (ALTO., TENORE., BASSO., QVINTO.) | MADRIGALS | OF | 5. and
6. parts, apt for the | Viols and voices. | *Made & newly publiſhed* | BY | *Thomas Weelkes of the
Coledge* | *at Wincheſter,* | Organist. | [Orn. 6] | AT LONDON | Printed by Thomas Eſte, the
aſſigne | of Thomas Morley. | 1600.

[in Ti. 8a[SESTO. (C$_2$: CANTO., ALTO., TENORE., BASSO., QVINTO.,) |
MADRIGALS | OF | 6. parts, apt for the Viols | and voices. | *Made & newly publiſhed* | BY |
Thomas Weelkes of the Coledge | *at Wincheſter,* | Organist. | [Orn. 6] AT LONDON | Printed by
Thomas Eſte, the aſſigne | of Thomas Morley. | 1600.

4° upright: Canto: [A]$_2$, B–D$_4$ [$3 (−C$_2$) signed]. Alto, tenore, bassus, quinto, the same. Sesto:
A$_4$, D$_4$ [$3 (A$_2$ missigned C$_2$) signed].

Crown & Oval: 20[crown 2 | 22]2; 20[oval 4 | 24 | 6] (Christ Church: basso: [A]), see Heawood 1024.

Bibliothèque nationale (Rès Vm^7 654, canto). Bodleian Library (2 copies) (Mal. 970; Douce Mm
361, quinto, sesto). British Library (55.b.20 [9], canto). Christ Church, Oxford (449–455).
Folger Library (2 copies) (STC 25206 copy 1; STC 25206 copy 2, alto, quinto). Harvard University (STC 25206, lacks quinto). Huntington Library (34003). Library of Congress (M1490
W43, lacks sesto). Royal College of Music (I.D.28).

STC2 25206; *ESTC* S111680; *RISM* W-485

39. Morley, *Madrigals to Fovre Voices* (2d ed.), 1600

[in Ti 8a] CANTVS. (TENOR., ALTVS., BASSVS.) | MADRIGALS | TO | FOVRE
VOICES | Publiſhed by Thomas | *Morley.* | NOW NEWLY IMPRINTED | with ſome
Songs added by the | Author. | [Orn. 6] AT LONDON | Printed by Thomas Eſte, the
aſſigne | of Thomas Morley. | 1600.
                NOTE: li. 11: "LONDON" (no colon)

4° upright. Cantus: A–C$_4$, D$_2$ [$3 signed]. Altus, tenor, the same. Bassus: A–C$_4$ [$3 signed].

Crown & Oval: 20[crown 2 | 22]2; 20[oval 4 | 24 | 6] (Archbishop Marsh's: cantus: C), see
Heawood 1024.

Archbishop Marsh's Library (Z.14.3 [3], cantus, altus). Edinburgh University (De.6.102 [1], tenor,
altus). Huntington Library (62691). Hamburg (Scrin. A/585 [3]).

STC2 18128; *ESTC* S110063; M-3695

39a. Morley, *Madrigals to Foure Voices* (2d ed.), 1600 [*c*1611–1612]

[in Ti 8a] CANTVS. (TENOR., ALTVS., BASSVS.) | MADRIGALS | TO | FOVRE
VOICES | Publiſhed by Thomas | *Morley.* | NOW NEWLY IMPRINTED | with ſome
Songs added by the | Author. | [Orn. 6] | AT LONDON: | Printed by Thomas Eſte, the
aſſigne | of Thomas Morley. | 1600.

NOTE: li. 11: "LONDON:" (colon)

4° upright. Cantus: A–C$_4$, D$_2$ [$3 signed]. Altus, tenor, the same. Bassus: A–C$_4$ [$3 signed].

*Shield*FM (1610):17[shield 3 | 20 | 20 | 6]14; 15[tail "1610" 5 | 15] 20 (Royal College: altus: B), it is simi-
lar to Heawood 571. See Allan H. Stevenson, "Watermarks Are Twins," *Studies in Bibliography* 4
(1951–1952): 74 and Fig. 3.4.

Bodleian Library (2 copies) (Mal. 975; Douce Mm 361 [7], tenor). British Library (K.3.m.11, tenor,
bassus). Folger Library (STC 18128, cantus). Manchester Central Library (BR 470 M v.61,
cantus). Royal Academy of Music (Spencer Collection, tenor). Yale University (M1584 M864
M18 1600, tenor).

40. *Triumphes of Oriana*, 1601

[in Ti. 8a] CANTVS. (ALTVS., TENOR., BASSVS., QVINTVS., SEXTVS.) | MADRI-
GALES | [rule] | The Triumphes of Oriana, | to 5. and 6. voices: com- | poſed by diuers ſeuer-
all | aucthors. | Newly publiſhed by Thomas Morley, | Batcheler of Muſick, and one of | the gentlemen of hir |
Maieſties honorable | Chappell. | [in Com. 3] 1601. | IN LONDON | PRINTED BY
THOMAS ESTE, | the aſsigne of Thomas Morley. | [rule] | ⸿Cum priuilegio Regiæ
Maieſtatis.

NOTE: li. 7 "*Morley,*" (with comma); li. 9: "*hir*"

4° upright. Cantus: [A]$_2$, B–D$_4$, E$_2$ [$3 signed]. Quintus, tenor, bassus, the same. Sextus: [A]$_2$,
D$_4$, C$_2$ [$3 signed].

Crown: 19[crown 5 | 24 | 5]19; 19[base 2 | 24 | 7]17 (British Library: cantus: B).

Bibliothèque nationale (Rès vm^7 656, cantus). British Library (K.3.i.15). Cambridge University
(Syn.6.60.6 [3], bassus). Christ Church, Oxford (449–454). Folger Library (STC 18130). Harvard University (STC 18130, lacks sextus). Royal Academy of Music (Spencer Collection,
tenor). Royal College of Music (I.D.20, lacks cantus).

STC2 18130; ESTC S94236; RISM 1601/16

40a. *Triumphes of Oriana*, 1601 [*c*1605–1606]

[in Ti. 8a] CANTVS. (ALTVS., TENOR., BASSVS., QVINTVS., SEXTVS.) | MADRI-
GALES | [rule] | The Triumphes of Oriana, | to 5. and 6. voices: com- | poſed by diuers ſeuer-
all | aucthors. | Newly publiſhed by Thomas Morley | Batcheler of Muſick, and one of | the gentlemen of her |
Maieſties honorable | Chappell. | [in Com. 3] 1601. | IN LONDON | PRINTED BY
THOMAS ESTE, | the aſsigne of Thomas Morley. | [rule] | ⸿Cum priuilegio Regiæ
Maieſtatis.

NOTE: li. 7: "*Morley*" (without comma); li. 9: "*her*"

4° upright. Cantus: [A]$_2$, B–D$_4$, E$_2$ [$3 signed]. Quintus, tenor, bassus, the same. Sextus: [A]$_2$, B$_4$,
C$_2$ [$3 (B$_2$ missigned D$_2$, B$_3$ missigned B$_2$) signed].

Crown: 19[crown 5 | 24 | 3]21; 16[base 8 | 24 | 5]19 (Bodleian Library [MS] Mus. Sch. E. 454: altus:
E), see Heawood 1020.

Bodleian Library (3 copies) (Mal 974; [MS] Mus. Sch. E. 453–458; Douce Mm 361 [16], altus [−E]). Cambridge University (2 copies) (Syn.7.203, quintus, tenor, sextus, altus; Pet. A.3.13 [4] quintus). Edinburgh University (De.6.98–106). Folger Library (STC 18130.2, altus, sextus). Harvard University (STC 18130, sextus). Huntington Library (62689). Royal College of Music (2 copies) (I.D.20, cantus; I.D.20 [a]). University of Illinois (uncat. 1601, tenor, bassus, quintus). Yale University (M1579 M864 T83 1601).

*STC*2 18130.5; *ESTC* S110049

41. Morley, *Canzonets a 3* (2d ed.), 1602

[in Ti. 7a] CANZONETS. | OR | LITTLE SHORT | SONGS TO THREE | VOYCES: PVB-LISHED | BY | THOMAS MORLEY, | *Bacheler of Muſicke, and one* | of the Gent. of hir Maieſties Royall | CHAPPEL. | ❡NOW NEWLY IMPRINTED | with ſome Songs added by the | AVTHOR. | [in Com.3] 1602. | IN LONDON | PRINTED BY THOMAS ESTE, | the aſsigne of Thomas Morley. | [rule] | ❡Cum priuilegio Regiæ Maieſtatis. | [in Ti. 7a] [CANTVS] (ALTVS., BASSVS.)

4° upright. [Cantus]: [A]$_2$, B–E$_4$, F$_2$ [$3 signed]. Altus, bassus, the same.

Crown: 19[crown 5 | 24 | 5]19; 19[base 2 | 24 | 7]17 (British Library: altus: D).

British Library (K.3.1.9, altus). Cambridge University (Syn.6.60.6 [1], bassus).

*STC*2 18122; *ESTC* S102534; *RISM* M-3692

42. Robinson, *Schoole of Musicke*, 1603

[li. 1–3 in Ti.10] In God reioyce, | With Inſtrument | and voyce. | THE | SCHOOLE OF MVSICKE: | WHEREIN IS TAVGHT, THE PER- | FECT METHOD, OF TRVE FINGE- | ring of the *Lute, Pandora, Orpharion, and Viol de* | *Gamba;* with moſt infallible generall rules, | both eaſie and delight- | full. | Alſo, a method, how you may be your owne inſtructer for | Prick-ſong, by the help of your *Lute,* without any | other teacher: with leſſons of all ſorts, for | your further and better in- | ſtruction. | Newly compoſed by *Thomas Robinſon,* | Luteniſt. | [li. 21–23 in Ti. 10] LONDON: Printed by *Tho. Este,* for Simon | Waterſon, dwelling at the ſigne | of the Crowne in Paules | Churchyard. 1603.

2°: A–O$_2$ [$2 (−E$_2$, F$_2$) signed].

Mixed stock of various crown marks, including: *Crown*IR: 26 × 24 (British Library: G); *Crown:* 5 × 24 (British Library: K); and *Crown:* 19 × 25 (Royal College: G).

British Library (K.2.d.1). Cambridge University (Syn.3.60.1). Royal College of Music (II.f.9).

*STC*2 21128; *ESTC* S101591; *RISM* R-1800

43. *Whole Booke of Psalmes,* 1604

[Ti. 4] [li. 1–3 xylographic, in Com. 2] THE | WHOLE BOOKE OF | PSALMES:- | WITH THEIR WON- | ted Tunes, as they are ſung | in Churches, composed into | foure parts: | Being so placed, that foure may ſing each | one a ſeuerall part in this booke. VVherein the Church tunes | are carefully corrected, & thervunto added other short tunes | vſually ſung in London and most places in this Realme. | VVith a Table in the beginning of this Booke, of | ſuch Tunes as are nevvly added, vvith the | number of each Pſalme placed to | the sayd Tune. | COMPILED BY X. SVNDRY AUTHORS, | vvho haue ſo laboured heerin, that the vnskilful vvith | ſmall practice may attaine to ſing that part, vvhich | is fittest for their voyce. | [Orn. 2] | IN LONDON: | printed by Thomas Eſte for the | companie of Stacioners, | [in Com. 3] 1604.

8°: A–R$_8$, S$_4$ [$5 signed].

*Crown/Grapes*IB:17[crown 3 | 20 | 2]18; 2[grapes IB 16.5]2 (Aberdeen: E), see Heawood 125, with a distinctive twin (or related mark): *Crown*IB/*Grapes:* 2[grapes 16]2; 20[crown 2 | 22] (Aberdeen: C).

Aberdeen University (TR.I.6v4.W2). Bodleian Library (Ps verse 1604 f.1). Boston Public Library (Benton 16.3). British Library (3433.b.11). Edinburgh (Cwn.749). University of Illinois (uncat. 1604). Yale University (Vp49 6).

STC2 2515; *ESTC* S90686

44. *Whole Booke of Psalmes, Collected, etc.,* 1604

[in Ti. 11] The | VVhole Booke of | PSalmes. | Collected into English mee- | ter by Tho. Sternh. Iohn Hop- | kins and others, cofnerred with | the Hebrue, with apt notes to | Sing them withall- | Iames V. | *If any be afflicted let him pray, & if* | *any be merry, let him Sing PSalmes.* | LON-DON | Printed by *Thomas ESte* for the | Companie of Stacioners. | 1604.

> NOTE: Toward the end of his career, East printed a number of monophonic *Whole Booke of Psalmes* editions, most of which do not name him but can possibly be attributed through his typographic materials. Some are mixed copies, and here his work will be detectable only on some gatherings. *STC2* attributes one *Psalmes* edition to both East and John Windet on this kind of typographical evidence (*STC2* 2522.3). There are in addition four anonymously printed editions of the *Psalmes* that have particularly close ties to East's 1604 edition (*STC2*: 2519.5, 2522.5, 2525.5 and 2529.5). These editions are all part of the uncataloged Hetherington Collection at the University of Birmingham.

4° in 8s. A–M$_8$ [$4 signed].

*Pot*PM: 2[pot 21]2; 4[16 base]5 (British Library: B).

British Library (C70.c4). University of Birmingham (Hetherington Collection [uncat]).

STC2 2514; *ESTC* S90685

45. East, *Madrigales,* 1604

[in Ti 8a] CANTVS. (ALTVS., QVINTAS., TENOR., BASSVS.) | MADRIGALES | TO | 3. 4. and 5. parts: apt for | Viols and voices. | *Newly compoSed by* | *Michaell ESte.* | [in Com. 3] 1604. | IN LONDON | PRINTED BY THOMAS | ESTE.

4° upright. Cantus: [A]$_2$, B–D$_4$ [$3 signed]. Bassus, quintus, the same. Altus: [A]$_2$, B$_4$ [$3 signed]. Tenor: [A]$_2$, B–C$_4$ [$3 signed].

Unmarked, chainlines 26–28, with remnants including: *Fleur-de-lis:* 2[flower 20]6 (Bodleian: cantus: B); and *Crown:*11[7]7; 9[8]8 (Christ Church: altus: B).

Aberdeen University (II.784.Gib, lacks quintus). Bodleian Library ([MS] Mus.Sch.E.453–457 [9]). British Library (2 copies) (K.2.d.17, bassus; K.2.d.3*, lacks quintus). Christ Church, Oxford (2 copies) (225–230; 449–454). Folger Library (STC 7460, cantus, tenor). Library of Congress (M1490 E14 M3 Case). York Minster (P7s, quintus).

STC2 7460, *ESTC* S118566; *RISM* E-6

46. Bateson, *English Madrigales,* 1604

[in Ti. 8a] CANTVS. (ALTVS., TENOR., BASSVS, QVINTAS., SEXTVS.) | The firSt Set of English | MADRIGALES: | to 3. 4. 5. and 6. | voices. | *Newly compoSed by Thomas BateSon* | practitioner in the Art of MuSicke, and | Organist of the Cathedral Church | of ChriSt | in the Citie of | CheSter. | [in Com. 3] 1604. | IN LONDON | PRINTED BY THOMAS | ESTE.

4° upright. Cantus: [A]$_2$, B–D$_4$, E$_2$ [\$3 signed]. Altus, bassus, the same. Sextus: [A]$_2$e, B$_4$(–B$_4$) [\$3 signed]. Quintus: [A]$_2$, B–C$_4$ [\$3 signed].

Crown 19[crown 5 | 24 | 3]21;16[base 8 | 24 | 5]19 (Huntington Library: cantus: B); and *Letter*R: 21[3 | 24 | 3]19; [24]4 (Huntington: cantus: C), with several other related (twin and variant) marks.

Bodleian Library ([Ms] Mus.Sch.E.470–473, lacks cantus and sextus). British Library (1+ copies) (K.3.h.3; Harl. 5919 [222], bassus tp). Cambridge University (Pet.A.3.13 [1], quintus). Christ Church, Oxford (449–454). Folger Library (STC 1586, cantus, altus, sextus, bassus). Harvard University (STC 1586, altus). Huntington Library (34008). Newberry Library (Case VM1579 B32f). Royal College of Music (I.D.14 [2]). University of California, Los Angeles (M1579 B3).

STC2 1586; ESTC S101050; RISM B-1277

47. Byrd, *Gradualia I,* 1605

GRADVALIA: | AC | CANTIONES SACRAE, | quinis, quarternis, trinifque | vocibus concinnatæ. | [rule] CONTRATENOR. [rule] | *Authore Guilielmo Byrd, Organiſta* | *Regio, Anglo.* | *Dulcia defectâ modulatur carmina linguà* | *Cantator Cygnus funeris ipſe ſui.* [in margin] Martalis. | lib. 13. Epig. | [in Com. 3] 1605. | LONDINI, | Excudebat Thomas Eſte.

4° upright. Superius; A$_2$, B–E$_4$, ^{2}B–D$_4$, ^{3}A–B$_4$, ^{3}C$_2$ [\$3 signed]. Tenor and bassus, the same. Medius A$_2$, B–E$_4$, ^{2}B–D$_4$, ^{2}E$_2$ [\$3 signed]. Contratenor: A$_2$, B–E$_4$, F$_2$ [\$3 signed].

Crown/GrapesIB 19[crown 3 | 22 | 3]19; 5[grapes IB 12]5 (York: superius: 2B); CrownPHCH/Grapes [crown PHCH 20]; 3[grapes 15]2 (York: medius: E): with numerous remnants (possible twins and variants), including: CrownIB/Grapes [crown IB 20]; 3[grapes15]2 (York: contratenor: D).

Cambridge University (Syn 6.60.6, bassus [–A]). York Minster (P2/1–5 [2]).

STC2 4243.5; ESTC S91271; RISM B-5217

47a. Byrd, *Gradualia I,* 1610 (reissue)

[Orn. 14] GRADVALIA, | AC | CANTIONES SA- | cræ, quinis, quaternis, triniſque | vo-cibus concinnatæ. | *LIB. PRIMVS.* | *Authore* Gulielmo Byrde, *Organiſta* | *Regio, Anglo* | EDITIO Secunda, priore emendatior. | *Dulcia defectâ modulatur carmina linguâ* | *Cantator Cygnus funeris ipſe ſui.* Martialis. | [rule] SVPERIVS. (British Library, K.2.f.7, *see note below*) [rule] | [Orn. 15] | LONDINI, | Exudebat *H. L.* Impenſis RICARDI REDMERI, | *Stella aurea in D. Pauli Coemeterio.* | 1610.

> NOTE: New title pages only. The reissued *Gradualia I* and *Gradualis II* title pages contain nu-merous typographical variants (not listed earlier). As Philip Brett has explained, Humphrie Lownes, the printer, probably set up as many title pages for these volumes as space would allow in a single forme (it is also possible that he set the title pages of both volumes at once, in which case he may have used two formes) (see *BE* 5, p. xvi).

British Library (3 copies) (K.2.f.7; R.M. 15.d.1; D.101.b, superius, medius, bassus). Cambridge University (Syn.6.61.15, superius). Christ Church, Oxford (489–494). Lincoln Cathedral (Mm.4.5–9).

STC2 4244; ESTC S115710

48. Pilkington, *Songs or Ayres,* 1605

[in Ti. 10, with 4-part canon in top compartment] THE | FIRST BOOKE OF | Songs or Ayres of 4. parts: | vvith Tableture for the | Lute or Orpherian, with | the Violl de- | Gamba. | *Newly compoſed by Francis Pilkington,* | Batcheler of Muſick, and Luteniſt: and one | of the Cathedrall

Church of Chriſt, | in the Citie of Cheſter. | [in Ti. 10] LONDON: | Printed by T Eſte, dwelling in | Alderſgate ſtreete, and are | ther to be ſould. 1605.

2°: [A]₂, B–M₂ [$2 signed].

*Letter*R: 32 × 19 (Glasgow University: A), with a distinctive twin (or related mark): *Letter*R: 27 × 19 (Glasgow University: B).

British Library (K.3.i.11). Folger Library (STC 19922). Glasgow University (R.x.12). Huntington Library (13569).

*STC*2 19922; *ESTC* S111835; *RISM* P-2370

Wilbye, *First Set of English Madrigals*, 1598 [*a*1605–1606]

Triumphes of Oriana, 1601 [*a*1605–1606]

Morley, *First Book of Balletts*, 1595 [*a*1605–1606]

49. Danyel, *Songs for Lute*, 1606

[Ti. 10, with Orn. 7 in top compartment] SONGS | FOR THE LVTE VIOL | and Voice: | Compoſed by I. Danyel, | Batchelar in Muſicke. | 1606. | TO Mʳⁱˢ Anne Grene. | [Orn. 2] | [in Ti. 10] LONDON | Printed by T.E. for Thomas Adams, | At the ſigne of the white Lyon, | in Paules Church-yard.

2°: [A]₂, B–L₂ [$2 signed].

Unmarked paper, chainlines 26–29, mixed with *Fleur-de-lis* 28 × 18 (British Library: C).

British Library (K.2.g.9). Folger Library (STC 6268). Huntington Library (34971).

*STC*2 6268; *ESTC* S106686; *RISM* D-906

50. Morley, *Canzonets a 3* (3d ed.), 1606

[in Ti. 7b] CANZONETS. | *OR* | LITTLE SHORT | *SONGS TO THREE* | *VOYCES:* | PVB-LISHED | BY | THOMAS MORLEY, | Bacheler of Muſicke, and one | of the Gent. of her Maieſties Royall | CHAPPEL. | ❡NOW NEWLY IMPRINTED | with ſome Songs added by the | AVTHOR. | [in Com. 3] 1606. | IN LONDON | PRINTED BY THOMAS ESTE, | the asſigne of William Barley. | [in Ti. 7b] CANTVS. (ALTVS., BASSVS.)

4° upright. Cantus: [A]₂, B–E₄, F₂ [$3 signed]. Altus, bassus, the same.

Fleur-de-lis: 4[18 base]4; 4[flower 18]4 (Royal College of Music: I.D.14 (9): bassus: B), with remnants including: unmarked, chainlines *c*26–29; and *Shield:*18[shield 6 | 24 | 5]19 (Cambridge: altus: F).

Bodleian Library (Douce Mm 361 [10], bassus [imp]). British Library (1+ copies) (Case.8.i.12; Harl. 5936 [364], altus tp). Cambridge University (Syn.5.60/12–14). Edinburgh University (De.105–106 [1], cantus, altus). Folger Library (2 copies) (STC 18123 copy 1; STC 18123 copy 2, cantus). Harvard University (STC 18123). Huntington Library (62690). Newberry Library (Case Vm 1579 M86 c3). Royal College of Music (2 copies) (I.D.14 [9]; II.E.39). University of California, Los Angeles (M1583 .M86 1606).

*STC*2 18123; *ESTC* S110047; *RISM* M-3693

51. Byrd, *Psalmes, Sonets & Songs*, n.d. [*a*1606–1607]

SVPERIVS. (MEDIVS., CONTRATENOR., TENOR., BASSVS.) | Pſalmes, Sonets, & ſongs of ſadnes and | pietie, made into Muſicke of fiue parts: whereof, ſome | of them going abroad among di-uers, in vntrue coppies, are | heere truely corrected, and th'other being Songs very rare | and newly compoſed, are heere publiſhed, for the recreation | of all such as delight in Muſicke: By William Byrd one | of the Gent: of the Queenes Maieſties | Royall Chappell. | [Orn. 1] | *Printed at London by Thomas Eſte* | dwelling in Alderſgate ſtreet, ouer | againſt the ſigne of the George.

4° upright. Superius: [A]₂, B–F₄, G₂ [$3 signed]. Medius, contratenor, tenor, bassus, the same.

Unmarked paper, chainlines 26–29.

Bibliothèque nationale (Rès. Vm⁷ 119, superius, bassus). Bodleian Library (Douce MM. 361 [4], contratenor). British Library (2 copies) K.2.f.2, lacks contratenor; RM.15.d.3, lacks contratenor). Britten-Pears (2 copies) (uncat. lacks contraten, uncat. contratenor only) Cambridge University (2 copies) (Syn.5.58.1, lacks superius; SSS.35.16, bassus). Christ Church, Oxford (489–493). Edinburgh University (De.6.96, superius). Folger Library (*STC* 4254, bassus). Harvard University (*STC* 4254, bassus). Huntington Library (14222). Library of Congress (M1490.B92 [Case]). Lincoln Cathedral (Mm.4. 5–9, superius [G, H], contratenor, tenor [–[], bassus [F–H]). Manchester Central Library (BR 360 Bz76, superius, medius). Newberry Library (Case Vm1579.B99p). Royal College of Music (I.d.1, lacks tenor). University of Illinois (xM784.1 B99p, medius).

*STC*2 4254; *ESTC* S106994; *RISM* B-5210

52. Byrd, *Gradualia II,* 1607

[li. 1 is xylographic] *GRADUALIA* | *SEU* | *CANTIONEM SACRARUM* | *Quarum aliæ ad Quatuor, aliæ verò ad* | *Quinque et Sex voces editæ* ſunt. | *Liber Secundus.* | Authore Gulielmo Byrde, Organista | Regio, Anglo. | *Muſica Diuinos profert modulamine Cantus:* | *Iubilum in Ore, favvm in Corde, et in Aure melos.* | [rule] | CANTVS Primus. (CANTVS Secundus., CONTRATENOR., [TENOR.], SEXTVS., BASSVS.) | [rule] | *Excudebat Thomas Eſte Londini, ex aſsignatione* | *Gulielmi Barley. 1607.*

4° upright. Cantus primus: [A]₂, B–H₄ [$3 signed]. Cantus secundus, contratenor, [tenor], sextus, bassus, the same.

Unmarked paper, chainlines 26–29, mixed with *Fleur-de-lis:* 4[18 base]5; 4[flower 17]3 (British Library: bassus: C).

British Library (K.2.f.6, lacks tenor).

*STC*2 4244.5; *ESTC* S115707; *RISM* B-5219

52a. Byrd, *Gradualia II,* 1610 (reissue)

[Orn.14] GRADVALIA, | SEV | CANTIONVM SA- | crarum: quarum aliæ ad Quatuor, aliæ | verò ad Quinque & Sex voces editæ ſunt. | *LIB. SECVNDVS.* | *Authore* Gulielmo Byrde, Organista | *Regio, Anglo.* | Ex Noua & accuratiſsima eiuſdem Authoris | recognitione. | *Muſica Diuinos profert modulamine Cantus:* | *Iubilum in Ore, fauum in Corde, & in Auremelos.* | [rule] | CANTVS Primus (British Library, K.2.f.8, *see note 44a*) | [rule] | [Orn. 15] | Excubedat *H. L.* Impenſis RICARDI REDMERI, | *ad Inſigne Stelle aureæ in Diui Pauli* | *Coemeterio.* 1610.
NOTE: See 44a.

British Library (2 copies) (K.2.f.8; D.101.c, cantus primus, sextus, bassus). Cambridge University (Syn.6.61.16, cantus primus). Christ Church, Oxford (489–494). Folger Library (STC 4243.2, sextus). Lincoln Cathedral (Mm.4.5–9, lacks sextus). Westminster Abbey.

*STC*2 4245; *ESTC* S126045

53. Croce, *Musica Sacra,* 1608

[in Ti. 8c] CANTVS. (ALTVS., TENOR., BASSVS., QVINTAS., SEXTVS.) | MVSICA SACRA: | TO | Sixe Voyces. | *Compoſed in the Italian tongue* | BY | GIOVANNI CROCE. | *Newly Engliſhed.* | [Orn. 2] | IN LONDON | PRINTED BY THOMAS ESTE, | the asſigne of William Barley. | 1608.

4° upright. Cantus: A–C₄ [$3 (A₂ unsigned) signed]. Altus, tenor, bassus, quintus, sextus, the same.

Shield & Castle 3[shield 3 | 18 | 20 | 18]3; 1[tail 20]1 (Huntington Library: cantus: A): the mark is similar to Heawood 578 and Churchill 264 but does not have PG initials.

Bodleian Library (2 copies) ([Ms] Mus.Sch.E.460–469; Wood 481, sextus). British Library (2 copies) (K.3.h.9; RM.15.f.1 [6], lacks bassus). Cambridge University (2 copies) (Syn.7.60.12, quintus, with altered tp; Syn.5.60.21, cantus). Chapin Library (Music: 2 Croce). Christ Church, Oxford (449–454). Folger Library (STC 6040). Harvard University (STC 6040). Huntington Library (13102, cantus [C₄ imp]). King's College, Cambridge (Rowe 316). University of Illinois (uncat. 1608, 2 bassus, quintus, 2 sextus). University of Michigan (M1490.C943 1608a).

STC2 6040; *ESTC* S105136; *RISM* C-4486

53a. Croce, *Musica Sacra*, 1611 (reissue)

[Ti. 12] *QVINTVS.* (British Library Harl. 5927 [68]) | [rule] | MVSICA SACRA: | TO | Sixe Voices. | Compoſed in the Italian | Tongue, | [rule] By GIOVANNI CROCE. [rule] | Newly Englished. | [Orn. 16] | AT LONDON, | Printed by H. L. for MATHEW | LOWNES. | 1611.
    NOTE: New title page only. Like the reissued *Gradulia* volumes, the extant title pages of this volume contain numerous typographical variants (see 44a).

British Library (Harl. 5927 [68], quintus tp). Cambridge University (Syn.6.61.17, sextus). University of Illinois (uncat., quintus).

STC2 6041; *ESTC* S118634

54. Weelkes, *Balletts and Madrigals I*, 1608

[in Ti. 8b] CANTVS. (ALTVS., TENOR., BASSVS, QUINTVS.) | BALLETTS | AND | MADRIGALS | TO | fiue voyces, with | one to 6. voyces : newly publiſhed | BY | Thomas Weelkes. | [Orn. 6] | IN LONDON | PRINTED BY THOMAS ESTE, | the asſigne of William Barley. | 1608.

4° upright. Cantus: [A]₂ B–D₄ [$3 signed]. Altus, tenor, bassus,the same. Quintus: [A]₂, B–D₄, E₂ (−E₂) [$3 signed].

Unmarked paper, chainlines 26–29, mixed with *Fleur-de-lis* 4[18 base] 5; 3[flower 18]5 (Edinburgh University: altus: B).

British Library (2+ copies) (K.3.k.14; 55.b.20 [15], altus; Harl. 5936 [367] bassus tp). Cambridge University (Syn.7.60.202). Edinburgh University (De.6.98–106). Folger Library (2 copies) (STC 25204 copy 1, lacks tenor; STC 25204 copy 2, altus, quintus). Harvard University (STC 25204, cantus, tenor, bassus). Library of Congress (M1490 N4). Newberry Library (Case VM 1579 W396, cantus). Royal College of Music (uncat).

STC2 25204; *ESTC* S103041; *RISM* W-482

55. Youll, *Canzonets*, 1608

[in Ti. 7d] CANZONETS | TO THREE VOYCES | NEWLY COMPOSED | BY | HENRY YOVLL | PRACTICIONER IN | THE ART OF | MVSICKE. | [in Com. 3] 1608 | IN LONDON | PRINTED BY THOMAS ESTE, | the aſsigne of William Barley. | [in Ti. 7d] CANTVS. (ALTVS., BASSVS.)

4° upright. Cantus: [A]₂, B–E₄ [$3 signed]. Altus, bassus, the same.

Unmarked paper, chainlines 26–29,mixed with *Fleur-de-lis* 4[18 base] 5; 4[flower 18]4 (Bodleian: bassus: C).

Bodleian Library (Antiq.e.E, bassus). British Library (K.3.k.21). Cambridge University (Syn.60.1–2). Folger Library (STC 26105, cantus). University of Illinois (uncat. 1608, altus).

STC2 25204; *ESTC* S101871; *RISM* Y-114

Morley, *Madrigals to Fovr Voices*, (2d ed.), 1600 [*c.*1610–1611]

Wilbye, *First Set of English Madrigals*, 1598 [*c.*1610–1611]

NOTES

INTRODUCTION

1. See Richard Agee, *The Gardano Music Printing Firms, 1569–1611* (Rochester, NY: University of Rochester Press, 1998); Jane A. Bernstein, *Music Printing in Renaissance Venice: The Scotto Press (1539–1572)* (New York: Oxford University Press, 1998); Mary S. Lewis, *Antonio Gardano: Venetian Music Printer, 1538–1569: A Descriptive Bibliography and Historical Study*, vol. 1: *1538–1549* (New York and London: Garland, 1988), vol. 2: *1550–1559* (New York and London: Garland, 1997); Henri Vanhulst, *Catalogue des éditions de musique publiées à Louvain par Pierre Phalèse et ses fils, 1545–1578* (Brussels : Palais des académies, 1990); Robert Lee Weaver, *Waelrant and Laet: Music Publishers in Antwerp's Golden Age* (Warren, MI: Harmonie Park, 1995); and his *A Descriptive Bibliographical Catalog of the Music Printed by Hubert Waelrant and Jan de Laet* (Warren, MI: Harmonie Park, 1994). See also the following standard studies: Samuel F. Pogue, *Jacques Moderne: Lyons Music Printer of the Sixteenth Century* (Geneva: Droz, 1969); Suzanne G. Cusick, *Valerio Dorico: Music Printer in Sixteenth-Century Rome* (Ann Arbor, MI: UMI Research Press, 1981); Kristine K. Forney, "Tielman Susato, Sixteenth-Century Music Printer: An Archival and Typographical Investigation" (Ph.D. diss., University of Kentucky, 1978); Daniel Heartz, *Pierre Attaingnant, Royal Printer of Music: A Historical Study and Bibliographical Catalogue* (Berkeley and Los Angeles: University of California Press, 1969); and Stanley H. Boorman, "Petrucci at Fossombrone: A Study of Early Music Printing, with a Special Reference to the Motetti de la Corona (1514–1519)" (Ph.D. diss., University of London, 1976).

2. Great Britain, Public Records Office, London (hereafter PRO), Court of Requests, Req 2. 202/63, *Thomas East vs. George Eastland* (1601); the case is summarized in Margaret Dowling, "The Printing of John Dowland's 'Second Booke of Songs or Ayres,'" *The Library* 4th ser., vol. 12 (1932): 365–380.

3. Thomas Milles, "The Custumers Alphabet and Primer . . ." (London, 1608), I.iv.

4. Steve Rappaport, *Worlds within Worlds: Structures of Life in Sixteenth-Century London* (Cambridge: Cambridge University Press, 1989).

5. The classic article on patronage at court is J. E. Neale, "The Elizabethan Political Scene," *Proceedings of the British Academy* 34 (1948): 97–117. See also Wallace T. MacCaffrey, "Place and Patronage in Elizabethan Politics," in S. T. Bindoff, J. Hurstfield, and C. H. Williams (eds.), *Elizabethan Government and Society: Essays Presented to Sir John Neale* (London: Athlone, 1961), 95–126; Simon Adams, "Eliza Enthroned? The Court and Its Politics," in Christopher Haigh (ed.), *The Reign of Elizabeth I* (Athens: University of Georgia Press, 1987), 56–58; the essays in John Guy (ed.), *The Reign of Elizabeth I: Court and Culture in the Last Decade* (Cambridge: Cambridge University Press, 1995); David Bergeron, *English Civic Pageantry, 1558–1642* (Columbia: University of South Carolina Press, 1971), 11–64; and Curt Breight, "Realpolitik and Elizabethan Ceremony: The Earl of Hertford's Entertainment of Elizabeth at Elvetham, 1591," *Renaissance Quarterly* 45 (1992): 20–48. On music patronage see Glenn A. Philipps, "Crown Musical Patronage from Elizabeth I to Charles I," *Music & Letters* 58 (1977): 29–42; and David Price, *Patrons and Musicians of the English Renaissance* (Cambridge: Cambridge University Press, 1981).

6. For a thorough treatment of the economic and social life of late Tudor London, see Rappaport, *Worlds within Worlds.* The following works also contain useful introductions to city governance: Lawrence Manley, *Literature and Culture in Early Modern London* (Cambridge: Cambridge University Press, 1995), 1–21; and Penry Williams, *The Later Tudors: England, 1547–1603* (Oxford: Clarendon Press, 1995), 169–175. The relationship between city and crown has been widely discussed: see, for example, Frank Freeman Foster, *The Politics of Stability: A Portrait of the Rulers in Elizabethan London* (London: Royal Historical Society, 1977),133–151; Rappaport, *Worlds within Worlds,* 185–186; Ian Archer, *The Pursuit of Stability: Social Relations in Elizabethan London* (Cambridge: Cambridge University Press, 1991), 32–39; and Valerie Pearl, *London and the Outbreak of the Puritan Revolution: City Government and National Politics* (London: Oxford University Press, 1961).

7. The music patents are transcribed in Robert R. Steele, *The Earliest English Music Printing: A Description and Bibliography of English Printed Music to the Close of the Sixteenth Century* (London: Bibliographical Society, 1903), 19 and 27–29. See discussions of the music monopoly in Joseph Kerman, *The Elizabethan Madrigal: A Comparative Study* (New York: American Musicological Society, 1962), 257–259; Donald W. Krummel, *English Music Printing 1553–1700* (London: Bibliographical Society, 1975), 10–30; Craig Monson, "Elizabethan London," in Iain Fenlon (ed.), *The Renaissance: From the 1470s to the End of the 16th Century* (London: Macmillan, 1989), 335–336; David Hunter, "Music Copyright in Britain to 1800," *Music & Letters* 67 (1986): 270; and Price, *Patrons and Musicians,* 178–189.

8. See, especially, Price, *Patrons and Musicians,* 178–189.

9. Steele, *Earliest English Music Printing,* 19.

10. M. A. Shaaber, "The Meaning of the Imprint in Early Printed Books," *The Library* 4th ser., vol. 24 (1943–1944): 120–141.

11. James Haar, "Orlando di Lasso, Composer and Print Entrepreneur," in Kate van Orden (ed.), *Music and the Cultures of Print,* afterword by Roger Chartier (New York: Garland, 2000), 125–162; Kristine K. Forney, "Orlando di Lasso's 'Opus 1': The Making and Marketing of a Renaissance Music Book," *Revue belge de musicologie* 39–40 (1985–1986): 33–60; and Henri Vanhulst, "Lassus et ses éditeurs: Remarques à propos de deux lettres peu connes," *Revue belge de musicologie* 39–40 (1985–1986): 80–100.

12. Musicologists, of course, would wish to see the composer's financial and musical needs faithfully served by the printer. Nonetheless, the general consensus among music bibliographers is that the continental composer was more often at the mercy of printers and patrons; see, for example, Agee, *Gardano Music Printing Firms,* 29–34; and Cusick, *Valerio Dorico,* 95–103.

13. After discussing all the privileges he knew of that were owned and operated by composers before (and during) Lasso's lifetime, Haar dismissed the whole slate as a "[a] rather scant list, its content mak[ing Lasso's seem] all the more extraordinary by contrast" ("Orlando di Lasso, Composer and Print Entrepreneur," 142).

14. Richard Helgerson, *Forms of Nationhood: The Elizabethan Writing of England* (Chicago: University of Chicago Press, 1992), 1.

15. Carlo Ginzburg, *The Cheese and the Worms: The Cosmos of a Sixteenth-Century Miller,* translated by John and Anne Tedeschi (New York: Penguin, 1982).

CHAPTER 1

1. Two recent examples are E. A. J. Honigmann, *Shakespeare: The "Lost Years"* (Totowa, NJ: Barnes and Noble, 1985); and Charles Nicholl, *The Reckoning: The Murder of Christopher Marlowe* (Chicago: Chicago University Press, 1995).

2. *Dictionary of National Biography*, 21 vols. (London: Oxford University Press, 1917–1938) (hereafter *DNB*), s.v. "Thomas East."

3. Ibid., s.v. "Michael East." Like Thomas, Michael also spelled his name "Est" and "Este." Furthermore, the two Easts did work together on several occasions; the elder East included the composer's music in the *Triumphes of Orianas* as well as in an edition devoted exclusively to Michael East's madrigals (*STC2* 7460). For early speculations about East's musical relations, see the John Bagford (1651?–1716) Papers, Harl. MSS 5414, 5419, 5892–5898, British Library, London. For a discussion of this collection, see Alec Hyatt King, "Fragments of Early Printed Music in the Bagford Collection," *Music & Letters* 40 (1959): 269–273.

4. On the view that East changed his name to Snodham, see Thomas East, *The Whole Book of Psalms: With Their Wonted Tunes, Harmonized in Four Parts . . .* , edited by Edward F. Rimbault (London: Musical Antiquarian Society, 1844), 5–7. The theory that Lucretia East was married to Thomas Snodham was perhaps first advanced in Joseph Ames (1689–1759), *Typographical Antiquities; or The History of Printing in England, Scotland, and Ireland*, augmented by William Herbert (London: William Miller, 1810–1819), 1006–1022.

5. *DNB*, s.v. "Thomas East."

6. Henry R. Plomer, "Thomas East, Printer," *The Library* 2d ser., vol. 3 (1901): 299.

7. Edward Arber (ed.), *A Transcript of the Registers of the Company of Stationers of London, 1554–1640 A.D.*, 5 vols. (Birmingham: The editor, 1875–1894).

8. The discovery of East's will was announced in Donald W. Krummel, *English Music Printing 1553–1700* (London: Bibliographical Society, 1975), 90. See also Miriam Miller's discussion of the document in *The New Grove Dictionary of Music and Musicians*, 29 vols., edited by Stanley Sadie and John Tyrell (New York: Grove, 2001) (hereafter *NG*), s.v. "Thomas East."

9. Peter Blayney is currently writing a much-anticipated study of the Stationers' Company. I owe a great debt to Faith Keymer's independent findings and collaborative efforts; see her "Thomas East, Citizen & Stationer of London: The Reconstruction of a Tudor Family Using Public Records," *PROphile* 11 (2000): 3–10.

10. John Harley, *William Byrd: Gentleman of the Chapel Royal* (Aldershot, Hants: Scolar, 1997), 14.

11. PRO, Court of the Star Chamber, C24/170, *Edward East vs. Richard East* (1584). The phrase "or thereabouts" was a tag line that appears in virtually all English court records of this era; thus the qualifying "in or about" could indeed be unduly conservative.

12. For a general discussion of the Radnage Easts, see Charles C. Jackson, *A History of Radnage* (West Wycombe: The author, 1970), 47–52.

13. PRO, C24/170.

14. PRO, Court of the Star Chamber, C24/233, *Thomas and Margaret Willet vs. Francis East* (1594).

15. See Margaret Dowling, "The Printing of John Dowland's 'Second Booke of Songs or Ayres,'" *The Library* 4th ser., vol. 12 (1932): 365–380.

16. *NG*, s.v. "Michael East."

17. For probate records with evidence that Michael East proved Mary Easte's will, see Cambridgeshire Public Records Office, Ely Consistory Registers, VC 23: 98 1611, "Probate and Will of Mary Easte, d.1611"; for a registry of Michael's father, William (Este's), will, see ibid.,VC 22: 14 1604, "Probate and Will of William Este, d.1604."

18. PRO, Feet of Fines, CP 25/2/161/2312/22, Eliz Hil.

19. For a bibliographical description of the two type ornaments of East's seal, see Ronald B. McKerrow, *Printers' & Publishers' Devices in England & Scotland 1485–1640* (London: Bibliographical Society, 1913), #206 and #209.

20. See Melvyn Paige-Hagg, *The Monumental Brasses of Buckinghamshire* (London: Monumental Brass Society, 1994), 180 and 255. For the locations of visitation manuscripts, see S. Friar,

Heraldry for the Local Historian and Genealogist (London: Alan Sutton, 1992). East arms appear in numerous visitation catalogs in Buckinghamshire, Berkshire, and Yorkshire.

21. See Jackson, *History of Radnage,* 47–52.

22. Plomer, "Thomas East," 299.

23. Guildhall Library, London, Ms. 16, 981, "Ironmongers' Company Presentment Book (1515–1680)": f. 12r (William Est, 4 Nov. 1527), f. 28r (Robert Este and Christopher Este, 14 Jan. 1538). Christopher does not resurface in any of the extant company records. I did, however, discover a suit between one Christopher Este and Robert and William Este (all of Bladlen, Bucks.) wherein Christopher sued to possess the land of their father, Jeffera Est. Presumably, therefore, Christopher won the case and returned to his land in Bucks. and did not continue to learn his trade in London (it is uncertain, however, if this is the same Christopher as the apprentice). See PRO, Req. 2. 14/81, Court of Requests, *Christopher Este vs. Robert and William Este* (1552).

24. In 1572 an indenture "made by the companie to Robert Este and Wm Skidmore" described Lewen's former dwelling as a "greate mansion house . . . in the parishe of St Nicholas Olave in London" (Guildhall Library, London, Ironmongers' Company Archive, Ms. 17, 003, F. 23v, "Indenture of Company Property to Robert Este and William Skidmore").

25. Skidmore's apprenticeship with Lewen began 18 January 1546; see Guildhall Library, "Ironmongers' Company," f.51r.

26. See Elizabeth Glover, *A History of the Ironmongers' Company* (London: Worshipful Company of Ironmongers, 1991), 49.

27. Ibid., 164.

28. Guildhall Library, London, Ironmongers' Company Archive, Ms. 16, 167, "Court Book (1555–1899)," f. 19v.

29. Ibid., f. 69v–72v.

30. Ibid., f. 155r, 157r, and 164r.

31. For a series of deeds for the "Blackhorse Alley" property in Aldersgate Street, see Guildhall Library, London, Deeds, Ms. 10, 905A, "Properties in Blackhorse Alley, Aldersgate Street, London (ca. 1500–1841)."

32. In 1590 Robert East allowed his house and property known as "Horsehead Alley" to be used by the Ironmongers' Company (Guildhall Library, "Court Book," f. 196).

33. Paige-Hagg, *Monumental Brasses,* 255.

34. Plomer, "Thomas East," 301–302.

35. See Arber, *Transcript,* vol. 1, 367, and vol. 2, 843.

36. Ibid., vol. 1, 111.

37. The standard history of the company is Cyprian Blagden, *The Stationers' Company: A History 1403–1959* (London: Allen and Unwin, 1960). The cultural role assumed by stationers is highlighted in Ian Gadd, "The Mechanicks of Difference; a Study in Stationers' Company Discourse in the Seventeenth Century," in Robin Myers and Michael Harris (eds.), *The Stationers' Company and the Book Trade 1550–1990* (New Castle, DE: Oak Knoll Press, 1997), 93–112. On the origins of and mechanisms for Tudor regulation of the book trade, see W. W. Greg, *"Ad Imprimendum Solem," The Library* 5th ser., vol. 9 (1954): 242–247. See also Peter W. Blayney, "William Cecil and the Stationers," in Myers and Harris, *The Stationers' Company,* 11–34; Graham Pollard, "The Early Constitution of the Stationers' Company before 1557," *The Library* 4th ser., vol. 18 (1937): 235–260; and D. F. McKenzie, "Stationers' Company Liber A: An Apologia," in Myers and Harris, *The Stationers' Company,* 35–64.

38. The effectiveness of political censorship by the state has recently been a matter of some debate: cf. Sheila Lambert, "State Control of the Press in Theory and Practice: The Role of the Stationers' Company before 1640," in Robin Myers and Michael Harris (eds.),

Censorship & the Control of Print: In England and France 1600–1910 (Winchester: St. Paul's Bibliographies, 1992), 1–32; and Anthony Milton, "Licensing, Censorship, and Religious Orthodoxy in Early Stuart England," *Historical Journal* 41 (1998): 625–651.

39. For East's election to the livery, see Arber, *Transcript*, vol. 2, 872. On 7 June 1603 East was elected to the court of assistants (*Records of the Court of the Stationers' Company 1602 to 1640*, edited by William A. Jackson [London: Bibliographical Society, 1957], 4). East, however, purchased a "dispensacon from all offices" with a cup of silver and linens in 1604 (Arber, *Transcript*, vol. 2, 838).

40. Guildhall Library, London, Original Wills, Box 3B (Ms. 9052 3B), f. 61, "Will of Thomas East, 21 July 1607."

41. J. Dover Wilson, "Richard Schilders and the English Puritans," *Transactions of the Bibliographical Society* 11 (1909–1911): 67.

42. Arber, *Transcript*, vol. 1, 324, and vol. 2, 81, 189, 205, and 224.

43. See Charles Welch, *History of the Worshipful Company of Pewterers of the City of London*, 2 vols. (London: Blades and Blades, 1902), vol. 1, 189–191, 197, 212–213, and 218, and vol. 2, 206. Hassel's wealthy widow, Agnes née Lamotte, is cited several times as well; see vol. 2, 268 and 281.

44. See Corporation of London Records Office, London, "Repertories of the Court of Aldermen," Rep. 16, f. 516v (15 November 1569) and rep. 17 f. iv (13 March 1570). I wish to thank Peter Blayney for bringing these documents to my attention.

45. Ibid.

46. In the probate record of Thomas Snodham's mother's will she was listed as "Maria Hasell *alias* Snodham." "Lucretia Hassell alias . . . Easte" was therein described as the sister of the deceased. See Guildhall Library, London, Commissary Court Act Book, Probate Records, "Maria Hasell *alias* Snodham," Ms. 9168/13/257 (27 April 1582).

47. Plomer, "Thomas East," 300–310. One of a number of books by East that has been studied rather thoroughly is his 1568 edition of *Mandeville's Travels* (Alfred Pollard, *A Short-Title Catalogue of Books Printed in England, Scotland, & Ireland and of English Books Printed Abroad 1475–1640*, 2d ed., 3 vols., revised and enlarged, begun by W. A. Jackson and F. S. Ferguson, completed by Katharine F. Pantzer [London: Bibliographical Society, 1976–1991] [hereafter *STC2*], 17250, another edition in 1582, *STC2* 17251). This was an illustrated edition, with woodcuts East had copied from an edition by Wynkyn de Worde. See Josephine Waters, "The Woodcut Illustrations in the English Editions of 'Mandeville's Travels,'" *Papers of the Bibliographical Society of America* 47 (1953): 59–63; and M. C. Seymour, "The Early English Editions of 'Mandeville's Travels,'" *The Library* 5th ser., vol. 19 (1964): 202–207. C. W. R. D. Moseley has even advanced the charming hypothesis that it was East himself who sponsored a play based on the book that has since been lost; see his "The Lost Play of Mandeville," *The Library* 5th ser., vol. 25 (1970): 47.

48. East registered music books in the Stationers' Company Registers for the atypical reason of establishing, rather than announcing, his exclusive right to the property (see chapter 6). He also took the unusual step of registering second editions of works he had premiered for others; see Arber, *Transcript*, vol. 2, 482, 439 (the books were registered with "an old copie extant in print"), and 449 (Arber noted here: "[T]his [is an] infrequent instance of the licensing of [a] second edition").

49. Ronald B. McKerrow, "Edward Allde as a Typical Trade Printer," *The Library* 4th ser., vol. 10 (1929): 121. Allde, like East, developed a particular interest in music publishing after serving for many years as a trade printer. See Arnold Hunt, "Book Trade Patents, 1603–1640," in Arnold Hunt, Giles Mandelbrote, and Alison Shell (eds.), *The Book Trade & Its Customers, 1450–1900: Historical Essays for Robin Myers*, introduction by D. F. McKenzie (New Castle, DE: Oak Knoll Press, 1997), 44. The London operations were probably based on

Italian models. Suzanne G. Cusick has made important discoveries about this issue in Rome. She argued that the Italian music printer Valerio Dorico "may not have had any financial interest [in music printing] beyond an expected fee for the technical services he offered" and concluded that his cultural role was essentially to function as a "*typografo* (trade printer) to the musicians of Rome." See her *Valerio Dorico: Music Printer in Sixteenth-Century Rome* (Ann Arbor, MI: UMI Research Press, 1981), 92 and 93.

50. McKerrow, "Edward Allde," 122–141.

51. H. S. Bennett, *English Books & Readers 1558 to 1603: Being a Study in the History of the Book Trade in the Reign of Elizabeth* (Cambridge: Cambridge University Press, 1965), 272.

52. East listed this property and his other lease in Cripplegate (to Thomas Hunt, Fishmonger) in his will (Guildhall Library, "Will of Thomas East").

53. Thomas Adams, "The Beginnings of Maritime Publishing in England, 1528–1640," *The Library* 6th ser., vol. 14 (1992): 212.

54. In the 1582 subsidy lists for St. Bennet's Parish, Thomas East and Henry Bynneman are listed together; see R. G. Lang, *Two Tudor Subsidy Rolls for the City of London: 1541 and 1582* (London: London Record Society, 1993), 182. An indication of the capital of each is reflected in the fact that East was assessed at £3, Bynneman at £10. East's onetime partner Henry Middleton was assessed at £8 and Robert East, the ironmonger who lived in the former mansion of Thomas Lewen, at £180, the second highest of all London citizens in 1582.

55. Bynneman probably did not print any music books by Byrd or Tallis. He did, however, attempt to sell a great number of copies of music books and music paper; see Mark Eccles, "Bynneman's Books," *The Library* 5th ser., vol. 12 (1957): 83 and 88, n. 2. Of the many editions printed by East and Bynneman see, for example, STC2: 18949, 19114, and 17577. Certain type that East either borrowed or bought from Bynneman appeared regularly in later editions by East; see Colin Clair, *A History of Printing in England* (London: Cassel, 1964), 315; and Iain Fenlon and John Milsom, "'Ruled Paper Imprinted': Music Paper and Patents in Sixteenth-Century England," *Journal of the American Musicological Society* (hereafter *JAMS*) 37 (1984): 145, n. 21.

56. These include East's "apostle" series and the beautiful inhabited series Day originally used in J. Cunningham's *Cosmographical Glasse* in 1559. For illustrations and bibliographical descriptions of these initials, see C. L. Oastler, *John Day, the Elizabethan Printer* (Oxford: Oxford Bibliographical Society, 1975), 45, Fig. 5, and 47, Fig. 6 (iii).

57. Among the romances to be published by East were an Elizabethan edition of Sir Thomas Malory's *La Mort d'Arthur* (1585) and a series of English translations of the works of Diego Ortuñez de Calahorra. East's editions of John Lyly's series of "Euphues" prose fiction are discussed in Plomer, "Thomas East," 303–304. Medieval texts reprinted by East, often as the only Tudor version, include *Bartholomeus de proprietatibus rerum* (1582), Malory's *La Mort d'Arthur*, and *Mandeville's Travels* (1568); see Plomer, "Thomas East," 300–303.

58. Tyler's translation is STC2 18859. East created a small industry with these romances. According to STC2, he published three volumes and numerous reprints as follows: *The Mirror of Princely Deeds* (London, 1578, 1582, 1599), *The Second Part of the Mirror of Princely Deeds* (London, 1583, 1585), and *The Third Part of the First Boke of the Mirror of Princely Deeds* (London, 1586: 2 editions). Another indication of the popularity of these is found in the stationers' registers. After he had published the first volume, East took the untranslated second book to be entered as protection from other publishers. The master and warden noted East's unusual tactic of registering a book in its pretranslated state by stipulating that it was to be printed "condiconally notwithstandinge that when the same is translated yt be brought to them to be pervsed, and yf any thinge be amisse therein to be amended" (Arber, *Transcript*, vol. 2, 414).

59. See Louise Schleiner, "Margaret Tyler, Translator and Waiting Woman," *English Language Notes* 29 (1992): 1–8.

60. See *STC2* 18859, A2–4v. East also wrote prefatory material for the other volumes in this series that he published.

CHAPTER 2

1. See Stanley H. Boorman, "Petrucci at Fossombrone: A Study of Early Music Printing, with a Special Reference to the Motetti de la Corona (1514–1519)" (Ph.D. diss., University of London, 1976); Catherine Chapman, "Andrea Antico" (Ph.D. diss., Harvard University, 1964); and Mary Kay Duggan, *Italian Music Incunabula: Printers and Type* (Berkeley and Los Angeles: University of California Press, 1992).

2. Ibid., 273–278.

3. The title page and colophon are undated: 1501 is the date that appears in its dedication. See Jean Marix, "Harmonice musices odhècaton A: Quelques prècisions chronologiques," *Revue de musicologie* 19 (1932): 236–241.

4. Iain Fenlon, *Music, Print and Culture in Early Sixteenth-Century Italy, the Panizzi Lectures, 1994* (London: British Library, 1995), 22.

5. Stanley H. Boorman, "The Salzburg Liturgy and Single-Impression Music Printing," in J. Kmetz (ed.), *Music in the German Renaissance: Sources, Styles and Contexts* (Cambridge: Cambridge University Press, 1994), 235–253.

6. See Alec Hyatt King, "The Significance of John Rastell in Early Music Printing," *The Library* 5th ser., vol. 26 (1971): 197–214; and John Milsom, "Songs and Society in Early Tudor London," *Early Music History* 16 (1997): 235–293.

7. Daniel Heartz, "A New Attaingnant Book and the Beginnings of French Music Printing," *Journal of the American Musicological Society* 14 (1961): 9–23.

8. For a statistical overview of the output of Venetian music-printing firms, see Tim Carter, "Music Publishing in Italy, c. 1580–c. 1625: Some Preliminary Observations," *RMA Research Chronicle* 20 (1986–1987): 19–37.

9. Richard Agee, *The Gardano Music Printing Firms, 1569–1611* (Rochester, NY: University of Rochester Press, 1998), 3–4.

10. Elizabeth Eisenstein, *The Printing Press as an Agent of Change: Communications and Cultural Transformations in Early-Modern Europe*, 2 vols. (Cambridge: Cambridge University Press, 1979), and *The Printing Revolution in Early Modern Europe* (Cambridge: Cambridge University Press, 1983). See also Lucien Febvre and Henri-Jean Martin, *The Coming of the Book: The Impact of Printing, 1450–1800*, translated by David Gerard, edited by Geoffrey Nowell-Smith and David Wootton (London: Humanities Press, 1976).

11. Mary S. Lewis, *Antonio Gardano: Venetian Music Printer, 1538–1569: A Descriptive Bibliography and Historical Study*, vol. 1: *1538–1549* (New York and London: Garland, 1988), vol. 2: *1550–1559* (New York and London: Garland, 1997); Agee, *The Gardano Music Printing Firms;* and Jane A. Bernstein, *Music Printing in Renaissance Venice: The Scotto Press (1539–1572)* (New York: Oxford University Press, 1998).

12. Daniel Heartz, *Pierre Attaingnant, Royal Printer of Music: A Historical Study and Bibliographical Catalogue* (Berkeley and Los Angeles: University of California Press, 1969), xviii–xix.

13. Bernstein, *Music Printing in Renaissance Venice,* 12.

14. Suzanne G. Cusick, *Valerio Dorico: Music Printer in Sixteenth-Century Rome* (Ann Arbor, MI: UMI Research Press, 1981).

15. On these music printers, see Kristine K. Forney, "Tielman Susato, Sixteenth-Century Music Printer: An Archival and Typographical Investigation" (Ph.D. diss., University of Kentucky, 1978); and Henri Vanhulst, *Catalogue des éditions de musique publiées à Louvain par Pierre Phalèse et ses fils (1545–1578)* (Brussels: Palais des académies, 1990).

16. See Gerald P. Tyson and Sylvia S. Wagonheim (eds.), *Print and Culture in the Renaissance:*

Essays on the Advent of Printing in Europe (Newark: University of Delaware Press, 1986). In their introduction, the editors note that "it will shortly become clear that printing was not quite as sweeping or instantaneous a revolution as had been usually thought" (8–9).

17. See John Milsom, "Songs and Society in Early Tudor London," *Early Music History* 16 (1997): 239. Milsom discusses newly discovered fragments of English printed music in this important article. The standard guide (in need of revision) to the music editions of this era remains Robert R. Steele, *The Earliest English Music Printing: A Description and Bibliography of English Printed Music to the Close of the Sixteenth Century* (London: Bibliographical Society, 1903). Steele discusses three additional music works of this era that were printed but are now lost (ghosts): a lute book of 1565, a citherne book of 1568 by Day, and Delamotte's *Introduction* of 1574 printed by Vautrollier. See, also, Bruce Pattison, "Notes on Early Music Printing," *The Library* 4th ser. Vol. 19 (1939): 378–418.

18. Milsom, "Songs and Society," 239. Milsom refers specifically to the time of Henry VIII.

19. Alec Hyatt King argued that Rastell was the first to use single-impression music type; see his "The Significance of John Rastell," 197–214. The 1570 music edition of Lasso's *Receuil* by Vautrollier was also of special historical importance. Using this work as evidence, Joseph Kerman corrected former contentions by showing that Vautrollier (rather than the composers) owned the music type used in the Tallis and Byrd *Cantiones* of 1575; see "An Elizabethan Edition of Lassus," *Acta Musicologica* 27 (1955): 74–75.

20. See J. Alpin, "The Origins of John Day's 'Certaine Notes,'" *Music & Letters* 62 (1981): 295–299.

21. Kerman, "Elizabethan Edition," 74; and Colin W. Holman, "John Day's 'Certaine Notes' (1560–65)" (Ph.D. diss., University of Kansas, 1991).

22. An account of the music of Marian exiles appears in Robin Leaver, *'Goostly Psalmes and Spirituall Songes': English and Dutch Metrical Psalms from Coverdale to Utenhove 1535–1566* (Oxford: Clarendon Press, 1991), 175–271.

23. H. Robinson (ed.), *Zurich Letters Comprising the Correspondence of Several English Bishops and Others, with Some of the Helvetian Reformers, during the Reign of Queen Elizabeth*, 2 vols. (Cambridge: Parker Society, 1842), vol. 1, 71, 40*–41*. These are translated in Leaver, *'Goostly Psalmes,'* 241.

24. Henry Machyn, *The Diary of Henry Machyn*, edited by J. G. Nichols (London: Printed for the Camden Society, 1848), 212. For this reference I am indebted to Nicholas Temperley, *The Music of the English Parish Church* (Cambridge: Cambridge University Press, 1979), 43.

25. See Rivkah Zim, *English Metrical Psalms: Poetry as Praise and Prayer 1535–1601* (Cambridge: Cambridge University Press, 1987), 112.

26. Ibid.

27. These editions are discussed in Temperley, *The Music of the English Parish Church*, 53–57. A bibliographical guide to them appears in Zim, *Metrical Psalms*, 211–259.

28. The clearest evidence for this is the several hundred editions listed for the *Whole Booke of Psalmes* in STC2. The connections between the psalms (as separated and set to music) and their original biblical source was an important factor in the book's widespread acceptance. The Act of Uniformity firmly resolved that only one version of the English Bible would be permitted in England, but no such law applied directly to a single musical version of the psalter. If they were never formally described in the statutes and laws of religious observance of the Elizabethan Settlement, these editions were sufficiently, if ambiguously, described in the Injunctions of 1559; see Temperley, *The Music of the English Parish Church*, 40–42. The title page of the 1561 edition by Day may have eradicated the ambiguity of the statute. Here it was clearly stated that the works were to be sung "according to the order appointd in the Queen Majesty's injunctions" (Zim, *Metrical Psalms*, 232). For a thorough guide to the music,

see Nicholas Temperley, *The Hymn Tune Index: A Census of English-Language Hymn Tunes in Printed Sources from 1535 to 1820*, 3 vols. (Oxford: Oxford University Press, 1998).

29. For a general history of the patents and the way these shaped the London printing trade, see Cyprian Blagden, *The Stationers' Company: A History 1403–1959* (London: Allen and Unwin, 1960). A full list of the patentees before 1640 appears in *STC2*, vol. 3, 195. Donald W. Krummel, *English Music Printing 1553–1700* (London: Bibliographical Society, 1975), 10–30, is the standard discussion of the complex relations caused by the patents of monopoly among stationers who printed music. See also Miriam Miller, "London Music Printing, c. 1570– c. 1640" (Ph.D. diss., University of London, 1969), 14–17.

30. Donald W. Krummel and Stanley Sadie (eds.), *Music Printing and Publishing*, Norton/ Grove Handbooks in Music (New York: Norton, 1990), s.v. "William Seres," by Miriam Miller. Only two editions with musical notation by Seres are known: Francis Seager, *Certayne Psalms*, 1553; and Christopher Tye, *Acts of the Apostles*, 1553; and they contain the same music font. For the hypothesis that Day's type was used for these books, see Krummel, *English Music Printing*, 42–46, and Leaver, *'Goostly psalmes'*, 244.

31. Krummel, *English Music Printing*, 11; Edward Arber, *A Transcript of the Registers of the Company of Stationers of London, 1554–1640 A.D.*, 5 vols. (Birmingham: The editor, 1875–1894), vol. 1, 124.

32. This patent appeared in Day's edition of the *Cosmological glasse* of 1559, dedicated to the queen. This edition itself was an extraordinarily beautiful example of printed work. Thus it would not be completely unreasonable to suppose that the comprehensive privilege Day won was due to his demonstrated capabilities to produce superior work.

33. For full texts of Day's patents, see Steele, *Earliest English Music Printing*, 22–23.

34. John Feather believes that the specific target of the complaints by the poor printers of the Stationers' Company was Day (*Publishing, Piracy and Politics: An Historical Study of Copyright in Britain* [London: Mansell, 1994], 21). Joseph Loewenstein provides a useful summary of the various methods by which the printing trade was regulated in "For a History of Literary Property: John Wolfe's Reformation," *English Literary Renaissance* 18 (1988): 390–394.

35. Arber, *Transcript*, vol. 1, 111; and see C. L. Oastler, *John Day, the Elizabethan Printer* (Oxford: Oxford Bibliographical Society, 1975), 40–42. On Day's music printing, see F. G. Edwards, "A Famous Music Printer, John Day, 1522–1584," *Musical Times* 47 (1906): 170–174, 236–239. On the connection between this complaint and Day's privilege of 1577, see Feather, *Publishing, Piracy and Politics*, 21; and Miller, "London Music Printing," 17.

36. The first printed collections of the *Whole Book of Psalmes* did not include music nota- tion. Scholars have speculated that either its music was originally composed with immediate publication in mind or it came from folk song or dance repertories that were ready at hand but for which sources do not survive. The latter conjecture is strengthened by the minuscule evidence of notated music from the ballad repertoire and the tradition of such *contrafacta* in the composition of Lutheran hymns; see Nicholas Temperley, "The Old Way of Singing: Its Origins and Development," *JAMS* 34 (1981): 516–518. Such a link with an oral tradition would help to explain the broad appeal of these settings of metrical psalms. Perhaps the practice of setting religious texts with tunes from secular song, which was established by Luther and others, might also have been followed for these Englished versions of the psalms. The title pages of the early editions by Day seem to suggest this by setting the psalm tunes as an anti- dote to other "ungodly Songes and Ballades, which tende only to the norishing of vyce, and corrupting of youth"; see Zim, *Metrical Psalms*, 232.

37. Sir John Stainer, "On the Musical Introductions Found in Certain Metrical Psalters," *Proceedings of the Royal Musical Association* 27 (1900–1901): 5.

38. Cyprian Blagden, "The English Stock of the Stationers' Company: An Account of Its Origins," *The Library* 5th ser., vol. 10 (1955): 184.

39. Harry Hoppe, "John Wolfe, Printer and Publisher, 1579–1601," *The Library* 4th ser., vol. 14 (1933): 256.

40. Richard Vernon, a former employee of Day, testified that the latter earned £250 annually from his privileged books (Oastler, *John Day*, 22).

41. Hoppe, "John Wolfe," 256.

42. For the dating of the "Complaynt," see W. W. Greg, *A Companion to Arber* (Oxford: Clarendon Press, 1967), #70.

43. Arber, *Transcript*, vol. 1, 111.

44. Arber provides a series of documents on the issue (vol. 1, 111–116, 140–144, and 246–248). They are supplemented by Greg, *Companion*, 124–134. For a narrative history of this famous dispute among London's stationers, see Lowenstein, "For a History," 396–405, which is based on a short documentary history by Greg (*Companion*, 117–123).

45. Loewenstein, "For a History," 396–405.

46. Greg, *Companion*, 123–125.

47. Several documents attest to the patentees' willingness to release certain titles to poor relief (Greg, *Companion*, p. 126 and #104). For the list of "released" titles, see Arber, *Transcript*, vol. 2, 787–788, and *STC2*, vol. 3, 199. The editors of *STC2* studied the list for evidence that the titles were reprinted in that year. They found that only a few titles were actually reprinted at that time, although three of Day's released titles did appear in 1584 editions.

48. These do not appear in the "poor relief" list; see *STC2*, vol. 3, 199.

49. W. W. Greg and E. Boswell, *Records of the Court of the Stationers' Company: 1576 to 1602 from Register B* (London: Bibliographical Society, 1930), 24.

50. Cyril Judge, *Elizabethan Book Pirates* (Cambridge, MA: Harvard University Press, 1934), 63.

51. This production method is described in Philip Gaskell, *A New Introduction to Bibliography* (Oxford: Clarendon Press, 1974), 116–117.

52. Arber, *Transcript*, vol. 2, 807–812.

53. Loewenstein, "For a History," 404.

54. Hoppe, "John Wolfe," 264–265.

55. Ibid., 255.

56. John Day's original intention was for his son to have a career in the church, but in 1577 Richard left his fellowship at Cambridge to join John in the book trade. At Day's Aldersgate shop, Richard served as an editor for his father's press, held a supervisor's role in the operation of presses alongside his stepmother, and helped maintain the financial records of the firm. Richard was listed with his father in the 1577 renewal of their royal patent. See PRO, *Court of the Star Chamber*, C24/180, *Richard Day vs. Alice Day* (1580–1581), Interr. 1, f.1. Richard Day's education is discussed in the *DNB*, s.v. "Richard Day." The remaining section on Richard Day's career is based on the 1585 and 1586 cases in the Star Chamber (PRO, C24/180–181). A summary of the case appears in Oastler, *John Day*, 65–68.

57. No editions by Richard Day appear in *STC2* after 1580. Some of his type, including a distinctive "apostle" series of initials, passed to East.

58. In a case between the assigns of Richard Day and William Ponson, it was revealed that eleven stationers were involved in one of the largest cases of piracy for which we now have a record. The assigns argued that Ponsonby and others had printed 4,000 copies of the *Psalmes* and had already bound 2,000 for sale. The court found that 10,000 copies of the *ABC* were also pirated. Whether this case reveals an increase in piracy or only a more accurate reflection of prior activities (due to more vigilant enforcement) is an open question. For a transcription of relevant cases, see Judge, *Elizabethan Book Pirates*, 149–155.

59. See Blagden, "English Stock," 163–185.

60. PRO, Patent Rolls C66/1463, m.2, "Music Privilege to Thomas Tallis and William

Byrd (1575)," transcribed in Steele, *Earliest English Music Printing,* 19, and Edmund H. Fellowes, *William Byrd,* 2d ed. (London: Oxford University Press, 1948), 9.

61. Denis Stevens, *Tudor Church Music* (New York: W.W. Norton, 1966), 43. See also Craig Monson, "Byrd and the 1575 Cantiones Sacrae," *Musical Times* 116 (1975): 1089–1091 and 117 (1976): 65–67; and Philip Brett, review of *Tallis and Byrd: Cantiones Sacrae (1575),* recording by Cantores in Ecclesia, director Michael Howard, *Musical Quarterly* 43 (1972): 149–153.

62. Facsimiles of the prefatory material and translations of the commendatory poems appear in William Byrd, *The Byrd Edition,* edited by Philip Brett, 20 vols. (hereafter *BE*), vol. 1: *Cantiones Sacrae (1575),* edited by Craig Monson (London: Stainer and Bell, 1976), xv–xxvi.

63. Fellowes, *William Byrd,* 10. The appeal of 1577 was apparently successful; the queen granted a property lease to Byrd in that year. See Fellowes, *William Byrd,* 11.

64. Arber, *Transcript,* vol. 1, 144.

65. The evidence for the failure as revealed in Barker's report and the composers' letter to the queen is often noted in general studies, and they are conveniently summarized in Monson, *Cantiones (1575),* v.

66. Mark Eccles, "Bynneman's Books," *The Library* 5th ser., vol. 12 (1957): 81–92.

67. Ibid., 88.

68. Ibid.

69. The book is listed twice in the catalogs of the Frankfurt fair; see John Harley, "New Light on William Byrd," *Music & Letters* 79 (1998): 478. It appears there with differing dates (1571 and 1578). This might be viewed as evidence that a new edition of the book was produced, but it is difficult to explain, then, why the composers would produce a new edition after explaining their "great loss" to the queen only one year earlier. More likely, the discrepant dates were caused by a publisher's reissue of the edition (i.e., a repackaging of the old edition with newly printed title pages) or, indeed, by scribal errors of a cataloger. For lists of the books sold at Frankfurt Fairs see James Thompson *The Frankfort Book Fair* (New York: Burt Franklin, 1911).

70. Fellowes, *William Byrd,* 8.

71. Ibid., 10.

72. Since the grant itself and the *Cantiones* edition were produced so close in time, it is possible that the composers referred also to the cost of gaining access to the queen through an intermediary in the court. The sum of 200 marks may have been a gratuity for the acquisition of the patent. For a discussion of the inner workings of the patronage system at Elizabeth's court and its hidden costs, see J. E. Neale, "The Elizabethan Political Scene," *Proceedings of the British Academy* 34 (1948): 97–117. Heybourne, alias Richardson, who contributed a commendatory poem for the composers in the book, was well placed to serve as an intermediary between the composers and the queen; see R. Marlow, "Sir Ferdinando Heybourne Alias Richardson," *Musical Times* 115 (1974): 736–739.

73. Dowling, "Dowland's 'Second Booke of Songs,'" 372–374.

74. See Monson, *Cantiones,* xxii.

75. The imprint lists Vautrollier at his address in the Blackfriars (see the facsimile of the title page in Monson, *Cantiones,* xv). In the absence of other data, this advertisement does remotely suggest that Vautrollier had a hand in the sales of the copies. Yet it contrasts with some imprints by East that explicitly denote the retailer, e.g., for Morley's *Canzonets a 3:* "Imprinted at London by Tho: East, the assigne of William Byrd: dwelling at Aldersgate street, at the signe of the black horse, and are there to be sold," see *STC2* 18121, [A]1r.

76. See Kerman, "Elizabethan Edition," 73; and Colin Clair, "Christopher Plantin's Trade-Connections with England and Scotland," *The Library* 5th ser., vol. 14 (1959): 28–45.

77. Arber, *Transcript,* vol. 1, 144.

78. Notable exceptions to this were the Chapel Royal and Cambridge and Oxford Universities. For a recent discussion of the continued circulation of Latin music after the 1559 Elizabethan Settlement, see John Milsom, "Sacred Songs in the Chamber," in John Morehen (ed.), *English Choral Practice 1400–1650* (Cambridge: Cambridge University Press, 1995), 161–199. Milsom argues here that the protestants were not all hindered from enjoying the music by the "Catholic agenda" in motet texts.

79. Joseph Kerman, "The Elizabethan Motet: A Study of Texts for Music," *Studies in the Renaissance* 9 (1962): 288–292, and *The Masses and Motets of William Byrd* (Berkeley: University of California Press, 1981), 35.

80. The most recent study of the Chapel Royal is David Baldwin, *The Chapel Royal Ancient & Modern* (London: Duckworth, 1990). Craig Monson, "Elizabethan London," in Iain Fenlon (ed.), *The Renaissance: From the 1470s to the End of the 16th Century* (London: Macmillan, 1989), 304–340, includes a useful discussion of the Chapel Royal in the Renaissance era.

81. See Monson, *Cantiones*, xv–xxvi.

82. Kerman, "The Elizabethan Motet," 289–295.

83. Harley, "New Light," 478.

84. Monson, *Cantiones*, iii.

85. The classic study of the philosophical underpinnings of such writing is E. M. W. Tillyard, *The Elizabethan World Picture* (London: Chatto and Windus, 1943). For the history of a growing national consciousness in forms of literature in the Elizabethan era, see Richard Helgerson, *Forms of Nationhood: The Elizabethan Writing of England* (Chicago: University of Chicago Press, 1992).

86. On this issue, see Brett, "Cantiones Sacrae," 150.

87. For the accounts of ambassadors in London, see Monson, "Elizabethan London," 308–311.

88. See Fellowes, *William Byrd*, 11–12.

89. See Monson, *Cantiones*, v–viii.

90. On manuscript and print culture, see J. W. Saunders, "The Stigma of Print: A Note on the Social Bases of Tudor Poetry," *Essays in Criticism* 1 (1951): 139–164; Daniel Traister, "Reluctant Virgins: The Stigma of Print Revisited," *Colby Quarterly* 26 (1990): 75–86; Harold Love, *Scribal Publication in Seventeenth-Century England* (Oxford: Clarendon Press, 1993); and Arthur Marotti, *Manuscript, Print, and the English Renaissance Lyric* (Ithaca: Cornell University Press, 1995).

91. Krummel, *English Music Printing*, 16.

92. Steele, *Earliest English Music Printing*, 28. Despite his annoyance with the uncontrollable competition, Morley kept the privilege for ruled music paper in his patent.

93. *The Catalogue of Manuscripts in the Library of St. Michael's College, Tenbury*, compiled by Edmund H. Fellowes (Paris: Editions de l'Oiseaux Lyre, 1934). These manuscripts are now at the Bodleian Library, Oxford University.

94. Iain Fenlon and John Milsom, "'Ruled Paper Imprinted': Music Paper and Patents in Sixteenth-Century England," *JAMS* 37 (1984): 139–163.

95. East's music paper was conveniently cataloged by editors of the *STC2* (7467.5).

96. Fenlon and Milsom, "'Ruled Paper Imprinted,'" 146–154.

97. Eccles, "Bynneman's Books," 87.

98. Alexander Rodger, "Roger Ward's Shrewsbury Stock: An Inventory of 1585," *The Library* 5th ser., vol. 13 (1958): 264.

99. Gerald D. Johnson, "William Barley, 'Publisher & Seller of Bookes,' 1591–1614," *The Library* 6th ser., vol. 11 (1989): 16.

100. See Kristine K. Forney, "Antwerp's Role in the Reception and Dissemination of the Madrigal to the North," in Angelo Pompillo et al. (eds.), *Atti del XIV Congresso della Società Internazionale di Musicologia: Trasmissione e Recezione delle Forme di Cultura Musicale, Bologna, 27 agosto– 1 settembre 1987* (Turin: Edizioni di Torino, 1990), vol. 1, 239–253.

101. See Joseph Kerman, *The Elizabethan Madrigal: A Comparative Study* (New York: American Musicological Society, 1962), 47–49.

102. Morley's compositional gleanings from continental sources are well known, but they have recently been clarified and further emphasized in Daniel Jacobson, "Thomas Morley and the Italian Madrigal Tradition: A New Perspective," *Journal of Musicology* 14 (1996): 80–91. Music of the nearby countries of France and the Netherlands had a similar effect; see Jane A. Bernstein, "The Chanson in England 1530–1640: A Study of Sources and Styles" (Ph.D. diss., University of California, Berkeley, 1974).

103. See Philip Brett, "Edward Paston (1550–1630): A Norfolk Gentleman and His Musical Collection," *Transactions of the Cambridge Bibliographical Society* 4 (1964): 51–69. On Arundel, see John Milsom, "The Nonsuch Music Library," in Chris Banks, Arthur Searle, and Malcolm Turner (eds.), *Sundry Sorts of Music Books: Essays on the British Library Collections presented to O. W. Neighbor on his 70th Birthday* (London: British Library, 1993), 146–182.

104. Milsom, "The Nonsuch Music Library," 146.

105. *STC2* 26094, A4r.

106. See Lydia Hamessley, "The Tenbury and Ellesmere Partbooks: New Findings on Manuscript Compilation and Exchange, and the Reception of the Italian Madrigal in Elizabethan England," *Music & Letters* 73 (1992): 177–221.

CHAPTER 3

1. Edward Arber (ed.), *A Transcript of the Registers of the Company of Stationers of London, 1554– 1640 A.D.*, 5 vols. (Birmingham: The editor, 1875–1894), vol. 1, 144.

2. See Josephine Waters, "The Woodcut Illustrations in the English Editions of 'Mandeville's Travels,'" *Papers of the Bibliographical Society of America* 47 (1953): 59–63.

3. PRO, Probate Records, PROB 11/156/61, "Will of Lucretia East, 1627."

4. *DNB*, s.v. "Richard Field."

5. Donald W. Krummel and Stanley Sadie (eds.), *Music Printing and Publishing*, Norton/ Grove Handbooks in Music (New York: Norton, 1990), s.v. "Pierre Haultin," by Donald W. Krummel.

6. Ibid.

7. One clear problem with this theory is Field's designation as "mercer" rather than "stationer" in the will (see earlier). Ursula Carlyle, assistant archivist to the Mercers' Company, kindly informed me in a correspondence of 6 November 1995 that it was not uncommon for nonmercers to so name themselves. Ms. Carlyle did discover one Richard Field who was admitted to the freedom of the Mercers' Company in 1606, however.

8. Donald W. Krummel, *English Music Printing 1553–1700* (London: Bibliographical Society, 1975), 84, n. 7. The edition is John Harrington, *A New Discourse on a Stale Subject*, R. Field (1596), *STC2* 12779.

9. On East's psalmbook font, see Krummel, *English Music Printing*, 61 (he was unaware of Field's use of this font). The version of Harrington's work wherein Field used East's psalter font is *STC2* 12779.5.

10. Krummel, *English Music Printing*, 61.

11. Using methods Mary S. Lewis has described in helpful detail (in her *Antonio Gardano: Venetian Music Printer, 1538–1569: A Descriptive Bibliography and Historical Study*, vol. 1: *1538–1549*

[New York: Garland, 1988], 63), I discovered standing type in the headers, signatures, and occasionally portions of the text underlay that appeared in multiple parts of the same edition. This indicates that, in such cases, East printed his part-books in vertical settings.

12. For an in-depth analysis of Elizabethan proofing, see Peter W. Blayney, *The Texts of 'King Lear' and Their Origins*, vol. 1: *Nicholas Okes and the First Quarto* (Cambridge: Cambridge University Press, 1982), 188–218. A useful collection of primary material in facsimile appears in J. K. Moore, *Primary Materials Relating to Copy and Print in English Books of the Sixteenth and Seventeenth Centuries* (Oxford: Oxford Bibliographical Society, 1992). See also Fredson Bowers, "Elizabethan Proofing," in *Essays in Bibliography, Text and Editing* (Charlottesville: University of Virginia Press, 1975), 241–242. The editors of *BE* have discussed East's editing in useful detail. Another excellent study is John Milsom, "Tallis, Byrd and the 'Incorrected Copy': Some Cautionary Notes for Editors of Early Music Printed from Movable Type," *Music & Letters* 77 (1996): 348–367.

13. Edwin Wolf, "Press Corrections in Sixteenth and Seventeenth Century Quartos," *Papers of the Bibliographical Society of America* 36 (1942), 188. See also W. W. Greg, "An Elizabethan Printer and His Copy," *The Library* 4th ser., vol. 4 (1923–1924): 102–118.

14. See Milsom, "Tallis, Byrd and the 'Incorrected Copy,'" 352–355.

15. On manuscript corrections and cancel slips, see ibid., 356–357. Milsom notes that a similarity in handwriting in multiple copies of an edition signals editing at the press. This circumstance obtained in East's hidden edition of the *Musica Transalpina I* (cf., for example, the incorrect minim similarly corrected with ink in *STC2* 26094.5, British Library copies K.3.k.9 and R.M.15.e.2, altus D1v, line 3). East used cancel slips several times in Byrd's *Gradualia* of 1605: In "Alma Redemptoris mater" a sharp is added by cancel slip to the F♯ semibreve over "genitorem" (*STC2* 4243, British Library RM.15.d.1, medius, 2D1r, line 9). A slip appears in the tenor part of "Gloria tibi domine," replacing the incorrect F with a G (*STC2* 4243, British Library RM.15.d.1, tenor, 3A1v, line 5). In the bassus part of "Suscepimus Deus," an "&" is replaced by a cancel slip with "eʃt" (*STC2* 4243, British Library RM.15.d.1, bassus, B1r, line 4). In Danyel's *Songs for Lute*, a semiminim is replaced by a cancel slip with the correct value of a minim for the F♯ over "beg'd" (*STC2* 6268, British Library, K.2.g.9, [A] 2v, line 3). In Byrd's *Gradualia* II of 1607, an incorrectly printed B♭ (a dotted semiminim) is replaced with the correct note, C, by a cancel slip (*STC2* 4244, British Library, K.2.f.8, cantus primus 3H2v, line 6).

16. The *Thomas East vs. George Eastland* suits of 1601 went before the Court of the King's Bench (PRO, K.B. 27/1364 /m. 534), the Court of Requests (PRO, Req. 2 /202/63; Req. 2/203/4), and the Court of Chancery (PRO, C2 Eliz. /E1/64). For a substantial account of this case, see Margaret Dowling, "The Printing of John Dowland's 'Second Booke of Songs or Ayres,'" *The Library* 4th ser., vol. 12 (1932): 365–380.

17. Further bibliographical implications of their actions are discussed in Francis R. Johnson, "Printers' 'Copy Books' and the Black Market in the Elizabethan Book Trade," *The Library* 5th ser., vol. 1 (1946): 97–105.

18. PRO, Req 2. 202/63.

19. Dowling did not seem to recognize that one of the witnesses in this case was the composer John Wilbye, although she does note the participation of notable musicians Johnson and Rosseter ("The Printing," 376).

20. PRO, Req 2. 203/4.

21. The error occurs on M1v, line 4. The cancel slip was found in the Royal College of Music (II.K.6) but does not appear in at least one other copy, where the accurate sign was actually printed by East (see, for example, Manchester Music Library, Rf 410 Ds 406).

22. PRO, Req 2. 202/63.

23. Ibid.

24. Ibid.

25. East was certainly not the only London printer to create hidden editions; see W. W. Greg, "On Certain False Dates in Shakespearean Quartos," *The Library* 2d ser., vol. 9 (1908): 113–132 and 381–409. H. K. Andrews and Peter Clulow discovered several hidden editions in their often-cited bibliographical studies of Byrd's editions; see H. K. Andrews, "The Printed Part-Books of Byrd's Vocal Music," *The Library* 5th ser., vol. 19 (1964): 1–10, and "Printed Sources of William Byrd's 'Psalmes, Sonets and Songs,'" *Music & Letters* 44 (1963): 5–20; and Peter Clulow, "Publication Dates for Byrd's Latin Masses," *Music & Letters* 47 (1966): 1–9. They did not detect that the following three works cited in their studies were also titles with hidden editions: Morley's *First Book of Balletts* (1595), Wilbye's *First Set of English Madrigals* (1598), and Morley's *Madrigalls to Fovre Voices*, 2d ed. (1600); see Clulow, "Publication Dates," 7–8. These last three hidden editions were discovered more recently. Philip Brett detected a hidden edition of Morley's *Balletts* of 1595; see his unpublished dissertation, "The Songs of William Byrd," (Ph.D. diss., Cambridge University, 1965), 215–216. The editors of *STC*2 determined that Wilbye's *English Madrigals* was produced in two hidden editions, and in the course of this study a hitherto unknown hidden edition was discovered: the falsely dated reprint of Morley's *Madrigalls to Fovre Voices*, 2d ed., 1600.

26. PRO, Req 2. 202/63.

27. The figure of £482. 8d. 3p, undoubtedly an estimate of East's estate at his death, was written at the bottom of the probate in East's original will (Guildhall Library, London, Original Wills, Box 3B [Ms. 9052. 3B], f. 61, "Will of Thomas East, 21 July 1607). In comparison, John Day, the highly successful general printer and sometime music printer, probably left his second wife alone more than £5,000 at his death in 1584. See C. L. Oastler, *John Day, the Elizabethan Printer* (Oxford: Oxford Bibliographical Society, 1975), 65. In the 1582 Lay Subsidy Roll for London (PRO, E179/251/16), East was taxed £3 while his neighbor and fellow stationer Henry Bynneman was taxed £10 and East's former partner, Henry Middleton, £8.

28. H. S. Bennett, *English Books & Readers 1558–1603* (Cambridge: Cambridge University Press, 1965), 272.

29. Allan H. Stevenson, *The Problem of the* Missale Speciale (London: Bibliographical Society, 1967), *passim*. For a recent application of paper-evidence methodology in musicology, see Peter Wright, "Paper Evidence and the Dating of Trent 91," *Music & Letters* 76 (1995): 487–509.

30. On the history and process of papermaking, see Dard Hunter, *Papermaking: The History and Technique of an Ancient Craft*, 2d ed. (London: Pleiades, 1947).

31. See Allan H. Stevenson, "Watermarks Are Twins," *Studies in Bibliography* 4 (1951–1952): 57–91.

32. See Table A1.3.

33. Stevenson, *The Problem of the* Missale Speciale, 94.

34. For London publishers at this time, paper was almost exclusively an imported commodity. Because of the vagaries of shipping and storing methods for large quantities of paper, the European papermakers sold their product to the London market from several mills in a region at once, thus meshing separately produced stocks. The detection of two editions with a constellation of similar marks provides persuasive evidence that they are from one stock of paper as delivered to the market. See ibid., 59–60.

35. Ibid., 94.

36. To produce these two editions East also included a token remnant of *Crown* 1 paper for certain [A] gatherings of both editions (see Table A1.3). Since this *Crown* 1 paper does not appear elsewhere in East's output, it links these two editions especially closely.

37. The editors of *STC*2 also surmise that Thomas Snodham, East's adopted son, printed the last hidden edition of Wilbye's *First Set*; see vol. 3, 316.

38. See Blayney, *The Texts of 'King Lear,'* 76 and 100.

39. See Andrews, "Printed Sources," 5–20; and " Printed Part-Books," 1–10; and Clulow, "Publication Dates," 1–9.

40. Andrews, "Printed Part-Books," 8.

41. Andrews, "Printed Sources," 11–12.

42. Krummel, *English Music Printing*, 15.

43. See Thomas G. Tanselle, "The Use of Type Damage as Evidence in Bibliographical Description," *The Library* 5th ser., vol. 23 (1968): 328–351.

44. Clulow, "Publication Dates," 5–8; and Andrews, "Printed Part-Books," 6.

45. Andrews, "Printed Sources," 6.

46. Andrews, "Printed Sources," 19–20, and "Printed Part-Books," 5–7.

47. The initials are actually woodblocks. For convenience' sake, they will be referred to as "type."

48. See Andrews, "Printed Sources," 20, and "Printed Part-Books," 6.

49. See Table A1.2.

50. See *STC2*, vol. 3, 230–249, for an in-depth study of and guide to stationers' addresses in East's era. According to *STC2* (vol. 3, 233), the B editions are the only ones to offer this address among the works of the entire group of London-based stationers in the years 1554 to 1650.

51. *NG*, s.v. "Thomas East," by William Miller and Jeremy Smith. The reference for this original will is Guildhall Library, London, Original Wills, Box 3B (Ms. 9052), f. 61. "Will of Thomas East, 21 July 1607." It was proved 30 April 1608 by the archdeaconry court of London; see Guildhall Library, London, Ms. 9050/4, f. 336v.

52. Guildhall Library, "Will of Thomas East." East's lessor for both Aldersgate Street properties was Sir Thomas Hunt, although by 1607 the leases had passed to Hunt's son Nicholas. Thomas Hunt was master of the Fishmongers' Company in 1592. In the Records of the Fishmongers' Company in Guildhall Library, Hunt's properties are discussed extensively; see, for example, Ms. 7259, "Deeds of Thomas Hunt's Essex Properties"; Ms. 6364, "Abstracts of Wills and Deeds," f. 37–39 (the abstract of Hunt's will); and Ms. 5570, "Court Minutes," vol. 1, f. 547–548 (a company viewing of some of Hunt's properties in Aldersgate Street).

53. Guildhall Library, "Will of Thomas East."

54. East gave the Aldersgate address for the first time in Byrd's *Songs of Sundrie Natures* edition of 1589; see also *STC2*, vol. 3, 56.

55. *STC2*, vol. 3, 233 and 56. For a bibliographical description of the two type ornaments of East's seal, see Ronald B. McKerrow, *Printers' & Publishers' Devices in England & Scotland 1485–1640* (London: Bibliographical Society, 1913), #206 and #209.

56. Guildhall Library, "Will of Thomas East."

57. See *The London Surveys of Ralph Treswell*, edited by John Scofield (London: Topographical Society, 1987), 7 and 36–37.

58. A facsimile of the "Ogilby and Morgan City of London Map" of 1676 appears in *The A to Z of Restoration London*, edited by Ralph Hyde (London: Topographical Society, 1992); see "Blackhorse Court," 14 (C72), and "George Inn," 25 (A99). Both, incidentally, were spared by the Great Fire of 1666.

59. East leased this property from Nowell Sotherton, Cursitor Baron of the Exchequer (who was himself a St. Botolph without Aldersgate parishioner; see *The London Surveys of Ralph Treswell*, 34–35). For further information on Sotherton see *The Judges of England 1272–1990: A List of Judges of the Superior Courts*, compiled by Sir John Sainty (London: Seldon Society, 1993), 137–139. Originally there was a note of the precise date on the seal of the Cripple-

gate lease in East's will (just the ending of the phrase remains), but unfortunately it was written on a portion of the document that has since been destroyed. Nonetheless, clearly legible in the extant will is a statement that the lease would begin "from the feaste of St Michael the archangel laste paste." Since the will itself is dated 5 February 1607/08, the lease began 29 September 1607; see Guildhall Library, "Will of Thomas East." Judging by the pattern set by East's use of the older Aldersgate address (see earlier), however, it would seem quite possible that he had begun to work at his Cripplegate address as early as 1605 or 1606.

60. *STC2*, vol. 3, 56. See also Henry R. Plomer, "Thomas East, Printer," *The Library* 2d ser., vol. 3 (1901): 300–309.

61. In the imprint of the *Psalmes*, for example, East noted that the copies were "to be sold at the dwelling house of the said Thomas East" (*STC2* 4253, [A]1r; a facsimile appears in Andrews, "Printed Sources," 7). For a case study of music sales in Europe at this time, see Tim Carter, "Music-Selling in Late Sixteenth-Century Florence: The Bookshop of Piero di Guiliano Morosi," *Music & Letters* 70 (1989): 483–501.

62. In a contract with the publisher George Eastland, East stipulated that he would keep a number of copies for his own trading purposes; see Dowling, "The Printing," 365–380.

63. *STC2*, vol. 3, 56.

64. Guildhall Library, "Will of Thomas East."

65. An exception was a musical treatise by William Bathe. This undated work provided too little paper or typographical evidence for conclusive results. In chapter 6, I consider circumstantial evidence that has to do with East's registrations and the timing of the music monopoly to place the work at the proper point in his production schedule.

66. Krummel and Sadie, *Music Printing and Publishing*, s.v. "Edition," by Stanley Boorman. For discussion of the reissues of Byrd's *Gradualia* editions, see Philip Brett (ed.), *Gradualia I (1605): The Marian Masses, BE* 5 (1989), xv–xvi. The reissue of Croce's *Musica Sacra* is noted in Krummel, *English Music Printing*, 94. For a discussion of the reissue of the Tessier chanson book, see John M. Ward, "Tessier and the 'Essex Circle,'" *Renaissance Quarterly* 29 (1976): 380.

CHAPTER 4

1. The swell of optimism at this time undoubtedly affected all business dealings in London, and Byrd and East were probably pleased that their venture coincided with an English victory. They had already taken steps to begin publishing music together in 1587, however, by registering Byrd's *Psalmes* at Stationers' Hall in November of that year (see Edward Arber, [ed.], *A Transcript of the Registers of the Company of Stationers of London, 1554–1640 A.D.*, 5 vols. [Birmingham: The editor, 1875–1894], 477).

2. According to *STC2*, East produced the following editions in 1588: his fifth edition of Lyly's *Euphues and His England* for Gabriel Cawood (*STC2* 17074); two military works for the publisher Thomas Wight, one by Cataneo (*STC2* 4791) and an English translation of Machiavelli's *Art of War* (*STC2* 17166); *Andria*, the classical play by Terence, for Thomas Woodcock (*STC2* 23895); a work by Arcaeus for Thomas Cadman (*STC2* 723); and two books East published himself (George Etherege's *In libros aliquot parli Aeginaletae*, [*STC2* 7498] and John Lyster's *A Rule How to Bring Up Children* [*STC2* 17122]).

3. A sermon by Laurence Chaderton contains East's initials, and thus it is listed in the *STC2* 4928 as a work East may have printed for Thomas Waldegrave.

4. H. K. Andrews's hypothesis that the B2 edition of Byrd's *Psalmes* was printed by East (*STC2* 4254) in 1599 ("Printed Sources of William Byrd's 'Psalmes, Sonets and Songs,'" *Music & Letters* 44 [1963]: 20) is no longer tenable (see chapter 7). Peter Clulow has shown

that 1599 is a possible date for the hidden editions of Byrd's Masses (see his "Publication Dates for Byrd's Latin Masses," *Music & Letters* 47 [1966)]: 1–9), but I suggest later that the year 1600 better fits the evidence.

5. This novel edition contained music by Byrd, John Bull, and Orlando Gibbons. It was reprinted in 1646, 1651, and 1655. For a discussion of the *Parthenia*, with an edition of the music, see John Bull, *Keyboard Music*, vol. 2, edited by R. T. Dart, Musica Britannica no. 19 (London: Stainer and Bell, 1963).

6. See Arber, *Transcript*, vol. 1, 111.

7. *NG*, s.v. "William Byrd," by Joseph Kerman.

8. Joseph Kerman, *The Elizabethan Madrigal: A Comparative Study* (New York: American Musicological Society, 1962), 261.

9. The most comprehensive study of Watson's life appears in Charles Nicholl, *The Reckoning: The Murder of Christopher Marlowe* (Chicago: University of Chicago Press, 1995), 177–184. Nicholl argues persuasively that Watson was brought up a Catholic. On John Case and his role as an apologist for music in the Anglican Church, see Nicholas Temperley, *The Music of the English Parish Church* (Cambridge: Cambridge University Press, 1979), 41–42.

10. The *Gratification* is transcribed with reconstructed parts in Philip Brett (ed.), *Madrigals, Songs and Canons*, BE 16 (1986). Byrd's madrigals are discussed later.

11. Kerman, *The Elizabethan Madrigal*, 261.

12. Ibid.

13. The popularity of certain forms of the Italian madrigal in the Netherlands, and the screen through which this music passed to England, is the subject of Joseph Kerman, "Elizabethan Anthologies of Italian Madrigals," *JAMS* 4 (1951), 122–138. See also Kristine K. Forney, "Antwerp's Role in the Reception and Dissemination of the Madrigal to the North," in Angelo Pompilio et al. (eds.), *Atti del XIV Congresso della Società Internazionale di Musicologia: Trasmissione e Recezione delle Forme di Cultura Musicale, Bologna, 27 agosto–1 settembre 1987* (Turin: Edizioni di Torino, 1990), vol. 1, 239–253. On the Italian madrigal, see Alfred Einstein, *The Italian Madrigal*, 3 vols., translated by A. H. Krappe, R. H. Sessions, and O. Strunk (Princeton, NJ: Princeton University Press, 1949).

14. *STC2* 26094, [A]1r.

15. Conversely, Byrd's name and contribution may have been solicited by Yonge. He may have believed Londoners would be more inclined to buy the "foreign" product if it included the work and endorsement of a familiar English figure.

16. See *STC2* 25119, A1r, and *STC2* 4256, [A]2r–v.

17. *STC2* 25119, B4r. Each madrigal appears as the last work of the section (i.e., the first setting is the last work in the section for four voices and the second is the last composition for six voices). It is possible that East and Byrd decided to place Byrd's works last to emulate the same procedure of layout in the *Whole Booke of Psalmes*, which always ended with a "Prayer for the Queen"; see *STC2* 2488, T8.

18. This is clearly seen even in the sketchy manuscript transmission of Byrd's music before 1588. Many preprinted versions of his works in both English and Latin traditions appear in manuscripts. See Philip Brett (ed.), *Consort Songs*, Musica Britannica no. 22 (London: Stainer Bell, 1967), xx; and Joseph Kerman, *The Masses and Motets of William Byrd* (Berkeley: University of California Press, 1981), 38–45.

19. See Philip Brett (ed.), *Gradualia I (1605): The Marian Masses*, BE 5 (1989), xv–xvi.

20. For a special consideration of this dilemma, see John Milsom, "Sacred Songs in the Chamber," in John Morehen (ed.), *English Choral Practice, 1400–1650* (Cambridge: Cambridge University Press, 1995), 166–171.

21. See *STC2* 4253, [A]2r.

22. Arber, *Transcript*, vol. 2, 477.

23. That Byrd participated in the preparations for the *Musica Transalpina* before 1588, however, cannot be ruled out.

24. *STC2* 4253, [A]2r.

25. Ibid.

26. See Alan Brown (ed.), *Cantiones Sacrae I (1589), BE* 2 (1988), v.

27. *STC2* 4256, [A]2r–v.

28. *STC2* 4256, [A]2r.

29. See Brown, *Cantiones Sacrae I*, v.

30. See Thomas Morley, *A Plain and Easy Introduction to Practical Music*, edited by R. A. Harman, with a foreword by R. T. Dart (New York: Norton, 1952), 3.

31. Ibid., 292–294.

32. Ibid., 293 (italics added).

33. See *STC2* 4247 (1589), [A]4v, and *STC2* 4248 (1591), [A]4v.

34. See *STC2* 4247 (1589), [A]1v, and *STC2* 4248 (1591), [A]1v. A facsimile with transcription and translation of the 1591 dedication appears in Alan Brown (ed.), *Cantiones Sacrae II (1591), BE* 3 (1988), xvii.

35. When he mentions "our little musical-establishment" to Somerset, he evokes for music making the type of intimate atmosphere in which courtly poetry was confined; see Brown, *Cantiones Sacrae I*, xxi.

36. David Price, *Patrons and Musicians of the English Renaissance* (Cambridge: Cambridge University Press, 1981), 179.

37. See *The Lumley Library: The Catalogue of 1609*, edited by Sears Jayne and Francis Johnson (London: British Museum, 1956).

38. John Milsom discovered that the majority of the collection's music editions do not appear in the 1609 catalog because only the first volume of multiple-volume tracts was listed. For a reconstruction of this collection, see John Milsom, "The Nonsuch Music Library," in Chris Banks, Arthur Searle, and Malcolm Turner (eds.), *Sundry Sorts of Music Books: Essays on the British Library Collections Presented to O. W. Neighbor on His 70th Birthday* (London: British Library, 1993), 146–182.

39. See Thurston Dart, "A Suppressed Dedication for Morley's Four-Part Madrigals of 1594," *Transactions of the Cambridge Bibliographical Society* 3 (1963): 401–405.

40. See Mary S. Lewis, *Antonio Gardano: Venetian Music Printer, 1538–1569: A Descriptive Bibliography and Historical Study*, vol. 1: *1538–1549* (New York: Garland, 1988), 103–108; and Richard Agee, *The Gardano Music Printing Firms, 1569–1611* (Rochester, NY: University of Rochester Press, 1998), 29 ff.

41. On the special nature of Byrd's approach to print, see Philip Brett, "Text, Context and the Early Music Editor," in Nicholas Kenyon (ed.), *Authenticity and Early Music* (Oxford; Oxford University Press, 1988), 83–114. On di Lasso, see Kristine K. Forney, "Orlando di Lasso's 'Opus 1': The Making and Marketing of a Renaissance Music Book," *Revue belge de musicologie* 39–40 (1985–1986): 33–60.

42. James Binns, "STC Latin Books: Evidence for Printing-House Practice," *The Library* 5th ser., vol. 32 (1977): 1–27. See also idem, "STC Latin Books: Further Evidence for Printing House Practice," *The Library* 6th ser., vol. 1 (1979): 347–354; and James P. Hammersmith, "Frivolous Trifles and Weighty Tomes: Early Proof-Reading at London, Oxford, and Cambridge," *Studies in Bibliography* 38 (1985): 236–251.

43. Binns, "STC Latin Books" (1977), 4: the selection is from *STC2* 18029, A5v.

44. Binns provides an account of an author coaxing and cajoling the publisher Thomas James:

> This is a book with which I fell in love as soon as I set eyes on it . . . I conceived the plan of copying it out . . . just as it was. I straightway entrusted the manuscript to the printer, imploring him to print it. But he, like all those fellows of his profession, refused and denied my request, saying that he could not do this without great loss. I pressed my point unceasingly, and informed him that it was not such a big book, that all his typographical fortunes depended on it, that it was not a book but a little pamphlet; that it was small in size but of the greatest worth. Finally I implored and conjured him through the love he bore for books by virtue of being a printer, through the advantage and profit accruing from his position as a bookseller.

(After several years, the printer finally capitulated and the work was produced.) See "STC Latin Books" (1977), 8. The selection is from *STC2* 959, *2r–v.

45. Byrd may have unofficially assumed a position East usually filled with hired workers. Such a literary figure as Henry Chettle, the dramatist and friend of Shakespeare, was East's apprentice and may have worked for him as a press corrector; see Arber, *Transcript*, vol. 2, 81. Joseph Moxon described the position of "Corrector" of the press as a full-time one (*Mechanick Exercises on the Whole Art of Printing [1683–4]*, 2d ed., edited by Herbert Davis and Harry Carter [London: Oxford University Press, 1962], 247). Hieronymus Hornschuch was such a figure of an earlier period. In a quarto edition, Hornschuch described his position in great detail, although his writing may be less pertinent here since he worked in France, not England; see *Hornshuch's Orthotypographia, 1608*, edited and translated by Philip Gaskell and Patricia Bradford (Cambridge: Cambridge University Press, 1972).

46. *STC2* 4253, [A]2r.

47. See Andrews, "Printed Sources," 19; and Clulow, "Publication Dates," 9. Many editors of the *BE* mention the high quality of East's work with musical texts.

48. The restricted markets and immediate utilitarian function of music books are discussed in Stanley H. Boorman, "Early Music Printing: Working for a Specialized Market," in Gerald P. Tyson and Sylvia S. Wagonheim (eds.), *Print and Culture in the Renaissance: Essays on the Advent of Printing in Europe* (Newark: University of Delaware Press, 1986), 222–245.

49. On music-printing practices of Renaissance firms on the continent, see Forney, "Orlando di Lasso's 'Opus 1,'" and Stanley H. Boorman, "The 'First' Edition of the 'Odhecaton A,'" *JAMS* 30 (1977): 183–207 (both of which are pioneering works on hidden musical editions). On Vautrollier's proofing techniques in the *Cantiones*, see John Milsom, "Tallis, Byrd and the 'Incorrected' Copy: Some Cautionary Notes for Editors of Early Music Printed from Movable Type," *Music & Letters* 77 (1996): 348–367.

50. A very conservative estimate is that there were the following ten errors corrected with slips in the *Songs* volume of 1589 (*STC2* 4256): Tenor: D3v, E2v, F2r; Bassus: C (in gutter of British Library K.2.f.3), E2v, H1r, and H2 (in gutter of British Library K.2.f.3); Contratenor: C2v, D2v; and Superious: B3v. These slips are still in place in some copies, but some may now be missing; I found single-note slips in the gutter of the University of Glasgow copy (Euing R.a.9) that are not in a British Library copy (K.2.f.3), for example. Also, a large slip in a British Library copy (K.2.f.3, Bassus, F2r) is no longer in place in the London University (Littleton) copy although the yellowed surface reveals that the latter obviously once held this slip.

51. See Milsom's comment to this effect in his "Tallis, Byrd and the 'Incorrected' Copy,"

348. Morley's music has not been as thoroughly studied. On Morley's proofing, however, Donald Krummel noted:

> It was also possible for the compositor to work with the editor or the composer looking over his shoulder; for some complicated texts, like Morley's *Plain and Easie Introduction*, it is hard to imagine how the copy could otherwise have been set at all. (*English Music Printing*, 14)

52. No slips were found in the *Musica Transalpina* editions.

53. The carefully edited editions of his *Gradualia* suggest that Byrd's special influence over East in matters of correcting the press extended beyond the term of his monopoly; see Brett, *Gradualia I*, xxi.

54. *STC2* 4253, [A]2v.

55. See Binns, "STC Latin Books" (1977), 3.

56. See Andrews, "Printed Sources, 11–19."

57. An alternative theory, which is not mutually exclusive to an editorial program, is that the work was reprinted twice because so many copies were sold that to replenish them required new impressions. (On reprinting and popularity, see Donald W. Krummel, "Musical Functions and Bibliographical Forms," *The Library* 5th ser., vol. 31 [1976]: 336; and Kerman, *Elizabethan Madrigal*, 263–264.) This latter theory is generally applicable to reprints, but the *Psalmes* may be an exception. No other extant work by East was reprinted as many times within such a short period of time, and despite the three editions, the same volume was reprinted twice again in undated editions many years later (*STC2* 4254). This suggests the unlikely condition that the *Psalmes* was, in fact, the single most popular music book East ever produced. Perhaps the long wait for music printing in England did excite demand to such a degree, but the more modest reprinting schedules of the *Musica Transalpina* of the same year of 1588 (reprinted in 1596–1597) and Byrd's own *Songs* of 1589 (reprinted in 1596–1597) in East's lifetime argue against such a thesis.

58. *STC2* 4253, [A]2v.

59. For records that pertain to Byrd's recusancy in Essex, see J. G. O'Leary, "William Byrd and His Family at Stondon Massey," *Essex Recusant* 7 (1965): 23. For an important recent study that incorporates new evidence, see David Mateer, "William Byrd's Middlesex Recusancy," *Music & Letters* 78 (1997): 1–14.

60. O'Leary, "William Byrd at Stondon Massey," 19.

61. William Weston, *The Autobiography of an Elizabethan*, edited by Philip Caraman (London: Longmans, 1955), 234.

62. *NG*, s.v. "William Byrd," by Joseph Kerman.

63. See Table A1.5.

64. The full list of editions of the Masses and all extant copies are tabulated in Clulow, "Publication Dates," 3.

65. See William Byrd, *Mass a 3: STC2* 4249, *Mass a 4: STC2* 4250, and *Mass a 5: STC2* 4251. The hidden editions of the three- and four-voiced Masses mimic the signatures of the first edition.

66. Although the topic is most intriguing, it is very difficult to find the evidence necessary to study the distribution of Byrd's Masses; see chapter 6. One promising approach (not attempted here) is to study the editions themselves for evidence of ownership (as it may appear in bindings and annotations within the books). On the copies of the Masses in the collections of Lincoln Cathedral Library, with note of bindings and conglomerate books, see Iain Fenlon, "Michael Honywood's Music Books," in Banks, Searle, and Turner, *Sundry Sorts of Music Books*, 183–200.

67. A recent study is Sheila Lambert, "State Control of the Press in Theory and Practice: The Role of the Stationers' Company before 1640," in Robin Myers and Michael Harris (eds.), *Censorship & the Control of Print in England and France 1600–1910* (Winchester: St. Paul's Bibliographies, 1992), 3.

68. See Alison Shell, "Catholic Texts and Anti-Catholic Prejudice in the 17th-Century Book Trade," in Myers and Harris, *Censorship & the Control of Print*, 35.

69. Clulow, "Publication Dates," 1. The hidden editions of the Masses were produced after Byrd's monopoly had ended in 1596 and will be discussed in chapter 6.

70. Ibid., 6–7. East first printed the four-voiced Mass in 1593; in the next year he printed the three-voiced; and, last, he printed the five-voiced Masses, which were probably completed late in 1595.

71. Clulow, "Publication Dates," 7.

72. Ibid.

73. See *STC2* 4253, [A]2v.

74. There was a problem with the layout of the Cantus volume in the first edition of the *Musica Transalpina* that East quietly corrected in the hidden edition.

75. As was brought out in litigation with the novice publisher Eastland, East stipulated that he would get the property rights after the first edition of Dowland's *Second Booke of Songs* was sold (PRO, Court of Request, Req 2/203/4, m. 9; and PRO, Court of Chancery C2/Eliz/E1/64, *Thomas East vs. George Eastland* (1601), m. 9). And, more significant, through the arbitration of the court of the Stationers' Company East argued for and won the rights to his registered titles as an element in the settlement, which required him to work as an assign for the draper-turned-stationer William Barley in 1606; see *Records of the Court of the Stationers' Company, 1602 to 1640*, edited by William A. Jackson (London: Bibliographical Society, 1957), 19–20.

76. The *East vs. Eastland* case reveals that for the Dowland volume Eastland paid more money to the music monopolist Morley than to East (and Morley had exactly nothing to contribute to the production); see Dowling, "The Printing," 371.

CHAPTER 5

1. This information is conveniently summarized in Margaret Dowling, "The Printing of John Dowland's 'Second Booke of Songs or Ayres,'" *The Library* 4th ser., vol. 12 (1932): 373.

2. Ibid., 368.

3. These imprints with East's address as the place where they were to be sold appear in *STC2* 4253, [A]1r, and *STC2* 4256, [A]1r. The colophon of the quintus part of the *Musica Transalpina* lists East's address at the "sign of the Black Horse"; see *STC2* 20694, H4v.

4. Edward Arber (ed.), *A Transcript of the Registers of the Company of Stationers of London, 1554–1640 A.D.*, 5 vols. (Birmingham: The editor, 1875–1894), vol. 1, 144.

5. Byrd claimed that he was "induced" by the carelessness of scribes to publish the Latin "Songs," but not before he had "brought them to the lathe and made [them] more correct," (Alan Brown [ed.], *Cantiones Sacrae I* [1589], BE 2 [1988], xxi).

6. *STC2* 4253, [A]2v.

7. The medius part for all the psalms, for example, has the phrase "The first singing part" in the header; see *STC2* 4253, C1r–C4v (i.e., the entire C gathering).

8. Philip Brett, "The Consort Song, 1575–1625," *Proceedings of the Royal Musical Association* 88 (1961–1962): 73–88; Joseph Kerman, "'Write All These Down': Notes on a Byrd Song," in A. Brown and R. Turbet (eds.), *Byrd Studies* (Cambridge: Cambridge University Press, 1992), 112–128; and David Brown, "William Byrd's 1588 Volume," *Music & Letters* 38 (1957): 371–375.

9. See Joseph Kerman, *The Elizabethan Madrigal: A Comparative Study* (New York: American Musicological Society, 1962), 103–117.

10. Byrd's stated plan was to make his music available for the vocal groups who performed madrigals, but he also encouraged all musicians, amateur and professional, to perform his music by whatever means they had at their disposal (*STC2* 4253, [A]2v).

11. On Hatton's glittering prominence as the queen's favorite and his sudden rise to great power in 1587, see Wallace T. MacCaffrey, *Queen Elizabeth and the Making of Policy, 1572–1588* (Princeton, NJ: Princeton University Press, 1981), 447–458.

12. Christopher Barker, for example, used his position as queen's printer in the 1580s to force his personal views on the regulatory policies of the Stationers' Company. Similarly, when John Wolfe (one of the most ambitious, active, and successful men of the company) eventually attained the position of queen's printer in 1592, he virtually retired from all other printing ventures; see Harry Hoppe, "John Wolfe, Printer and Publisher, 1579–1601," *The Library* 4th ser., vol. 14 (1933): 266–271.

13. Ibid., 259–264.

14. See Cyprian Blagden, "The English Stock of the Stationers' Company: An Account of Its Origins," *The Library* 5th ser, vol. 10 (1955): 184. The *ABC*, also owned by the Day printing dynasty, may have been the more valuable property. It was apparently so vigorously used by young students of the era that few copies survive; see C. L. Oastler, *John Day, the Elizabethan Printer* (Oxford: Oxford Bibliographical Society, 1975), 22. Thus the fact that *STC2* lists only the Sternhold-Hopkins Psalter for the work of the "Assignees of Richard Day" may be misleading evidence; see H. Anders, "The Elizabethan 'ABC with the Catechism,'" *The Library* 4th ser., vol. 16 (1935–1936): 32–48. Nonetheless, the complete collection of psalms was probably then the most prized single property of the trade; see James Doelman, "George Wither, the Stationers' Company and the English Psalter," *Studies in Philology* 90 (1993): 74–77.

15. PRO, Patent Rolls, "Music Privilege to Thomas Tallis and William Byrd (1575)," C66/1463, m.2, transcribed in Edmund H. Fellowes, *William Byrd*, 2d ed. (London: Oxford University Press, 1948), 10.

16. Donald W. Krummel, *English Music Printing 1553–1700* (London: Bibliographical Society, 1975), 23.

17. Ibid.

18. A brief discussion of Puckering and his role as patron of music appears in Thurston Dart, "A Suppressed Dedication for Morley's Four-Part Madrigals of 1594," *Transactions of the Cambridge Bibliographical Society* 3 (1963): 401–405.

19. *STC2* 2482, A1r–v.

20. See J. Alpin, "The Origins of John Day's 'Certaine Notes,'" *Music & Letters* 62 (1981): 295–299.

21. Arber, *Transcript*, vol. 2, 477.

22. *STC2* 4253, [A]1r.

23. In this volume, Byrd set metrical translations of Psalms 2, 32, 38, 51, 102, 130, and 143 to music. These three-voiced works were the first of the anthology and filled gathering B of the tenor, bassus, and superius parts; see *STC2* 4256.

24. *STC2* 6220, [A]1r.

25. Krummel, *English Music Printing*, 22. See also Dart, "Suppressed Dedication," 404; and Hoppe, "John Wolfe," 259–264.

26. For a facsimile and discussion of this font, see Krummel, *English Music Printing*, 61–62.

27. *STC2* 2482, A2v.

28. The music of Cobbold, Farmer, Cavendish, Johnson, and Kirbye also appeared in Morley's *Triumphs of Oriana* of 1601, (*STC2* 18130). Johnson and Blancks were noted under the

heading of "Music" in Francis Meres, *Palladis Tamia: Wit's Treasury* (London, 1598; reprint, New York: Garland, 1973), 288–289. This, incidentally, was a miscellany with the first references to all eleven plays that Shakespeare completed by 1598.

29. See Robert Illing, *Est's Psalter*, vol. 1: *Commentary and Transcriptions* (Adelaide: Libraries Board of South Australia, 1969), 5.

30. These appear together as a thematic index in an appendix at the end of the volume (*STC2* 2482, T8v [p. 288]).

31. Illing, *Est's Psalter*, vol. 1, 9.

32. See Thomas East, *The Whole Book of Psalms: With Their Wonted Tunes, Harmonized in Four Parts . . .*, edited by Edward F. Rimbault (London : Musical Antiquarian Society, 1844).

33. See *STC2* 2482, A1r–v.

34. Krummel, *English Music Printing*, 78.

35. See James Binns, "STC Latin Books: Evidence for Printing-House Practice," *The Library* 5th ser., vol. 32 (1977): 3.

36. See Robert Illing, "Barley's Pocket Edition of Est's Metrical Psalter," *Music & Letters* 49 (1968): 219–223.

37. See Nicholas Temperley, *The Music of the English Parish Church* (Cambridge: Cambridge University Press, 1979), 41–42.

38. In the *Psalmes* edition, Byrd printed his famous "Reasons Briefly Set Downe by th'Auctor, to Perswade Every One to Learne to Sing" (*STC2* 4253, [A]2v).

CHAPTER 6

1. Thomas Morley, *A Plaine and Easie Introduction to Practicall Musicke* (London: Peter Short, 1597), [A]2v. For R. A. Harman's transcription of this poem and the other two commendatory works in the treatise and his theory that "I.W." is John Wootton, see Thomas Morley, *A Plain and Easy Introduction to Practical Music*, edited by R. A. Harman, with a foreword by R. T. Dart (New York: Norton, 1952), 4.

2. On Elizabethan dedications, see H. S. Bennett, *English Books & Readers 1558 to 1603: Being a Study in the History of the Book Trade in the Reign of Elizabeth* (Cambridge: Cambridge University Press, 1965), 30–40.

3. For puns on Morley's name in the commendatory poems, see Morley, *Plain and Easy*, 4.

4. By 1596 Byrd had lived in Essex for three years. During these years, Byrd became less active in London and at the court. This may well explain his apparent lack of interest in renewing the music grant in 1596.

5. Joseph Kerman first formulated this interpretation in his striking work on the English madrigal. He responded to romanticized assertions about music as a ubiquitous element of a so-called merry Tudor England and advanced a more sober interpretation. His seminal study culminated in a withering assessment of the level of interest taken by Renaissance London music consumers in the music books of their countrymen. See his *The Elizabethan Madrigal: A Comparative Study* (New York: American Musicological Society, 1962).

6. David Brown, "Thomas Morley and the Catholics: Some Speculations," *Monthly Musical Record* 89 (1959): 55.

7. *NG*, s.v. "Thomas Morley," by Philip Brett.

8. Thurston Dart, "A Suppressed Dedication for Morley's Four-Part Madrigals of 1594," *Transactions of the Cambridge Bibliographical Society* 3 (1963): 401–405. See also Donald W. Krummel, *English Music Printing 1553–1700* (London: Bibliographical Society, 1975), 21–26.

9. For statistics that concern the madrigal production of Venetian printers in this era, see Tim Carter, "Music Publishing in Italy, c. 1580–c. 1625: Some Preliminary Observations," *RMA Research Chronicle* 20 (1986–1987): 19–37.

10. *NG*, s.v. "Thomas Morley."

11. Morley, *Plain and Easy*, 292–294.

12. Dart, "Suppressed Dedication," 403.

13. Ibid., 404.

14. See Kerman, *The Elizabethan Madrigal*, 136.

15. During East's lifetime, two editions of Morley's music were printed by Short and two were published by Barley; see Miriam Miller, "London Music Printing, c. 1570–c. 1640" (Ph.D. diss., University of London, 1969), 85 and 92. East printed six editions of Morley's music and two anthologies of other composers published by him: the *Madrigals to Five Voyces*, which marked one of the last of the "Englished" madrigal series, and the *Triumphes of Oriana*, a famous collection that memorialized Elizabeth I.

16. According to Thurston Dart, "The true English madrigal was created almost single-handed by . . . Morley. . . . The astonishing flowering of English madrigal during the next thirty years was very largely due to the skill, enterprise and discernment of this one remark-able musician" ("Suppressed Dedication," 401).

17. An important study of Bathe's theories, with a discussion of the issues involved in dating the editions, is Jessie Ann Owens, "Concepts of Pitch in English Music Theory, c. 1560–1640," in Cristle Collins Judd (ed.), *Tonal Structures in Early Music* (New York: Garland, 1998), 183–246. See also Bernarr Rainbow, "Bathe and His Introductions to Musicke," *Musical Times* 123 (1982): 243–247; and Paul J. Nixon, "William Bathe and His Times," *Musical Times* 124 (1983): 101–102.

18. Many of these registers were transcribed by Arber. The original records are now available in microfilm; for a guide to these, see Robin Myers, *The Stationers' Company Archive: An Account of the Records 1554–1984* (Winchester: St. Paul's Bibliographies, 1990).

19. See Leo Kirschbaum, "The Copyright of Elizabethan Plays," *The Library* 5th ser., vol. 14 (1959): 232–234.

20. There is an extensive literature on the registers and related issues of intellectual property. Of particular value are the following works by W. W. Greg: "Entrance, License and Publication," *The Library* 4th ser., vol. 25 (1944–1945): 1–14; "Entrance and Copyright," *The Library* 4th ser., vol. 26 (1945–1946): 308–310; and *Some Aspects and Problems of London Publishing between 1550 and 1650* (Oxford: Oxford University Press, 1956), 41–62. Greg's statistical studies of the registrations and subsequent publications were extended in Maurine Bell, "Entrance in the Stationers' Register," *The Library* 6th ser., vol. 16 (1994): 50–54. John Feather discusses the link between the registers and systems of copyright in *Publishing, Piracy and Politics: An Historical Study of Copyright in Britain* (London: Mansell, 1994), 10–36, and "From Rights in Copies to Copyright: The Recognition of Authors' Rights in English Law and Practice in the Sixteenth and Seventeenth Centuries," *Cardozo Arts & Entertainment Law Journal* 10 (1992): 455–473. See also Leo Kirschbaum, "Authors' Copyright in England before 1640," *Papers of the Bibliographical Society of America* 40 (1989): 40–45.

21. For the following discussion of the stationers' role in developing rights to copy I have drawn on the works of Greg and Feather listed earlier, but I am also especially indebted to Joseph Loewenstein, "For a History of Literary Property: John Wolfe's Reformation," *English Literary Renaissance* 18 (1988): 390–394.

22. For a recent historiographical study of Elizabethan censorship and the governmental use of the registers, see Sheila Lambert, "State Control of the Press in Theory and Practice: The Role of the Stationers' Company before 1640," in Robin Myers and Michael Harris (eds.), *Censorship & the Control of Print: In England and France 1600–1910* (Winchester: St. Paul's Bibliographies, 1992), 1–32.

23. For a list of manuscripts and printed copy with evidence of licensing still extant, see

J. K. Moore, *Primary Materials Relating to Copy and Print in English Books of the Sixteenth and Seventeenth Centuries* (Oxford: Oxford Bibliographical Society, 1992), 35–64.

24. The classic economic study of the London Companies is William Herbert, *The History of the Twelve Great Livery Companies of London . . .* (London: The author, 1836–1837). See also I. G. Doolittle, *The City of London and Its Livery Companies* (Dorchester: Gavin, 1982).

25. Edward Arber (ed.), *A Transcript of the Registers of the Company of Stationers of London, 1554–1640 A.D.*, 5 vols. (Birmingham: The editor, 1875–1894), vol. 3, 76–77. East, with characteristic care and parsimony, took pains to relist his nine-year-old registry of Byrd's *Psalmes*, even though it was technically unnecessary. In this way, he reaffirmed his standing as the rightful owner of that "copy" among stationers. Beyond his clever inclusion of Byrd's *Psalmes* in the registry of 1596, East also listed his Italian editions of Morley's *Canzonets* and *Balletts* with parallel English versions as one unit. This saved him a registration fee for what might properly have been seen as two separate editions. Morley's *Canzonets a 3* and his *Madrigalls* appear there, too; thus East was to list all of the six editions he printed with music by Morley. The music books missing from the list are the sets of duos by Farmer and Whythorne, Damon's collections of psalms, East's own *Whole Booke of Psalmes*, the broadside edition of the *Gratification* and the undated (and unsigned) editions of Byrd's Masses. See Table A1.4.

26. See, for example, Lillian Ruff and Arnold Wilson, "The Madrigal, the Lute Song and Elizabethan Politics," *Past & Present* 44 (1969): 20–22.

27. Statistical surveys of the London printing trade of this era have shown that fewer than half of the works produced at this time in the city were ever registered. The common view in bibliographical scholarship is therefore that registration was not compulsory; see Bell, "Entrance in the Stationers' Register," 51.

28. Arber, *Transcript*, vol. 3, 379.

29. Ibid., 392.

30. Joseph Kerman made a similar argument more than three decades ago but was unable to account comprehensively for the pattern of registrations and nonregistrations (*The Elizabethan Madrigal*, 265).

31. Byrd's volume was titled *Psalmes, Sonets & Songs*, and Mundy's was titled *Songs and Psalmes*.

32. See Robert R. Steele, *The Earliest English Music Printing: A Description and Bibliography of English Printed Music to the Close of the Sixteenth Century* (London: Bibliographical Society, 1903), 27–29.

33. Gerald D. Johnson, "William Barley, 'Publisher & Seller of Bookes,' 1591–1614," *The Library* 6th ser., vol. 11 (1989): 32.

34. See John M. Ward, "Barley's Songs without Words," *Lute Society Journal* 12 (1970): 14.

35. Barley has attracted the interest of many bibliographers and musicologists; see, for example, John Livesay, "William Barley: Elizabethan Printer and Bookseller," *Studies in Bibliography* 8 (1956): 218–225; and J. A. Lavin, "William Barley, Draper and Stationer," *Studies in Bibliography* 21 (1969): 214–223. Unfortunately, this surprisingly strong interest has resulted in some confusion over Barley's role. Gerald Johnson goes far to give the first clear picture of Barley's career in "William Barley," 10–46.

36. By the same token, it was not permissible for a draper to actually produce books, for that would intrude upon the special privilege granted by the queen only to stationers. East, therefore, had the advantage of the right to print music not available to Barley and Morley, who had to hire printers to work for them. Surprisingly, since he was surely to some extent a rather nefarious figure, Barley very probably honored the stipulation that he could not print the books he traded. Instead, he had music printed "for" him. This was the essential corrective argument advanced by J. A. Lavin as he reacted to John Livesay's study; see Lavin, "William Barley, Draper," 225. For a study of the interaction of the drapers and stationers in

matters of bookselling, see Gerald D. Johnson, "The Stationers versus the Drapers: Control of the Press in the Late Sixteenth Century," *The Library* 6th ser., vol. 10 (1988): 1–17.

37. Morley, *Plain and Easy*, 130–131.

38. See Ward, "Barley's Songs," 17, n. 6.

39. Anthony Holbourne, preface to *The Cittharn School* (London, 1597).

40. See *NG*, s.v. "Antony Holbourne," by David Brown.

41. The *Canzonets* by Morley was yet another music collection produced in 1597 that contained music with special arrangements for lute. Thanks in no small measure to Morley, 1597 was quite a propitious year for Elizabethan lutenists. On Carey, see David Price, *Patrons and Musicians of the English Renaissance* (Cambridge: Cambridge University Press, 1981), 80; and *DNB*, s.v. "George Carey."

42. Like Holbourne's and Morley's works, the texts of the music in Dowland's edition alluded to intimate activities of the court, including some elegiac tributes to the recently deceased dancer "bonny boots," who was probably Sir Henry Noel. See David Greer, "'Thou Court's Delight': Bibliographical Notes on Henry Noel," *Lute Society Journal* 17 (1975): 49–59.

43. Donald W. Krummel and Stanley Sadie (eds.), *Music Printing and Publishing*, Norton/Grove Handbooks in Music (New York: Norton, 1990), s.v. "Peter Short," by Miriam Miller.

44. Krummel, *English Music Printing*, 12–13.

45. For evidence of careful editing in the "Introduction," see O. E. Deutsch, "The Editions of Morley's 'Introduction,'" *The Library* 4th ser., vol. 23 (1943): 127–129.

46. For Short's registration of the *Introduction* by Morley, see Arber *Transcript*, vol. 2, 241.

47. See PRO, Court of Requests, Req 2. 202/63, *Thomas East vs. George Eastland* (1601), and the summary of the case in Dowling, "The Printing," 365–380.

48. Ibid.

49. *Repertoire international des sources musicales* (hereafter *RISM*), Series A. 1: *Einzeldrücke vor 1800*, 9 vols., edited by Karl-Heinz Schlager (Kassel: Bärenreiter, 1971), lists nine editions of the Lasso Latin duos (or motets and ricercares) to the year 1610. The original edition, *Novae aliquot*, was printed in Munich by Adam Berg (*RISM* 1577c). For a modern edition of the original Berg volume, with facsimiles, see Orlando di Lasso, *The Complete Motets*, vol. 11: *Novae aliquot, ad duas voces cantiones (Munich, 1577)*, edited by Peter Berquist (Madison, WI: A-R Editions, 1995). East's version follows the number and order of works of the Berg edition. He also followed the text underlay of the original very carefully; see facsimiles [xix] and [xxi]. As in the Berg edition, East included an index with "cum" and "sine" designations for the works with and without texts. (These were later designated respectively as "motets" and instrumental "ricercare" by Venetian printers.) The chief difference between the editions by East and Berg was that East changed the layout of pages to fit an upright quarto format and, for that reason, his line endings are not the same as the Berg edition. Overall, it would seem likely that the printer's copy for East's work was the Berg edition.

50. See Peter N. Schubert, "A Lesson from Lassus: Form in the Duos of 1577," *Music Theory Spectrum* 17 (1995): 1–26.

51. For a discussion of Elizabethan educational institutions, see Robert Wienpahl, *Music at the Inns of Court during the Reigns of Elizabeth, James, and Charles* (Ann Arbor, MI: University Microfilms International, 1979).

52. See Gustav Ungerer, "The French Lutenist Charles Tessier and the Essex Circle," *Renaissance Quarterly* 28 (1975): 198–201.

53. Ibid., 194–195. In 1582 Guilliaume Tessier, on a similar quest, dedicated his work to the queen.

54. By 1597 Essex had a reputation, albeit tainted, as the queen's favorite. He was also the

military hero of Calais and Cadiz and the leader of one of the two most powerful factions in the queen's court.

55. John M. Ward points out the ambiguities in the documentary evidence of Tessier's putative advance in the Essex coterie in "Tessier and the 'Essex Circle,'" *Renaissance Quarterly* 29 (1976): 378–384.

56. Perhaps Tessier was interested in something more sinister than simply musical performance and tutelage and hoped to serve the earl as a spy, although no reports to Essex have been attributed to him. If so, it was appropriate that Tessier made his appeal through Bacon. Bacon was the man responsible for recruitment, organization, and management of Essex's intelligence service. See Charles Nicholl, *The Reckoning: The Murder of Christopher Marlowe* (Chicago: University of Chicago Press, 1995), 222–223.

57. See Price, *Patrons and Musicians*, 79.

58. Ibid., 81.

59. Ibid., 79.

60. See *NG*, s.v. "John Wilbye," by David Brown.

61. See Glenn A. Philipps, "Patronage in the Career of Thomas Weelkes," *Musical Quarterly* 62 (1976): 46–57.

62. Ibid., 55.

63. The issue status of the Tessier volume (but not its implications) is discussed in Ward, "Tessier and the 'Essex Circle,'" 380, n. 6.

64. In 1597 East also printed a lecture by John Bull, a member of the Chapel Royal and thus a colleague of Morley, who was appointed to the prestigious post of professor of music at Gresham College in Oxford. This venture also seems to be part of the "aspiring" nature of East's music-publishing program in these years. Only the title page of this book survives. An offset of the first page of the lecture may be seen, however, on the verso of the title page; see Alec Hyatt King, "Fragments of Early Printed Music in the Bagford Collections," *Music & Letters* 40 (1959): 269.

65. *STC2* 26095, [A]2r.

66. *Calendar of the Manuscripts of the . . . Marquis of Salisbury . . . Preserved at Hatfield House, Hertfordshire*, 24 vols. (hereafter *Salisbury MS*), vol. 8, 273.

67. Steele, *Earliest English Music Printing*, 27–29.

68. W. W. Greg and E. Boswell, *Records of the Court of the Stationers' Company: 1576 to 1602 from Register B* (London: Bibliographical Society, 1930), 65.

69. See Miriam Miller, "London Music Printing, c. 1570– c. 1640" (Ph.D. diss., University of London, 1969), 23.

70. Morley was at pains to explain the whole issue of paper in his letter of 1598; for instance, see *Salisbury MS*, vol. 8, 273.

71. Ibid.

72. See Robert Illing, "Barley's Pocket Edition of Est's Metrical Psalter," *Music & Letters* 49 (1968): 219–223.

73. See Krummel, "English Music Printing," 23.

74. *Salisbury MS*, vol. 9, 373. See also Krummel, "English Music Printing," 24.

75. *Salisbury MS*, vol. 9, 373.

76. The original contracts are no longer extant; however, vestiges of Morley's contracts with both printers appeared in two sources: Peter Short's three-year contract was printed in his second edition of Dowland's *First Booke of Songs* (see Miller, "London Music Printing," 83), and East's contract was explained at length in his litigation with George Eastland; see Dowling, "Dowland's 'Second Book of Songs,'" 365.

CHAPTER 7

1. See John E. Parish, *Robert Parsons and the English Counter-Reformation* (Houston: Rice University, 1966), 63–66; and Francis Edwards, *Robert Persons, the Biography of an Elizabethan Jesuit, 1546–1610* (St. Louis: Institute of Jesuit Sources, 1995). Persons was also the author, or co-author, under the pseudonym R. Doleman, of a compendious treatise titled *A Conference about the Next Succession to the Crowne of Ingland* ... (Antwerp, 1594). Advertised as a disinterested work on the succession, it was perceived by many, including some English Catholics, to have as its main purpose the elevation of the Infanta of Spain, Isabel Clara Eugenia, to the English throne; see Joel Hurstfield, "The Succession Struggle in Late Elizabethan England," in S. T. Bindoff, J. Hurstfield, and C. H. Williams (eds.), *Elizabethan Government and Society: Essays Presented to Sir John Neale*, (London: Athlone, 1961), 374. For a different interpretation, however, see Leo Hicks, S.J., "Father Robert Persons, S.J., and 'The Book of Succession,'" *Recusant History* 4 (1957): 104.

2. For a guide to the scholarly literature on Byrd's Masses see the following: Edmond H. Fellowes, *William Byrd*, 2d ed. (London: Oxford University Press, 1948); Joseph Kerman, *The Masses and Motets of William Byrd* (Berkeley: University of California Press, 1981); and Richard Turbet, *William Byrd, a Guide to Research* (New York: Garland, 1987).

3. The standard study of Essex is W. B. Devereux, *Lives and Letters of the Devereux, Earls of Essex*, 2 vols. (London: J. Murray, 1853). On the Essex Revolt, the most thorough account is Mervyn James, *Society, Politics and Culture: Studies in Early Modern England* (Cambridge: Cambridge University Press, 1986), 416–465.

4. Lillian Ruff and Arnold Wilson, "The Madrigal, the Lute Song and Elizabethan Politics," *Past & Present* 44 (1969): 3–51, and "Allusion to the Essex Downfall in Lute Song Lyrics," *Lute Society Journal* 12 (1970): 31–36.

5. The meshing of art and politics in Tudor London was once a thriving scholarly concern in studies of Shakespeare and other writers of the Elizabethan and early Stuart era. For a useful summary of studies on Elizabethan art and politics before the mid–twentieth century, see David Bevington, *Tudor Drama and Politics: A Critical Approach to Topical Meaning* (Cambridge, MA: Harvard University Press, 1968), 14–26. The rise of Deconstructionism brought such investigations into disfavor, but in recent years they have reemerged to become a matter of great scholarly interest thanks to the efforts of a group of literary scholars known as New Historicists. Two volumes generally credited as inaugural works of the new historicism in literary studies are: Wesley Morris, *Toward a New Historicism* (Princeton, NJ: Princeton University Press, 1972); and *The New Historicism*, edited by H. Aram Veeser (New York: Routledge, 1989). The rise of print culture has been a topic of great interest to this group: see, for example, John Wall, "The Reformation in England and the Typographical Revolution: 'By This Printing ... the Doctrine of the Gospel Soundeth to All Nations,'" in Gerald P. Tyson and Sylvia S. Wagonheim (eds.), *Print and Culture in the Renaissance: Essays on the Advent of Printing in Europe* (Newark: University of Delaware Press, 1986), 208–221, and other essays in this collection. Legal, economic, and other practical conditions that affected the creation and dissemination of various forms of art in the Renaissance (conditions similar to those encountered by East and the composers of London's music trade) have been thoroughly studied by students of English Renaissance drama; see, for example, Steven Mullaney, *The Place of the Stage: License, Play, and Power in Renaissance England* (Chicago: University of Chicago Press, 1988).

6. The lines of religious affiliations and sympathies in Elizabethan England were by no means hard and fast; see Christopher Haigh, *English Reformations; Religion, Politics and Society under*

the Tudors (Oxford: Clarendon Press, 1993), 285–295. Perhaps it should be mentioned in this context that Thomas East did have contacts with Edmund East, a renowned recusant and likely relative, and that he visited him on Christmas Day, 1580; see PRO, Court of the Star Chamber, C24/170, *Edward East vs. George East* (1584). I believe it may well have been through such recusant connections that Byrd and East actually met and formed their partnership, but in the absence of more documentation it is still difficult to assert this with confidence.

7. See Alistair Fox, "The Complaint of Poetry for the Death of Liberality: The Decline of Literary Patronage in the 1590s," in John Guy (ed.), *The Reign of Elizabeth I: Court and Culture in the Last Decade*, (Cambridge: Cambridge University Press, 1995), 248.

8. For an in-depth study of the music in Byrd's works in these collections, see Kerman, *Masses and Motets.*

9. Joseph Kerman, "The Elizabethan Motet: A Study of Texts for Music," *Studies in the Renaissance* 9 (1962): 293–298. See also David Mateer, "William Byrd's Middlesex Recusancy," *Music & Letters* 78 (1997): 1–14.

10. Philip Brett (ed.), *Gradualia I (1605): The Marian Masses, BE* 5 (1989), ix.

11. Craig Monson, "Byrd, the Catholics and the Motet: The Hearing Reopened," in Dolores Pesce (ed.), *Hearing the Motet: Essays on the Motet of the Middle Ages and Renaissance* (Oxford: Oxford University Press, 1997), 348–374.

12. William Weston, *The Autobiography of an Elizabethan*, edited by Philip Caraman (London: Longmans, 1955), 69–71, 76–77. Another example of Byrd's musical participation in an illegal Jesuit-sponsored gathering is documented at White Webbs, Middlesex, in 1604; see Philip Caraman, *Henry Garnet, 1555–1606, and the Gunpowder Plot* (New York: Farrar, Straus, 1964), 317.

13. Kerman, "The Elizabethan Motet," 278.

14. John Milsom, "Sacred Songs in the Chamber," in John Morehen (ed.), *English Choral Practice, 1450–1650*, (Cambridge: Cambridge University Press, 1995), 166–171.

15. Edward Arber (ed.), *A Transcript of the Registers of the Company of Stationers of London, 1554–1640 A.D.*, 5 vols. (Birmingham: The editor, 1875–1894), vol. 3, 76.

16. For a description of the conditions of Catholic worship in the Elizabethan era, see Adrian Morey, *The Catholic Subjects of Elizabeth I* (Totowa, NJ: Rowman and Littlefield, 1978), 148–151; and Michael Hodgetts, *Secret Hiding Places* (Dublin: Ventas, 1989). On the evolution of Catholic worship during the Elizabethan era, see concise discussions in: Haigh, *English Reformations*, chapters 14 and 15; and Alan Dures, *English Catholicism, 1558–1642: Continuity and Change* (London: Longmans, 1983), 1–39.

17. "An act (1581) to retain the Queen's Majesty's subjects in their due obedience made the saying or hearing of the mass punishable by a fine of 100 or 200 marks" (*Recusants in the Exchequer Pipe Rolls 1581–1592*, extracted by Dom Hugh Bowler, edited by Timothy J. McCann [London: Catholic Record Society, 1986], 1).

18. Peter Clulow, "Publication Dates for Byrd's Latin Masses," *Music & Letters* 47 (1966): 6.

19. Ibid.

20. Facsimiles of the *Gradualia* prefatory material appear in Brett, *Gradualia I (1605)*, BE5 xxxi–xxxiv.

21. James Jackman provided a liturgical analysis of these collections in his "Liturgical Aspects of Byrd's 'Gradualia,'" *Musical Quarterly* 49 (1963): 237–259. For the *Gradualia* registration, see Arber, *Transcript*, vol. 3, 279.

22. *DNB*, s.v. "Thomas Bancroft."

23. P. M. Handover, *The Second Cecil: The Rise to Power, 1563–1604 of Sir Robert Cecil, Later First Earl of Salisbury* (London: Eyre and Spottiswood, 1959), 153.

24. Gladys Jenkins, "The Archpriest Controversy and the Printers, 1601–1603," *The Library* 5th ser., vol. 2 (1948): 183.

25. Edwards, *Robert Persons*, 254–255. In a recent article, Teruhiko Nasu has independently considered the question of Bancroft and his role as licenser of the *Gradualia*; see "The Publication of Byrd's *Gradualia* Reconsidered," *Brio* 32 (1995): 109–120. For delving into the question of Bancroft's reasons for licensing the book, this is a most welcome addition to the literature. On those reasons, however, my view differs from Nasu's. Whereas he finds a positive role for Bancroft, whom he sees as another of Byrd's patrons, I would tend to see the bishop's role differently—as frankly sinister and antagonistic to Byrd.

26. See Thomas Greaves Law, *A Historical Sketch of the Conflicts between Jesuits and Seculars in the Reign of Queen Elizabeth* (London: D. Nutt, 1889); and Jenkins, "Archpriest Controversy," 183–186. For a recent review of the controversy from the Jesuit perspective, see Edwards, *Robert Persons*, chapters 11–21, *passim*.

27. According to *STC2*, East printed the following (mostly religious) works for Thomas Man: *The (Scottish) Confession of Faith*, 1603 (*STC2* 22024.3); Richard Greenham, *Three Very Fruitfull and Comfortable Sermons*, 1604 (*STC2* 12324.5); Anthony Rudd, *A Sermon Preached at Greenwich*, 1604 (*STC2* 21433.5); John Bate, *The Royal Priesthood of Christians*, 1605 (*STC2* 1590); Arthur Dent, *A Pastime for Parents*, 1606 (*STC2* 6622); John Dod and Robert Cleaver, *A Plaine and Familiar Exposition*, 1606 (*STC2* 6954); Henry Hollard (Vicar of St. Brides), *The Historie of Adam*, 1606 (*STC2* 13587); William Whately, *The Redemption of Time*, 1606, 1607, and 1608 (*STC2*: 25318, 25319, and 25319.3); William Borton, *The Christians Heavenly Treasure*, 1608 (*STC2* 4168); and Jean Taffin, *Of the Markes of the Children of God*, 1608 (*STC2* 23653).

28. Snodham printed works by Robert Cleaver (*STC2* 18063), William Whately (*STC2* 15709), Thomas Wilson (*STC2* 12108), and Jean Taffin (*STC2* 1013) for Man.

29. Another strong possibility, not altogether exclusive of the first, was that James's accession brought with it a period of relative tolerance for Catholics and Bancroft simply relaxed his role as a censor and permitted Byrd's music to be published to reflect the more magnanimous spirit of the times; see David H. Willson, *King James VI and I* (London: Jonathan Cape, 1956), 217–222.

30. See Peter le Huray, *Music and the Reformation in England, 1549–1660* (Cambridge: Cambridge University Press, 1978), 234.

31. See *NG*, s.v. "William Byrd," by Joseph Kerman.

32. Clulow, "Publication Dates," 8.

33. Ibid.

34. Ibid.

35. Ibid.

36. For East's paper, see Table A1.3 and appendix 4.

37. Margaret Dowling, "The Printing of John Dowland's 'Second Booke of Songs or Ayres,'" *The Library* 4th ser., vol. 12 (1932): 370.

38. Ibid., 366.

39. When the music patent was in force, East never allowed a music book to leave his press without an indication of the patent holder for whom he worked as an assign (with the important exception of the years circa 1593–1596), see Table A1.5.

40. See Jeremy L. Smith, "The Hidden Editions of Thomas East," *Notes, Quarterly Journal of the Music Library Association* 53 (1997): 1090–1091.

41. Allan H. Stevenson, *The Problem of the Missale Speciale* (London: Bibliographical Society, 1967), 94.

42. PRO, State Papers, S.P. 12/274 , f. 250–261, "Examinations of Gervase Pierrepoint, Rich. Thimbleby, Edward Forset, John Wiborowe and John Balls (23–24 April 1600)." See *Calendar of State Papers, Domestic Series of the Reigns of Edward VI, Mary, Elizabeth and James I* (hereafter *Cal. S.P. Dom.*), 12 vols., *1598–1601* (London: H.M.S.O., 1869), 423–425. The letter is

transcribed in full in *Calendar of the State Papers Relating to Scotland* (hereafter *Cal. S.P. Scot.*), vol. 3, part 2: *1597–1603*, edited by J. D. Mackie (Edinburgh: H.M.S.O., 1969), 613–617.

43. Unlike Persons, in 1597 Angus had officially subscribed to the Protestant "Confession of Faith" under pressure from James VI, the king of Scotland. As a Scotsman and Catholic, Angus maintained an allegiance not only to the king but also to the Jesuit cause, and this made him the ideal recipient of Persons's letter; see William Fraser, *The Douglas Book*, 4 vols. (Edinburgh: T. and A. Constable, 1885), vol. 2, 399.

44. Fraser contends that Persons's letter was confiscated at the time of the arrests, see *The Douglas Book*, vol. 2, 399. Other copies surfaced soon after this. In an intelligence report intercepted after the first examinations yet before the end of April, the reporter mentions that this letter was received by James and sent to the queen (*Cal. S.P. Dom., 1598–1601*, 427). Another copy of the same letter resurfaced in Liège 30 April 1600. John Petit wrote to the spy Thomas Phelippes: "I send you ... a copy of a letter written by Father Parsons to the Earl of Angus in Scotland" (*Cal. S.P. Dom., Addenda, 1580–1625*, 405). Such an important letter would obviously have been copied often. Nonetheless, the court's quick reaction to the espionage of East's apprentices may well have been what caused the confiscation and preservation of the particular copy that was read at East's house.

45. Primary documents on these men may be found in the State Papers and Acts of the Privy Council (cited in specific detail later). Also see *DNB*, s.v. "Edward Forset." (It is clear from this article that there were two men with this name who have been conflated in some studies.) Forset continued as a staunch recusant well into the reign of James I; see John J. LaRocca, ed., *Jacobean Recusant Rolls for Middlesex* (London: Catholic Record Society, 1997), Recusant Roll 15-E377/26, 1617–1618. On the Thimblebys, see J. W. F. Hill, *Tudor and Stuart Lincoln* (Cambridge: Cambridge University Press, 1956), 70–82; and John Bossy, *The English Catholic Community 1570–1850* (New York: Oxford University Press, 1976), 173–175. Pierrepoint is mentioned often in books on Campion; see, for example: Richard Simpson, *Edmund Campion: A Biography* (London: Williams and Norgate, 1867), 157–158.

46. Simpson, *Campion*, 157–158; and Evelyn Waugh, *Edmund Campion*, 2d ed. (London: Longmans, 1961), 162–163.

47. In 1589 Thimbleby took a bond to remain under the house arrest of Edward Billesby (of the town of Billesby, Lincoln) before the Court of the High Commission; see *Acts of the Privy Council of England* (hereafter *A.P.C.*), 32 vols., edited by J. R. Dasent, *1588–9*, (London: H.M.S.O., 1907), 318. In 1591 Thimbleby was still under Billesby's charge (*A.P.C., 1591*, 142). Pierrepoint was to have "lycence to repaier into the country for some necessaries" in 1589 (*A.P.C., 1588–9*, 383), but he was imprisoned, along with John Thimbleby, at Banbury later that year (*A.P.C., 1588–9*, 414–415). For another of Pierrepont's terms in prison see *A.P.C., 1581–1582*, 194. On 12 February 1584, Pierrepont was tortured on the rack; see *Cal. S.P. Dom., 1581–1590*, edited by Robert Lemon (London: H.M.S.O., 1865), 159.

48. On 24 August 1582, a report was filed that concerned observances of Mass at the Marshalsea in the "chambers of Mr. Shelly, Mr. Pierpoint, and Mr. Denton." The report goes on to note: "Their supersititous stuff, their abominable relics, and their vile books, have been taken away" (*Cal. S.P. Dom., 1581–1590*, 68). Pierrepoint's messages and letters were under suspicion later in 1582; see *Cal. S.P. Dom., 1581–1590*, 86. On 10 January 1584, there was a "collection of the papers and writings found about Jervais Perpoint and his lodging in the Marshalsea," whereupon several books and letters were confiscated (*Cal. S.P. Dom., 1581–1590*, 151).

49. Both apprentices were from the island of Ely. Wiborowe had been presented by East to his company on 6 March 1598 and John Balls on 25 December 1593; see Arber, *Transcript*, vol. 2, 224 and 189.

50. Wiborowe explained that he "came into the work-house before his fellow, and thus heard some speeches that [Balls] did not" (*Cal. S.P. Dom., 1598–1601, 424*).

51. All three recusants were arrested and examined on the same day; see *Cal. S.P. Dom., 1598–1601, 425*.

52. *Cal. S.P. Dom., 1598–1601, 434–435.*

53. The single most powerful jurist of his day and the leading prosecutor of recusants in England, John Popham, Lord Chief Justice, personally began the inquisitions and attended several others with his colleagues. (On Popham and recusants, see Elliot Rose, *Cases of Conscience: Alternatives Open to Recusants and Puritans under Elizabeth I and James I* [Cambridge: Cambridge University Press, 1975], 64–65.) Other examinations were conducted by Stephen Soame, who would later become lord mayor of the City of London, and Sir Edward Coke, the queen's attorney general, who would also have a prominent role in the prosecution of Lord Essex after his ill-fated revolt; see Edward Cheyney, *A History of England: From the Defeat of the Armada to the Death of Elizabeth*, 2 vols., 2d ed. (Gloucester, MA: Peter Smith, 1967), vol. 2, 548. Perhaps the strongest indication of the importance of this episode at East's house, in the eyes of the court, was the fact that Coke took his own notes during the last examinations of these men; see *Cal. S.P. Dom., 1598–1601, 434–435*. Most of the similar notes of examinations preserved in the State Papers survive only in scribal copies. The government's interest in the affair was surely based on the significance of the letter they confiscated and its author, Persons, yet this reflects again on the stature of the men who met at East's, for it was they who began the dissemination of the important news of this letter to Catholics in England.

54. In 1600 Persons's seeming turn in support from the Infanta to the Scottish king would surely have been treated seriously by Angus and, more important, by Catholic Englishmen. Not only English Protestants and Puritans but also many Catholics in England would have preferred any other successor to the Infanta of Spain. Even at the end of her reign, many English Catholics still hoped for greater toleration from Elizabeth herself, and they did not wish to be seen to encourage a successor from an antagonistic country. In 1598 a group of Loyalists headed by the priest William Bishop even drafted a "Protestation of Allegiance" in the hope of increased tolerance. For the same purpose, in April 1599 William Warton, a Loyalist priest, submitted to the attorney general a denunciation of the Jesuits for attempting to secure a Spanish succession. By the turn of the century, English Catholics were probably most anxious for any news about prospects for normalizing their situation once a new monarch came to the throne; see Arnold O. Meyer, *England and the Catholic Church under Elizabeth*, 2d ed., translated by Rev. J. R. McKee, introduction by John Bossy (London: Routledge, 1967), 456–458; and Dures, *English Catholicism*, 35–40.

55. In the last years of Elizabeth's reign, the Scottish king was known to be strongly frustrated by the queen's refusal to make a solid and public commitment to his succession claim. This drove him to explore the possibility of foreign Catholic support, even that of the pope, in case he should feel moved to exert his claims by force. Persons was well informed about these approaches and was attempting to capitalize on them. His plan was therefore not as unrealistic as it appears with the benefit of hindsight; see *Cal. S.P. Scot., 1597–1603, 613–616*, and *Cal. S.P. Dom., 1598–1601, 427*. See also Helen G. Stafford, *James VI of Scotland and the Throne of England* (London: Appleton, 1940), 231, 234–240, and 291; Hicks, "Father Robert Persons, S.J.," 112; and Willson, *King James VI and I*, 144.

56. *Cal. S.P. Dom., 1598–1601, 424.*

57. See Dowling, "The Printing," 369–370.

58. *Cal. S.P. Dom., 1598–1601, 424.*

59. That Pierrepoint was not in residence at East's but rather at a goldsmith's shop in

London (who was listed as "Tirrey") makes it possible to speculate that he, too, was in the process of collecting materials for the Mass. His objective may have been to commission and purchase the necessary religious paraphernalia at the same time the Thimblebys were obtaining the appropriate music for the illegal Catholic ritual. Together this group may have been planning a service to the religious community of their coreligionists by collecting and distributing necessary materials for the celebration of the Mass. Further investigation of the activities of the goldsmith Tirrey may reveal his connection to Catholic markets for metal arts.

60. *A.P.C., 1600–1601*, 85.

61. Ibid., 475.

62. Ibid., 768.

63. James, *Society, Politics and Culture*, 434.

64. Penry Williams, *The Later Tudors: England, 1547–1603* (Oxford: Clarendon Press, 1995), 325–327. Essex was also a member of the Privy Council, a longtime favorite of the queen, and the owner of a lucrative monopoly for sweet wines. With so many affiliations and resources, it is not surprising that Essex stood at the center of a network of patronage and clientage so extensive that it was operated by four secretaries. The number of solicitations to Essex for his support was generally so great that he was once embarrassed to discover that he had helped to find a position for someone who was sponsored by an enemy; see Paul E. J. Hammer, "Patronage at Court, Faction and the Earl of Essex," in John Guy (ed.), *The Reign of Elizabeth I: Court and Culture in the Last Decade*, (Cambridge: Cambridge University Press, 1995), 70.

65. See Fox, "Complaint of Poetry," 231. Fox's figures are based on Franklin B. Williams's study, *An Index of Dedications and Commendatory Verses in English Books before 1641* (London: Bibliographical Society, 1962).

66. All dedications to Essex of the 1590s are listed in Fox, "Complaint of Poetry," 248. Included there are East's editions of Thomas Watson's *Italian Madrigalls Englished*, 1590 (*STC2* 25119) and John Mundy's *Songs and Psalmes*, 1594 (*STC2* 18284).

67. The summary of Essex's career in this and the following two paragraphs is based on Arthur F. Kinney, *Elizabethan Backgrounds: Historical Documents of the Age of Elizabeth I* (London: Archon, 1975), 317–323, and James's extensive analysis of the final years of the courtier's life in *Society, Politics and Culture*.

68. Kinney, *Elizabethan Backgrounds*, 323.

69. See *DNB*, s.v. "Robert Devereux."

70. Bevington, *Tudor Drama and Politics*, 26.

71. Ibid., 34.

72. The Hayward volume was elaborately dedicated to the earl, with the reference between Essex and Henry specified. The queen's pithy remark on the matter was unambiguous; she simply stated, "I am Richard II"; see John Nichols, *The Progresses and Public Processions of Queen Elizabeth*, 3 vols. (London: The author, 1823), vol. 3, 552–553. For more on the famous connection between Hayward and Essex, see E. M. Albright, "Shakespeare's 'Richard II,' Hayward's 'History of Henry IV' and the Essex Conspiracy," *PMLA* 46 (1931): 694–719; Ray Heffner, "Shakespeare, Hayward and Essex," *PMLA* 45 (1930): 754–780; and S. L. Goldberg, "Sir John Hayward, 'Politic' Historian," *Review of English Studies* 6 (1955): 233–244.

73. When John Wolfe, the printer of Hayward's *Henry IV*, was examined before the Privy Council, he explained that the "people [were] calling for it exceedingly." It was Essex himself who informed the Archbishop of Canterbury that the book had political implications of a serious nature and ordered that the dedication to him be removed. But Essex had waited

long enough for Wolfe to have already sold over 600 copies of the book with the dedication in place; see *Cal. S.P. Dom., 1598–1601*, 450–451. Similarly, the Richard II play by Shakespeare and perhaps another based on Hayward's book were public successes thanks to the Essex faction, and this came to the attention of the queen herself, who noted that one version of the work had been played "40tie times in the open streets"; see James, *Society, Politics and Culture*, 419, n.10.

74. Ruff and Wilson, "The Madrigal," 3–51.

75. Ibid., 9; and idem, "Allusion to Essex," 31–36.

76. See David Price, *Patrons and Musicians of the English Renaissance* (Cambridge: Cambridge University Press, 1981), 155, n. 3.

77. See Ruff and Wilson, "The Madrigal," 6.

78. Ibid., 38; and idem, "Allusion to Essex," 34.

79. Earl of Essex to the queen: "I speak the words of my soul, yet cannot utter that which most concerns me, and should give my full heart greatest ease; therefore I say to myself 'Lie still, look down, and be silent'"; see *Cal. S.P. Dom., 1598–1601*, 457. Essex also revealingly wrote: "The prating tavern haunter speaks of me what he lists; the frantic libeller writes of me what he lists; *they print me and make me speak to the world, and shortly they will play me upon the stage*" (*Cal. S.P. Dom., 1598–1601*, 435, italics added).

80. See Donald W. Krummel and Stanley Sadie (eds.), *Music Printing and Publishing*, Norton/Grove Handbooks in Music (New York: Norton, 1990), s.v. "Peter Short," by Miriam Miller.

81. See Dowling, "The Printing," 374.

82. Ruff and Wilson, "The Madrigal," 35.

83. Dowling, "The Printing," 375.

84. Ibid., 376. Dowling finds it "curious that Cotton, after selling copies to Frank at about 1s. 5 1/2d. apiece, should buy them back at double that price." But it may be that since Frank was a leather seller, Cotton had the books bound by Frank and thus paid Frank for that service.

85. There was a man named Fanshaw involved in a tavern brawl over the Essex Revolt; see *Salisbury MS*, vol. 11, 190. But it is not clear whether he was defending the honor of Cecil or Essex in the exchange.

86. Dowling, "The Printing," 371.

87. See Francis R. Johnson, "Printers' 'Copy Books' and the Black Market in the Elizabethan Book Trade," *The Library* 5th ser., vol. 1 (1946): 97–105.

88. Arber, *Transcript*, vol. 3, 167.

89. Dowling, "The Printing," 368.

90. *Cal. S.P. Dom., 1598–1601*, 545–546. For Cromwell's financial problems during his stay in the Tower, see *Cal. S.P. Dom., 1598–1601*, 601.

91. PRO, Acts of the Privy Council, PC 2/26, f. 333, "Letter to the Leiutennant of the Tower" (1601) (see *A.P.C., 1601–1604*, 143).

92. On Cromwell's career, see *DNB*, s.v. "Edward Cromwell."

93. Snodham reprinted the Scottish edition of George Ker, *A Discouerie of the Conspiracie of Scottish Papists* (London, 1603) (*STC2* 14939), and the copies were sold at East's house. These were confessions of Ker and others who were involved in the Spanish Blanks conspiracy. The conspiracy involved Scottish Catholics as well placed as Lord Angus, who later played a minor role as the addressee of a seditious letter by Persons confiscated at East's house in 1601, discussed earlier. John Hayward's *An Answer to the First Part of a Certaine Conference* (London, 1603) was printed by East and Snodham for S. Waterson and C. Burbie (*STC2* 12988).

It was entered in the Stationers' Company Registers on 7 April 1603 by Waterson; see Arber, *Transcript*, vol. 3, 364. Hayward had been imprisoned at the end of Elizabeth's reign for his historical writings associated with the Essex Revolt. In his dedication to the king, the author admitted that he had offended the last monarch so conspicuously with his writings but would now go to great lengths to ingratiate himself with the new king. This book is a long disputation of the arguments of Persons's *Conference*. The latter book, of course, was a topic of intense discussion at the meeting at East's house and was the chief reason that Persons chose to write a letter to his fellow Catholic Lord Angus.

94. John Savile's *King James His Entertainment at Theobalds* (London, 1603) was printed by "T. Snodham" but sold at the house of "T. Este" and it was entered to Snodham 14 May 1603 (see *STC2* 17261). East's book on the tobacco controvery is J.H., *Work for Chimny-sweepers: Or A warning for Tabacconists* (London, 1602). This was a work East printed for Thomas Bushell; see *STC2* 12571.5. The second edition of this book (*STC2* 12571) was probably a hidden edition published by East and sold at his house. This is the only hidden edition I have discovered thus far among East's editions of general literature. On the early Stuart tobacco controversy, see Willson, *King James VI and I*, 289–303.

CHAPTER 8

1. See William Hyde Price, *The English Patents of Monopoly* (Cambridge, MA: Harvard University Press, 1913).

2. See Arnold Hunt, "Book Trade Patents, 1603–1640," in Arnold Hunt, Giles Mandelbrote, and Alison Shell (eds.), *The Book Trade & Its Customers, 1450–1900: Historical Essays for Robin Myers*, introduction by D. F. McKenzie (New Castle, DE: Oak Knoll Press, 1997), 44. The music grant (once thought to have become extinct in 1606) was renewed by William Stansby, Richard Hawkins, and George Latham, "citizens and stationers of London," in 1635 (p. 54).

3. *Cal. S.P. Dom., 1603–10*, 609. For a discussion of the events that led to this grant, see Cyprian Blagden, "The English Stock of the Stationers' Company in the Time of the Stuarts," *The Library* 5th ser., vol. 12 (1957): 167.

4. *Cal. S.P. Dom., 1603–10*, 609.

5. Cyprian Blagden has pointed out that it was not until the establishment of the Latin Stock that the English Stock was designated as such; see *The Stationers' Company: A History 1403–1959* (London: Allen and Unwin, 1960), 92, n. 1.

6. For an overview of the wholesale effects of this grant on company policy, see *Records of the Court of the Stationers' Company, 1602 to 1640*, edited by William A. Jackson (London: Bibliographical Society, 1957), viii–xi.

7. The company raised the sum of £9,000 among its members for the purchase of pre-existent patents; see Blagden, *The Stationers' Company*, 75–77. It seems not to have been properly noted that music was of interest to the company before the time of the Stock's official charter: Eastland sold copies of Dowland's *Second Booke of Songs* to the Stationers' Company in 1600; see Margaret Dowling, "The Printing of John Dowland's 'Second Booke of Songs or Ayres,'" *The Library* 4th ser., vol. 12 (1932): 374. East used the company's estimates of the worth of these items to argue that Eastland's pricing was extravagant. From this and evidence presented by Blagden, it would seem very clear that the company's publishing interests were far-reaching; the grant of 1603 was not so much the initiation of a new institution as authorization of a plan that was well under way before James's accession.

8. See *Records of the Court*, ix.

9. I base this on Blagden's comments in his 1960 work, *The Stationers' Company*, 75.

10. *Records of the Court,* ix. In her will of 1627, Lucretia East noted:

> I the said Lucretia Este have at this present in stocke in the hands of the Company of Stationers of London the somme of one hundred and three score pounds which of right ought and is to bee paid by the said Company within the space of one whole yeare next after my decease at fower quarterly payments by fourtie pounds a payment. (PRO, Probate Reocrds, PROB 11/156, "Will of Lucretia East, 1627.")

11. See Robert Illing, *Est-Barley-Ravenscroft and the English Metrical Psalter* (Adelaide: Libraries Board of South Australia, 1969), 2−4; and *STC2* 2515.

12. See James Doelman, "George Wither, the Stationers' Company and the English Psalter," *Studies in Philology* 90 (1993): 74−77.

13. For the conflicts between patentees of the two music monopolies before 1603, see chapter 5.

14. See *Records of the Court,* viii.

15. *STC2* 2514 . See, for example, the conglomerate editions of the *Book of the Common Prayer* and the *Whole Booke of Psalmes* in the British Library (3433.b.11: 1 and 2 [quarto editions of 1604]) and the conglomerate volume of a similar set in Archbishop Marsh's Library (P2a: 1 and 2 [folio editions of 1607]).

16. *STC2* 2522.3. Windet, who printed this volume with East as a temporary partner, inherited the business of John Wolfe and was the chief printer among the assignees of Richard Day. After 1603 Windet also began to print music traditionally associated with the music patent; see Miriam Miller, "London Music Printing, c. 1570−c. 1640" (Ph.D. diss., University of London, 1969), 111−114.

17. The copy of *STC2* 2514 in the British Library (3433.d.12) is bound with Barker's *Book of the Common Prayer* and has paper with a similar *Grapes* IB (I) mark. Similarly, Barker's *Common Prayer* folio of 1607 and *STC2* 2522.3 in Archbishop Marsh's Library (P2a) have similar *Grapes* IB (II) marks.

18. See W. W. Greg, *A Companion to Arber* (Oxford: Clarendon Press, 1967), 55−56 and 161.

19. For the mid-seventeenth century activities of the Stationers' Company regarding this property, see Doelman, "George Wither," 75−77.

20. *A Prognostication for Ever* (London, 1582, 1598, and 1605), *STC2*: 439.17, 439.18, and 439.19.

21. See *STC2*: 532.6, 452.5, 532.7, 434.19, and 532.5.

22. *Records of the Court,* 71.

23. Robert R. Steele, *The Earliest English Music Printing: A Description and Bibliography of English Printed Music to the Close of the Sixteenth Century* (London: Bibliographical Society, 1903), 29.

24. See Hunt, "Book Trade Patents," 44 and 54.

25. Thomas Deloney, *Strange Histories* (London, 1602), was published by Barley (see *STC2* 6566). Apparently because this contained a phrase or so of music, Barley listed Morley in the imprint as the patent holder.

26. *STC2* 7095. For a list of music editions produced in the 1603−1606 era, see Gerald D. Johnson, "William Barley, 'Publisher & Seller of Bookes,' 1591−1614," *The Library* 6th ser., vol. 11 (1989): 43−44. Johnson does not include East's hidden editions and reissues in this list.

27. See Miller, "London Music Printing," 84.

28. *STC2* 21128.

29. For East's contract with Morley, see Dowling, "The Printing," 366.

30. By the turn of the century, books of lute songs had become popular enough in London to attract a number of new publishers to the music field. With the death of Morley and the resultant lapse in the force of the music patent, these publishers became much more vis-

ible. Among these new music publishers, some, like Matthew Selman and Waterson, treated music books as a relatively minor concern. Waterson published a handful of music books, which included East's edition of Robinson's *Schoole of Musicke* in 1603; see Johnson, "William Barley," 48. Selman had only a single publication in music, Robert Jones's *Second Book of Songs* (printed by Short), but he had also bought illicitly produced copies of Dowland's *Second Booke of Songs* from East's two apprentices, Balls and Wiborowe, in 1601; see Dowling, "The Printing," 371. Therefore, Selman and perhaps Waterson, too, may have stocked more music books than their publication record suggests. Conversely, some other book traders newly attracted to music, namely Thomas Adams and John Browne, eventually published a substantial number of books that they vigorously traded. As their careers progressed, these men solicited the trade-printing work of nearly all the music printers active in the first quarter of the seventeenth century; see Johnson, "William Barley," 48.

31. Donald W. Krummel and Stanley Sadie (eds.), *Music Printing and Publishing*, Norton/Grove Handbooks in Music (New York: W. W. Norton, 1990), s.v. "Thomas Snodham," by Miriam Miller.

32. *STC2* 6268.

33. Edward Arber (ed.), *A Transcript of the Registers of the Company of Stationers of London, 1554–1640 A.D.*, 5 vols. (Birmingham: The editor, 1875–1894), vol. 3, 319.

34. Ibid., 246.

35. See Table A1.3 and appendix 4.

36. See Table A1.3 and appendix 4.

37. Arber, *Transcript*, vol. 3, 246.

38. See Roy C. Strong, "Queen Elizabeth I as Oriana," *Studies in the Renaissance* 6 (1959): 251–260.

39. Lillian Ruff and Arnold Wilson, "The Madrigal, the Lute Song and Elizabethan Politics," *Past & Present* 44 (1969): 21–23.

40. Some other possible reasons that come to mind, unlikely though they seem, include: (1) if we assume that East had printed the first edition but that it had been sold not at his shop but elsewhere, then perhaps he wished to print a hidden edition in order to compete with the actual bookseller, not necessarily because the first edition had sold well and the stock needed replenishing; or (2) perhaps some yet-to-be-discovered "silent" publisher requested a complete edition of some work for private purposes that were somehow completely divorced from the concept of market demand.

41. See Joseph Kerman, *The Masses and Motets of William Byrd* (Berkeley: University of California Press, 1981), 118.

42. See Philip Brett (ed.), *Gradualia I (1605): The Marian Masses*, BE 5 (1993), xvi.

43. H. K. Andrews had originally placed the *Psalmes* production in the fallow period of 1599, when Byrd was five years along a ten-year gap in relations with East; see his "Printed Sources of William Byrd's 'Psalmes, Sonets and Songs,'" *Music & Letters* 44 (1963): 19–20, and "The Printed Part-Books of Byrd's Vocal Music," *The Library* 5th ser., vol. 19 (1964): 5–7.

44. David Mateer, "William Byrd, John Petre and Oxford, Bodleian MS Mus. Sch. E. 423," *RMA Research Chronicle* 29 (1996): 21.

45. It is a most confounding puzzle how Barley obtained his power in the music patent in the first place. Without tangible evidence at hand, it is only possible to speculate on this matter, especially since the entire issue may have had as much to do with selling music editions as with the publishing of new editions of music books that were generally still available for study. The only clue Barley has left for historians is that he was the first to work with Morley once the composer obtained the patent in 1598; see Johnson, "William Barley," 29. Perhaps Barley's priority in time kept East from making a claim for the patent.

46. *Records of the Court*, 19.

47. Ibid., 20.

48. *STC2* 4258 (published by W. Hall and T. Haviland). The larger implications of the *East vs. Barley* incident have been discussed in two articles by Gerald D. Johnson, who is only the latest of an unexpectedly large number of Barley biographers; see his "William Barley" and "The Stationers versus the Drapers: Control of the Press in the Late Sixteenth Century," *The Library* 6th ser., vol. 10 (1988): 1–17.

49. Johnson, "William Barley," 24.

50. Johnson, "The Stationers versus the Drapers," 1.

51. Donald W. Krummel, *English Music Printing 1553–1700* (London: Bibliographical Society, 1975), 30. Johnson has observed that the reason East's reprint of Morley's *Canzonets* was produced in 1606 with a mention of Barley's patent was probably due to this case; see his "William Barley," 33.

52. See, for Morley's fees, Dowling, "The Printing," 366, and, for Barley's fees from East's reprints, *Records of the Court*, 20. Table A1.2 is a list of East's hidden editions with proposed times of publication.

53. See Johnson, "William Barley," 33.

54. *Records of the Court*, 19.

55. Johnson recognizes that the particular case involved reprinting. Yet by setting these fees against Morley's, he implies that Morley's and Barley's fees are comparable; see his "William Barley," 32. David Price tends to assume that Barley charged all music printers the single fee based on this case; see his *Patrons and Musicians of the English Renaissance* (Cambridge: Cambridge University Press, 1981), 181.

56. See *Records of the Court*, 20; and Dowling, "The Printing," 366.

57. In this case, East paid Morley's fee but charged the amount to Eastland. In the end, Eastland did not repay East for handling this fee, despite the fact that he had signed a bill of debt to East for that amount; see Dowling, "The Printing," 370.

58. See Arber, *Transcript*, vol. 3, 340 and 360–361. An overview of East's registrations appears in Table A1.5.

59. Jeremy L. Smith, "From 'Rights to Copy' to the 'Bibliographic Ego': A New Look at the Last Early Edition of Byrd's 'Psalmes, Sonets & Songs,'" *Music & Letters* 80 (1999): 511–519.

60. Guildhall, Original Wills, Box 3B (Ms. 9052 3B), f. 61, "Will of Thomas East, 21 July 1607."

61. *Records of the Court*, 20.

62. Guildhall, "Will of Thomas East."

63. Her legacy as the widow of a shareholder of the English Stock came to £160 per year.

64. *Records of the Court*, 36.

65. On the Snoden (Snodham, Snowden, etc.) family, see Peter W. Blayney, *The Texts of 'King Lear' and Their Origin*, vol. 1: *Nicholas Okes and the First Quarto* (Cambridge: Cambridge University Press, 1982), 15–21.

66. PRO, Probate Records, PROB 11/148, "Will of Elizabeth Snodham, 1626."

67. Guildhall, "Will of Thomas East."

68. Arber, *Transcript*, vol. 3, 413.

69. Miller, "London Music Printing," 103.

70. See Johnson, "William Barley," 45.

71. Arber, *Transcript*, vol. 3, 450.

72. Ibid.

73. See (and cf.) ibid., 450 and 465.

74. Miller, "London Music Printing," 83.

75. Although two hidden editions of Byrd's *Psalmes* were also printed, that volume was probably reproduced as much for Byrd's sake as for his audience's; see chapter 4.

76. See Figure 3.4.

77. Allan H. Stevenson, *The Problem of the* Missale Speciale (London: Bibliographical Society, 1967), 94.

78. See Miller, "London Music Printing," 104.

79. In Adams's case, Barley brought a suit against the publisher quite similar to the one he had earlier instituted against East; see *Records of the Court*, 39–40.

80. Johnson, "William Barley," 35.

81. For repositories with these reissued copies, see *STC2*: 4243.5, 4244.5, 6041, and 23918.3.

82. See Brett, Gradualia 1 (1605), xv–xvi.

CONCLUSION

1. See Thomas Whythourne, *The Autobiography of Thomas Whythourne*, edited by James Osbourn (London: Oxford University Press, 1962), 220. For general comments on the lack of musical proofreading at this time, see Donald W. Krummel, *English Music Printing 1553–1700* (London: Bibliographical Society, 1975), 73.

2. Joseph Kerman's important critical survey of music publishing for this era in *The Elizabethan Madrigal: A Comparative Study* (New York: American Musicological Society, 1962), 257–259, has been very influential; see, for example, David Price, *Patrons and Musicians of the English Renaissance* (Cambridge: Cambridge University Press, 1981), 178–189. For a controversially narrow political interpretation of the music-publishing conditions of Elizabethan England, see Lillian Ruff and Arnold Wilson, "The Madrigal, the Lute Song and Elizabethan Politics," *Past & Present* 44 (1969): 3–51.

3. John M. Ward contests this negative view of Barley in his "Barley's Songs without Words," *Lute Society Journal* 12 (1970): 18.

4. Krummel, *English Music Printing*, 33.

5. See Kerman, *The Elizabethan Madrigal*, 258.

APPENDIX 2

1. See Table A1.2 for a list of the hidden editions discussed in this section.

2. The very few variants that affect the music and text in hidden editions of Byrd's Mass editions are discussed in Peter Clulow, "Publication Dates for Byrd's Latin Masses," *Music & Letters* 47 (1966): 9. Other hidden editions of this list have variants that generally conform to those he noted.

3. For the dates of these and all hidden editions discovered in East's output thus far, see Table A1.2.

4. The original editions of these larger works were all from East's first years of music printing (1588–1589) and thus were produced during Byrd's tenure as monopolist. It is at least possible that Byrd was less concerned about East's independent printing ventures than Morley, who was by all accounts an ambitious entrepreneur. On typographical changes in hidden editions of Byrd's *Psalmes*, see H. K. Andrews, "Printed Sources of William Byrd's 'Psalmes, Sonets and Songs,'" *Music & Letters* 44 (1963): 6–13. In the hidden edition of Byrd's *Songs*, one striking typographical change is the consistent use of type ornaments rather than rules of empty staff lines to fill extra spaces on various pages; c.f. *STC2* 4256 and 4256.5: Tenor: C2^r, E1^r, F1^r, and F2^r.

5. See Andrews, "Printed Sources," 11–15.

6. See *STC2* 4256 and 4256.5: Tenor: C3^v, lines 4–5, and *STC2* 18121: British Library; K.3.i.7. (a hidden edition) and *STC2* 18121: British Library R.M.15.e.2: Altus; B3v, lines 5–6.

7. There were twenty-four cases discovered where the stem of the note on the middle line faced downward, for example, in one page of the hidden edition of Morley's *Madrigals.* Yet on the same page of the original they were consistently presented with the stem upward: cf. *STC2* 18128: British Library; K.3.m.11 and Edinburgh Library: De.6.102 (1): Tenor; B4v (a hidden edition).

8. In the case of the first pair of hidden editions (Byrd's *Songs* and Morley's *Canzonets*), the presence of a token remnant of paper in both editions also suggests they were produced concurrently; see Table A1.3.

9. See, for example, Andrews, "Printed Sources," 11–15; and Clulow, "Publication Dates," 9. *STC2* provides a convenient note that distinguishes each hidden edition in its catalog (usually this is a single change in spelling found on the respective title page or dedication of each edition).

10. Andrews, "Printed Sources," 11–15.

11. The signature of the hidden edition is as follows: cantus; $A-D_4$, altus; $A-B_4$ C_2; tenor; $A-D_4$; bassus; A_2, $B-D_4$; quintus A_2 B_4; sextus $A-D_4$. By allowing East's compositors to complete the parts in four complete gatherings, it would seem that the addition of the dedication (with a table on its verso) made the sextus and tenor parts less difficult to prepare at the press; see *STC2*: 25319.7 and 25319.

12. George Kirbye, *First Set of Madrigals (1597)*, edited by Edmund H. Fellowes, revised by Thurston Dart and Philip Brett (London: Stainer & Bell, 1960), ii.

13. Kirbye, *First Set of Madrigals (1597)*, ii.

14. Andrews, "Printed Sources," 11.

APPENDIX 4

1. A standard guide to bibliographical catalogs and checklists is Philip Gaskell, *A New Introduction to Bibliography* (Oxford: Clarendon Press, 1972).

2. Stephen Spector, "Introduction," in Stephen Spector (ed.), *Essays in Paper Analysis,* (Washington, DC: Folger Shakespeare Library, 1987), 7–23.

Select Bibliography

A to Z of Restoration London, The. Edited by Ralph Hyde. London: Topographical Society, 1992.

Acts of the Privy Council of England. Edited by J. R. Dasent. 32 vols. London: H.M.S.O., 1890–1907.

Adams, Simon. "Eliza Enthroned? The Court and Its Politics." In Christopher Haigh (ed.), *The Reign of Elizabeth I*, 55–78. Athens: University of Georgia Press, 1987.

Adams, Thomas. "The Beginnings of Maritime Publishing in England, 1528–1640." *The Library* 6th ser., vol. 14 (1992): 207–219.

Agee, Richard. *The Gardano Music Printing Firms, 1569–1611.* Rochester, NY: University of Rochester Press, 1998.

Albright, E. M. "Shakespeare's 'Richard II,' Hayward's 'History of Henry IV' and the Essex Conspiracy." *Proceedings of the Modern Language Association* 46 (1931): 694–719.

Alpin, J. "The Origins of John Day's 'Certaine Notes.'" *Music & Letters* 62 (1981): 295–299.

Ames, Joseph. *Typographical Antiquities; or The History of Printing in England, Scotland, and Ireland.* Augmented by William Herbert. London: William Miller, 1810–1819.

Anders, H. "The Elizabethan 'ABC with the Catechism.'" *The Library* 4th ser., vol. 16 (1935–1936): 32–48.

Andrews, H. K. "The Printed Part-Books of Byrd's Vocal Music." *The Library* 5th ser., vol. 19 (1964): 1–10.

———. "Printed Sources of William Byrd's 'Psalmes, Sonets and Songs.'" *Music & Letters* 44 (1963): 5–20.

Arber, Edward (ed.). *A Transcript of the Registers of the Company of Stationers of London, 1554–1640 A.D.* 5 vols. Birmingham: The editor, 1875–1894.

Archer, Ian. *The Pursuit of Stability: Social Relations in Elizabethan London.* Cambridge: Cambridge University Press, 1991.

Bagford, John. Papers. Harl. MSS 5414, 5419, 5892–5898. British Library, London.

Baldwin, David. *The Chapel Royal Ancient & Modern.* London: Duckworth, 1990.

Bell, Maurine. "Entrance in the Stationers' Register." *The Library* 6th ser., vol. 16 (1994): 50–54.

Bennett, H. S. *English Books & Readers 1558 to 1603: Being a Study in the History of the Book Trade in the Reign of Elizabeth.* Cambridge: Cambridge University Press, 1965.

Bergeron, David. *English Civic Pageantry, 1558–1642.* Columbia: University of South Carolina Press, 1971.

Bernstein, Jane A. "The Chanson in England 1530–1640: A Study of Sources and Styles." Ph.D. diss., University of California, Berkeley, 1974.

———. *Music Printing in Renaissance Venice: The Scotto Press (1539–1572).* New York: Oxford University Press, 1998.

Bevington, David. *Tudor Drama and Politics: A Critical Approach to Topical Meaning.* Cambridge, MA: Harvard University Press, 1968.

Binns, James. "STC Latin Books: Evidence for Printing-House Practice." *The Library* 5th ser., vol. 32 (1977): 1–27.

———. "STC Latin Books: Further Evidence for Printing-House Practice." *The Library* 6th ser., vol. 1 (1979): 347–354.

Blagden, Cyprian. "The English Stock of the Stationers' Company: An Account of Its Origins." *The Library* 5th ser., vol. 10 (1955): 163–185.

———. "The English Stock of the Stationers' Company in the Time of the Stuarts." *The Library* 5th ser., vol. 12 (1957): 167–186.

———. *The Stationers' Company: A History 1403–1959.* London: Allen and Unwin, 1960.

Blayney, Peter W. *The Texts of 'King Lear' and Their Origins.* Vol. 1: *Nicholas Okes and the First Quarto.* Cambridge: Cambridge University Press, 1982.

———. "William Cecil and the Stationers." In Robin Myers and Michael Harris (eds.), *The Stationers' Company and the Book Trade 1550–1990,* 11–34. New Castle, DE: Oak Knoll Press, 1997.

Boorman, Stanley H. "Early Music Printing: Working for a Specialized Market." In Gerald P. Tyson and Sylvia S. Wagonheim (eds.), *Print and Culture in the Renaissance: Essays on the Advent of Printing in Europe,* 222–245. Newark: University of Delaware Press, 1986.

———. "The 'First' Edition of the 'Odhecaton A.'" *Journal of the American Musicological Society* 30 (1977): 183–207.

———. "Petrucci at Fossombrone: A Study of Early Music Printing, with a Special Reference to the Motetti de la Corona (1514–1519)." Ph.D. diss., University of London, 1976.

———. "The Salzburg Liturgy and Single-Impression Music Printing." In J. Kmetz (ed.), *Music in the German Renaissance: Sources, Styles and Contexts,* 235–253. Cambridge: Cambridge University Press, 1994.

Bossy, John. *The English Catholic Community 1570–1850.* New York: Oxford University Press, 1976.

Bowers, Fredson. "Elizabethan Proofing." In *Essays in Bibliography, Text and Editing,* 241–250. Charlottesville: University of Virginia Press, 1975.

Breight, Curt. "Realpolitik and Elizabethan Ceremony: The Earl of Hertford's Entertainment of Elizabeth at Elvetham, 1591." *Renaissance Quarterly* 45 (1992): 20–48.

Brett, Philip. "The Consort Song, 1575–1625." *Proceedings of the Royal Musical Association* 88 (1961–1962): 73–88.

——— (ed.). *Consort Songs.* Musica Britannica no. 22. London: Stainer Bell, 1967.

———. "Edward Paston (1550–1630): A Norfolk Gentleman and His Musical Collection." *Transactions of the Cambridge Bibliographical Society* 4 (1964): 51–69.

———. Review of *Tallis and Byrd: Cantiones Sacrae (1575),* Recording by Cantores in Ecclesia, Director Michael Howard. *Musical Quarterly* 43 (1972): 149–153.

———. "The Songs of William Byrd." Ph.D. diss., Cambridge University, 1965.

———. "Text, Context and the Early Music Editor." In Nicholas Kenyon (ed.), *Authenticity and Early Music,* 83–114. Oxford: Oxford University Press, 1988.

Briquet, Charles-Moïse. *Les Filigranes, Dictionnaire historique des marques du papier des leur apparition vers 1282 jusqu'en 1600. Avec 39 figures dans le texte et 16,112 fac-similés de filigranes.* 4 vols. 2d ed. New York: Hacker Art Books, 1966.

Brown, David. "Thomas Morley and the Catholics: Some Speculations." *Monthly Musical Record* 89 (1959): 53–61.

———. "William Byrd's 1588 Volume." *Music & Letters* 38 (1957): 371–375.

Bull, John. *Keyboard Music.* 2 vols. Edited by R. T. Dart. Musica Britannica nos. 14 and 19. London: Stainer and Bell, 1963 and 1970.

Byrd, William. *The Byrd Edition.* 20 vols. Edited by Philip Brett. London: Stainer Bell, 1976–.

Calendar of State Papers, Domestic Series of the Reigns of Edward VI, Mary, Elizabeth and James I. 12 vols. London: H.M.S.O., 1856–1872.

Calendar of the Manuscripts of the . . . Marquis of Salisbury . . . Preserved at Hatfield House, Hertfordshire. 24 vols. London: H.M.S.O., 1883–1976.

Calendar of the State Papers Relating to Scotland. Vol. 13, part 2: *1597–1603.* Edited by J. D. Mackie. Edinburgh: H.M.S.O., 1969.

Cambridgeshire Public Records Office, Ely Consistory Registers. VC 23: 98 1611 "Probate and Will of Mary Easte, d.1611."

————. VC 22: 14 1604 "Probate and Will of William Este, d.1604."

Caraman, Philip. *Henry Garnet, 1555–1606, and the Gunpowder Plot.* New York: Farrar, Straus, 1964.

Carlyle, Ursula. Letter to the author. 6 November 1995.

Carter, Tim. "Music Publishing in Italy, c. 1580–c. 1625: Some Preliminary Observations." *RMA Research Chronicle* 20 (1986–1987): 19–37.

————. "Music-Selling in Late Sixteenth-Century Florence: The Bookshop of Piero di Guiliano Morosi." *Music & Letters* 70 (1989): 483–501.

Catalogue of Manuscripts in the Library of St. Michael's College, Tenbury, The. Compiled by Edmund H. Fellowes. Paris: Editions de l'Oiseaux Lyre, 1934.

Chapman, Catherine. "Andrea Antico." Ph.D. diss., Harvard University, 1964.

Cheyney, Edward. *A History of England: From the Defeat of the Armada to the Death of Elizabeth.* 2 vols. 2d ed. Gloucester, MA: Peter Smith, 1967.

Churchill, W. A. *Watermarks in Paper in Holland, England, France, etc., in the XVII and XVIII Centuries and Their Interconnection.* 2d ed. Amsterdam: M. Hertzberger, 1967.

Clair, Colin. "Christopher Plantin's Trade-Connections with England and Scotland." *The Library* 5th ser., vol. 14 (1959): 28–45.

————. *A History of Printing in England.* London: Cassel, 1965.

Clulow, Peter. "Publication Dates for Byrd's Latin Masses." *Music & Letters* 47 (1966): 1–9.

Corporation of London Records Office, London. "Repertories of the Court of Aldermen." Rep. 16. f. 516v (15 November 1569) and rep. 17 f. 1v (13 March 1570).

Cusick, Suzanne G. *Valerio Dorico: Music Printer in Sixteenth-Century Rome.* Ann Arbor, MI: UMI Research Press, 1981.

Dart, Thurston. "A Suppressed Dedication for Morley's Four-Part Madrigals of 1594." *Transactions of the Cambridge Bibliographical Society* 3 (1963): 401–405.

Deutsch, O. E. "The Editions of Morley's 'Introduction.'" *The Library* 4th ser., vol. 23 (1943): 127–129.

Devereux, W. B. *Lives and Letters of the Devereux, Earls of Essex.* 2 vols. London: J. Murray, 1853.

di Lasso, Orlando. *The Complete Motets.* Vol. 11: *Novae aliquot, ad duas voces cantiones (Munich, 1577).* Edited by Peter Berquist. Madison, WI: A-R Editions, 1995.

Dictionary of National Biography. 21 vols. London: Oxford University Press, 1917–1938.

Doelman, James. "George Wither, the Stationers' Company and the English Psalter." *Studies in Philology* 90 (1993): 74–82.

Doleman, R. [Robert Persons]. *A Conference about the Next Succession to the Crowne of Ingland . . .* Antwerp, 1594.

Doolittle, I. G. *The City of London and Its Livery Companies.* Dorchester: Gavin, 1982.

Dowling, Margaret. "The Printing of John Dowland's 'Second Booke of Songs or Ayres.'" *The Library* 4th ser., vol. 12 (1932): 365–380.

Duggan, Mary Kay. *Italian Music Incunabula: Printers and Type.* Berkeley and Los Angeles: University of California Press, 1992.

Dures, Alan. *English Catholicism, 1558–1642: Continuity and Change.* London: Longmans, 1983.

East, Thomas. *The Whole Book of Psalms: With Their Wonted Tunes, Harmonized in Four Parts . . .* Edited by Edward F. Rimbault. London: Musical Antiquarian Society, 1844.

Eccles, Mark. "Bynneman's Books." *The Library* 5th ser., vol. 12 (1957): 81–92.

Edwards, F. G. "A Famous Music Printer, John Day, 1522–1584." *Musical Times* 47 (1906): 170–174, 236–239.

Edwards, Francis. *Robert Persons, the Biography of an Elizabethan Jesuit, 1546–1610.* St. Louis: Institute of Jesuit Sources, 1995.

Einstein, Alfred. *The Italian Madrigal.* 3 vols. Translated by A. H. Krappe, R. H. Sessions, and O. Strunk. Princeton, NJ: Princeton University Press, 1949.

Eisenstein, Elizabeth. *The Printing Press as an Agent of Change: Communications and Cultural Transformations in Early-Modern Europe.* 2 vols. Cambridge: Cambridge University Press, 1979.

————. *The Printing Revolution in Early Modern Europe.* Cambridge: Cambridge University Press, 1983.

Essays in Paper Analysis. Edited by Stephen Spector. Washington, DC: Folger Shakespeare Library, 1987.

Feather, John. "From Rights in Copies to Copyright: The Recognition of Authors' Rights in English Law and Practice in the Sixteenth and Seventeenth Centuries." *Cardozo Arts & Entertainment Law Journal* 10 (1992): 455–473.

————. *Publishing, Piracy and Politics: An Historical Study of Copyright in Britain.* London: Mansell, 1994.

Febvre, Lucien, and Henri-Jean Martin. *The Coming of the Book: The Impact of Printing, 1450–1800.* Translated by David Gerard. Edited by Geoffrey Nowell-Smith and David Wootton. London: Humanities Press, 1976.

Fellowes, Edmund H. *William Byrd.* 2d ed. London: Oxford University Press, 1948.

Fenlon, Iain. "Michael Honywood's Music Books." In Chris Banks, Arthur Searle, and Malcolm Turner (eds.), *Sundry Sorts of Music Books: Essays on the British Library Collections, Presented to O. W. Neighbor on His 70th Birthday,* 183–200. London: British Library, 1993.

————. *Music, Print and Culture in Early Sixteenth-Century Italy, the Panizzi Lectures, 1994.* London: British Library, 1995.

————, and John Milsom. "'Ruled Paper Imprinted': Music Paper and Patents in Sixteenth-Century England." *Journal of the American Musicological Society* 37 (1984): 139–163.

Forney, Kristine K. "Antwerp's Role in the Reception and Dissemination of the Madrigal to the North." In Angelo Pompilio, Donatella Restani, Lorenzo Bianconi, and F. Alberto Gallo (eds.), *Atti del XIV Congresso della Società Internazionale di Musicologia: Trasmissione e Recezione delle Forme di Cultura Musicale, Bologna, 27 agosto–1 settembre 1987,* 1, 239–253. Turin: Edizioni di Torino, 1990.

————. "Orlando di Lasso's 'Opus 1': The Making and Marketing of a Renaissance Music Book." *Revue belge de musicologie* 39–40 (1985–1986): 33–60.

————. "Tielman Susato, Sixteenth-Century Music Printer: An Archival and Typographical Investigation." Ph.D. diss. University of Kentucky, 1978.

Foster, Frank Freeman. *The Politics of Stability: A Portrait of the Rulers in Elizabethan London.* London: Royal Historical Society, 1977.

Fox, Alistair. "The Complaint of Poetry for the Death of Liberality: the Decline of Literary Patronage in the 1590s." In John Guy (ed.), *The Reign of Elizabeth I: Court and Culture in the Last Decade,* 231–252. Cambridge: Cambridge University Press, 1995.

Fraser, William. *The Douglas Book.* 4 vols. Edinburgh: T. and A. Constable, 1885.

Friar, S. *Heraldry for the Local Historian and Genealogist.* London: Alan Sutton, 1992.

Gadd, Ian. "The Mechanicks of Difference; a Study in Stationers' Company Discourse in the Seventeenth Century." In Robin Myers and Michael Harris (eds.), *The Stationers' Company and the Book Trade 1550–1990,* 93–112. New Castle, DE: Oak Knoll Press, 1997.

Gaskell, Philip. *A New Introduction to Bibliography.* Oxford: Clarendon Press, 1972.

Ginzburg, Carlo. *The Cheese and the Worms: The Cosmos of a Sixteenth-Century Miller.* Translated by John and Anne Tedeschi. New York: Penguin, 1982.

Glover, Elizabeth. *A History of the Ironmongers' Company.* London: Worshipful Company of Ironmongers, 1991.

Goldberg, S. L. "Sir John Hayward, 'Politic' Historian." *Review of English Studies* 6 (1955): 233–244.

Great Britain, Public Records Office, London. Acts of the Privy Council. PC 2/26. f. 333. "Letter to the Leiutennant of the Tower (1601)."

———. Court of Chancery. C2 Eliz. /E1/64. *Thomas East vs. George Eastland* (1601).

———. Court of Requests. Req. 2/14/81. *Christopher Este vs. Robert and William Este* (1552).

———. Court of Requests. Req. 2 /202/63. *Thomas East vs. George Eastland* (1601).

———. Court of Requests. Req. 2/203/4. *Thomas East vs. George Eastland* (1601).

———. Court of the King's Bench. K.B. 27/1364. *Thomas East vs. George Eastland* (1601).

———. Court of the Star Chamber. C24/170. *Edward East vs. Richard East* (1584).

———. Court of the Star Chamber. C24/180–181. *Richard Day vs. Alice Day* (1580–1581).

———. Court of the Star Chamber. C24/233. *Thomas and Margaret Willet vs. Francis East* (1594).

———. Feet of Fines. CP 25/2/161/2321/22. Eliz. Hil.

———. Lay Subsidy Roll. E179/251/16. "London, 1582."

———. Patent Rolls. C66/1463. m.2. "Music Privilege to Thomas Tallis and William Byrd (1575)."

———. Probate Records. PROB 11/148. "Will of Elizabeth Snodham, 1626."

———. Probate Records. PROB 11/156/61. "Will of Lucretia East, 1627."

———. State Papers. S.P. 12/274. f. 250–261. "Examinations of Gervase Pierrepoint, Richard Thimbleby, Edward Forset, John Wiborowe and John Balls (23–24 April 1600)."

Greer, David. "'Thou court's delight': Bibliographical Notes on Henry Noel." *Lute Society Journal* 17 (1975): 49–59.

Greg, W. W. "*Ad Imprimendum Solem.*" *The Library* 5th ser., vol. 9 (1954): 242–247.

———. *A Companion to Arber.* Oxford: Clarendon Press, 1967.

———. "An Elizabethan Printer and His Copy." *The Library* 4th ser., vol. 4 (1923–1924): 102–118.

———. "Entrance and Copyright." *The Library* 4th ser., vol. 26 (1945–1946): 308–310.

———. "Entrance, License and Publication." *The Library* 4th ser., vol. 25 (1944–1945): 1–14.

———. "On Certain False Dates in Shakespearean Quartos." *The Library* 2d ser., vol. 9 (1908): 113–132, 381–409.

———. *Some Aspects and Problems of London Publishing between 1550 and 1650.* Oxford: Oxford University Press, 1956.

———, and E. Boswell. *Records of the Court of the Stationers' Company: 1576 to 1602 from Register B.* London: Bibliographical Society, 1930.

Guildhall Library, London. Archdeaconry Court of London. Probate Records. "Thomas East." Ms. 9050/4 f. 336v. (30 April 1608).

———. Commissary Court Act Book. Probate Records. "Maria Hasell *alias* Snodham." Ms. 9168/13/257 (27 April 1582).

———. Deeds. Ms. 10, 905A. "Properties in Blackhorse Alley, Aldersgate Street, London (ca. 1500–1841)."

———. Ironmongers' Company Archive. Ms. 16, 967. "Court Book (1555–1899)."

———. Ironmongers' Company Archive. Ms. 16, 981. "Ironmongers' Company Presentment Book (1515–1680)."

———. Ironmongers' Company Archive. Ms. 17, 003. f. 23v. "Indenture of Company Property to Robert Este and William Skidmore."

———. Original Wills. Box 3B (Ms. 9052 3B), f. 61. "Will of Thomas East, 21 July 1607."

———. Records of the Fishmonger's Company. Ms. 7259, 6364; 5570.

Guy, John (ed.). *The Reign of Elizabeth I: Court and Culture in the Last Decade.* Cambridge: Cambridge University Press, 1995.

Haar, James. "Orlando di Lasso, Composer and Print Entrepreneur." In Kate van Orden (ed.), *Music and the Cultures of Print,* afterword by Roger Chartier, 125–162. New York: Garland, 2000.

Haigh, Christopher. *English Reformations: Religion, Politics and Society under the Tudors.* Oxford: Clarendon Press, 1993.

Hamessley, Lydia. "The Tenbury and Ellesmere Partbooks: New Findings on Manuscript Compilation and Exchange, and the Reception of the Italian Madrigal in Elizabethan England." *Music & Letters* 73 (1992): 177–221.

Hammer, Paul E. J. "Patronage at Court, Faction and the Earl of Essex." In John Guy (ed.), *The Reign of Elizabeth I: Court and Culture in the Last Decade,* 63–78. Cambridge: Cambridge University Press, 1995.

Hammersmith, James P. "Frivolous Trifles and Weighty Tomes: Early Proof-Reading at London, Oxford, and Cambridge." *Studies in Bibliography* 38 (1985): 236–251.

Handover, P. M. *The Second Cecil: The Rise to Power 1563–1604, of Sir Robert Cecil, Later First Earl of Salisbury.* London: Eyre and Spottiswood, 1959.

Harley, John. "New Light on William Byrd." *Music & Letters* 79 (1998): 475–488.

———. *William Byrd: Gentleman of the Chapel Royal.* Aldershot, Hants: Scolar, 1997.

Heartz, Daniel. "A New Attaingnant Book and the Beginnings of French Music Printing." *Journal of the American Musicological Society* 14 (1961): 9–23.

———. *Pierre Attaingnant, Royal Printer of Music: A Historical Study and Bibliographical Catalogue.* Berkeley and Los Angeles: University of California Press, 1969.

Heawood, Edward. *Watermarks, Mainly of the 17th and 18th Centuries.* 2d ed. Hilversum: Paper Publications Society, 1969.

Heffner, Ray. "Shakespeare, Hayward and Essex." *Proceedings of the Modern Language Association* 45 (1930): 754–780.

Helgerson, Richard. *Forms of Nationhood: The Elizabethan Writing of England.* Chicago: University of Chicago Press, 1992.

Herbert, William. *The History of the Twelve Great Livery Companies of London . . . .* London: The author, 1836–1837.

Hicks, Leo, S. J. "Father Robert Persons, S.J., and 'The Book of Succession.'" *Recusant History* 4 (1957): 104–137.

Hill, J. W. F. *Tudor and Stuart Lincoln.* Cambridge: Cambridge University Press, 1956.

Hodgetts, Michael. *Secret Hiding Places.* Dublin: Ventas, 1989.

Holbourne, Anthony. *The Cittharn School.* London, 1597.

Holman, Colin W. "John Day's 'Certaine Notes' (1560–65)." Ph.D. diss., University of Kansas, 1991.

Honigmann, E. A. J. *Shakespeare: The "Lost Years."* Totowa, NJ: Barnes and Noble, 1985.

Hoppe, Harry. "John Wolfe, Printer and Publisher, 1579–1601." *The Library* 4th ser., vol. 14 (1933): 241–288.

Hornschuch, Hieronymous. *Hornshuch's Orthotypographia, 1608.* Edited and translated by Philip Gaskell and Patricia Bradford. Cambridge: Cambridge University Press, 1972.

Hunt, Arnold. "Book Trade Patents, 1603–1640." In Arnold Hunt, Giles Mandelbrote, and Alison Shell (eds.), *The Book Trade & Its Customers, 1450–1900: Historical Essays for Robin Myers,* introduction by D. F. McKenzie, 27–54. New Castle, DE: Oak Knoll Press, 1997.

Hunter, Dard. *Papermaking: The History and Technique of an Ancient Craft.* 2d ed. London: Pleiades, 1947.

Hunter, David. "Music Copyright in Britain to 1800." *Music & Letters* 67 (1986): 269–282.

Hurstfield, Joel. "The Succession Struggle in Late Elizabethan England." In S. T. Bindoff, J. Hurstfield, and C. H. Williams (eds.), *Elizabethan Government and Society: Essays Presented to Sir John Neale,* 369–396. London: Athlone, 1961.

Illing, Robert. "Barley's Pocket Edition of Est's Metrical Psalter." *Music & Letters* 49 (1968): 219–223.

———. *Est-Barley-Ravenscroft and the English Metrical Psalter.* Adelaide: Libraries Board of South Australia, 1969.

———. *Est's Psalter.* 2 vols. Adelaide: Libraries Board of South Australia, 1969.

Jackman, James. "Liturgical Aspects of Byrd's 'Gradualia.'" *Musical Quarterly* 49 (1963): 237–259.

Jackson, Charles C. *A History of Radnage.* West Wycombe: The author, 1970.

Jacobson, Daniel. "Thomas Morley and the Italian Madrigal Tradition: A New Perspective." *Journal of Musicology* 14 (1996): 80–91.

James, Mervyn. *Society, Politics and Culture: Studies in Early Modern England.* Cambridge: Cambridge University Press, 1986.

Jenkins, Gladys. "The Archpriest Controversy and the Printers, 1601–1603." *The Library* 5th ser., vol. 2 (1948): 180–186.

Johnson, Francis R. "Printers' 'Copy Books' and the Black Market in the Elizabethan Book Trade." *The Library* 5th ser., vol. 1 (1946): 97–105.

Johnson, Gerald D. "The Stationers versus the Drapers: Control of the Press in the Late Sixteenth Century." *The Library* 6th ser., vol. 10 (1988): 1–17.

———. "William Barley, 'Publisher & Seller of Bookes,' 1591–1614." *The Library* 6th ser., vol. 11 (1989): 10–44.

Judge, Cyril. *Elizabethan Book Pirates.* Cambridge, MA: Harvard University Press, 1934.

Judges of England 1272–1990, A List of Judges of the Superior Courts. Compiled by Sir John Sainty. London: Seldon Society, 1993.

Kerman, Joseph. "Elizabethan Anthologies of Italian Madrigals." *Journal of the American Musicological Society* 4 (1951): 122–138.

———. "An Elizabethan Edition of Lassus." *Acta Musicologica* 27 (1955): 7–76.

———. *The Elizabethan Madrigal: A Comparative Study.* New York: American Musicological Society, 1962.

———. "The Elizabethan Motet: A Study of Texts for Music." *Studies in the Renaissance* 9 (1962): 273–308.

———. *The Masses and Motets of William Byrd.* Berkeley: University of California Press, 1981.

———. "'Write All These Down': Notes on a Byrd Song." In A. Brown and R. Turbet (eds.), *Byrd Studies,* 112–128. Cambridge: Cambridge University Press, 1992.

Keymer, Faith. "Thomas East, Citizen & Stationer of London: The Reconstruction of a Tudor Family Using Public Records." *PROphile* 11 (2000): 3–10.

King, Alec Hyatt. "Fragments of Early Printed Music in the Bagford Collections." *Music & Letters* 40 (1959): 269–273.

———. "The Significance of John Rastell in Early Music Printing." *The Library* 5th ser., vol. 26 (1971): 197–214.

Kinney, Arthur F. *Elizabethan Backgrounds: Historical Documents of the Age of Elizabeth I.* London: Archon, 1975.

Kirbye, George. *First Set of Madrigals (1597).* Edited by Edmund H. Fellowes. Revised by Thurston Dart and Philip Brett. London: Stainer & Bell, 1960.

Kirschbaum, Leo. "Author's Copyright in England before 1640." *Papers of the Bibliographical Society of America* 40 (1989): 40–45.

———. "The Copyright of Elizabethan Plays." *The Library* 5th ser., vol. 14 (1959): 231–250.

Kirwood, A. E. M. "Richard Field, Printer, 1589–1624." *The Library* 4th ser., vol. 12 (1931): 3–39.

Krummel, Donald W. *English Music Printing, 1553–1700.* London: Bibliographical Society, 1975.

———. "Musical Functions and Bibliographical Forms." *The Library* 5th ser., vol. 31 (1976): 327–350.

———, and Stanley Sadie, (eds). *Music Printing and Publishing.* Norton/Grove Handbooks in Music. New York: Norton, 1990.

Lambert, Sheila. "State Control of the Press in Theory and Practice: The Role of the Stationers' Company before 1640." In Robin Myers and Michael Harris, (eds.), *Censorship & the Control of Print: In England and France 1600–1910,* 1–32. Winchester: St. Paul's Bibliographies, 1992.

Lang, R. G. *Two Tudor Subsidy Rolls for the City of London: 1541 and 1582.* London: London Record Society, 1993.

Lavin, J. A. "William Barley, Draper and Stationer." *Studies in Bibliography* 21 (1969): 214–223.

LaRocca, John J. (ed.). *Jacobean Recusant Rolls for Middlesex (London).* London: Catholic Record Society, 1997.

Law, Thomas Greaves. *A Historical Sketch of the Conflicts between Jesuits and Seculars in the Reign of Queen Elizabeth.* London: D. Nutt, 1889.

le Huray, Peter. *Music and the Reformation in England, 1549–1660.* Cambridge: Cambridge University Press, 1978.

Leaver, Robin. *'Goostly Psalmes and Spirituall Songes': English and Dutch Metrical Psalms from Coverdale to Utenhove 1535–1566.* Oxford: Clarendon Press, 1991.

Lewis, Mary S. *Antonio Gardano: Venetian Music Printer, 1538–1569: A Descriptive Bibliography and Historical Study.* vol. 1: *1538–1549,* New York and London: Garland, 1988, vol. 2: *1550–1559*: New York and London: Garland, 1997.

Livesay, John. "William Barley: Elizabethan Printer and Bookseller." *Studies in Bibliography* 8 (1956): 218–225.

Loewenstein, Joseph. "For a History of Literary Property: John Wolfe's Reformation." *English Literary Renaissance* 18 (1988): 389–412.

London Surveys of Ralph Treswell, The. Edited by John Scofield. London: Topographical Society, 1987.

Love, Harold. *Scribal Publication in Seventeenth-Century England.* Oxford: Clarendon Press, 1993.

Lumley Library, The: The Catalogue of 1609. Edited by Sears Jayne and Francis Johnson. London: British Museum, 1956.

MacCaffrey, Wallace T. "Place and Patronage in Elizabethan Politics." In S. T. Bindoff, J. Hurstfield, and C. H. Williams (eds.), *Elizabethan Government and Society: Essays Presented to Sir John Neale.* 95–126. London: Athlone, 1961.

———. *Queen Elizabeth and the Making of Policy, 1572–1588.* Princeton, NJ: Princeton University Press, 1981.

Machyn, Henry. *The Diary of Henry Machyn.* Edited by J. G. Nichols. London: Printed for the Camden Society, 1848.

Manley, Lawrence. *Literature and Culture in Early Modern London.* Cambridge: Cambridge University Press, 1995.

Marix, Jean. "Harmonice musices odhècaton A: Quelques prècisions chronologiques." *Revue de musicologie* 19 (1932): 236–241.

Marlow, R. "Sir Ferdinando Heyborne alias Richardson." *Musical Times* 115 (1974): 736–739.

Marotti, Arthur. *Manuscript, Print, and the English Renaissance Lyric.* Ithaca, NY: Cornell University Press, 1995.

Mateer, David. "William Byrd, John Petre and Oxford, Bodleian MS Mus. Sch. E. 423." *RMA Research Chronicle* 29 (1996): 21–46.

———. "William Byrd's Middlesex Recusancy." *Music & Letters* 78 (1997): 1–14.

McKenzie, D. F. "Stationers' Company Liber A: An Apologia." In Robin Myers and Michael Harris (eds.), *The Stationers' Company and the Book Trade 1550–1990*, 35–64. New Castle, DE: Oak Knoll Press, 1997.

McKerrow, Ronald B. "Edward Allde as a Typical Trade Printer." *The Library* 4th ser., vol. 10 (1929): 121–162.

———. *Printers' & Publishers' Devices in England & Scotland 1485–1640.* London: Bibliographical Society, 1913.

———, and F. S. Ferguson. *Title-Page Borders Used in England & Scotland 1485–1640.* London: Bibliographical Society, 1932.

Meres, Francis. *Palladis Tamia: Wit's Treasury.* London, 1598; reprint, New York: Garland, 1973.

Meyer, Arnold O. *England and the Catholic Church under Elizabeth.* 2d ed. Translated by Rev. J. R. McKee. Introduction by John Bossy. London: Routledge, 1967.

Meynell, Francis, and Stanley Morison. "Printers' Flowers and Arabesques." *Fleuron* 1 (1923): 1–43.

Miller, Miriam. "London Music Printing, c. 1570–c. 1640." Ph.D. diss., University of London, 1969.

Milles, Thomas. "The Custumers Alphabet and Primer . . . ." London, 1608.

Milsom, John. "The Nonsuch Music Library." In Chris Banks, Arthur Searle, and Malcolm Turner (eds.), *Sundry Sorts of Music Books: Essays on the British Library Collections Presented to O. W. Neighbor on His 70th Birthday*, 146–182. London: British Library, 1993.

———. "Sacred Songs in the Chamber." In John Morehen (ed.), *English Choral Practice, 1400–1650*, 161–199. Cambridge: Cambridge University Press, 1995.

———. "Songs and Society in Early Tudor London." *Early Music History* 16 (1997): 235–293.

———. "Tallis, Byrd and the 'Incorrected' Copy: Some Cautionary Notes for Editors of Early Music Printed from Movable Type." *Music & Letters* 77 (1996): 348–367.

Milton, Anthony. "Licensing, Censorship, and Religious Orthodoxy in Early Stuart England." *Historical Journal* 41 (1998): 625–651.

Monson, Craig. "Byrd and the 1575 Cantiones Sacrae." *Musical Times* 116 (1975): 1089–1091; 117 (1976): 65–67.

———. "Byrd, the Catholics and the Motet: The Hearing Reopened." In Dolores Pesce (ed.), *Hearing the Motet: Essays on the Motet of the Middle Ages and Renaissance*, 348–374. New York: Oxford University Press, 1997.

———. "Elizabethan London." In Iain Fenlon (ed.), *The Renaissance: From the 1470s to the End of the 16th Century*, 304–340. London: Macmillan, 1989.

Moore, J. K. *Primary Materials Relating to Copy and Print in English Books of the Sixteenth and Seventeenth Centuries.* Oxford: Oxford Bibliographical Society, 1992.

Morey, Adrian. *The Catholic Subjects of Elizabeth I.* Totowa, NJ: Rowman and Littlefield, 1978.

Morley, Thomas. *A Plain and Easy Introduction to Practical Music.* Edited by R. A. Harman, with a foreword by R. T. Dart. New York: Norton, 1952.

———. *A Plaine and Easie Introduction to Practicall Musicke.* London: Peter Short, 1597.

Morris, Wesley. *Toward a New Historicism.* Princeton, NJ: Princeton University Press, 1972.

Moseley, C. W. R. D. "The Lost Play of Mandeville." *The Library* 5th ser., vol. 25 (1970): 46–49.

Moxon, Joseph. *Mechanick Exercises on the Whole Art of Printing (1683–1684)*. 2d ed. Edited by
Herbert Davis and Harry Carter. London: Oxford University Press, 1962.

Mullaney, Steven. *The Place of the Stage: License, Play, and Power in Renaissance England*. Chicago:
University of Chicago Press, 1988.

Myers, Robin. *The Stationers' Company Archive: An Account of the Records 1554–1984*. Winchester:
St. Paul's Bibliographies, 1990.

———, and Michael Harris (eds.). *The Stationers' Company and the Book Trade 1550–1990*. New
Castle, DE: Oak Knoll Press, 1997.

Nasu, Teruhiko. "The Publication of Byrd's *Gradualia* Reconsidered." *Brio* 32 (1995): 109–120.

Neale, J. E. "The Elizabethan Political Scene." *Proceedings of the British Academy* 34 (1948):
97–117.

New Grove Dictionary of Music and Musicians, The. 29 vols. Edited by Stanley Sadie and John
Tyrell. 2d ed. New York: Grove, 2001.

New Historicism, The. Edited by H. Aram Veeser. New York: Routledge, 1989.

Nicholl, Charles. *The Reckoning: The Murder of Christopher Marlowe*. Chicago: University of
Chicago Press, 1995.

Nichols, John. *The Progresses and Public Processions of Queen Elizabeth*. 3 vols. London: The
author, 1823.

Nixon, Paul J. "William Bathe and His Times." *Musical Times* 124 (1983): 101–102.

Oastler, C. L. *John Day, the Elizabethan Printer*. Oxford: Oxford Bibliographical Society, 1975.

O'Leary, J. G. "William Byrd and His Family at Stondon Massey." *Essex Recusant* 7 (1965):
18–23.

Owens, Jessie Ann. "Concepts of Pitch in English Music Theory, c. 1560–1640." In Cristle
Collins Judd (ed.), *Tonal Structures in Early Music*, 183–246. New York: Garland, 1998.

Paige-Hagg, Melvyn. *The Monumental Brasses of Buckinghamshire*. London: Monumental Brass
Society, 1994.

Parish, John E. *Robert Parsons and the English Counter-Reformation*. Houston: Rice University, 1966.

Pattison, Bruce. "Notes on Early Music Printing." *The Library* 4th ser., vol. 19 (1939): 378–413.

Pearl, Valerie. *London and the Outbreak of the Puritan Revolution: City Government and National Politics*.
London: Oxford University Press, 1961.

Philipps, Glenn A. "Crown Musical Patronage from Elizabeth I to Charles I." *Music & Letters*
58 (1977): 29–42.

———. "Patronage in the Career of Thomas Weelkes." *Musical Quarterly* 62 (1976): 46–57.

Plomer, Henry R. *English Printers' Ornaments*. London: Grafton, 1924.

———. "Thomas East, Printer." *The Library* 2d ser., vol. 3 (1901): 298–310.

Pogue, Samuel F. *Jacques Moderne: Lyons Music Printer of the Sixteenth Century*. Geneva: Droz, 1969.

Pollard, Alfred. *A Short-Title Catalogue of Books Printed in England, Scotland, & Ireland and of English
Books Printed Abroad 1475–1640*. 3 vols. 2d ed. Revised and enlarged. Begun by W. A.
Jackson and F. S. Ferguson. Completed by Katharine F. Pantzer. London: Bibliographi-
cal Society, 1976–1991.

Pollard, Graham. "The Early Constitution of the Stationers' Company before 1557." *The Library* 4th ser., vol. 18 (1937): 235–260.

Price, David. *Patrons and Musicians of the English Renaissance*. Cambridge: Cambridge University
Press, 1981.

Price, William Hyde. *The English Patents of Monopoly*. Cambridge, MA: Harvard University
Press, 1913.

Rainbow, Bernarr. "Bathe and His Introductions to Musicke." *Musical Times* 123 (1982):
243–247.

Rappaport, Steve. *Worlds within Worlds: Structures of Life in Sixteenth-Century London.* Cambridge: Cambridge University Press, 1989.

Records of the Court of the Stationers' Company, 1602 to 1640. Edited by William A. Jackson. London: Bibliographical Society, 1957.

Recusants in the Exchequer Pipe Rolls 1581–1592. Extracted by Dom Hugh Bowler. Edited by Timothy J. McCann. London: Catholic Record Society, 1986.

Repertoire international des sources musicales. Series A. 1: *Einzeldrücke vor 1800.* 9 vols. Edited by Karl-Heinz Schlager. Kassel: Bärenreiter, 1971–.

Robinson, H. (ed). *Zurich Letters Comprising the Correspondence of Several English Bishops and Others, with Some of the Helvetian Reformers, during the Reign of Queen Elizabeth.* 2 vols. Cambridge: Parker Society, 1842.

Rodger, Alexander. "Roger Ward's Shrewsbury Stock: An Inventory of 1585." *The Library* 5th ser., vol. 13 (1958): 247–268.

Rose, Elliot. *Cases of Conscience: Alternatives Open to Recusants and Puritans under Elizabeth I and James I.* Cambridge: Cambridge University Press, 1975.

Ruff, Lillian, and Arnold Wilson. "Allusion to the Essex Downfall in Lute Song Lyrics." *Lute Society Journal* 12 (1970): 31–36.

———. "The Madrigal, the Lute Song and Elizabethan Politics." *Past & Present* 44 (1969): 3–51.

Saunders, J. W. "The Stigma of Print: A Note on the Social Bases of Tudor Poetry." *Essays in Criticism* 1 (1951): 139–164.

Schleiner, Louise. "Margaret Tyler, Translator and Waiting Woman." *English Language Notes* 29 (1992): 1–8.

Schubert, Peter N. "A Lesson from Lassus: Form in the Duos of 1577." *Music Theory Spectrum* 17 (1995): 1–26.

Seymour, M. C. "The Early English Editions of 'Mandeville's Travels.'" *The Library* 5th ser., vol. 19 (1964): 202–207.

Shaaber, M. A. "The Meaning of the Imprint in Early Printed Books." *The Library* 4th ser., vol. 24 (1943–1944): 120–141.

Shell, Alison. "Catholic Texts and Anti-Catholic Prejudice in the 17th-Century Book Trade." In Robin Myers and Michael Harris (eds.), *Censorship & the Control of Print: In England and France 1600–1910,* 33–58. Winchester: St. Paul's Bibliographies, 1992.

Simpson, Richard. *Edmund Campion: A Biography.* London: Williams and Norgate, 1867.

Smith, Jeremy. L. "From 'Rights to Copy' to the 'Bibliographic Ego': A New Look at the Last Early Edition of Byrd's 'Psalmes, Sonets & Songs.'" *Music & Letters* 80 (1999): 511–530.

———. "The Hidden Editions of Thomas East." *Notes, Quarterly Journal of the Music Library Association* 53 (1997): 1059–1091.

Sopher, Alan. "A Handlist of Works Printed by Thomas East." Diploma in Librarianship diss., University of London, 1959.

Spector, Stephen. "Introduction." In Stephen Spector (ed.), *Essays in Paper Analysis,* 7–23. Washington, DC: Folger Shakespeare Library, 1987.

Stafford, Helen G. *James VI of Scotland and the Throne of England.* London: Appleton, 1940.

Stainer, Sir John. "On the Musical Introductions Found in Certain Metrical Psalters." *Proceedings of the Royal Musical Association* 27 (1900–1901): 1–50.

Steele, Robert R. *The Earliest English Music Printing: A Description and Bibliography of English Printed Music to the Close of the Sixteenth Century.* London: Bibliographical Society, 1903.

Stevens, Denis. *Tudor Church Music.* New York: Norton, 1966.

Stevenson, Allan H. *The Problem of the Missale Speciale.* London: Bibliographical Society, 1967.

———. "Watermarks Are Twins." *Studies in Bibliography* 4 (1951–1952): 57–91.

Strong, Roy C. "Queen Elizabeth I as Oriana." *Studies in the Renaissance* 6 (1959): 251–260.

Tanselle, Thomas G. "The Use of Type Damage as Evidence in Bibliographical Description." *The Library* 5th ser., vol. 23 (1968): 328–351.

Temperley, Nicholas. *The Hymn Tune Index: A Census of English-Language Hymn Tunes in Printed Sources from 1535 to 1820.* 3 vols. Oxford: Oxford University Press, 1998.

———. *The Music of the English Parish Church.* Cambridge: Cambridge University Press, 1979.

———. "The Old Way of Singing: Its Origins and Development." *Journal of the American Musicological Society* 34 (1981): 516–518.

Thompson, James. *The Frankfort Book Fair.* New York: Burt Franklin, 1911.

Tillyard, E. M. W. *The Elizabethan World Picture.* London: Chatto and Windus, 1943.

Traister, Daniel. "Reluctant Virgins: The Stigma of Print Revisited." *Colby Quarterly* 26 (1990): 75–86.

Turbet, Richard. *William Byrd, a Guide to Research.* New York: Garland, 1987.

Tyson, Gerald P., and Sylvia S. Wagonheim (eds.). *Print and Culture in the Renaissance: Essays on the Advent of Printing in Europe.* Newark: University of Delaware Press, 1986.

Ungerer, Gustav. "The French Lutenist Charles Tessier and the Essex Circle." *Renaissance Quarterly* 28 (1975): 190–203.

Vanhulst, Henri. *Catalogue des éditions de musique publiées à Louvain par Pierre Phalèse et ses fils, 1545–1578.* Brussels: Palais des académies, 1990.

———. "Lassus et ses éditeurs: Remarques à propos de deux lettres peu connes." *Revue belge de musicologie* 39–40 (1985–1986): 80–100.

Wall, John. "The Reformation in England and the Typographical Revolution: 'By This Printing . . . the Doctrine of the Gospel Soundeth to All Nations.'" In Gerald P. Tyson and Sylvia S. Wagonheim (eds.), *Print and Culture in the Renaissance: Essays on the Advent of Printing in Europe,* 208–221. Newark: University of Delaware Press, 1986.

Ward, John M. "Barley's Songs without Words." *Lute Society Journal* 12 (1970): 5–22.

———. "Tessier and the 'Essex Circle.'" *Renaissance Quarterly* 29 (1976): 378–384.

Waters, Josephine. "The Woodcut Illustrations in the English Editions of 'Mandeville's Travels.'" *Papers of the Bibliographical Society of America* 47 (1953): 59–63.

Waugh, Evelyn. *Edmund Campion.* 2d ed. London: Longmans, 1961.

Weaver, Robert Lee. *A Descriptive Bibliographical Catalog of the Music Printed by Hubert Waelrant and Jan de Laet.* Warren, MI: Harmonie Park, 1994.

———. *Waelrant and Laet: Music Publishers in Antwerp's Golden Age.* Warren, MI: Harmonie Park, 1995.

Welch, Charles. *History of the Worshipful Company of Pewterers of the City of London.* 2 vols. London: Blades and Blades, 1902.

Weston, William. *The Autobiography of an Elizabethan.* Edited by Philip Caraman. London: Longmans, 1955.

Whythourne, Thomas. *The Autobiography of Thomas Whythourne.* Edited by James Osbourn. London: Oxford University Press, 1962.

Wienpahl, Robert. *Music at the Inns of Court during the Reigns of Elizabeth, James, and Charles.* Ann Arbor, MI: University Microfilms International, 1979.

Williams, Franklin B. *An Index of Dedications and Commendatory Verses in English Books before 1641.* London: Bibliographical Society, 1962.

Williams, Penry. *The Later Tudors: England, 1547–1603.* Oxford: Clarendon Press, 1995.

Willson, David H. *King James VI and I.* London: Jonathan Cape, 1956.

Wilson, J. Dover. "Richard Schilders and the English Puritans." *Transactions of the Bibliographical Society* 11 (1909–1911): 65–89.

Wolf, Edwin. "Press Corrections in Sixteenth and Seventeenth Century Quartos." *Papers of the Bibliographical Society of America* 36 (1942): 188–209.

Woodfield, Denis. *Surreptitious Printing in England 1550–1640.* New York: Bibliographical Society, 1973.

Wright, Peter. "Paper Evidence and the Dating of Trent 91." *Music & Letters* 76 (1995): 487–509.

Zim, Rivkah. *English Metrical Psalms: Poetry as Praise and Prayer 1535–1601.* Cambridge: Cambridge University Press, 1987.

Index